THE
PLAYBOY®
INTERVIEWS

OTHER BOOKS IN **THE PLAYBOY INTERVIEWS** SERIES

THE
PLAYBOY®
INTERVIEWS

THE COMEDIANS

EDITED BY STEPHEN RANDALL AND
THE EDITORS OF *PLAYBOY* MAGAZINE

PRESS™
Milwaukie

M Press
10956 SE Main Street
Milwaukie, OR 97222
mpressbooks.com

Portions of this book are reprinted from issues of *Playboy* magazine.
Cover and series design by Tina Alessi & Lia Ribacchi

Library of Congress Cataloging-in-Publication Data

The Playboy interviews : the comedians / edited by Stephen Randall and the editors
of Playboy magazine. -- 1st M Press ed.
    p. cm. -- (The Playboy interviews)
  Includes index.
  ISBN-13: 978-1-59582-066-2
  ISBN-10: 1-59582-066-3
  1. Stand-up comedy--United States. 2. Comedians--United States--Interviews. I.
Randall, Stephen. II. Playboy (Chicago, Ill.)
PN1969.C65P53 2007
792.702'80922--dc22
[B]
                                    2007000782

ISBN 978-1-59582-066-2
First M Press Edition: September 2008

10 9 8 7 6 5 4 3 2 1

Printed in U.S.A.

CONTENTS

INTRODUCTION

By Stephen Randall
Deputy Editor, Playboy *magazine*

One night, Steve Martin was onstage trying out a new joke about his girlfriend. In the bit, she complained, "I don't think you respect me as a woman."

"What are you talking about?" responded Martin. "You are the best hog I ever had."

Naturally, the audience booed, and Martin quickly retorted, "Hey, wait a minute, comedy is not pretty."

That ad-lib took on a life of its own. It became the title of one of Martin's comedy albums and more or less sums up the entire profession. Probably no other art form looks so effortless and yet requires so much work. It's easy to be the funny guy at the office, but when you're onstage in front of hundreds of strangers—or talking to a TV camera—you find out that not only is comedy not pretty, many times it's just plain ugly.

Everyone knows that comedians are an odd bunch. They're almost always smart, with a writer's gift for words, a soldier's belief in discipline and an inpatient's litany of neuroses. No matter how talented, they are often angry, confused, depressed, self-absorbed and off-kilter. A comedian who appears carefree on camera can seem tortured at home.

No one knows this better than the comics themselves. Jim Carrey promises in his *Playboy Interview* that he'll never end up being an angry old man like George Carlin. Carlin denies he's angry, saying, "Angry is getting into a fistfight, which I've never done. Angry? Not me." Even genial Jerry Seinfeld tells *Playboy*, "I'm annoyed. If you're not cranky and annoyed, you can't be a comedian."

For comedy connoisseurs, this is an amazing lineup, representing almost all aspects and eras of 20th century American comedy. Groucho Marx cut his teeth in vaudeville. Jon Stewart has redefined how Americans get their news. Don Rickles single-handedly reinvented the Las Vegas lounge act. Seinfeld, Bill Cosby, and Tina Fey took the sitcom to creative and commercial heights (and became rich doing so). Martin and Woody Allen have conquered stand-up, albums, movies and books. Carlin, Carrey, Robin Williams and Chris Rock are comedians who leave other comics awestruck.

You know these people, and yet you don't. Yes, they are funny folks who can't help but try to make you laugh—and given who they are, they succeed. They are also extremely serious people, who are often surprisingly removed from their public personas. Because the goal of every *Playboy Interview* is to provide a multifaceted look at its subject, you'll meet performers who live to bring happiness, but may not be so happy themselves.

Steve Martin was right, even when tossing off a casual ad-lib. Comedy might not be pretty, but it certainly is interesting.

THE
PLAYBOY®
INTERVIEWS

DON RICKLES

A candid conversation with the asp-tongued "Mr. Warmth"

With the following probe into the poisonous psyche of comedian Don Rickles, the checkered career of our interviewer this month, the intrepid Sol Weinstein, hits an all-time low. Undaunted by the hate mail in response to his demented *Playboy Interview* with Woody Allen (May 1967), the cockamamie creator of that one-man blintzkrieg Israel Bond (whose superspy misadventures premiered in *Playboy*) foolishly accepted our assignment—he was the only one who'd take it—to confront "The Merchant of Venom" in his lair at Las Vegas's Sahara Hotel. When his wounds had healed, Sol sent us this report—COD—scrawled in body paint on the torso of a topless waitress:

"I lounged on the lawn of Twin Hangnails, my ancestral estate in Levittown, Pennsylvania, chuckling fondly whilst my beloved dog, Mimi, part Saint Bernard, part Chihuahua, nibbled on a new Alpo mixture fast gaining favor among our furry friends because it tastes like a mailman's ankle. My daughter sat entranced at the activities of her 1969-model Barbie and Ken dolls, which, because they came accoutered with a full array of battery-powered working parts, were teaching her all she'd ever need to know about the facts of life. Stooping over his mother's flowerbed, my typical suburban son deftly plucked an azalea here, a jonquil there, to afford the sun and rain a clear shot at his cannabis garden. In a hammock reclined the fair Mrs. Weinstein, knitting a sampler, Love Levittown, Haight Ashbury, and humming the catchy score from Ingmar Bergman's *The Silence*. Such was the bucolic bonhomie of this lazy-daisy day when the accursed phone burred inside. 'It's *Playboy* calling, Stallion Thighs,' chirped my missus. 'Wonder who the interviewee is this trip?' I mused. Sonny Tufts? Judge Crater?

"On came the same hard-nosed *Playboy* editor who'd dispatched me on Woody Allen's trail in 1967. He spat two words into the receiver, heard my audible gulp and added, in a softer voice, '*Playboy*, of course, will furnish you full combat pay plus a week's R&R in Sun City.'

"The phone tumbled from my hand; I turned albino-white. Recovering myself, I gritted my gums, snarled and punched my wife in the mouth, yanked the bowl from Mimi's slavering jaws and sent her off yapping with a brutal kick, pushed my son into a thorn bush and broke my daughter's heart by tearing Barbie and Ken apart at the moment of truth.

"'For the love of heaven,' whimpered the wife through a shattered $4000 periodontia job, 'what's come over you?'

"'When I went on the Woody assignment, I got into an appropriate mood by thinking small. Now I've been asked to interview Don Rickles.'

"My brood began to chant the Kaddish, the Hebraic prayer for the dead. The ever-practical Mrs. Weinstein doubled my life insurance and made a hasty arrangement to connect with a lover, specifying that the employment agency send over any gamekeeper named Mellors.

"Of course, the Rickles job meant that once again I would have to postpone a series of big-league projects in order to satisfy Hefner's sadistic caprice: (a) my screenplay for Sam Katzman about a teenybopper's hopeless love for a robot, *Gidget Balls Gadget* (in a tragic final scene, he dies of rust); (b) my novel of a Middle Earth nun, *Hobbit Kicks the Habit*; (c) a bonanza from the sale of a naked photo of Raul Castro to *Ramparts* for use as a gatefold; (d) my brilliantly reasoned treatise for the U.S. Public Health Service in which I proved an irrefutable causal link between standing on ground zero at an H-bomb test and death; and (e) my offer to labor at the side of Dr. Christiaan Barnard on the world's first soul transplant, Ray Charles's into George Wallace's.

"The next day's post brought a plane ticket (one way) from *Playboy*, some publicity stills showing Rickles dropping napalm on Disneyland and a copy of the tyrant's best-selling Warner-7 LP, *Hello Dummy!* I had seen many a controversial album labeled 'Not Suitable For Air Play,' but never one that admonished 'Not Suitable For Play

Anywhere.' Nevertheless, I slapped it onto my phonograph, which slapped me back, and I then listened in fear and trembling to a scathing half hour of ethnic invective. But before the first side had hissed to a close, the machine pressed its reject button and self-destructed. Unfortunately, I'd also left my window open during the audition; a forest of For Sale signs cropped up throughout the neighborhood as I packed my suitcase.

"So it was on to Vegas and the Sahara via a blushing-pink, highly seductive Braniff jet (which was attacked in midair over Nashville by a randy TWA 707). After wolfing down a delicious Braniff platter of baked storm window, I dug into the authorized biography of Rickles supplied by Grove Press.

"Born in Jackson Heights, New York, to a solidly middle-class couple who'd owned their own janitor, I learned, Rickles had overcome his initial 'shyness' by involving himself in scholastic theatrics, i.e., the lead in Victor Herbert's The Red Mill, the classic operetta about a Communist takeover of a Social Democrat granary. After graduation from Newtown High School with a diploma in license-plate manufacture, he had spent his semen first class with the Navy in the Philippines during World War II, alternating between fighting the Japanese and writing continuity for Tokyo Rose's nightly broadcasts.

"His postwar training ground in comedy was 'the toilets,' those 10th-rate nightclubs—such as Filopowicz's Hawaiian Paradise in Hamtramck, Michigan—that have served as the compost heap for thousands of flowering showbiz careers. Then came a prominent booking at the famed Slate Brothers Club in L.A. as a last-minute replacement for another comic, who had become violently stricken after receiving a box of Girl Scout cookies from Rickles. In the audience that first night was Frank Sinatra, who found himself the target of Rickles's sniping: 'Hi, Frank! Remember the good old days when you had a voice?' For reasons best known to himself, Sinatra instantly became a Rickles nut and began to drag in his Rat Pack nightly to boost attendance. Soon the nettlesome New Yorker was a ranking raja of the hate set and all of show business was thronging the joint for the right to be lashed by Rickles's forked tongue. Realizing he'd fallen into the right bag, Don has been excoriating his auditors ever since.

"It took nine years, however, before the TV tycoons became sufficiently courageous to spring the sulphuric Rickles wit on unsuspecting home audiences. After debuting on the Johnny Carson show and demolishing the host, he soon became a familiar fright wig on TV's other big variety shows—Joey Bishop's, Merv Griffin's, Mike Douglas's, etc., and he hit the heights of hostility in a memorable 13-minute stint on *The Dean Martin Show* last year, castigating a gaggle of gagging celebrities who'd been invited by the thoughtful Martin for the express purpose of having their careers destroyed before 30 million viewers.

"Rickles's confreres in the nightclub fraternity have since bestowed the warmest accolades upon him at numerous 'trade' fetes. Among them were Joe E. Lewis, the famed Aristotle of the Bottle, who croaked: 'Don Rickles is in a class by himself—because decent people won't associate with him'; and Jack E. Leonard, who accuses Rickles of 'doing my act so long I'm going to make a citizen's arrest.' But perhaps the most effusive encomium came from Jackie Kannon, no slouch in the venom league himself: 'Don Rickles has given diarrhea an exciting new egress.' Firmly established as the Torquemada of the tongue, Rickles now fronts his own half-hour show each Friday night on ABC-TV, is co-hosting a number of *Kraft Music Hall* specials and has been promised that his face will soon grace a stamp—North Vietnamese.

"When I met him in Vegas, Rickles was packing them in—personally, with the help of a cattle prod—at the Sahara's Casbar Theater. One glance at the bullet-headed bawd ramming his jack boots onto the stage, and occasionally onto a ringsider's hand, convinced me that someone had cut Mussolini down from the rope and infused him with a second, even more heinous existence. Indeed, as Rickles thrust out his belligerent jaw, a column of Fascisti rolled their tanks through the crowd, weeding out defectives for shipment to a labor camp.

"His press agent had guaranteed me an interview at poolside; so the following afternoon, I waddled through a field of strewn-about keno losers to the star's webbed feet and kneeled in obeisance, as is the custom, while he munched angrily on a chef's salad.

"'Cheap bastards,' rasped the satrap of the Sahara. 'I ask them for Thousand Island dressing and they give me 963 islands.' Flinging the plate into the waiter's face, he snarled, 'Tell Del Webb I hope his next hotel is built on a minefield in Syria.'

"The beauteous Mrs. Rickles, who sat beside him, flashed a look that said, 'He really isn't this way all the time'; whereupon, Rickles proffered his right hand to me in greeting, while he dumped hot coffee onto my leg with his left. I looked back at Mrs. Rickles, whose despairing eyes said, 'I guess he really is that way all the time.'

"Before he would agree to the interview, he insisted on a set of preconditions that seemed reasonable enough. He would squat under a huge umbrella, his feet in a bucket of ice, while I would lie staked out in the 115-degree Vegas sun and howl in merriment each time he dropped a colony of sauba ants into my navel, which he had smeared with Smucker's quince jelly. Satisfied of my eagerness to please, Rickles showed his fangs in a mirthless smile and spake thusly."

RICKLES: You have 15 minutes, dummy. I shall grant a few additional moments if you don't prove to be a complete idiot, and perhaps as long as half an hour if you amuse me.

PLAYBOY: Fair enough, Don. Why don't we begin by—

RICKLES: What's with this "Don" bit? Since when did you become an equal? It's *Mister* Rickles to you. And what's with this "we"? All I see is one blinking, nail-chewing little spy writer from Levittown who pathetically needs to conduct a successful interview with a superstar to save his flagging career. And who's that dwarf with the camera?

PLAYBOY: That's Carl Iri, our Japanese-American photographer. He just wants to take a few candid shots of you while we talk.

RICKLES: Okay—but what's he got in that case, photos of direct hits on Pearl Harbor? Tell him to kiss my Sessue Hayakawa.

PLAYBOY: Mr. Rickles, we'd like to start by—

RICKLES: Did anybody ever tell you that you have exciting shoulders?

PLAYBOY: You're the first *guy* to comment on them. Shall we get on with the interview?

RICKLES: You really need this, don't you, kid? You desperately want to halt your downslide back to oblivion, right?

PLAYBOY: Well. . . .

RICKLES: Then blow in my ear. Would you like to call me "Don"?

PLAYBOY: It would certainly make for a friendlier dialog.

RICKLES: Then do it. Say, did anyone ever tell you that you have a finely turned pair of ankles? I particularly like the way your veins stand out when you arch your instep, just like the tributaries of the Amazon gleaming in the midday sun. You're a bewitching boy—but I detect a definite gaminess emanating from this room. Doesn't big-spender Hefner give you enough to buy a decent deodorant?

PLAYBOY: As a matter of record, that aroma is English Leather.

RICKLES: You must have gotten it from Lord Cornwallis's saddle at the Battle of Yorktown. And that bathing suit: It looks like it was cut from a casing on Hebrew National Salami.

PLAYBOY: Don, we—

RICKLES: I've warned you once.

PLAYBOY: But you said we could call you Don.

RICKLES: That was before I got downwind from you.

PLAYBOY: Okay, Mr. Rickles. We'd like to begin by—

RICKLES: Before we go any further, I'd like to tell you that I've read your Israel Bond spy stories in *Playboy*, and an Ian Fleming you're not. You're not even an Irving Fleming.

PLAYBOY: Since you'd like to get personal, we've caught your act, and we've heard funnier material on a sinking lifeboat.

RICKLES: Let me have that stubby, gnawed pencil of yours for a second. I just want to mark this down: "Semiunknown spy writer flattens big-time super-Jew with devastating putdown, thus grabbing a one-to-nothing lead in the top of the first." Go ahead.

PLAYBOY: For years, the moguls of the television industry shied away from you. Why?

RICKLES: I had one major problem. I was hilarious wherever I performed. They had a cardinal rule on TV: Who needs laughter? They preferred to see some guy on a game show hit a buzzer and correctly identify the days of the week in order, thus winning three weeks in Borneo. On one of those shows I won the trip, but who can fox trot with a Pygmy? Speaking of Pygmies, I knew right away I'd have trouble selling myself when I met the powers that be in the television industry; they were dressed in Robert Hall suits, Thom McAn no-scuffs and T-shirts without sleeves, and they had these tiny pimples on the backs of their necks. Their biggest kick was getting up at five A.M. to watch the daily farm reports and shouting, "Oh, look, Abner! The heifer is making doo-doo on the sow! Whoopee!"

PLAYBOY: What prompted the breakthrough that's made you one of the medium's hottest attractions?

RICKLES: Somebody at one of these TV agencies came up with a wild new concept. He called it "talent." They hanged him at high noon on a scaffold in Rockefeller Plaza for such blasphemy, but it did help me crack through at last.

PLAYBOY: You've scored resoundingly on all the variety shows. What kind of relationship do you have with the various hosts?

RICKLES: Let's start with Johnny Carson, who's a peachy guy. I had dinner at his home one night; he made us all sit on the floor and shuck corn. Those Midwest guys never forget their taproots. The first time I ever saw Johnny in swim trunks, I enrolled him in a Borscht Belt health club; a substantial Jewish meal has saved more than one gentile comic from malnutrition. Mike Douglas is a charming fellow, too. Runs a real wholesome, family-type operation. I spent a day in his dressing room sewing nametags on his shorts so he could go to summer camp, and I gave him some animal crackers to eat on the train. Mike's an ex–Kay Kyser band singer who used to perform on those remote broadcasts from hotels in Pittsburgh during the golden days of radio. The announcer would say, "And now, Mike Douglas steps to the microphone to ask the musical question . . ." and Mike would forget the question. No matter what the leader had scheduled, he'd sing "Ramona."

Recently, I've started appearing with Merv Griffin, another ex-band singer, whose only hit record was *I've Got a Lovely Bunch of Cocoanuts*, which gives you an indication of *his* musical tastes. Merv used to sit in a high chair above the Freddy Martin band, banging his spoon and screaming, "I want my Farina, I want my Farina!" I'm generally forced to spend an hour with him before each show convincing him that he's tall. His fondest memento is a daguerreotype taken of him in the company of Blue Barron, Shep Fields and Harry Horlick at a Lawrence Welk barbecue, watching Harry James's lip go bad.

PLAYBOY: Are you as fond of Joey Bishop?

RICKLES: Occasionally, Joey nods to me, starts to engage me in conversation, then decides he'd better not, because I might make him laugh and then his jaw would crack. Seriously, though, I hate to admit it, but Joey has definitely eclipsed me as a star with his new country-and-western album. When I see him, I'll have to give him a bucket of grits.

PLAYBOY: You're well acquainted with most of the funnymen in this business. Who, in your opinion, are the genuine powerhouse comics?

RICKLES: Jack Haskell, Regis Philbin and Strom Thurmond. With a possibility of their being joined by Bud Collyer, "Mr. One-Liner."

PLAYBOY: This TV season, you're co-hosting some specials on the *Kraft Music Hall*. Since Kraft has somewhat of a conservative image, why do you think they decided to engage your services?

RICKLES: Probably because I was very impressive in my interview with producers Dwight Hemion and Gary Smith. I wore a dark, conservative suit with a Reagan button, Florsheim shoes and, instead of a hanky in my breast pocket, a grilled-cheese sandwich. And I was humming the Parkay margarine song. One of these Kraft shows will feature Alan King, a delightful performer who has done for the suburbs what Nasser did for Egypt. Also with me will be Eddy Arnold, who secretly fathered all the Sons of the Pioneers.

PLAYBOY: Many critics thought your appearance on the last Emmy Awards show saved it from being a complete bomb. Did you agree?

RICKLES: Completely. If I'd been in charge, there would have been some drastic changes in the format. I would have done 90 minutes of cute patter, mailed everybody their awards and then shown a test pattern. I don't know how interested some guy in Fort Wayne is in seeing someone get an Emmy for the best cable pulling during a Miss Universe telecast, the best bulb screwing, the best drawing of Charlie Brown by a Czechoslovakian illustrator or the sexiest lighting for an Excedrin commercial. And they waste so much time on the Emmy show. The announcer introduces the West Coast moderator, who introduces the East Coast moderator. Then the West Coast moderator and the East Coast moderator spend five minutes introducing themselves to the announcer, who proceeds to introduce the caterer, who introduces the headwaiter and ultimately the guy who dunks the wienies at the steam table.

PLAYBOY: There was some talk that your own performance in a *Run for Your Life* segment last season might win you an Emmy, but this never panned out. Why?

RICKLES: Because my competition wasn't exactly the three top balloon squeezers on Ted Mack's *Amateur Hour*. I was up against the likes of Sir John Gielgud and Rod Steiger, and there was even a rumor that God was entered in my category. I was promised a consolation prize, though. If anybody dropped his Emmy, I was first in line for the pieces. The statuette is supposed to be a high-priced, gold-plated creation designed especially for the Emmy show, but when I saw Dick Van Dyke knocking his against the wall to get attention, I knew it couldn't be worth much. The brass inscription fell off, and underneath it I saw the words, "To You, Claudette Colbert, for Your Stunning Performance in *It Happened One Night*."

But I did enjoy working with Ben Gazzara on *Run for Your Life*, and I've given his producer a perfect way to extend the series. The doctor says to the doomed Paul Bryan, "We've made a horrible mistake and read the wrong x-rays. You never did have a terminal illness, just a mild case of house-itosis. So come back next Thursday for a fumigation and you can do another 39 weeks." Incidentally, kid, this interview is going on too long and it's too brilliant to waste on a clod like Hefner. Screw him. Let's sell it to Olympia Press as a dirty book.

PLAYBOY: That's twice you've maligned Hefner. What have you got against him?

RICKLES: You wouldn't print it if I told you.

PLAYBOY: Come, now, Don, *Playboy* is nothing if not fair.

RICKLES: I agree with the first part of that statement.

PLAYBOY: How can you be so vindictive, when Hef had you as his personal guest at the Mansion?

RICKLES: Hef had me as his guest for one reason: He wanted to play trick-or-treat with me in the dark. Did you ever see Hefner in heat? It reminds me of a melting Fudgsicle flanked by two jellybeans. He wouldn't leave me alone all the nights I stayed there. Kept sneaking into my room with those hot, lovesick Methodist eyes boring into mine. Wanted to know if I'd like my pillow fluffed up, offered to rub Bengay into my tummy. What a weirdo. When he isn't making passes at his guests, he sits around that *meshuganah* Mansion all day in those brown pajamas, writing about the sex life of a guppy. The man is definitely bananas. He must be a gay dog at W.C.T.U. meetings. To be frank with you, I didn't find it amusing when he put a rubber band on his ass and kept telling me, "I'm an airplane, Don. Make me take off!" And that bedroom of his. It looks like a Polish janitor's. He keeps jumping up, grabbing oily rags and polishing the trophy he won from *Good Housekeeping* for installing a "dancing waters" fountain in his bidet. I personally think that any guy who hangs around Bunnies all day should be retired to a carrot farm.

PLAYBOY: Why shouldn't Hef hang around with Bunnies?

RICKLES: He claims he's too intellectual, too high-principled to molest these unfortunates, but I've seen his bathroom towels marked His and Hers and Hers and Hers and Hers and. . . .

PLAYBOY: That ran once as a *Playboy* cartoon. Hef has always wondered where you get your material. Have you ever been privileged to attend any of his famous Sunday-night movie screenings at the Mansion?

RICKLES: Yes. What a thrill. He still thinks John Boles is big in the business. Hef's idea of a stag film is *Bambi*. He nudged me in the ribs while it was playing one night and cried, "Look, Don! The deer is running from the forest fire!" His brother had to keep explaining the story line to him, and that's no bargain, because his brother is a hockey puck. These Sunday-night movie sessions generally wind up with a festival of rib-splitting cartoons. I must say, it's a trifle dismaying to see Hugh M. Hefner, Playboy of the Western World, sex symbol of America's heartland, running around hitting his nose against the walnut paneling and singing, "Ha-ha-ha-ha-ha, ho-ho-ho-ho-ho! It's the Woody Woodpecker song!" Now I'm told he's sunk some of his ill-gotten lucre into a gigantic Playboy resort in Lake Geneva, Wisconsin, which is so square it's been turned down by Shriners' conventions. He can't even get the Holiday Inn crowd.

PLAYBOY: Have you ever been given a tour of the Woo Grotto downstairs at the Mansion?

RICKLES: That's where old Bunnies go to drown at the advanced ages of 20 and 21, when Hef doesn't want them anymore. When I visited the Woo Grotto, Lon Chaney was crawling around with his *Phantom of the Opera* makeup still on. And once in a while, you'd see a dead plumber floating by.

PLAYBOY: Did Hef play his $20,000 stereo rig for you?

RICKLES: He spent 20 big ones just so he can pick up reruns of Don McNeill's *Breakfast Club* without static. He keeps the volume up so high you'd think he invited Johnny Belinda for lunch. But he doesn't even listen; he usually spends the day up in his office answering letters from subscribers, those typical queries: "Dear Hef: I'm a zookeeper and I'm having an affair with an anteater. Is this wrong?" And Hef always answers: "Not if the anteater is a consenting adult."

PLAYBOY: Why are you painting such an unflattering portrait of Hef?

RICKLES: Are you kidding? Those are his better points. Let me tell you about some of his less charming qualities—like the way he lets his porridge drip down his leg when he eats, the disgusting noise he makes when he sucks his Ovaltine through a Flavor-straw, the tantrums he throws when his valet won't lift him on his "horsie." On top of that, I happen to know that Hefner puts silicone in his malteds to make his breasts harder. I could go on, but I don't want to embarrass him.

PLAYBOY: That's very thoughtful. May we change the subject now?

RICKLES: Not till I tell you this theory I have about Hefner. I think he and Howard Hughes are one and the same.

PLAYBOY: This is a serious charge. Can you support it?

RICKLES: Have you ever seen both of them together? They never appear in public. They have the same initials. They both made their fortunes in questionable enterprises. They both wear white sneakers and like to consummate big business deals at the bottom of abandoned zinc mines. And they both subsidize Holy Roller sects in Lubbock, Texas. I rest my case.

PLAYBOY: Do you mean to say that Hefner has done nothing for society?

RICKLES: Well, during World War I, he did block doughboys' hats.

PLAYBOY: If we didn't know you better, we'd think you didn't like him.

RICKLES: That's not entirely true. We did have a barrel of fun once when we hand-wrestled one night, but he started to weep when I broke his pipe. Up until then, he thought he was Popeye. With a body like his, he needs all the spinach he can get. Incidentally, do I get a free subscription to the magazine for consenting to this interview?

PLAYBOY: You'll be lucky to get a copy of the interview.

RICKLES: Tell your peerless leader I hope he gets rhino fungus in any areas he considers important to his manhood—or his womanhood, as the case may be.

PLAYBOY: Let's get off this sour-grapes, knock-Hefner kick. You know he could ruin you if he wanted to.

RICKLES: The only thing Hefner could ruin is a rug, if he drooled on it.

PLAYBOY: Let's talk about that famous 13-minute shot on *The Dean Martin Show* that alienated not only Hefner but the entire entertainment industry. Are you grateful to Dean for that opportunity?

RICKLES: Not really. He didn't even know I was on the show. When we were introduced, he thought I was Sam Levenson. All he said to me was, "Bring me more ice, more ice." Dean's lovable, all right, but it's tough to be with him. You get seasick trying to talk to him on an angle. And it's difficult to make yourself heard over the popping of corks. His idea of fun would be to be abandoned in the Mojave Desert with Arnold Palmer, playing putt and pitch. It was kicks, however, to needle all the celebrities that Martin's staff had packed the audience with—especially Pat Boone, who cried so hard he inadvertently cleaned his white bucks.

PLAYBOY: On the strength of that success, ABC assigned you to your own *Don Rickles Show*. How did you settle on a format?

RICKLES: We took the best elements from *The Gale Storm Show, Lamp Unto My Feet, The Hollywood Squares* and Lyndon Johnson's farewell speech to his troops and unified them into a veritable laff riot. If it doesn't turn out that way, you can contact me at the Charley Grapewin Home for Actors. Probably neither you nor Hef owns a TV set, so if you want to watch me on Friday nights, go down to Sears and have them turn one on for you. I do an opening monolog, then talk with five or six people who have oddball occupations—like the Man from Glad or a professional nose groomer—or somebody who's connected in some weird way with a big star, like Sinatra's dentist or Sammy Davis's rabbi or Don Adams's telephone-shoe repairman. Each week it'll be something different, a heckle session, or a sketch, or a stunt. It'll be a loose format that will enable me to be constantly brilliant. My head writer, Pat McCormick, is assisted by Eddie Reider, Frankie Ray and Jack Riley, who used to be the gag writers on *Sermonette*.

PLAYBOY: It would seem you've reached the pinnacle in television. Do you have any desires as yet unfulfilled in show business?

RICKLES: Well, I have my own TV show; my album *Hello Dummy!* is a red-hot item; I own a few apartment houses; I make a tremendous weekly stipend; I'll be moving soon from the Sahara's Casbar Theater to the hotel's main room, the Congo, with a 12-figure, three-year contract—or is it a three-figure, 12-year contract?—and I've just been named a presidential advisor on comedy. Maybe now, just *maybe*, they'll consider me worthy enough to be the host on the *Hollywood Palace*. It could happen very soon—if Guy Madison and John Forsythe drop out.

PLAYBOY: One of your biggest boosters has been Don Adams, star of *Get Smart*. What do you think of him?

RICKLES: He's one of my dearest friends, but I wish he'd stop kissing my ring; it loosens the stone. Some guys worshiped Mantle, Gehrig, Williams; I've always been Don's idol. It's a terrible bore, but every so often I break down and spend an evening with him, strictly as a mercy mission. He always wants to play spin the bottle or pink belly, but I tell him to grow up; so we usually go out and roll a crippled newsboy.

PLAYBOY: Frank Sinatra had much to do with your early success. Why does he brook insults from you that he wouldn't take from any other comedian?

RICKLES: He knows I have complete prints of *Johnny Concho* and *The Kissing Bandit* in my vault and that I can arrange to have them run on any *Saturday Night at the Movies*, thus sending him back into limbo forever. Did you see Frank in those flicks? For years he gave criminals a bad name. And I have other holds on him. I know for a fact he's a virgin and that the biggest sexual kick he gets is touching the noodles in my mother's chicken soup. That's how he gets in heat.

PLAYBOY: Your act and your private conversation are studded with that phrase, "in heat." Why?

RICKLES: Don't knock it if you haven't tried it. And in your case, I don't think you have. The last sexual experience you had was in a laundry hamper with wet towels on top of you. Give me that pencil back: "Super-Jew floors slope-browed interviewer with roundhouse right to the groin, overcoming deficit to grab two-to-one lead going into the top of the third."

PLAYBOY: That was a foul blow. Getting back to Sinatra—

RICKLES: When you interview somebody, do you always keep your hand on his knee?

PLAYBOY: You're not concentrating on the interview.

RICKLES: Forget the interview. Keep it up and I'll grab you by the ankles and make a wish.

PLAYBOY: Getting back to Sinatra: By bringing his Rat Pack to your café performances, he gave your career a big shot in the arm. Now that you're just as towering as Sinatra [*Rickles insisted on this description as a condition of his permission to publish the interview—Ed.*], have you considered forming your own Rat Pack?

RICKLES: I have, and—to answer your next question—Hefner's not going to be a member.

PLAYBOY: Who will be?

RICKLES: My second in command will be Criswell of *Criswell Predicts*, who told me that, according to his astrological calculations, Mount Everest will not be climbed this year by a cardiac patient. Also in the gang will be Huntz Hall, Jane Withers, Snooky Lanson and Pat Nixon. Our court jester will be "Scatman" Caruthers; and Frank Sinatra Jr. wants desperately to be our technical advisor. We plan to dash about in a gay, insane social whirl, speeding from White Tower Restaurant to Howard Johnson's in a fleet of Tucker Torpedoes and planting all sorts of zany quips in Earl Wilson's column, like "Don Rickles said it was so hot in Manhattan today that when he drove by Grant's Tomb, the door was open!" We'll also be a bunch of crazy cutups—tying strings to wallets, squirting water from our boutonnieres, wearing ties that light up and say, "Will You Kiss Me in the Dark, Baby?" And we'll throw wild hen fests and smoke cigarettes and talk catty and play cribbage and go off our diets and stay up till all hours. We'll set the tone for society with our hip talk—expressions like "Ain't we got fun?" and "Monkeys is da cwaziest people." And we'll be the envy of Carnaby Street with our Mod outfits: the kind of expensive but casual separates that Bogart wore in *The African Queen*.

PLAYBOY: Don't you plan to invite your pal Bill Cosby to join the Rickles Rat Pack?

RICKLES: Well, some of my best friends are ex-television spies, but this is an exclusive club. Nothing personal, you understand.

PLAYBOY: You appeared as a guest star on an episode of I Spy. What was it like to work with Cosby and Robert Culp?

RICKLES: It was like being Nancy Drew on safari with the Hardy Boys. What a sick relationship: They're Frick and Frack with Lugers. When lunchtime came, Culp did the cooking and I waited tables while Cosby sat and ate. That's when I knew equality had arrived in America. They offered me the part of a ruthless, overbearing nightclub owner who pushes people around and despoils women. Anxious for a chance to change my image, I jumped at the part. Anybody who really knows me off-stage can tell you I'm so docile that I ask permission to go to the bathroom. Sometimes when I hear a bell, I think it's time to go to geography class.

We filmed this particular I Spy episode on location in the shade of Cosby's 500-pound friend, Fat Albert. For background music we used Cosby's LP, *Old Silverthroat Sings*, which reaches a new high-water mark in popular singing. Bill is really representative of the *new* Negro: He has a natural lack of rhythm. But he does move well, due to his early days as a quarterback at Temple University in Philadelphia. He's the only spy I know who says, "Take this grenade on a hand-off, run out into the flat and bomb the secondary."

PLAYBOY: From the intrigue of I Spy to the folksiness of *The Andy Griffith Show* was quite a jump, but you managed it in another acting role last year. As a big-city sophisticate, why were you hired to appear on such a hayseed series?

RICKLES: Andy originally hired me because he wanted somebody to play the jew's-harp; the way he played it, it came out too gentile. Anyway, I've always had a masochistic desire to get in touch with the real America. Andy and I sat around the ole cracker barrel in Mayberry's general store, just a-whittlin' and a-chewin' the fat: "Lookee thar, Andy, a cricket! Let's watch him for a few days." When things got dull, we moseyed on down to the drugstore and listened to the Alka-Seltzer fizz.

PLAYBOY: This kind of homey humor is conspicuous by its absence from your best-selling album *Hello Dummy!*, which has been described as too incendiary for air play. Is it?

RICKLES: Absolutely not. As a matter of fact, I'm getting plenty of air play for *Hello Dummy!* on several FM stations in Andorra and Madagascar.

And the album has been number one for the past 30 weeks at Thule Air Force Base in Greenland. I must confess I had trouble at first getting U.S. stations to spin it, until the record company had the good sense to send out sample discs to all the deejays containing carefully culled 10-second excerpts. Great bits like "And here he is—Don Rickles!" That one got tons of air play. And "Hi, folks!" and "You've been a wonderful audience, folks" and "Well, goodnight, folks." Listeners haven't been offended in the least by these savage samples of my lethal wit.

PLAYBOY: Another milestone in your meteoric career has been your recent headlining at the Copacabana. Was this appearance valuable to you as a performer?

RICKLES: The Copa is still the most prestigious date in New York, because you get coverage from Gotham's widely read syndicated columnists. They all sit at front-row tables, writing their reviews, which their editors can't read too well because they've only recently learned how to block-print. I have to help Earl Wilson a lot with his capital T's and I's. He still can't figure out which one has the long straight line going across the top.

PLAYBOY: Though it's only about 10 miles from the Copa, you've come a long way since you were graduated *summa cum laudemouth* from high school in Jackson Heights. Tell us something about your early life there.

RICKLES: I'm the product of a passionate interlude between a couple whose Atwater Kent radio failed one night. Unable to pick up *Amos 'n' Andy*, they found themselves with time on their hands and begot me. I was born in 1926; but when my mother took her first look at me, she began to holler, "You'll never amount to anything, you dummy; you'll end up like your cousin Sol, a buttonholer in the garment district." When she kept nagging me, I decided to run away—but the Doberman wouldn't let me out of the closet. After my birth, she and my father got in touch with me on various occasions, which was decent of them, considering that I resided in the same apartment.

PLAYBOY: Are you saying they didn't love you?

RICKLES: Well, I was left on the doorstep with a note pinned to my Dr. Dentons: "Please kidnap." Within an hour, I was spirited away; within two hours, I was dumped back on the doorstep with another note: "Keep him. Please find enclosed check for $10,000." They used the money to send me to military school in French West Africa. And there were other hints of their disaffection. In the den they furnished for me was a tiny rocking chair with arm clamps and a metal *yarmulke* attached to a pair of electrodes. My toy soldiers shot real bullets; and one Hanukkah they gave me a kiddie car with a bomb wired to the ignition.

PLAYBOY: How did you express your gratitude for their kindnesses?

RICKLES: When I grew older, I would book them on Florida cruises during the hurricane season. And I used to go to Mass on Seder in a Polish church, where I would eat pork chops with dairy silver and hold hands with my Negro sweetheart.

PLAYBOY: Have you taken a trip back to the old neighborhood?

RICKLES: Yes, and each time I do, the same guys are still sitting on top of the same Pepsi Cola cooler in the corner delicatessen. Apparently their asses are frozen to it, because they were sitting there when I left in 1939. They try to hide their envy in subtle ways, like telling me that no matter how many times I go on *The Dean Martin Show*, I'll still never make their *fakokteh* softball team. My old rabbi, on the other hand, whom I saw on my last visit, has never displayed an iota of envy. He said to me, "Duvid"—that's my Jewish name—"I always thought you'd grow up to be famous, because you were outstanding in the annual Purim play." The Purim holiday celebrates the victory of the Jews over the wicked Persian overseer, Haman, when Good Queen Esther and Mordecai conned the king into hanging Haman. I got rave notices as the queen.

PLAYBOY: Is it true, as Thomas Wolfe wrote, that "You can't go home again?"

RICKLES: Who the hell was Thomas Wolfe? Did he marry a *shiksa*? As for going home again, I never went home when I lived there. It was a stuffy, lower-middle-class flat in a dank cell block on a sunless side street directly over the subway. You had to time your conversations between trains. I don't expect Hefner to know too much about this kind of life, since he was raised in a silo with a Guernsey for a wet nurse. He'd think a dumbwaiter is a guy who doesn't know how to uncork a wine bottle. We had a German super who used to yell up the dumbwaiter: "It iss Crizz-z-z-muz. Vere iss mein Crizz-z-z-muz prezent?" We used to drop it down to him in a large brown garbage bag attached to an anvil. The place had a lot of charm if you like to listen to your neighbors going to the bathroom—and if you like the *ambiance* of cabbage soup, which wafted from the apartment of the Hungarians on the ground floor, killed flies and darkened the wallpaper in the hall two shades. All this we were able to afford because my dad was a truly big success in the insurance field.

PLAYBOY: What was his approach?

RICKLES: Soft sell, basically. He'd tell a client, "Herbie, I saw your cardiogram and you have about an hour left. Sign here on the dotted line." And they did, thus enabling him to bankroll my bar mitzvah.

PLAYBOY: Can you re-create the solemnity of that day in which you bound yourself to the faith of your forefathers?

RICKLES: The synagogue was so crowded that half the services were held in a church three blocks away; but we had a reciprocal deal with each other's spillovers, so it worked out. My speech was somewhat unorthodox—if you'll excuse the expression: "Honorable Father and Mother, worthy Rabbi"—and then I blanked out, forgot all my lines; but I was a real trouper even then. Without a pause, I went into my crowd-pleasing impression of W.C. Fields in *The Bank Dick*, topped myself by cracking my knuckles to the tune of "A Yiddisha Momme" and somersaulted off the stage. What's the Jewish word for excommunication?

PLAYBOY: Did you make out any better at school in Jackson Heights?

RICKLES: I was king of the hill at P.S. 148. As classroom monitor, I turned in a daily truancy list containing the names of anyone who defied me—including the teacher, a shriveled-up old maid who came complete with bun, steel-rimmed glasses and a dress that had enough flowers on it to give you a hay-fever attack. She never dared to flunk me, because I threatened to tell the others that she pasted eight-by-10 glossies of Edgar Kennedy to her bodice. After school, I usually sauntered home, had my glass of milk and watched the water from the clothes hanging over the stove drip into my Orphan Annie mug. A good afternoon for me was going over to the schoolyard and making juice loans to the gentile kids. Otherwise, I spent the mid-1930s campaigning for Alf Landon; I was the only Jewish kid in the block to do so. It was the same as coming out for Hitler. But I was never too hip about Roosevelt, anyway. I thought he was a boulevard.

PLAYBOY: Did you play any of those fabled street games that Bill Cosby talks about in his monologs?

RICKLES: We played Johnny on a pony: I was the kid whose *tuchus* ended up on the fire hydrant. The idea of the game is that five guys bend over and 10 guys jump on them. I remember thinking at the time, "We should be playing this game with broads." Stickball was another of my big talents; my next-door neighbor was Polish, so I always had a broom to use. But all of our neighbors were friendly and helpful. One of them was Italian, so we always had plenty of oil for my dad's car: Giuseppe just shook it out of his hair, right into the crankcase.

PLAYBOY: Speaking of broads, when did you start to become aware of the fair sex?

RICKLES: At a synagogue dance, when the kids laughed at me for lindy-hopping with a bridge chair. So I asked Bernice Sachs to dance. Bernice's father was so rich he used to stand up in the synagogue every Jewish holiday and yell, "I donate $10,000—anonymous!" When I returned home from my first date with her, I had a noticeable hickey on my neck; my mother thought an Irish kid had bit me in a fight. That first experimentation with love wasn't a howling success; Bernice begged me to rip off her dress, but my main concern was if my comedy was going over. I thought I'd outgrown that problem until years later, on my wedding night, when my wife failed to laugh when I was ready to make my big move, and I knew it was back again.

PLAYBOY: You were doing comedy routines on your wedding night?

RICKLES: Yeah—the old Adam and Eve bit. Except we didn't have any fruit.

PLAYBOY: Let's move from one combat zone to another. Your biography cites your heroic accomplishments in the Navy during World War II. Would you care to tell us about them?

RICKLES: No, I'd really rather not toot my own horn that way.

PLAYBOY: But—

RICKLES: Well, if you insist. I was stationed in the Philippines for three years. There were only two Jewish kids on the boat, a PT tender called the *USS Cyrene*. It used to be a dock until they put a bottom under it. It was so humid in the tropics that the crew spoiled. Every time we got a taste of action, the rest of the guys would look at the two of us and cry, "Do us a miracle. Part the seas and get us the hell out of here."

PLAYBOY: Seriously, did you really see any action?

RICKLES: Yes, we hissed at the enemy, cursed at him, even fired our weapons at him. That's how we destroyed our ship's movie screen. I was personally responsible for the death of Richard Loo in *The Purple Heart*, and my buddy got Philip Ahn in *Wings Over Burma*. Tell your buck-toothed photographer this is all in fun.

PLAYBOY: Who was your commanding officer on this magnificent fighting vessel?

RICKLES: A guy who'd come to us directly from a sea-scout meeting. He thought a sandbar was candy. The atmosphere on board was a trifle strained. We kept looking at each other under the shower, imagining the other guy was Betty Grable on a Bob Hope camp tour. One of the gang had definite effeminate tendencies. He kept on skipping up and down the deck, screeching, "Oh, let *me* fold the flag!" There was another guy who was always attempting suicide; we had to keep cutting him down from the bulkhead.

PLAYBOY: Who was he?

RICKLES: The morale officer. The whole tour was worse than *Mister Roberts*. If any of us had tried to write a book about it, the others would have killed him for reminding them of it.

PLAYBOY: After the war, you studied at the American Academy of Dramatic Arts. What did you learn there?

RICKLES: How to use makeup effectively. I swabbed it on so liberally I was always being solicited by members of the vice squad. Have you ever seen a policeman expose himself? It's what they call a "cop-out."

PLAYBOY: With this sort of high-caliber dramatic training under your belt, you launched your career in those premiere-showcase supper clubs that comedians refer to as "the toilets." What were they like?

RICKLES: Really high-class places. They smelled like a pair of sneakers after a basketball doubleheader at the Garden. And the owners were the kind of guys who wore $5000 pinkie rings and beerstained undershirts. They'd sit in the front row and spit at the acts. The clientele wore double-breasted Chester Morris suits with Hoover buttons—and this was in the 1950s. It was the first time I'd ever seen grown men wearing brown patent-leather shoes with white anklet socks. And always on their ties was a figure of Roy Rogers's horse. You wouldn't often see Grace Kelly there dancing with Adolphe Menjou.

Many of these gin mills were sailor joints in Washington, D.C., which featured bubble dancers like Monique LaVine, who was in big trouble when her bubble pipe didn't work; you know how opium residue can clog a pipe. We had specialty acts like Zokina and Her King Cobra, which turned out to be a garter snake with dewlaps. It was retarded, too. Instead of slithering over Zokina's oiled body, it ate its own basket. And one of the strippers, Flora LaVerne, had so many stretch marks on her body she looked like the Mississippi River delta from 30,000 feet up. Occasionally, brawls would erupt, which I avoided by lying on the floor and pretending to be a mound of cigarette butts.

PLAYBOY: Did it work?

RICKLES: You get out of line once more and I'll fix it so you never play the glockenspiel again. The marquee outside these fun spots was a real ego booster. It was a kick to spot your name in lights—if you could see it through all the dead moths on the bulbs. My accommodations were swanky, too. To dress, I had to stand on top of a bus boy. The four-piece combo—piano, bass, drums and spittoon—were all Sammy Kaye rejects. No matter what request the customers hollered for—"Stardust," "Body and Soul," "Moonglow"—they broke into "Take Me Out to the Ball Game." They started a wonderful musicians' quiz called "Find the Melody." Generally, there was also a girl singer named Lola Lane or Tish Burdue, who had the sexy, throbbing vocal quality of a wino retching through a kazoo. And the food served in these places could best be described as Forest Lawn for flies. An occasional ribbon of flypaper dangling in the soup added a distinctive Duncan Hines touch. The only reason the place was never condemned by the Board of Health was because they didn't have the guts to go in there and check. The parking-lot attendant had his fun and games, too. You pulled up, gave him the keys to your car and went inside. It was your job to find it the following day at the demolition derby on Route 31 outside Bethesda, Maryland.

PLAYBOY: Were any of these "toilets" operated by hoods?

RICKLES: Perhaps, but I've never worried about the mob element, because I'm a personal friend of Efrem Zimbalist Jr.

PLAYBOY: Plays a hell of a zimbal, doesn't he?

RICKLES: Give me that pencil. "*Playboy* punster zings in 'zimbal' joke on unsuspecting comedian to take a four-to-three lead in the top of the seventh." You have a quicksilver mind, my child. I both respect and hate you for that. Why don't you dive headfirst into a vat of pickled hair? But to tell you the truth, the gangster image has never frightened me, because I happen to know that Warren Beatty has trouble with the firing mechanism on a cap pistol.

PLAYBOY: Many people who know you primarily as a nightclub performer are surprised these days to see you popping up on some of the *Late Show* movies. Would you like to discuss some of your early film successes?

RICKLES: Hollywood first beckoned to me in 1956 by starring me in a war thriller, *Run Silent, Run Deep*, which also featured Clark Gable and Burt Lancaster in supporting roles. They were adequate in the film, but I got tired of carrying them. The plot concerned an American sub in the Bongo Straits that was trying to fool a Japanese destroyer into thinking they'd sunk us by using the old submarine's trick—disgorging garbage from the torpedo tubes. To this day, I'm bitter about how Clark and Burt looked at each other and said, "We're out of garbage. Let's throw out Rickles."

I also did *The Rat Race* with Tony Curtis, one of our great Cary Grants. When I knew Tony, he was one of the boys; today, he wears love beads and challenges women to duels. Then they threw me into a couple of high-class vehicles called *Muscle Beach Party* and *Beach Blanket Bingo*, produced by American International Pictures, which specialized in low-budget quickies that were shot for a price range of $40 to $50: add $5 if they were in color. This gave me a chance to work with my idols Annette Funicello and Frankie Avalon, who got me admitted to their day nursery as a fringe benefit. My dialog consisted of yelling "Surf's up! Surf's up!" every 25 minutes. But Frankie and Annette had to rehearse their lines for hours. It was hard for them to remember "Run, Spot, run!" They want me to act in their new one, *Kiss My Sandbox*.

PLAYBOY: Now that you're a big star in your own right, have you been offered any meatier parts?

RICKLES: Only the ones they throw into my cage. Actually, yes, my agent has been deluged with movie offers, but unfortunately none of them are talkies. I've been asked to co-star with Lyle Talbot in *I Was in Heat for a Werewolf*. And Paramount wants me to redo the Quasimodo role with two humps. There was also some talk about me starring in *Planet of the Apes* because the producers thought they could save money on makeup, but I turned it down because they offered me peanuts. Give me that pencil. "Super-Jew lobs in 'peanuts' ad lib, streaks into five-to-four lead in the top of the eighth."

PLAYBOY: Until Hollywood discovers your potential as a sex star, fans can see you at your unexpurgated best only in Las Vegas. For the benefit of those who've never sojourned in this manmade jewel on the desert, could you fill them in on the atmosphere?

RICKLES: You know you're getting into Vegas when the pilots start betting among themselves that they'll clear the mountain. And the weather can be quite distressing. During a typical Vegas sandstorm, I often put a hanky over my mouth and go out looking for Rommel's tanks. The heat can be appalling, too. It hit 125 degrees here at the Sahara one afternoon and the pool had to be rushed to the hospital with heat prostration. In other parts of the world, the hotels bear dignified names—Hilton, Statler, Plaza, St. Regis. Here, the owners have delusions of grandeur. They call them Sahara, Aladdin, Thunderbird, Caesars Palace. The only hotel in town that makes any sense is called the Mint. They hit it right on the head. The residents of this town have one shining philosophy: Roll the customers, but do it legal. In my hotel, the Sahara—

PLAYBOY: *Your* hotel? We're sure Del Webb would take umbrage at that claim.

RICKLES: Del Webb doesn't get laughs—not intentionally, anyway. I put this hotel on the map. Before I came here, they had thrilling lounge acts like Milo Waslewski and His Accordionettes, featuring Wanda Kropnik, the first topless eggsucker.

PLAYBOY: Since you started working in Vegas, nude shows have taken over most of the big showrooms. As a devoutly religious man, how do you feel about making your living in this sexually liberated atmosphere?

RICKLES: Well, it was a shock to discover that many of the girls are not wearing their dresses at a decent, respectable mid-calf length, and that there is gambling going on here openly and nobody is saying a thing about it. And the language is revolting. I don't believe I've ever heard the words "hell" and "damn" used so casually and by people of such obvious breeding. I'll definitely have to write an exposé for the *Watchtower* on these developments.

PLAYBOY: We hear a good deal about your storied confrontations in Vegas with Fat Jack Leonard, who likes to call himself the "fastest mouth in the West." Can you set the scene for one of these showdowns?

RICKLES: Somehow, the word gets out that both Jack and I are in town and a hush falls over the Strip. Saloonkeepers board up their establishments. Kids and old ladies are hustled off the streets: even hustlers are hustled off the streets. Danny Thomas kneels in his combination chapel-and-nightclub and prays for our souls. Then at high noon, Jack and I start a measured walk down the Strip toward each other. I can see by the way his cheeks are puffed up that he has 20 new one-liners jammed in his mouth. I myself have 25, including five that Shecky Greene sent over on the Wells Fargo wagon. We've agreed to start spewing lines at the count of three; but at two, Jack cheats, spits his lines out and I get knocked off as usual. I know Jack claims I've been doing his act, but at least I've been trying to improve it.

PLAYBOY: With or without Jack's help, you've cornered the market on the ethnic insult. How did you uncover this mother lode of malice?

RICKLES: What do you mean, ethnic insult? May your yam nose get caught under a West German steam iron; may your bird shrivel up into a pea pod; may a Green Beret drive a personnel carrier over your kumquats. But to answer your question, pal, it happened one night when the audience bolted toward me carrying their knives and forks with them. I had an idea it wasn't for the purpose of asking for autographs, so I hurled a few ethnic gibes to fend them off. About half of them reeled back, and the rest began to laugh at them, which they took as deadly slander; in a moment, they were at each other's jugulars. Then I called the police and had them all arrested for starting a race riot.

PLAYBOY: Is it really necessary for you to be so hostile?

RICKLES: Would you rather I came onstage like Art Linkletter and sang 4-H cookie-baking songs? If I did that, my audience would consist of two Cuban waiters in the back, slapping at mosquitoes with their napkins.

PLAYBOY: What have you been saying lately to the various ethnic groups in your audience?

RICKLES: If I see an Italian in the audience, I tell him, "Domenico, spit out the nails and tell me if my shoes are ready." To the Poles: "You're wonderful people. When Jewish-owned cars break down, who else has the strength to push them back to the garage? And thanks for giving us the *Warsaw Concerto*."

PLAYBOY: To Mexicans?

RICKLES: "Every time you get the runs, Manuel, stop over at the state highway department. They need someone to make the white lines down the middle of Route 66. If you don't like that, you can kiss my *tacos*." That's Castilian for *tuchus*.

PLAYBOY: Do you spare those of your own faith?

RICKLES: No, why should I? I usually say something like, "If you took that roll of bills out of your pants pocket, you'd look like a eunuch."

PLAYBOY: How about the WASPs?

RICKLES: I always know when WASPs are in the audience. They're the ones still wearing World War II discharge buttons. They order corned beef on white bread with a glass of milk and a pickle. They call each other "Mother" and "Father." The Negroes call them Mother, too, only they pronounce it different.

PLAYBOY: Ever get any Arabs in the crowd?

RICKLES: Sometimes. It would be the easiest thing for me to malign the Arabs, to get cheap laughs at their expense, but I tell them, "Look, we're all part of humanity, so let's bury the animosities of the past." Then I tell Achmed and Abdullah to stand up in the spotlight and take a bow.

PLAYBOY: Do they?

RICKLES: Yes. And as soon as they do, I yell, "Open fire!"

PLAYBOY: Have you ever reduced anyone in your audience to tears?

RICKLES: One night some old broad yelled out, "You're great, you're great!"; so I cut her up with a hundred insults. I just can't stand people who fawn—though I must admit, it was a rotten way to treat my own mother.

PLAYBOY: Must there be celebrities in your audience for you to be at your best?

RICKLES: Oh, no. Human beings have a habit of laughing, too.

PLAYBOY: A guy like you seems to beg for hecklers. What devastating lines do you direct against a really rowdy specimen?

RICKLES: I say, "Please try to be more polite. Your frequent interruptions have a deleterious effect on my timing and thus diminish my overall effectiveness as a humorist." He generally runs off crying.

PLAYBOY: Aren't you afraid of being assaulted physically when you toss off barbs like that?

RICKLES: Not really. I tell any hostile elements in the audience, "If you strike me, a squadron of Mirage bombers will level your home." I have also studied Korean *Fung Kyu*, the deadliest form of openhanded combat. With one blow of my left hand, I can shatter every bone in a child's body.

PLAYBOY: Do you work yourself into a rage before you come onstage?

RICKLES: My, my, the cockamamie interviewer is so clever he asks his questions in rhyme. Why don't you swing with a Burma-Shave sign and get splinters in your thighs? My usual procedure before facing a Sahara crowd is to allow myself to be bitten by a vicious dog. Working with rabies germs coursing through my veins helps my comedic flow.

PLAYBOY: Are you aware that a growing number of your devotees would like to see you committed to an institution?

RICKLES: Yes, I can understand how lonely it gets for them in those cages; they're just as entitled to a little entertainment as anyone else.

PLAYBOY: In view of your seething hostility, it seems logical to ask if you've ever submitted to psychiatric evaluation.

RICKLES: A guy named Lennie once recommended it to me. He also wanted me to pet rabbits and fluffy chickens and, like an idiot, I listened. Next thing I remember, two guys in white coats were jamming a thermometer into me and I was making like Johnny Weissmuller and diving into a sink. My first headshrinker was the great Jivaro psychiatrist Calypso Bwanamakuba. I gave him up fast when I saw some of his former patients hanging from his belt. I ended up with a Freudian analyst, but I gave him up, too, when I walked in on him one day and found him making love on his couch. Alone.

PLAYBOY: Some entertainers possess legendary fixations—like a well-known pop singer who reportedly takes showers several times a day and insists on carrying freshly laundered money. Did your analyses uncover any special quirks?

RICKLES: Several. I can never work a nightclub that's on fire—an odd hang-up, but that's how it is. I must sleep in my closet to ascertain that my clothes aren't plotting against me. I must have food and drink on any day of the week ending in "d-a-y." And no optometrist who has ever memorized the South African constitution or played bop alto in the Cedar Rapids Jazz Festival can be allowed to examine my eyes. I also have two major phobias—spiders and height; if I ever had to stand on top of a 1000-foot spider, I think I'd die. And one lesser hang-up: I will never use chili-pepper suppositories unless the seeds have been removed.

PLAYBOY: That's the umpteenth anal reference you've made in this interview, suggesting a rather sick fixation. Do you tell enema jokes, too?

RICKLES: I never mention enemas; that's not my bag. Incidentally, is this how Hefner gets his jollies? "Hey, guys, let's get Rickles to talk about enemas!" He must sit around his bedroom in the nude, humming. With some of the fruity clothes he wears, he'd be better off. What the hell can you say about a midget who sits around in Bunny ears and trap-door pajamas screaming, "Don, you wanna see me play dump truck?" May he take a high colonic with an open umbrella.

PLAYBOY: You know, Don, you can dish out the insults, but can you take it when some enraged listener strikes back?

RICKLES: Try me, yo-yo.

PLAYBOY: You're . . . you're a *terrible* person!

RICKLES: Oh, God, did you have to excoriate me like that? I must call up my rabbi for spiritual solace in this, my darkest hour.

PLAYBOY: "Interviewer's incisive invective shatters Superswine's façade, thus enabling interviewer to take a six-to-five edge going into the top of the ninth." Let's continue. A man who abuses as many people as you do must have a good attorney. Who's yours?

RICKLES: A sharp cookie named Paul Caruso, who predicted Caryl Chessman would get off free. Paul thinks the Supreme Court is a garden apartment in downtown L.A. And he has a unique way of influencing the jury. During his final summation, he distributes Italian ices. I once saw Paul get a guy out of a rape charge by using a shrewd strategy. He proved that his client couldn't possibly have attacked the girl because at the exact time the alleged offense took place he was selling atomic secrets to the Russians.

PLAYBOY: You seem to be well fixed in the legal department. Who steers your artistic career?

RICKLES: Joe Scandore, another Italian, which shows you how much faith I have in my own people. Joe has always been a mite too hungry for that 10 percent commission. He once booked me into the Roxy Theater in New York City while the wrecking ball was hitting the building. He always thought I worked better in debris. And to this day, I'm still irate over his booking me into the officers' club in Stuttgart, Germany.

PLAYBOY: Why? Some of those Service-club gigs pay very well.

RICKLES: In 1944? Another thing leads me to believe he may not be the proper manager to shepherd my career. His favorite comedian is Tennessee Ernie Ford. I don't question Joe's intellectual qualifications, though. He did get a master's in potty training at Syracuse University.

PLAYBOY: Your professional life looks set. May we now delve into your married life? Until fairly recently you were a confirmed bachelor. What induced you to take the plunge?

RICKLES: It happened when I met Barbara Sklar, a very pretty brunette who was a secretary for a big show-business agency, supplementing her income by standing on Lexington Avenue in a torn dress, whimpering, "Paper, mister? Daily paper?" She's from Philadelphia, where their big thrill is watching the Liberty Bell on hot days, hoping the cracks will get fused together. She's so quiet I hardly know she's even with me, which makes for a blissful marriage.

PLAYBOY: Did you have an elaborate wedding?

RICKLES: It was an orthodox wedding, but kind of weird. I don't think the rabbi liked me; he put the wineglass on the floor for me to step on, as is traditional at these mergers, but he insisted that I do it with my shoes off. And the service was quite prolonged; by the time it was over I had cheated on her three times. My family was great about the whole thing, though; they gave us generous presents. Her family's contribution to the proceedings was taking pictures of my family giving us the gifts; then they sent my family the bill for the film. Because Barbara's a little frugal, we took the economy-jet honeymoon trip to Europe, which consisted of circling over London, Paris and Rome without landing.

PLAYBOY: You spent your honeymoon in the air?

RICKLES: Yeah, but it wasn't so bad. We just flipped the occupied switch and curled up in the head. For some reason, she was rather hesitant about lovemaking. She said, in an accusing tone, "I had no idea you were going to do *that*." But since then she's become quite sophisticated about love. Her favorite phrase is, "Let's do *that*."

PLAYBOY: What's "*that*"?

RICKLES: She feels that when we indulge in amorous activities we should be in the same room. It's a little kinky, but I go along with it.

PLAYBOY: In preparing for the love act, do you peruse any sex manuals?

RICKLES: Usually I go off by myself and read one to make sure I don't flunk. Afterward, she grades my performance; 95 is passing. I haven't failed yet.

PLAYBOY: You've been married for several years now. Has any of the excitement worn off?

RICKLES: Not at all. Today, just like when we were married, strange things happen when our lips meet. My Timex goes back one hour; the night-light flutters in bossa-nova tempo; the shower curtain flings itself open so the tub can watch; and sometimes my cousin comes over, looks at us, lights an Olympic torch and cries, "Let the games begin!"

PLAYBOY: Which sex manuals do you consult—Theodoor Van de Velde, Eustace Chesser, Albert Ellis?

RICKLES: The writings of Sonny Liston. He was always good at working in close.

PLAYBOY: Apart from lovemaking, how do you spend your time at home?

RICKLES: I usually sit around watching my wife prepare exotic cuisine. Her favorite dish is a day-old bun with a side order of lard. She reads all those Julia Child cookbooks, like *100 Exciting Ways to Prepare Salt*. On a typical day at home, the fan magazines would find us cuddling together as we dice onions and chat about hemming curtains for the nursery.

PLAYBOY: Are you a good babysitter for your daughter?

RICKLES: Not bad. Mindy Beth and I change each other every four hours.

PLAYBOY: Is she being brought up according to Dr. Spock?

RICKLES: Yes, but it's pretty hard to carry a picket sign when you're teething. Spock's advice is sound for the most part, but when it doesn't work, I go back to my mother's old method: I deprive Mindy of food and water and lock her in a suitcase.

PLAYBOY: What kind of future do you have planned for her?

RICKLES: Marriage to a rich guy with a heart condition; but with my luck, she'll wind up a taxi dancer. Just warn Hefner that if she ever becomes a Bunny and lives in his Mansion, he won't look too attractive with stumps for hands.

PLAYBOY: The word is that since you became a star you've gone Hollywood with a snazzy penthouse in Beverly Hills. Is that slander true?

RICKLES: Don't say penthouse. I prefer to say "top floor," because that phrase won't make my friends think I've outgrown them. Which I have.

PLAYBOY: Did you hire a decorator to furnish the place?

RICKLES: Several. The first one was Tiny Tim's effeminate brother. He wanted to tiptoe through my tulips, so I threw him out. Our second decorator was a jovial, burly type in a tweed jacket who puffed on a briar. Did a hell of a nice job, too; except I didn't like the way she kept fondling Barbara.

PLAYBOY: Have you become a patron of the arts since you started coming into big money?

RICKLES: Yes, I have. While scouring the galleries for a frame worthy of my 20-foot self-portrait, I discovered a great artist, a Dutch genius named Van Gogh.

PLAYBOY: We'll bite. You mean Vincent?

RICKLES: No, Sylvia, his mother—a great undiscovered talent. I've added her greatest masterpiece to my collection, the immortal *Hair Drier Breast-Feeding Its Young*. A very passionate lady; she got that from her son, who was once so incensed at his mistress that he cut off part of his body and mailed it to her.

PLAYBOY: His ear?

RICKLES: If that's what you want to believe, go right ahead.

PLAYBOY: Your book collection is the talk of the literati. Do any first editions adorn your shelves?

RICKLES: Many—children's classics, mostly. Like *Heidi Is Horny, Porky Pig Goes Kosher, Little Jack Horner Sits in the Corner and Watches His Thumb Die, Doctor Dolittle Goes Both Ways with the Pushmi-Pullyu* and my personal favorite, *Chitty-Chitty Gang Bang*.

PLAYBOY: Who runs this *soigné* household?

RICKLES: Cockimoto, our Japanese houseboy, who does a bang-up job but sometimes embarrasses us by staging those Oriental tea ceremonies. The narcotics squad has raided us three times. And it's chilling to see him interrogating my guests: "Where is your aircraft carrier, Yankee pig?" Tell that Japanese photographer to stop pointing that zoom lens at my navel. If he wants Okinawa back, he can have it.

PLAYBOY: What kind of showbiz luminaries show up at your celebrated parties?

RICKLES: Mostly animal acts that never made it on *The Ed Sullivan Show*. But Ed should do his own act on that show; he's the only guy I know who shaves with his arms folded. I don't want to knock him, though.

He's one of my dearest friends, so you know how lonely I am. His wife, who interprets for him, is amazing; she's the only one who has the guts to tell him he looks great.

PLAYBOY: Your eleemosynary instincts have been lauded throughout the years. What charities do you support?

RICKLES: Mostly the Etta Rickles Cabana Chair Fund, which keeps my mother in Miami Beach. And the United Jewish Appeal, of course; although during the six-day war, for the sake of fair play, I started a United Arab Appeal drive with a gigantic rally at the city dump. We raised damn near $3, most of it in pledges from Syrian bellhops who work in Jewish hotels. But I knew the Jews would have to win the war in six days; after all, on the seventh day He rested, too.

PLAYBOY: In your act you talk so much about your God that many people think He's a personal friend. Are they right?

RICKLES: Last week my mother-in-law turned into a pillar of salt; draw your own conclusions. But to be perfectly honest with you, our God hasn't shown up yet; I'll know Him when He does, though, because He'll be wearing a top hat and tails and do a couple of tap numbers with Moshe Dayan's daughter.

PLAYBOY: How can you be sure He hasn't appeared already?

RICKLES: Because we haven't had a Jewish president.

PLAYBOY: Would you want to be the first Jew to occupy the White House?

RICKLES: No, I wouldn't want to step down. I will say, however, that under a Jewish president we'd never have any wars. He'd give the enemy a couple hundred bucks and settle out of court.

PLAYBOY: Still, if you *were* president, how would you exercise your power?

RICKLES: I'd force Everett Dirksen to flush out his sinuses on *Meet the Press*. Maybe make Captain Kangaroo read *The 120 Days of Sodom* to his kiddies some Saturday morning. And insist that Kate Smith sing lead with the Jefferson Airplane—naked. And every place I'd go, I'd be surrounded with drooling fawners begging me, "Don, let me go on your TV show!" But the hell with Barbara's family.

PLAYBOY: In April of this year, *Playboy* ran a series of sardonically witty horoscopic profiles. What's your astrological sign?

RICKLES: I was born under the sign of Taurus the Bull, which gives me a tendency to charge the audience and gore the maitre d'. At the Sahara, the latter happens to be Johnny Joseph, a man of Lebanese extraction, which gives me an added incentive.

PLAYBOY: Those born under your sign can boast a number of endearing virtues—stubbornness, irritability, avarice, insane jealousy—but nothing to indicate exceptional intellectual endowment. Yet you're known to have an inordinate admiration for your own mental powers. Since they say the stars never lie, do you think you might be wrong?

RICKLES: If the stars never lie, then you can believe me when I tell you that I'm brilliant. Let me put it to you this way. When I retire at night, my mind sleeps in a separate bed. I get a wakeup call from the hotel clerk at two P.M., but my mind isn't disturbed until 3:30. Since my career is predicated on the successful function of my mind, I defer to it in every way. I would never dare offend it; it might decide to leave me and relocate in Sinatra's body. Why should I make *him* a hit?

PLAYBOY: We concede that your mind is paramount, but we also can't help noticing that your physique has undergone a drastic change from its elephantine proportions of a few seasons back.

RICKLES: True, angel boy. Would you like to get a room together? The best way to describe my new slimmed-down body is to say that when I see it in the mirror, I touch and sigh. The mirror is so jealous it takes the Fifth when I ask it who's the fairest of them all. You may fondle it if you wish.

PLAYBOY: That would be sacrilege. We're told you've shed some 60 pounds. How did you do it?

RICKLES: I was going to try a crash diet, but I decided against it when I found out it called for me to run my car into a concrete abutment at 70 miles an hour. Then I tried sitting in a basin of cottage cheese, but all it did was excite me sexually. Organic foods were my next kick: breakfasts of Quaker Puffed Pebbles and Campbell's Cream of Jeans. Another diet called for skimmed water. I tried to get jobs that would guarantee exercise, like being a real-estate agent in Watts. Then I went on the famous weight-watcher diet, which allows you five fruits a day, but I abandoned it when I got 423 phone calls from Fire Island. I finally settled on the famous Minnesota Mining and Manufacturing Company diet—Scotch tape across the mouth; that did the trick.

PLAYBOY: Has weight reduction enhanced your virility, as it has for many middle-aged men?

RICKLES: Again with the damn sex questions? Why doesn't Hefner get his mind off smut and go mount a Fig Newton?

PLAYBOY: The reason Hef asked us to pump you for this sort of information is because of your reputation for great expertise in the field. We were hoping, in fact, that you'd use this podium, as a veteran sexual counselor for thousands of showgirls, to enlighten our readers with the facts about various myths pertaining to sex. What can you tell us, for example, about the legendary ill effects of autoeroticism?

RICKLES: Let me look it up in my diary. Let's see—oh, yes, here it is. As far as legends are concerned, my research tells me that prolonged autoeroticism will definitely cause blindness and excessive growth of hair. I would say that overindulgence in this practice makes one sluggish and could lead to expulsion from the volleyball team.

PLAYBOY: How about those behind-the-hand whispers about Oriental women?

RICKLES: They're true. Oriental women are built vastly different from Oriental men.

PLAYBOY: Thanks for clearing that up. We've also wondered whether it's true, as popular belief has it, that Greek love is practiced only by Greeks.

RICKLES: That's just a Greek myth.

PLAYBOY: Are you speaking from personal experience?

RICKLES: I'll have to back away from that question.

PLAYBOY: We'll mark that down as a yes. What are your other perversions?

RICKLES: Driving past schoolyards with the car door open, the backseat loaded with Milky Ways and Mars bars, and calling out to little girls. I lure them into the car, sell them the candy at outrageous prices and boot them out untouched.

PLAYBOY: What other perversions excite you?

RICKLES: Anything Danish—films, pornographic books, girls, coffeecakes. I also wanted to see that four-letter version of *Ulysses*, but I couldn't get the producer to lend me a print so I could show it in my bathroom.

PLAYBOY: Couldn't you have gone to see it at a theater?

RICKLES: That would take the fun out of it; and besides, I'm a little too old to sit in the balcony with my coat over my lap.

PLAYBOY: Do you have any secret cravings that involve animals?

RICKLES: I sometimes become aroused looking at a frog on a wet rock and watching his neck throb.

PLAYBOY: Did you ever make it with a frog?

RICKLES: Once. It convinced a Navy doctor I had been in the Philippines too long. On one other occasion, I had a burning yen to attack a chicken, but my mother said no for two reasons: It wasn't flicked, and it wasn't kosher.

PLAYBOY: Don, you've fielded our toughest questions with engaging frankness, but now we're going to hand you a blockbuster. Ordinarily, we wouldn't want to get this personal, but we think we know you well enough to spring it.

RICKLES: Wait—let me brace myself.

PLAYBOY: Ready?

RICKLES: Fire away.

PLAYBOY: What's your favorite color?

RICKLES: Look, pal, I didn't mind you asking me about my private life and even my sexual perversions, but this time you've gone too far.

PLAYBOY: Don't duck it. What's your favorite color?

RICKLES: The way things are going—black.

PLAYBOY: Another ethnic slur. A racist like you probably wouldn't even want his daughter to marry a Negro.

RICKLES: If you were a Negro, would you want me for a father-in-law?

PLAYBOY: Good point. Do you think intermarriage is the solution to the race problem?

RICKLES: No, I think all we have to do is make a new version of *Gone With the Wind*, starring Sidney Poitier as Rhett Butler, Sammy Davis Jr. as Ashley Wilkes, Lee Bouvier as Mammy and me as Prissy, Butterfly McQueen's unforgettable role as the faithful family retainer. Race relations might also improve if we could get bookies and jockeys to work closer together.

PLAYBOY: Many young people, black and white, feel that drastic reform of our social institutions will be necessary before racial justice can be achieved. Do you have any equally inspired ideas on how to make the New Politics a viable force in America?

RICKLES: Would you repeat the question?

PLAYBOY: Sorry to wake you. Many young people, black and white, feel that drastic reform of our social institutions will be necessary before racial justice can be achieved. Do you have any equally inspired ideas on how to make the New Politics a viable force in America?

RICKLES: I heard you the first time. I just couldn't believe you were such a pompous ass.

PLAYBOY: Don't know the answer, do you?

RICKLES: Egghead fruit. May your Phi Beta Kappa key get caught in your fly during commencement exercises.

PLAYBOY: May we conclude that you have nothing to say about the New Politics?

RICKLES: I don't have anything to say about the *old* politics. As far as I'm concerned, Nixon is the brand name for a dog repellent that keeps Fido off the furniture, Spiro Agnew sounds like a Romanian fungus and Johnson is a baby powder. As for Humphrey, who could vote for a cartoon character from *Joe Palooka*? Besides, who could trust a man who once sold Chapstick right over the counter in a Minneapolis drugstore?

PLAYBOY: Have you ever taken drugs yourself?

RICKLES: I tried something called LBJ once before I went onstage and the microphone cord turned into a bullwhip, sliced me in a key region and I finished my act sounding like Anna Maria Alberghetti.

PLAYBOY: What's your feeling about the hippie movement?

RICKLES: I don't worry about them. The unkempt hippie of today will be the mutual-fund salesman of tomorrow.

PLAYBOY: A man of your sagacity should certainly have some notion about how to close the generation gap. Do you?

RICKLES: I say this: Talk to your kid, see what's bugging him, give his fears and desires a sympathetic airing; then take him into the cellar and work him over with a rubber hose and I'm sure he'll come around.

PLAYBOY: A progressive panacea. What do you think about the new morality?

RICKLES: It's the same as the old morality except that they put it on film.

PLAYBOY: Speaking of films, you're an inveterate moviegoer. Apart from Danish stag reels, what kind of movies do you like?

RICKLES: Anything with Bruce Cabot or Buster Crabbe. I particularly liked a recent remake of *King Kong* in which, instead of falling from the Empire State Building, Kong marries Fay Wray and they move to the suburbs. But it doesn't work out because their sex life isn't all they dreamed it would be.

PLAYBOY: In addition to moviegoing, how do you like to relax?

RICKLES: You'd like me to say I read *Playboy* in the woodshed, wouldn't you? You're sadly mistaken. I relax by lying with the bedcovers over my head and playing "pup tent."

PLAYBOY: Last night during your act, you told a woman who gasped at your bawdy language, "What did you expect, lady? Billy Graham?" If Graham ever chanced to find himself in your audience, what would you do?

RICKLES: Convert, what else?

PLAYBOY: Would you clean up your material for his benefit?

RICKLES: No, but I'd wear a lightning rod to ground any bolts from the blue.

PLAYBOY: Do you think he'd enjoy your act?

RICKLES: I think he'd laugh his head off—and then ask the Almighty's forgiveness. But I don't think Sinatra would accept the apology.

PLAYBOY: You once remarked that you'd know you'd really made it in show business when "that guy in the Kansas wheat field" would recognize you on sight. If that day ever comes, how will you feel toward him?

RICKLES: If I thought he really and truly loved me, I'd plow his south 40 with my tongue—two rows at once.

PLAYBOY: Don, because you're basically a well-meaning pussycat at heart and because you always conclude your act with a sincere apology if you've hurt anyone's feelings, can we assume that all your vicious pillorying of Hef has been just in fun?

RICKLES: It's just my humble way of telling Hefner he's the laughingstock of two continents. In the others, nobody's heard of him yet.

PLAYBOY: But, Don—

RICKLES: Mr. Rickles to you. May Hefner do a half gainer and land on the head of the pin he should have written his *Philosophy* on. May his famous Playboy Club breakfast give his patrons the Aztec Two-Step and may the johns be out of order when it happens. May all the Bunnies' tails fall off from jungle rot.

PLAYBOY: But, Don—

RICKLES: As for you, flunky, may I say from the bottom of my heart that I've never liked you from the start. You're the kind of toady who bootlicks a star and then borrows money at the end of the night for passage on the Greyhound back to Omaha.

PLAYBOY: Do you mean to tell us you were insincere when you called us "angel boy" and invited us up to your room?

RICKLES: Face facts, dummy. You've been had. I find you about as attractive sexually as a dentist's drill. I was just stringing you along to snap Polaroids when I got you in heat, which I planned to send to your wife. Now that I've got what I want from you—the publicity from this interview, even in a six-bit girlie rag like *Playboy*—you can go eat a dish of Brillo for all I care. May you pass out and wake up in the bottom of a birdcage. As for that no-talent publisher of yours, he's the type who sits in his living room with his robe open reading *True Confessions*. May his next special girl turn out to be a special boy. May his electronic entertainment room short-circuit with his finger in a socket and give him a Rap Brown haircut. May his new television show win an Emmy as the greatest cultural series since *Ding Dong School*.

PLAYBOY: But, Don—

RICKLES: May the members of his editorial staff come back from a field trip to Tijuana with blue tongues. May all the gatefolds of the next issue fall out before they get to the newsstands, leaving the readers with a thrilling 50,000-word essay on Che Guevara's favorite cookout recipes. May Hefner leave that airless Mansion of his just once to see what the sun looks like—and get sunstroke. May all his yachts be lost in the Bermuda triangle. May his entire empire be taken over by the board of directors of *Jack and Jill* magazine. May all the performers at his Clubs start telling dirty jokes in Yugoslavian. May a herd of baboons break into the Clubs, eat the VIP dinner and throw up all over the Door Bunny. May God hurl a thunderbolt and—

PLAYBOY: Don, has anyone ever spoken to you about your breath?

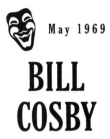

May 1969

BILL COSBY

A candid conversation with the kinetic comedian-actor-singer-entrepreneur

During this decade, no comedian—black or white—has come close to achieving the superstardom Bill Cosby has fashioned for himself in the short space of seven years. At 31, he commands a fee of $50,000 a week for nightclub dates; and on concert tours, he often earns three times that figure. Cosby has also vaulted to the top of two industries: He won four consecutive Grammys for his comedy albums and three Emmys in a row for his co-starring role as secret agent Alexander Scott on NBC's *I Spy*, his first attempt at acting. In 1967, Cosby recorded two albums of rhythm-and-blues vocals, with the perhaps predictable result that one of his cuts, "Little Old Man," was a top pop hit for more than two months. And in April of this year, Cosby began filming his first movie, a remake of *Here Comes Mr. Jordan*, in which he enacts the comic gangster role originally played by Robert Montgomery. So great is the demand for his services that NBC recently signed him to a five-year contract that will net him anywhere from $15 million to $50 million; it calls for, among other things, an annual Cosby TV special, two cartoon specials based on his subteen superheroes, Fat Albert and Old Weird Harold, and *The Bill Cosby Show*, beginning next fall, in which he will be featured each week as a San Francisco schoolteacher who moonlights as a detective.

Speaking of moonlighting, Cosby is also becoming as adept an executive as he is an entertainer. He and business partners Roy Silver and Bruce Campbell are assembling an entertainment conglomerate, based in Beverly Hills, whose net worth has already approached the $50 million mark. Among their properties: a record company (Tetragrammaton, which released the controversial John Lennon–Yoko Ono LP *Two Virgins*, featuring a frontal nude photo of the loving couple), a cartoon-animation studio, a public-relations firm, a talent-management corporation, a projected chain of Fat Albert hamburger stands and a motion-picture-production company that already has a five-film, $12 million contract with Warner Bros.–Seven Arts.

To everyone's surprise but his own, Cosby's emergence as a one-man industrial giant has had no adverse effect on his personality. On stage and off, he is informal, unpretentious and, to use his favorite adjective, cool. Married, the father of two daughters and with another child on the way, Cosby maintains that he's perfectly willing to sire as many as 20 girls before he stops trying for a son. The Cosbys live in a huge Spanish-style home in Beverly Hills, where Bill spends a good deal of time informally entertaining friends, most of whom, like trumpeter Miles Davis and Boston Celtic player-coach Bill Russell, are either black entertainers or black athletes.

Sports are a prime passion of his: Cosby watches as many televised football games as his wife will put up with and, during the year, plays charity exhibitions with a pickup basketball team—often on behalf of local black groups—throughout the Los Angeles area. No stranger to ghetto residents, Cosby gets a special kick out of working with youth. He sponsored a group of young Watts musicians in 1967, called them the Watts 103rd Street Rhythm Band and featured them as accompanists on a couple of his TV guest shots. To Cosby, it represents the way he can—and does—help other black people. His prospects in life not too many years ago, as he himself is the first to point out, were even dimmer than those of the Watts group before he aided them.

The eldest of three sons, Bill was born on July 12, 1937, in an area of Philadelphia that *Time* magazine once christened The Jungle. Bill's boyhood was typical of many a black youth's: He shined shoes, played street football and schoolyard basketball, took part in teen-gang wars and compiled a lackluster academic record from the moment he set foot in school ("William would rather clown than study," his sixth-grade teacher noted on a report card Cosby now keeps framed in his home). At Germantown High School, he was captain of the track and football teams, which took up most of his time; after he had to repeat his 10th year because of poor grades, Bill dropped out of school to join the Navy as a medical corpsman. "I read the Geneva convention and it says you can't shoot a medic," he explained later. "And we were very popular—first thing wounded guys in the field would shout was 'Medic!' 'What do you want?' I'd ask. 'My leg! My leg!' 'Sorry, but I don't make house calls.'"

All his kidding aside, Cosby felt that the military life was largely a waste of time. "The thing I really hated," he recently recalled, "is that a guy with one stripe more than another cat thinks he has the power of God over him—and he does. After my first few days in the navy, I knew I'd have to make it as a civilian. And for that, I needed an education."

Accordingly, Cosby enrolled in correspondence courses conducted by the Navy and soon earned a high school diploma. Just before his tour of duty was completed, he competed for the Navy in a track meet at Villanova University. Gavin White, at that time the track coach of Villanova's city rival, Temple University, was in the stands that afternoon. Cosby was introduced to White and asked if Temple would consider offering him a track scholarship when he got out of the Navy. White replied that it could be arranged, and it was.

A versatile college athlete, Cosby participated in more than a half-dozen events for Temple's track team, winning the Middle Atlantic Conference's high-jump competition with a leap of six feet and running the 100-yard dash in 10.2 seconds. As a second-string fullback on the varsity football squad, he was scouted for the New York Giants by Emlen Tunnell, who rated him as having a good chance to make the National Football League as a defensive safety.

Cosby decided to earn spending money by taking a job tending bar in a small downtown Philly cocktail lounge, where his comedy career began—inadvertently—when he found himself entertaining customers to pass the time. After trying out a few bits at campus parties, Bill did occasional stand-up routines in other bars and, on weekends, would journey up to New York's Greenwich Village in search of better-paying gigs, where he finally landed a $60-a-week job at the Gaslight Club in the summer of 1962. By autumn, Cosby was commuting regularly from Philadelphia to New York for weekend appearances in Village clubs. It wasn't long before comedy and college became incompatible. "Bill wanted to travel to a football game in Ohio by himself," recalls Temple athletic director Ernie Casale. "He couldn't make the team flight because of a show-business commitment. I told him that, realistically, he'd soon have to choose between Temple and show business. He made the choice right there and then."

Though he made the right decision, he wasn't too sure at the time; his mother didn't want him to leave college, and neither did he. "But I was making as much as $300 on weekends," he remembers, "and even though I wasn't sure how long it would last, I was determined to see it out." By 1963, Cosby had graduated to top Village spots such as The Bitter End; and that summer, Allan Sherman, who was guest-hosting *The Tonight Show* for vacationing Johnny Carson, caught his act and put him on network TV for the first time. A few weeks after that, Sherman co-produced Cosby's first album, *Bill Cosby Is a Very Funny Fellow . . . Right!* His career has been straight up ever since.

Over the years, Bill has been the subject of a series of limpid interviews; perhaps with the misguided intention of boosting a black comic who wasn't skewering whites onstage, writers and editors have often deleted his more trenchant offstage observations about the black man's place in America—almost to the point of making him seem an Uncle Tom. As a result, he roundly dislikes the press. "One magazine sent a guy out to spend three or four days with me. That cat and I talked for hours about what's happening to black people in this country, and I couldn't wait to see the issue. But it was really stupid, man. They were more interested in showing me playing basketball with my press agent than in what I had to say."

In an effort to reveal the real Cosby, *Playboy* dispatched Associate Editor Lawrence Linderman to accompany him on a series of one-night stands in the Midwest. Reports Linderman: "Cosby's life is incredibly departmentalized; aside from his personal appearances, he's constantly hopping across the country to show up for business conferences, TV guest shots, his friends' first nights and assorted film commitments. This schedule literally knocks him out. It isn't unusual to walk into Cosby's dressing room between performances and find him dozing in a straight-backed chair, a long-dead cigar propped between his lips. He stays that way until it's time to go on, then snaps awake instantly and gets himself 'up' on the way to the stage. Once there, he turns on and works as hard—physically—as any comedian I've ever seen. But the most impressive thing about watching Cosby perform is to realize how wide the appeal of his humor has become: The same routines that make him a hit in Harlem's Apollo go over just as big with all-white crowds in Las Vegas and Des Moines." The universality of Cosby's comedy provided the opening for our interview.

PLAYBOY: Both fans and critics often call your humor "color-blind." Do you think that's an accurate description?

COSBY: Well, I think there are some people who are disappointed when I don't tell my audiences that white people are mistreating black people. White critics will write about Cosby not doing any racial material, because they think that now is the time for me to stand up and tell my audiences what color I am and what's going on in America. But I don't see these people knocking the black elevator man in their building just because he isn't doing anything for civil rights by running that elevator; it wouldn't sell newspapers or magazines. The fact that I'm not trying to win converts onstage bugs some people, but I don't think an entertainer *can* win converts. I've never known any kind of white bigot to pay to see a black man, unless the black man was being hung. So I don't spend my hours worrying how to slip a social message into my act; I just go out and do my thing.

PLAYBOY: How would you describe it?

COSBY: My humor isn't jokes as much as situations. I tell stories and play the characters in those stories, like the one I wrote for you guys. This isn't something that came to me overnight. I don't think I hit my stride until my third album; up until then, I'd been doing what amounted to cartoon ideas. Some of my humor comes straight out of the newspapers, in a way. Take Noah and the ark. I once read about a mass murder; and when they captured the guy and asked him why he did it, he said, "The voice told me to do it." You'd be surprised at how many killings there are where a guy hears a voice that says, "Take up thy rifle, go out and *slay!*" Now, this is a country built on Christianity; if a guy sees a bolt of lightning, hears a crack of thunder and then a voice saying, "Go and smite thine enemies!"—which was always happening in the Bible—how many cats do you know who wouldn't go along with it? So I started to think about what would happen today if a guy was told by the voice to go build an ark. First of all, he'd doubt that the voice was real. So there's got to be conversation between him and the voice. Second, what are the neighbors going to think? And third, no rain has been falling and it's hard to build an ark, so Noah, who's a totally rational man, is going to be angry at himself for doing it. As he's hammering away, he's going to be thinking, "What the hell am I building an *ark* for?"

PLAYBOY: The recorded version of your Noah story is a tightly constructed and highly polished comedy routine; yet during nightclub performances—as with so much of your material—you vary the dialog and often the plot from night to night. Why?

COSBY: Well, I think I'm similar in my comedy to the way jazz musicians work. After you play a song through once, the solos start. I treat each of my characters as a song, and I start soloing when the character comes into the plot. I have certain notes to follow, but I can do different things with them—like chord changes. For instance, in my LP *To Russell, My Brother, Whom I Slept With*, there's a scene where the kid lies to his father about how his bed broke. On the record, the kid cries when he does it. But there are nights when the kid doesn't cry. It all depends on how I want the kid to explain it to his old man. And also, to an extent, I want my live performances to be different from my records. I can't stand to have somebody sitting out there with his lips moving with mine.

PLAYBOY: Most of your humor has to do with your childhood. Was it as happy as you make it seem?

COSBY: Are you kidding? The thing I most remember about being a kid was being poor. I remember the eviction signs, especially; they were doubly hard to take. I had buddies who'd tell me, "Hey, man, like, you're *really* poor; you didn't pay your rent." Now, I'm not saying my life was harder than anybody else's; I'm just telling you the way it was. I remember a Christmas when we had no Christmas tree, and you just can't get lower than that. We had an orange tree and there weren't any presents. And I remember taking a girl to the junior high school prom and I didn't have money to cover cab fare; I was hoping she'd ride the trolley car with me, in her gown. But something great happened: Her mother gave me $6 to help with the cab fare, because somehow she knew I didn't have any money. Maybe it wasn't all that tough to guess; I was wearing a blue double-breasted suit coat and a pair of black slacks. I wanted to keep my raincoat on, because I knew when I took it off, I'd be the only guy there who hadn't been able to come up with the bread to rent a tux. One house we lived in had no bathtub; my mother used to take out this big tub, put water in it and put it on top of the stove to heat up.

But when you're young, you have all kinds of energy and you forget the bad things and get on with the good: playing ball, going downtown with your friends to shine shoes and sell shopping bags, making $2 and coming back home. In that neighborhood, we never had an image to look up to, aside from a minister. Anybody else who came around was either the white insurance man or the white bill collector who was looking for his $2 for the plastic lamp he sold that was shaped like a cat with sparkling red eyes and a pink bottom. I know I didn't look up to any grownups. I would envy certain guys whose fathers had a sense of humor, whose fathers showed they cared for them.

PLAYBOY: What about your own father?

COSBY: Well, I love my father and he loves me, but the old man wasn't the outstanding part of my life. My parents got married in Philadelphia and my father started out with a middle-class paying job. But he was a heavy drinker when they married, and through booze and his own particular personality, he cared more about his buddies and what they thought of him than about taking care of his wife and kids. Somebody always seemed to rob my father on paydays between work and the house. So when he got home, I heard these terrible arguments between my mother and my father about where the money was. He'd say, "Well, you better take this, because that's all I have." And my mother would say, "But, Bill, you got paid today." And then he'd say, "Well, this is all I have, so don't ask me for any more." Then there were times when he'd come back the next day and say, "Gimme $10." And Mom would tell him she needed the money to buy food. And then an argument and maybe a fight. I remember my father beating my mother up three times. I was too small to do anything about it. These things are very, very painful to think about today.

PLAYBOY: Do you have any pleasant memories of those years?

COSBY: Well, I dug cars, and still do. But I didn't actually *have* one until I was 24 years old, when I bought an old Dodge for $75, and I loved it, *loved* it. It had the baldest tires in the world. A cue ball has more grip than those tires did. I called it the Black Phantom. I did everything with that car! When I was a teenager, it was a big thing when one of the guys in the neighborhood got a set of wheels. There was a guy named Charley Wades, whose father gave him a car. Now, Charley was almost like a cab driver; if you wanted to go to a party with him, you had to have some money to chip in for gas. Charley would say, "You can bitch about me charging you for the gas, but that's the only thing I'm charging you for. You're only giving me a quarter for gas, but what about my tires and my sparkplugs? What about my seats that you're rubbing your ass on? Where were you when I had to *reline* my seats? I didn't charge you nothing for that. So you're getting away clean, man."

And then there was the time Andy Patterson's father gave him a 1946 Olds, which, by the time Andy got it, was the saddest and slowest thing in north Philly. One night we double-dated and Andy had put old army blankets over the car seats. I don't know what kind of rodent eats foam rubber, but Andy had two of the biggest holes I ever saw in his front seat; and when he forgot to tell a chick about them, she just about disappeared when she sat down. The covers went over her head and her can hit the bottom of the car. We all laughed about it, pulled her out and then drove into a gas station. It's raining and cold and the gas-station guy is sitting in his little office when Andy honks the horn. The guy gets up, puts on his raincoat and hat and comes around the car, slips and falls flat on his behind. And we start laughing again. The guy gets up, soaking wet, and limps up to the window. Andy rolls it down and says, "Gimme 19 cents' worth of regular." And the guy walks away, goes back into his office and just sits there, shaking his head, just shaking his head. Those were the days when, to us, almost *nothing* mattered except cars.

PLAYBOY: Did you continue your romance with cars when you became successful?

COSBY: Three years after I bought the Black Phantom, I started appearing in big nightclubs and on TV shows, and the first thing I did was go out and buy a 1955 Mercedes-Benz 300SL for $5000. I put a down payment on it and drove across country, from Philadelphia to San Francisco. I figure I paid about $6000 in garage bills to keep it going, because each mechanic I met would say, "Umm, the car don't sound right, Bill," and I'd say, "Okay, fix it." And I would ride the buses again, waiting for the car to be fixed, because parts had to be flown in from places like Egypt and San Diego and Mars.

One night, I was playing the Crescendo in Los Angeles and Theodore Bikel came to see me—we'd been good friends in Greenwich Village—and he invited me to go out for coffee. So Theodore's car comes up and it's a Corvette with We Shall Overcome and Freedom Now bumper stickers plastered all over it—so many you couldn't even see the chrome. Then up comes my Mercedes and he says to me: "What the hell did the *Nazis* ever do for you?" The next day, I sold it for $2500 and bought a Chrysler Imperial. But that was too heavy a car, so I went to a Chrysler station wagon, then a Plymouth station wagon, and I didn't like either of them. Finally, I said to my wife, Camille: "Every car we get, we're trying to get away from the stereotype of the Negro with the Cadillac; but I don't care what anybody says, the Cadillac is the best car in the world, and I'm buying one." So I went and bought an Eldorado and it was great.

But it so happens that most of my friends are either entertainers or athletes, and Bill Russell came to the house when we had this two-door Eldorado, a $7500 car. My wife and I are up front and Russell and his girl are like two pretzels in the back. So we decided to get rid of it and I bought a Rover, which has a little more room in the back. Later, I owned a Rolls-Royce limousine for a while and drove it myself; but I got rid of it pretty quick, because a Rolls looks weird without a chauffeur up front and I didn't want anybody driving me around. I've always loved Ferraris, so I have one of those now. I gave my wife an Excalibur, and I also have a 1934 Aston Martin, but I wouldn't take that car out on the road. I got rid of the Rover, so now I own only three cars; I think I'm starting to come out of it.

PLAYBOY: Your success came quickly. Did you spend the bread as fast as it came in?

COSBY: When I really started making it, I did. Everything had to be gold—tie clips, cuff links; I even went through the diamond-ring bit—the whole thing, but only for a couple of months. That's all it takes to take the edge off your desire to own things. I don't think this is necessarily a phase for most people who start earning a lot of money; but if you've come from a poor neighborhood, you tend to start buying like there's no tomorrow. There are stores that thrive on that kind of thing, stores that challenge you to walk in. It's almost like that store is saying, "I don't think you can afford it." So a guy goes in and he says, "I can *too* afford it." Dunhill's is that kind of store. I bought ice buckets, all kinds of expensive ashtrays, a humidor, lighters and a clock that tells the time all over the world; it takes me about an hour to find out what time it is in California. I put most of that stuff in one room, which my wife calls Cosby's Dunhill.

PLAYBOY: Is being rich as much fun as you thought it would be?

COSBY: I don't really think of myself as being rich. To me, a rich cat is somebody who can retire and live off his money any time he wants to, and I can't. I'd like to wind up with an income of $50,000 a year when I retire; but with the tax structure the way it is, that's almost impossible to do, unless I make investments in things like land that over a long period of time will take good care of my money. I wouldn't blame you, though, if you said, "What's he complaining for? He's a millionaire."

PLAYBOY: Are you?

COSBY: Last year, I earned $2 million—but that isn't $2 million in the pocket. There's an agent fee, a manager, press, a building for my corporation—and an accountant from whom you learn you're really broke; that now, in fact, you're worse off, in a way, than if you'd just taken a gig as a schoolteacher. Almost every cent is spent; and every penny you make, you got Uncle Sam taking out 70 percent after expenses. And now there's cats coming to me because they've read some bullshit article about me, like *Newsweek*'s, saying I'm going to get $50 million from CBS for 20 years and that my record albums have earned, like, $3 million. So, as soon as cats hear this, they all got business deals to propose.

PLAYBOY: Do many of them try to put the touch on you?

COSBY: All of them—and they don't just ask for five bucks, either. They want it all. First time a guy says to me, "Hey, you got a minute?" right away I know I'm being hit for bread. It used to take me a while to get up the nerve to say it, but now I can do it automatically: "Here's my card. See me at the office and I'll listen to you." I usually have to shout this over the sound of the band at some jazz joint, because that's where they've decided I've got to hear their plan. Well, 90 percent of these cats, when you say that to them, come back with, "If you don't want to hear it now, man, then forget it, 'cause I got a good thing going." But let's say a cat has something legitimate; if I tell him the bread isn't there—which it isn't—he won't believe me, and he's going to wind up putting me down. But let me tell you that in 1968, I had to scrape up—and get a loan from the bank for—$833,000 in taxes.

PLAYBOY: In spite of the tax bite, you still have what most people would consider a lot of money at your disposal. How do you spend it?

COSBY: Quickly. My home cost $250,000, plus $100,000 worth of furniture. But it's a *home*, not a palace with chandeliers hanging and white rugs and things you can't walk on or sit on. You come into my house and you can sit on my sofa and take your shoes off and plop your feet up on the table. *People* live there, not a maid and a butler—*people*. It's comfortable; nothing is closed off. My Ferrari cost $17,000, and it's air conditioned, because I remember Philly summers riding around with friends of mine in an old 1946 Chevy; we would be sweating and we'd have to drive fast to make some breeze. I like groovy steaks; I like to serve a great wine to my friends when they come by, even though I don't drink. I remember one time when I was a kid and read that Mitzi Gaynor was going to get $50,000 for playing a week in Las Vegas and saying to myself, "God, that's a lot of bread." It was so totally out of proportion to what I dreamed of, even when I started making $400 a week. There's a tremendous gap between where I used to live and what I used to do and where I am now. And I dig it.

PLAYBOY: In the midst of your own luxury, do you ever feel guilty when you think about the poverty in which most black Americans are forced to live?

COSBY: When I first started making big money, I felt guilty, I guess. But now I feel that I've really put together a hell of a one-man antipoverty program. I took my talent and I put it to work, and today, I've brought up, by the bootstraps, the economic conditions of a mother, a father, two brothers, aunts, uncles, grandfathers and other family members, and then reached out to help close friends. The next step is to help out other black people. This doesn't simply mean giving them $500,000—although I give plenty. But to me, reaching out to black people means to open up my particular part of the industry. My production companies will have black apprenticeship programs and will use black actors, directors and stagehands. After they've demonstrated their talents and people dig 'em, they can then go on their own, which is why I tour with talented black performers like the Pair Extraordinaire and Leon Bibb. When they meet my audience, the people remember their names. So I don't feel guilty about having bread. Now, when I meet a guy in the ghetto, of course he's going to be envious, but he doesn't necessarily resent me for it; there's a whole lot of cats in the ghetto to whom I Spy was something to be proud of, in a way. I certainly was, and I can only thank one man for making it happen: Sheldon Leonard.

PLAYBOY: How did you meet him?

COSBY: It was really funny, man, and it wasn't funny. I went into this business after hearing Mel Brooks and Carl Reiner do their 2000-year-old-man routine. I loved their flow of humor, the looseness of it and the fact that any second, a piece of greatness could suddenly be created. So I decided to go into show business to do this kind of comedy. I figured I'd eventually need a partner, but then I go on television, do two or three guest shots, and suddenly I'm playing at the Crescendo in Los Angeles. Remember, now, I'm in show business for two years, and Carl Reiner comes by to see the show and afterward he says, "I loved your show, man." Well, of course, I'm stunned. Like, Carl Reiner—one half of the 2000-year-old-man thing—came to see me! Now, this is before militancy and Watts and Detroit, when it was still something else for a white star to come see a black man. And he says, "My producer, Sheldon

Leonard, wants to see you. He couldn't be here tonight, but he loves your work."

The next morning, I went to Sheldon's office, hoping that perhaps he would give me a guest shot on *The Dick Van Dyke Show*. Now, mind you, I couldn't act at all; I'd never done any acting, except a couple of lies to my mother. So I walked into Sheldon's office and he talks to me, not about doing a *Van Dyke Show* but about a new series that would co-star a black man and a white man. They're going to be spies and they're going to travel to Hong Kong. Now, here I am, my first time in California, only the third time I've ever been out of Pennsylvania, and this guy is talking about Hong Kong. That knocked me out of my chair more than the series. I said, "Travel to Hong Kong? This program is going to pay my way to Hong *Kong*?" And Sheldon is telling me he thinks I've got the particular personality that will work for his show and that all I have to do is put the same thing on TV that I do in my stand-up act, and that'll be my job. Then he says, like, "Can you act?" And I say, "You must be high. You didn't see me when I did *Othello* in Central Park last year, did ya?" And he smiles and all I'm thinking about is, "Hong Kong, Hong *Kong*, man. I'm gonna see the original Chinese people, the ones I've read about." So I get back to my manager, Roy Silver, and I tell him, "Don't let this cat off the hook, 'cause if he's blowing smoke, we're not letting him get out of it." Well, Sheldon said he'd get in touch with me a year later. And he did.

PLAYBOY: Before the show actually got under way, it was reported that you didn't want to play a hip valet, since no matter how hip you were, you'd still be a white man's servant. Was this true?

COSBY: I had to find out a lot of things from Sheldon before I signed. Like, was I going to carry a gun? I wanted to make sure that I didn't have to go off into the bushes when an *I Spy* fight started. They said I didn't. So Bob Culp and I fought the international Communist conspiracy on an equal basis. I must tell you, though, that the show wouldn't have been what it was if it hadn't been for Bob.

PLAYBOY: Had you met him before you started working together?

COSBY: No. I met him when the show began filming. But he did send me a letter not too long after Sheldon had first talked to me, when I was playing Mister Kelly's in Chicago. The letter said that two guys going to do a series must get married, that they *are* married. Right away, this was actor talk, and I had only been in the business around three years. Here was an actor telling me I have to marry him. That upset me a little.

PLAYBOY: How did it go when you finally got together with Culp?

COSBY: The first time I saw Bob was the first day we read for the series; I walked in and we shook hands, but we didn't really have a chance to talk before they gave us scripts. Then it was the moment of truth for me: All of the fears, anxieties and apprehensions were bubbling and boiling, because now I had to prove myself. Although the producers were with me, they were really listening to see if I could act. I'd never read a single line for Sheldon Leonard—and when you think about that, about a producer banking half a million dollars on a guy whose comedy routine he liked, it becomes a hell of a gamble. Well, they listened, and I was embarrassed, because I was no good—*really* no good. I fumbled and mumbled and couldn't concentrate or do anything right.

But afterward, Bob and I got together and talked and, at Bob's suggestion, we agreed to make the relationship between the white character, Kelly Robinson, and the black man, Alexander Scott, a *beautiful* relationship, so that people could see what it would be like if two cats like that could get along. Bob's a fine actor and a fine human being. He could have made it rough for me; he could have made me paranoid with criticism, because my ego came into play. At the time, I was a pretty well-known, up-and-coming comic; and if he'd been rough on me, it would have been too easy for me to say to myself, "What do I need all this for?" In other words, if Bob hadn't been the great guy he is, I might have copped out.

PLAYBOY: Were you still nervous when the filming actually began?

COSBY: It was really weird, man. As a comedian, I can walk out in front of 5000 people and not worry about a thing. Not a *thing*, believe me. But to stand up and face a camera and crew of maybe 15 guys and get uptight about it—to me, that's weird. It took a lot of weeks before I felt relaxed and able to do my thing without being self-conscious.

PLAYBOY: How did you feel about playing and, in a real sense, glamorizing a CIA agent?

COSBY: Well, actually, the CIA never let us say we were CIA agents.

PLAYBOY: But, in effect, you were, weren't you?

COSBY: In effect, yes. But the important thing to me, man, was to get a black face on the screen and let him be a hero. I would have done it regardless of what the CIA's image was at the time—and the series was conceived and drawn up well before the CIA got to be a heavy. I was very, very happy—forget the CIA—that a black man was able to be on an equal basis with the show's white hero.

PLAYBOY: One continuing criticism of the show's stories was that Bob Culp always got the girls, which seemed to make him a little more equal than you. Did you resent that?

COSBY: If you weren't a steady viewer, you might have missed some of Scotty's love stories. But that concerned me less than the fact that Sheldon Leonard didn't hire me as a token. He said he wanted to use a Negro. Now, at that particular time, how was the black man accepted by the public? I'll tell you: Before we even got the first show on the air, writers and poll takers had picked us to wind up 97th out of 100 shows. We originally were going to work *I Spy* like a funny Lone Ranger and Tonto, wherein I would supply the humor. I accepted that, man, because that's the way it was: There was *nothing* else going. I felt I could surely bring some things out in this character, because here was a guy who carried a gun and knew karate, so at least he was going to be able to shoot and fight. As long as Scotty wasn't going to let the other cat beat up the bad guys after he got knocked out, as long as he wasn't going to be carried home so he could do the paperwork, I felt it would be okay. Bob, by the way, wrote the first *I Spy* script in which I was interested in a woman—who turned out to be Eartha Kitt.

PLAYBOY: How did you develop the character of Scott?

COSBY: Well, the first thing I decided was to make this guy, who was so intelligent on paper, a real human being. If you know a guy who has a PhD or a master's, you know he kind of respects what he has, but he doesn't talk as if he's always conscious of the degree. He'll say "ain't" and "got" and "I'm gonna," all the time knowing technically, grammatically what's going on. So I decided to make Alexander Scott this kind of guy—a guy who grew up in the ghetto, who went to school and took on middle-class values, who was trying to live like the white middle class. But he always knew he was black, with a real degree of black pride.

PLAYBOY: When did you feel you had Scott really pegged?

COSBY: After about the seventh story, I felt I could kind of walk into it. It was almost as if I just woke up one morning, went to work and knew it was *cool.*

PLAYBOY: Did you feel, as many critics did, that *I Spy*'s scripts were often secondary to the banter between you and Culp?

COSBY: Bob and I—and the producers—wanted the shows to have stronger stories, but we never really got them. They became watered-down mystery plots. And in our third year, a couple of the shows turned out to be walking *National Geographic* magazines; our backs would be to the camera and you could see the Aegean over our shoulders. Or we'd be looking over the edge of a beautiful cliff on the Mediterranean.

PLAYBOY: Were you relieved or disappointed when the show was canceled after its third season?

COSBY: Both. When I first got the news, I felt, like, "I'm free"; but after a few minutes, I started thinking about all those hours I would have off. I started thinking about our producers—Sheldon Leonard, Morton Fine and David Friedkin—and how unhappy they had to be. About all the grips and people who made a living from the show. And then I wondered about all the things we could have—and should have—done on the show. But that isn't the way TV is set up. We were there to make the dollar. The only way I can look at it is that we were in 74th place after three years and to go into a fourth season wouldn't have made much sense. So NBC decided to shoot a brand-new show that went an hour and cost only half as much as I *Spy*. Finally, it was just a matter of economics. But we had some new things in mind for the fourth year, and I'm kind of sorry we didn't get a chance to do them.

PLAYBOY: What were they?

COSBY: Well, our producers had opened their eyes and ears to us. It was easier for Bob and me to kidnap a producer and lock him up in his room than for Columbia students to get their grievances taken care of. We got Sheldon to agree to more love stories for me in the fourth season, also to more scripts for Bob carrying a whole show by himself. And, for dessert, we wanted to bring the boys together in a couple of stories where there'd be no script, no nothing; they'd just walk around kind of improvising. So it would have been a new show.

PLAYBOY: To a very real extent, your role in I *Spy* helped open up the television industry to black performers. Do you think the representation of Negroes on TV has improved enough since you began the series in 1965?

COSBY: Well, we've certainly come a long way from black cats who were bug-eyed, afraid of ghosts and always saying things like "Feet, don't leave me now." Guys like Mantan Moreland, Stepin Fetchit and Willie Best never hit anybody, never fought back and were always scared white. And we don't see the mass stupidity of *Amos 'n' Andy* anymore. That show still gets to me, man. Each time I name an *Amos 'n' Andy* character, try to imagine these guys as white, and you won't be able to: You had Lightnin', who was slow in every possible way; Calhoun, the lawyer who never got anybody out of trouble and never went into court prepared; Kingfish, the conniver, who was always saying, "Yeah, but brother Andy . . ."; and Andy himself, who wasn't too bright, either. Like, *nobody* on that show was bright except Amos, the cab driver, who we hardly ever heard from. And then there was Kingfish's wife, Sapphire; every time he came through that door, she'd be chewing him out for something. Now, audiences weren't supposed to laugh *with* these people; they were supposed to laugh *at* them, because they were so dumb. And while that show was on, there was nothing else on the air to counterbalance these stereotypes. It was almost as if Poles were exclusively presented as characters in Polish jokes. Well, you're just not going to believe that all Polish people are really dumb; but if that's all you got to see about 'em, you might start to believe it. And they'd understandably resent it. Or the same thing about Jewish people hoarding money. You have to show things besides stereotypes.

PLAYBOY: Do you think that a series with a nonstereotyped all-black cast could be successful on TV today?

COSBY: Probably not. The kind of show you mean would have to be about the life of a black family, with all its struggles. But if you're really going to do a series about a black family, you're going to have to bring out the heavy; and who is the heavy but the white bigot? This would be very painful for most whites to see, a show that talks about the white man and puts him down. It would strike indifferent whites as dangerous; it would be called controversial and they probably wouldn't want to tune in. But when there's a right and a wrong, where's the controversy? The white bigot is *wrong*. The indifferent person sitting on the fence is *wrong*. Instead of having occasional shows that present the black viewpoint on educational channels, the networks should be in there pitching now.

PLAYBOY: Isn't the widening employment of black actors in featured roles on various series a hopeful sign that television's racial stereotyping is coming to an end?

COSBY: I think it's a positive thing that most of the new shows have a black member of the cast; when I started *I Spy*, about the only blacks on TV were maids and butlers. It's still tokenism, but I would rather see a cat who is standing tall as a token than nobody at all. And the acceptance of black people on television means that when enough shows are seen by enough whites, they'll get used to it, with the result that black people will be able to do more things in this society. There's also the important matter of black identification. Let's forget hatred and bigotry for the moment; let's pretend they don't exist. Now, I have black skin.

When I look at TV, I have to identify with what I see, and all I saw when I was growing up was the white upper class or white middle class or white lower class. So it was white America that I identified with, that I studied and tried to emulate as I grew up. Now, a black kid can try to act like a white American, but there's just no way he can *be* a white American. So when TV begins to feature black people, it's performing a great service to the black community; that's the way I felt about being in *I Spy*.

PLAYBOY: You won three consecutive Emmys for *I Spy*, and your comedy LPs won you four consecutive Grammys. Which meant more to you?

COSBY: They all mean the same to me: that I'm a winner; that I've been chosen by the people of my profession, regardless of who they are, as the best. I think if I could take the awards and do what I really wanted with them, I'd probably Scotch-tape them onto the hood of my car and kind of drive around with a little smile on my face. Because I'm really proud of them, man. But you're supposed to be very cool about these things and tuck the Emmys and the Grammys away in the corner of some room, so that nobody will think you're vain and conceited. The greatest moment of an award, though, is when they announce your name, the moment when you're expected to say thank you. Then it's on to the next thing; you can't hang around bathing your body in the reflection of a trophy.

PLAYBOY: One of the things you seem to be going on to next is singing. You have two vocal LPs out, and one of your singles, "Little Old Man," was a pop hit two years ago. Are you going to try to make it as big in singing as you have in comedy?

COSBY: No; singing is just something I like to do. I like rhythm and blues and I'm thinking about cutting another blues album, but I don't even come close to having any kind of a voice. It's just a hobby—like some guys like to golf. They don't play a good game, but they're out on the course every morning. I don't shoot a good game of rhythm and blues, but I got my cap and clubs and shoes, and I go sing.

PLAYBOY: Your first film—a remake of *Here Comes Mr. Jordan*—will be released sometime this fall. Do you have the same trepidations about going into movies that you did before you became a television star?

COSBY: Not as many as then, but I'm entering a new field, and that means I've got a new audience to win over; it doesn't matter about past awards or that when you play a city, you draw 17,000 people for a one-night stand. This is a new thing and you've got to make a new impression. But I hope to have better scripts than I did on TV, and I hope to do things that have broader scope.

PLAYBOY: At this point, how would you assess yourself as an actor?

COSBY: I think I have a personality talent. I can play a sensitive guy and also a funny guy, caught in a funny situation. You won't see me going into Brando-ish depths or trying to compete with Sir Laurence Olivier on Shakespeare. But I feel I have the intelligence and the talent to be a big star; I really believe that. This isn't conceit; it's just that I know what I can do and, by this time, I also know that by doing things the way I want to do them, people will be for me.

PLAYBOY: Do you ever worry that your popularity will wane and that you'll no longer be able to earn the kind of money you're presently pulling in?

COSBY: I have a *great* fear of winding up broke; I guess that would be about the most embarrassing thing that could happen to me. Because, if I *do* wind up broke, my mother will blame it all on the cigars I smoke; my father will say it's because of all the expensive things I bought at Dunhill's; and my wife will say it's from all the charitable organizations I've given to. So to avoid all that, as I said before, I'm involved in long-range investments—like land—that will eventually bring me an income of about $50,000 a year. Maybe one day, I'll have made such heavy bread that even Sam won't be able to penetrate it, and then I hope I'll be set for the rest of my life. Because I really do plan to get out of show business within five years or so.

PLAYBOY: Completely?

COSBY: No, I'm not going to make a total break with show business, because, to me, that would almost be like castration. I think I'll be doing occasional TV specials and appearances, a little less than the kind of thing Bob Hope does. I'm going to just take my little bundle and let all those handshaking, graft-taking $30,000-a-year politicians know they won't have to worry about *me* standing in any unemployment line.

PLAYBOY: What will you do with yourself?

COSBY: I plan to teach in a junior high school, which is where kids become glandularly aware of being male and female. Early adolescence is a very difficult time of life for ghetto kids, because people to look up to, like I said earlier, are scarce in a poor neighborhood. In middle- and upper-middle-class neighborhoods, kids have their fathers to look up to—college graduates or skilled workmen. In lower-class neighborhoods, kids look up to the gambler's skills—skills that work openly against the law. Poor kids have no image that teaches them the value of education. It has to do with what they're taught in history classes, too; I'd want to show kids there are black heroes to be proud of, so they have a different kind of cat to look up to. Because, let's face it, most of the black people we admire are running that race or hitting that ball or dribbling it down-court. And so black girls hope to marry a guy who'll become a professional athlete. And the guy hopes to become a pro, goes to college without knowing about or being ready for college, plays ball and often never graduates. Without teaching a subject in particular, I want to help put those kids on to finding out what they really want to do in life.

PLAYBOY: But schools aren't set up for classes without any particular subject.

COSBY: No, they're not—but that doesn't mean they won't be. In small towns, the church and the school are the center of things; functions are held at both and the pastor and the teacher know all the parents. No school is like that in the big cities. Instead, school is the building whose windows you break in the summertime; it's the building with the yard where you play penny poker games. It isn't the connecting ground it should be for kids. Children grow up thinking that all teachers are Ichabod Cranes, but teachers are just underpaid human beings who aren't supposed to strike. For every successful human being, there are at least three or four teachers who inspired them to become what they are today; but the teachers never get any of the credit. When I was in school, I remember a teacher telling me I'd better study or else I'd grow up to be a garbageman. If you look at what the average garbage collector makes and what the average schoolteacher makes, I think the garbageman is probably telling his kids they'd better *not* study or else they're going to wind up as schoolteachers.

PLAYBOY: In last December's *Playboy Interview*, Black Panther leader Eldridge Cleaver said that unless black demands for equality are quickly met, the result will be "a second Civil War . . . plunging America into the depths of its most desperate nightmare." In view of your plans to teach black children, form black production companies and continue your entertainment career, it would seem that you don't agree with Cleaver's evaluation of America's future.

COSBY: I'm not in favor of raising guns, but I don't think Cleaver would be, either, if he thought there was any other way to solve the racial situation in this country. A lot of black men feel that way, and I can't say they're wrong, because America's resistance to giving the black man a fair shake is almost unbelievably strong. And when black people keep butting their heads against the stone wall of racism, there are those who feel they *have* to become violent.

Look, there can't be an argument over the fact that we should have equality in America. But the white man doesn't want us to have it, because then he'll be giving up a freedom of his—to reject us because of color. I really believe that black people could march until the end of the world and the majority of whites still wouldn't want to give up what they see as their precious right to be racists. Whites should realize that, under these conditions, it's only natural for some of those marchers to finally say, "Shit, man, this ain't gettin' us nowhere. The best thing to do is throw a goddamn bomb into the building." When Martin Luther King was murdered, I felt that his death made the nonviolent approach appear irrelevant to many black people.

PLAYBOY: Stokely Carmichael and others said that Dr. King's murder marked the passing of nonviolence. Do you agree with them?

COSBY: Martin Luther King was a good teacher of the nonviolent philosophy and a great leader. I think his philosophy is still as meaningful today as when he was alive. It was well before his death that Stokely broke away from nonviolence, and it was well before his death that violent, militant groups came into being. But I don't think people can arbitrarily be put into neat categories of violent or nonviolent. I can tell you that I *don't* believe in letting black people get pushed around when they're in the right. If a lot of black people no longer believe in nonviolence, it's because they've lost all faith and trust in white men. Black people have lain in the streets and they've let whites hit them in the head with everything from clubs to ketchup bottles. They've let themselves be called niggers and have still somehow managed to walk tall and show that they still believe in nonviolence, that this philosophy makes them better than those who torment them. But they've taken all this abuse, and for what? How far has it really gotten them? Many intelligent and educated black people are tired, just plain tired, of being noble, of not striking back. And I think that a lot of white people secretly *hope* that the Negro will renounce nonviolence.

PLAYBOY: Why?

COSBY: Because it would give whites an excellent reason to go ahead and strike; they think force is the easiest way to solve the problem. Not necessarily a war, but some law that would quietly march us off into concentration camps until we learned that this is *their* country.

PLAYBOY: As you know, most whites think the concentration-camp theory is a myth.

COSBY: Look, it's possible to have concentration camps in Chicago—or in almost any large city—by simply blocking off the ghetto, putting barbed wire around it and not letting anybody in or out. This isn't going to happen until we give the whites a little more of a reason for putting us in a concentration camp, but it isn't too far away. Black people are not going to stop burning their own neighborhoods for a while, but if nothing is accomplished as a result of this, they'll become even more desperate; and when there's nothing left to burn in black neighborhoods, they're going to spread out—into white neighborhoods, into downtown districts, to hit those stores. Farfetched as it may sound, black people will actually go to war if they're driven to it. Not *all* black people, but the ones who feel they're willing to give up their lives in order to mess up this country, to bring America to its knees. I'm not talking about just burning some buildings but about black guerrillas cutting wires, darkening the cities, ending communications. All-out war.

PLAYBOY: Of course, black people couldn't possibly win such a war. Don't you think it could result only in massive repression and bloodshed?

COSBY: Yes, I do, and there's just no arguing that point. The terrible thing is that there's no way the troops are going to be able to distinguish between the bomb throwers and people who are peacefully sitting in their homes.

PLAYBOY: Do you think this war can be averted?

COSBY: That's up to the white man. He's at the point now where he will either have to allow the black man his civil rights or try to wipe him out. History has shown, I think, that in order for the black man to achieve a positive response to his protests, he has to keep escalating his methods of dissent, not because he wants to but because the white establishment *forces* him to. We have been forced to go from singing to sit-ins to marching to letting them beat us up, to watching them burn and bomb our churches and assassinate our leaders and, now, into being coerced into burning our own neighborhoods. The next step is to start slaughtering us en masse, and the step after that is out-and-out war.

PLAYBOY: Malcolm X often claimed that "the squeaky hinge gets the oil"—that America redresses black grievances only in response to violence. But if shooting were to break out tomorrow on a national scale, do you think it's likely that the white establishment, with its domestic order threatened, would respond by ensuring equality for black people?

COSBY: Well, this much is certain: It'll be the hinge's loudest possible squeak. But I really think that, all along, the white man has been oiling the hinge with the secret intention of slamming the door. And when he finally slams it shut for good—and has his genocidal war—he won't have to worry about the squeak anymore. What will be left won't exactly be a country, but at least the place will be well run. Except that America will have to find someone else to dance to its music. The Mexicans will folk-dance for a while, and then there's the Puerto Ricans, and then the Chinese people will be dancing; but soon enough, *that* squeaky-hinged door will be slammed shut, too—and padlocked.

PLAYBOY: Do you think the world will sit by and quietly watch while all this is happening?

COSBY: As long as most of the world powers are white, why not? When the French, Poles and Czechs come off the boat, they're welcomed to America, "the land of the free, the home of the brave." The Statue of Liberty welcomes them, but it doesn't welcome the man who was *born* here—the black man. There's no lamp lit for him; so the black man has to climb up there and light it himself. World opinion? If all these European countries are so groovy, then how come when their guys get off the boat, they turn out to be bigots?

PLAYBOY: If the world *is* ready to passively witness genocide in the U.S., doesn't black violence, as preached by militants like Rap Brown, strike you as ill advised, to say the least?

COSBY: Rap and the other militants all speak the truth when they let America know that the black man is not going to take any more bullshit; we've been here for 300 years and we've had it with waiting. But when Rap makes a speech and says we should get guns and use them on Whitey, it doesn't strike me as a cool move tactically. I, for one, would never let people know I was planning to shoot at them. If you mean it, you just don't talk about it. This goes back to my street-corner days. Unless he's got another card to pull out, it's not the brightest cat in the world who stands around telling a guy, "I'm gonna get a gun and blow your head off." When the guy sees you don't have that gun yet, he pops you right in the teeth or, if *he's* got a gun, he uses it on *you.*

PLAYBOY: Do you think the easy accessibility of firearms in America heightens racial tensions?

COSBY: The way I look at it is that guns are sold to protect whites against blacks. The leaders of bigotry have got to keep the poor, ignorant white cat really upset and nervous, so that their friends the gun manufacturers can sell him some guns and maybe even some bazookas as well.

PLAYBOY: But you'd have to admit that the black militants' threats are at least one of the reasons whites are buying guns.

COSBY: Yes, and *you* have to admit that every time the black man has made a nonviolent move to gain acceptance, he's been laughed at or cursed or hosed down or killed.

PLAYBOY: You seem to be saying that race war is inevitable. Is that what you believe?

COSBY: I hope it's not inevitable, but I don't know. I think if we really want to make sure nothing like it ever happens, we have to get on the stick now, and just maybe it can be avoided. Because we know the answers.

PLAYBOY: What are they?

COSBY: Well, if it's not too late already, one answer is through black political power, such as what happened in Cleveland with Carl Stokes and in Gary with Richard Hatcher being elected mayor. But that doesn't solve the problems even in those cities, because if the administration doesn't have black people on its board of directors or as city planners, there's very little that a mayor can actually do. Supposedly, the mayor has power, but he's only as powerful as the various city boards that go along with him.

PLAYBOY: Do you think that elected officials such as Stokes and Hatcher will be able to persuade white city board members to go along with them on plans for improving black neighborhoods?

COSBY: If they're not able to, it won't be because they haven't tried. They were elected by black people; and if they want to be re-elected, they'll have to produce. But the black politician of today knows that his people don't really trust him. Especially if he has a white man over him, in which case he'll be called the white man's politician.

PLAYBOY: Do you think that many black legislators *are* white men's politicians?

COSBY: It used to be like that because of a policy that dates back to the days of slavery, when one black man on a plantation would be allowed to work indoors. He was called the house nigger and lived and ate well, and wouldn't do anything to make the boss angry, or else he'd wind up in the fields pickin' that cotton. Black politics has always had a little of this house-nigger mentality, but now it's changing. You can see it in a cat like Julian Bond, who could have been a house nigger but who, in effect, said, "Now, look, I don't *mind* working in the house, but I just want you to know a couple of things," for which they tried to throw him out of the house—Georgia's statehouse. But there's still a lot of resentment and envy of the black politician, because the guys working in the fields know that the cat in the house is eating real good. They know he's not getting chitlins or the last part of the pig thrown to him.

PLAYBOY: Do you feel that the majority of recently elected black congressmen are working as hard as they can to advance the cause of black equality?

COSBY: I'd rather see guys like S.C.L.C.'s Jesse Jackson or even Rap Brown in Congress than some of the black cats who are there now. I think Rap would make one hell of a vice president; to use Dick Gregory's line, *nobody* would shoot the president then. Most black congressmen seem like they're just trying to belong. But here again, what they may be doing is walking that tightrope to prove it can be done, to make it easier for other black men to get elected. You can never tell what a guy's philosophy may really be, because while we're putting him down, he might just be quietly paving the way for other black legislators. That's sometimes in the nature of a great sacrifice, especially when we, as selfish individuals, tend to look only at immediate results. So I'd really like to believe that a man like Senator Brooke is giving the cats in the senate a fast shuffle, so that he can clear a path for more black senators. If he's doing that, then beautiful. But if he's really into the whole Republican thing, if he was genuine during his campaign for Nixon and for that great friend of the black man, Spiro T. Agnew, then Brooke hasn't done a thing for us.

PLAYBOY: What do you think is the single most imperative issue that should receive top priority from black legislators?

COSBY: Justice. Police forces and the courts have to be overhauled and improved—*really* improved. I no longer expect a white policeman to jump in and protect a black man from being struck by a white, because I think their sense of white brotherhood—another way of saying racism— prevents them from identifying with the black or from just remaining objective. Police will turn their heads away when bricks, rocks or fists are thrown at a black man by whites. Not long ago, a white Chicago woman kicked a black man in the behind and punched him in the neck because he wanted Negro kids bused to school; when the guy defended himself against her, the cops arrested *him*. In that case, as in so many others, law and order protected the white aggressor.

PLAYBOY: Surely you don't think *all* white cops are racist.

COSBY: Look, let's first talk about what a very difficult thing it is to be a policeman. And let's talk about a policeman who is straight, who goes about his job with an open mind. But because he's a cop, he's got a problem, because he is being judged the way we black people don't like to be judged; in other words, when you see a policeman, he's a *cop*. And if he's a white cop, he has a white family and he identifies with white people; cops aren't machines, you know, when it comes to race relations.

PLAYBOY: Is there any way you see that white cops and black people could begin getting along better?

COSBY: I think relations would improve if a scientist could invent a mechanized helmet cops could wear, which would see to it that they enforced the law equally for all and which would get them working to wipe out crime and corruption in *every* part of society. Then the policeman would really be the upholder of law and order; he'd be a fighter for justice; he'd be what we want him to be—Batman. But a cop can't command a neighborhood's respect when he accepts bribes that range from petty cash to some fairly heavy bread.

PLAYBOY: Wouldn't police forgo bribes if cities raised their salaries; and wouldn't they be better equipped to deal with black people if they were also required to have special schooling in community relations?

COSBY: Sure, but a better answer for me is to put black cops in black neighborhoods. Black cops may be hated as much or even more than white cops by a lot of people in the ghetto, but I still think it's advisable for at least two reasons: Kids could grow up seeing black men in positions of authority, and ghetto streets wouldn't wind up in charge of a scared white cat who thinks the answer to problems is to hit people in the head because he's "tired of letting them get away with it," which is how white cops talk among themselves. Listen, if a guy doesn't want to be arrested by the police, it's easy for two cops to get the cat into a car without punching and beating on him with a nightstick. I once saw a policeman stop a harmless old black drunk who was mouthing off at him, and the cop just punched him out. Now, this to me is not law enforcement, because I don't think a guy learns anything when he's beaten up—except to hate. He certainly doesn't learn respect for the law; and when he gets to court, if he has any respect for the law left, the judges finish that off.

PLAYBOY: Are you saying that the courts are prejudiced?

COSBY: Cats with dough don't commit armed robbery or most of the crimes poor people commit. Yet rich guys' crimes—like embezzling a bank or moving a million dollars' worth of heroin a year—hurt a hell of a lot more people than some guy who sticks up a candy store and gets away with $12; so I think something's a little wrong there. When the rich man comes to court, he's got the best lawyers money can buy. But the poor man, the black man, gets a lawyer who's not necessarily interested in the case and may even consider it a pain in the ass. And then there's the whole thing about under-the-table payoffs to judges, which I won't attempt to document but which exist. What I'm saying is that there are two kinds of justice in this country: one for the rich and one for the poor—and blacks are poor. When the black people keep getting shafted by cops and courts, how can they have respect for people who are supposed to represent the law? So justice is first on my list. After that, I think white people will have to show us they believe that a policy of segregation is wrong—and that'll mean giving the black man an equal shot at decent housing, jobs and education.

PLAYBOY: You say segregation is wrong, yet many civil rights groups now restrict their membership to blacks only. If whites want to help and are rejected by Negroes, where do you suggest they go?

COSBY: Into their own communities to teach their own people what they feel.

PLAYBOY: Doesn't that still add up to turning away committed whites?

COSBY: All the unkept promises and half-truths of whites to blacks have resulted in a great deal of justifiable distrust. I think it's right for the black man to be in charge of his own organizations, even at the risk of alienating white friends; if those white friends resent that, I wonder about the sincerity of those friendships. But I'm not really worried about black bigotry, because it started only recently, when we finally understood that it was impossible to live anywhere in America without encountering racism. As soon as some real progress is made, it'll be hard to find a black bigot, because the black man won't have the time to be hating anyone. He'll be too busy going after that trade apprenticeship or skilled job.

PLAYBOY: Do you feel that the present generation of young whites is at odds with its parents on the race issue?

COSBY: I think that the white college radicals we read so much about are a very tiny percentage of the young people. Most white kids grow up listening to their parents call black kids niggers, and they learn to do the same thing, and quickly. Which is why I think white kids who want to help black people should work in their own communities. Blacks don't have a chance to wipe out the ignorance that's responsible for a lot of prejudice.

PLAYBOY: In line with that thought, a recent poll indicated that most white people believe there's no real difference in the way they grow up and the way blacks grow up—and conclude that blacks themselves are totally responsible for all their social and economic problems. Do you think that if whites had more information about actual ghetto conditions, racial harmony would improve?

COSBY: It couldn't do any harm, but I find it hard to believe that white people don't know what life is like for the average American black. If a white guy sat down and objectively thought about the situation for a minute, how could he *possibly* think that blacks are growing up the same way he grew up? Did his mother have to pay more than $200 for a couch that costs white people $125? A guy in the slums buys a car for $150 and has to pay $400 a year insurance on it. The ghetto supermarkets sell food you can't find anywhere else; did you ever eat green meat and green bread? How many winters have white people spent with rats scurrying around their apartments at night, with windows boarded up but not keeping out the cold, and with no heat? Try to get a ghetto slumlord to fix up an apartment and you'll know what frustration and bitterness is.

PLAYBOY: Haven't a number of city governments begun cracking down on slumlords?

COSBY: Yes, but it doesn't do any good. It's fine to have a law on the books, but what good is it if a slumlord can get around it? If he can pay a city official $150 or $500 a year to keep his mouth shut when inspection time comes around, the law is worth nothing. And if the landlord is prosecuted, he'll hand money under the table to someone higher up than the city inspector. Or maybe he won't even bother to bribe anyone; after all, what difference will it make whether he spends $200 bribing a cat or paying that amount in the form of a fine? Here, again, black people wind up powerless, because they have no capital.

PLAYBOY: Then you advocate black capitalism?

COSBY: That's right. I think whites should begin to understand how personally destructive poverty is. Drive through Harlem sometime; if a cat's got no bread, he's just not going to look good. He'll look bad enough not having a job and having no money coming in; but if he comes out of a one-room apartment with three or four brothers, and his father has no job, how can he *possibly* look good? And when you're poor, nobody wants to have anything to do with you. This used to happen to me, even among black people. Before I became "somebody," I had my problems getting dates with girls. I had black girls reject me because I had only a glen-plaid suit and striped shirt and striped tie to wear on a date; that was all I owned in the way of dress-up clothing. That was all I could afford. There's a whole string of chicks in Philadelphia who are bread-conscious and turned me loose because I was hoping to become a schoolteacher, which would have given them a cat who was making $130 a week—if he made it through college. Chicks would put that down: "Schoolteacher? Nope, you're not in my bracket." There's probably girls today think, "Gee, I could have had him and I let him go. I sold Bill Cosby short at $12, and now he's $432 a share. Damn!" The point is: The poorer you are, the uglier you are. And that poverty creeps into every part of black people's lives: poor education, poor housing, poor sanitation, poor medical care and, as a result of all these, poor jobs. When society keeps on showing that it's more interested in property rights than in human rights, the result is looting and riots.

PLAYBOY: Do you think, as many law-enforcement officials have alleged, that looting and rioting are ever planned, in the same way that a civil rights march is planned, with the intention of forcing whites into remedial concessions?

COSBY: Looting and rioting are spontaneous things that happen with a crowd. They're not planned, coordinated actions. It all boils down to the fact that when the opportunity comes to get a free pair of pants or a television set, people go along with the crowd. If *you* were walking down a street and saw people running in and out of stores, getting away with things you never had—getting away clean, too—why *not* go in there and get that bicycle or sofa yourself? As far as rioting is concerned, let me put it to you this way: If a guy is walking along and all of a sudden a crowd of people comes up and they're shouting, the first thing he'll want to know is what they're yelling about—right? Then he hears what they're yelling about; maybe a cop shot an unarmed black kid or police turned off fire hydrants black kids were using to beat 90-degree heat in the ghetto. Things like that have actually caused riots. The man may get pulled into that mob and listen to their statements and he may well join them. Now, a mob is like a pack of animals, man, and things like sniping and arson are liable to happen when a bunch of people, who are justifiably bitter and frustrated, are set off by an incident that finally exhausts all of their patience. But in riots where there's sniping going on, how come the cats who wind up getting killed are all unarmed black bystanders?

PLAYBOY: Do you think looting and rioting will stop as soon as black people acquire a fair share of America's wealth?

COSBY: Absolutely. You know, when doctors have to treat a wound, they don't heal it by putting bacteria on it or by applying dirty bandages to it. The powers in this country know how to heal the race situation and they also know that, by doing so, they'd be solving the problems of our cities. When white people move out of the city, they're moving to better homes, better schools. Cities have no attractions to make people change their minds and move back. And even if the people do move back, where do they wind up living? In a lower-class ghetto area or next to one. So let's clean up the city's sores. And to clean them up, we need to make jobs available to the people who live there, who suffer and die there, who, like the middle-class whites who leave, also want to get out and live in better surroundings. If it means that we build factories in ghettos—forget smog and air pollution and all that other crap for the moment—then that's what we'll have to do. We'll have to build more hospitals and schools to improve the quality of ghetto life. That's the only way the city will be able to offer both its blacks and its whites the same things that are available in the suburbs; that's the only way people will stop leaving the city.

PLAYBOY: Do you think urban-renewal programs can help?

COSBY: Urban renewal usually means that buildings are torn down, people are moved to another area and then, for years, all you have are empty lots. That's a fact. And black people ask themselves the same questions whites would ask in the situation: Where are the homes we were promised? Why did you chase us out of there in the first place? How can any neighborhood become stable with this kind of thing going on?

PLAYBOY: But some new public housing *does* get built in ghettos. Aren't these suitable places to live?

COSBY: Well, a project is a little better than that apartment you've lived in where the landlord won't fix anything. But you can build low-rent housing without having it look and feel like a steel-and-brick concentration camp. You can put more elevators in and make sure the elevators work, so that little kids playing in the street who have to go to the john don't have to wait 10 minutes for an elevator and wind up urinating in the lobbies.

PLAYBOY: As you know, there are millions of whites who can't understand why a majority of black neighborhoods are so rundown and littered.

COSBY: Look, take a simple thing like garbage collection. You may have eight families living in what was once a one-family house—because rents are high and because the jobs available to ghetto blacks don't pay well. You're going to get an awful lot of trash from this house, because all these people are living there. Each family goes out, does its shopping and contributes its share of garbage, so you'd expect there'd be at least twice as much collection as there was before. But there's usually *half* as much garbage collection and, at that, those eight families have it good, compared with most of the people who live in black neighborhoods.

PLAYBOY: Do you think these conditions can be corrected through the poverty program?

COSBY: They could be, but they won't; I don't think that the poverty program can mean much when 70 percent of its bread goes into the pockets of the people who get paid to give it away. And now that poverty-program funds are under local supervision, it's become just another piece of political patronage. That's almost criminal.

PLAYBOY: How do you think federal funds *should* be used to help clean up and eventually eliminate the ghettos?

COSBY: The first thing we should do is study the findings and recommendations of the Kerner Commission. I don't think any recent government study has been more valid—or more ignored by the government—than that report. The fact is that if certain buildings went up in the ghetto, they would supply jobs for thousands of black men. The second move also has to do with jobs; I think we should discontinue the summer work programs for kids and concentrate on men.

PLAYBOY: Why?

COSBY: White legislators think that as long as a kid's energy is spent and his time taken up, he'll be too tired to throw a bomb. But that's bullshit, because a kid's got more energy than a grownup. And I know, man. I used to play basketball from nine in the morning until the sun went down. But the truth of the matter is that no parent can command a kid's respect if the parent doesn't have a strong game going for himself—if the father doesn't have a job. The kid will hear his mother chewing the old man out because he's not working. Or he'll hear them both moaning and groaning because there's no money coming in.

Listen, summertime should be when a kid can go out and hit that ball and swim and go hiking. Summertime is no books, no sitting in a classroom, and the biggest worry for parents is that their kid doesn't knock up somebody's daughter. I see summer as a time to have a ball, not a season to burn off energy so that you won't burn up the city. If the kid's working and the old man isn't, he's not the father, man; he's just an older guy who can beat you up. He can beat you up because he's bigger and stronger, but he certainly isn't anybody you can use as an example of what you want to be when you grow up.

So I believe all the job emphasis should be directed toward industrial corporations giving job-training programs to fathers who are out in the streets. If you take care of the father, then the kid has somebody to look up to. Black men *don't* need those dumb civic programs that send entertainers to perform in the ghetto every summer. Maybe they expect the cat in the audience to say to himself, "I enjoyed that show so much I'm not going to be militant anymore. As a matter of fact, that was such a good program that I don't care if I'm poor and can't get a job for the rest of my life. I'm gonna come early and get a better seat for next year's show. That is, if I don't starve to death between now and then."

PLAYBOY: Do you think a guaranteed annual income might be one answer to the poverty problem?

COSBY: I'm in favor of a guaranteed *job*; no man, black or white, really wants to be given a paycheck or handed a loaf of bread or a book of stamps. Men want to work and they want to be paid decent salaries. When I look at myself as a young man who can retire in a few years and receive an income from my investments, I still know that I could no more sit on my ass and let that check come in than I could lie paralyzed in bed for the rest of my life. I've got to do something with my hands, my feet and my brain. To me, it won't make any difference if it's a job as a part-time schoolteacher, paying $30 a week—because I'll still have that big dividend check coming in every week. But I'll be working. Jobs are what the black man wants. But if I'm washing down hospital wards, or sweeping floors in a restaurant, and if my paycheck at the end of the month is smaller than a relief check, why work? When a guy on welfare gets a job, he no longer gets welfare; would *you* work to lose money? We could set up better plans that would cost a lot less and be more helpful to this country if we really wanted to.

PLAYBOY: Have you any in mind?

COSBY: Sure. Men on relief should be taught skilled jobs. That's only half of it, though, because it isn't enough just to teach skills. We must also make sure there are jobs available to use the skills. And all of us also have to be grownup enough and intelligent enough to realize that all people are not the grooviest in the world and that even after you teach a guy a skill, he may not be able to hold a job or really want it. We have our con men and our criminals. No matter how cool your society is, you'll still have people who'll kill and rape and steal, regardless of color.

PLAYBOY: While we're still on the subject of color: Perhaps for the first time in America, the awareness of skin color is being used constructively in the "black is beautiful" concept. What does that phrase represent to you?

COSBY: With me, it isn't a matter of black is beautiful as much as it is that white is not *all* that's beautiful—which is what black men are taught. We need a self-love to throw off all that bullshit that's been laid on us for the past 300 years. And this is a groovy way to teach our kids to be proud of what they are. We black people have our own culture, which has always been laughed at because it's different from the white man's. I remember when I was in junior high school at Christmastime, and we'd been allowed to bring records in. I never owned any, but a couple of colored girls brought Mahalia Jackson's version of *Silent Night*, while the white kids brought things like the Mormon Tabernacle Choir singing *Hallelujah* and Bing Crosby's *White Christmas*. Well, the black treatment of a Christmas carol was something the white kids snickered at, because of their own ignorance; and, at the same time, we were embarrassed because it wasn't white. Mahalia just didn't sound like the Mormon Tabernacle Choir, and Clara Ward didn't sound like Bing Crosby. But this no longer happens, because of the black-is-beautiful re-education, because of the fact that our culture, our music is something to be proud of. We're into a different style, a different way of doing things, and we're not going to let anybody laugh at it just because his face is white. And we're not going to be ashamed of if. What we are is beautiful—what we are is black.

PLAYBOY: After centuries of being told they were inferior, have black people themselves had difficulty in accepting this new self-pride?

COSBY: It hasn't been easy to throw out all the brainwashing, but we're doing it. Let me give you a personal example: Black people from the South have a common accent; it's almost a foreign language. I can't speak it, but I understand it, because my 85-year-old grandfather speaks it. I remember hearing him use the word "jimmin" and I had to go up to my grandmother to find out what he was saying. She told me he was saying "gentlemen." That was black; it's the way my grandfather talks, the way my Aunt Min talks, because she was down South picking cotton while I was in Philadelphia picking up white middle-class values and feeling embarrassed about hearing people talk like that and wanting to send them to school to straighten them out. I now accept this as black, the same way I accept an Italian whose father from the old country has a heavy accent. I accept it as black the same way chitlins and crab fingers and corn bread and collard greens and hush puppies and hog jaws and black-eyed peas and grits are black. This is what we were given to eat; this was our diet in the South, and we've done some groovy things with it. Now even white people are talking about Uncle So-and-So's sparerib place.

PLAYBOY: Why do you think black food and black music have become so fashionable in much of white society today?

COSBY: White people are trying to get a little soul—which has to do with sentiment and sorrow, sympathy and guilt. It's like the hippies who go around dressed as if they're poor, although their parents live in big suburban homes. A lot of white people want soul and they think they can get it by eating the food, learning the dances, digging the music. Many white chicks feel they'll get soul if they ball a black man they don't even care about.

PLAYBOY: Do you think that's a major motivation for interracial sex?

COSBY: I can't really say. While soul is the attraction for the white person, I feel that the black goes to the white because of the white's status in this society; the black person is supposed to in some way *gain* from making love to a white. And the white is giving up status to make love to a black. It's almost like a materialistic thing now: If a white chick is with a black guy, she's saying, "Look at me, look what I'm giving up, look how I'm going against society. Man, am I *brave!*" Now, I'm not talking about love, just balling. If he or she wants to have soul, like, go on ahead and ball, but that ain't gonna make you soulful. I've been with white cats who've looked at black chicks I wouldn't be seen with anywhere and heard them say, "Man, she is *fantastic*-looking." And, by the same token, I've seen white girls look at a black man and say, "That guy's really beautiful." But what they mean—and I'm talking about whites who have a desire to make love to a black—is that they dig that African or extra blackness that says this person is 100 percent black. To them, this blackness represents soul.

PLAYBOY: Doesn't it represent the same thing to black people?

COSBY: Of course not. Ever since America was founded, we've been trying to overcome the dumb idea that skin color, of its own nature, determines the character of the person who's inside it. After all that's happened to the black man in this country, it would be even crazier for us to believe in racism than for whites to. Up until six years ago, black people, because of their identification with white society, didn't want to be black. In cities like Washington, D.C., in fact, there are many Negroes who still feel a great deal of resentment if a dark Negro comes to date a light-skinned girl. The parents of that girl want to keep breeding lighter, so they can finally get rid of that *badge* and walk free. But most black people have finally discovered they've been deluding themselves.

PLAYBOY: About what?

COSBY: Through the civil rights movement and through Martin Luther King Jr., America's racism was forced out into the open, so the world could see it. Black people found out that most whites just didn't *want* them to have a growing place in America's future. Once we found that out, we turned to ourselves for help, as we had to. It's like when a cat leaves home to see the world but gets robbed and can't find a job; the only place for him is back home. Well, we need to make a place for ourselves, a place where we can be received and accepted, and this is happening through black identification—realizing that one is black, not white, and being proud of it. But many black people today go to extremes in their rejection of white power, white imperialism and white values.

PLAYBOY: Which white values?

COSBY: The main white value—greed. Through greed, whites have been fooled into thinking that freedom for black people means they'll lose their jobs, their homes, even the clothes off their backs. Certain ideas have been laid on the white man to exploit his greed, and the windup is that whites, because of greed, think all black men are lazy and shiftless and everything else represented in racist stereotyping. But this has all been the result of lies, and white people now have to listen to the truth: Freedom, for *any* man, is a need like food and water. The black man needs his freedom and he is determined to get it—now. If white America chooses to withhold equality from the black man, the result is going to be disaster for this country. But if whites allow the black man the same civil rights they themselves take for granted, then they're *really* in store for a shock; this country will turn into the coolest and grooviest society the world has ever seen.

 December 1985

A candid conversation with America's superdad about his revolutionary true-to-life comedy series—and about racism, kids, humor and heroes

Go figure out America's taste in television. Last year, just when the nation seemed hopelessly addicted to prime-time programs that featured equal measures of sex, greed and hair spray, along came *The Cosby Show*—an unlikely series about a black obstetrician and his family—and suddenly, network executives were proclaiming that sitcoms weren't dead, after all. NBC, proud as a peacock at last, found itself presenting TV's top-rated weekly comedy series, while comedian Bill Cosby, riding the biggest wave of his career, had become America's favorite father figure.

As Dr. Heathcliff Huxtable, Cosby portrays a bright, funny physician who's deeply in love with his lawyer wife, Claire, played by Phylicia Ayers-Allen. Their TV children—four daughters and one son—mirror the real-life set of siblings Cosby has sired with his wife of almost 22 years, the former Camille Hanks. On *The Cosby Show*, Father knows best, but not to the point of parental infallibility: Cliff Huxtable often learns as much from his kids as they do from him. Some critics have carped that the show isn't "black" enough, which is to say that Dr. Huxtable isn't poor and doesn't go around exchanging high fives each time he delivers a baby or a solution to a family problem. The Huxtable children, meanwhile (judging by current TV standards and practices), are just plain weird: They actually love and respect their parents. Most people are not put off by all that. As John J. O'Connor recently noted in *The New York Times*, "At a time when so many comedians are toppling into a kind of smutty permissiveness, Mr. Cosby is making the nation laugh by paring ordinary life to its extraordinary essentials. It is, indeed, a truly nice development." In a cover story, *Newsweek* suggested that Cosby's magical rapport with children, huge popularity with grownups and fiercely creative imagination put him in the genius class.

How far Bill Cosby's career will continue to develop is anybody's guess, including the comedian's. For more than 20 years, Cosby has been a show-business staple whose body of work now includes 20 comedy albums (five of which won Grammys), five TV series (he won three Emmys for *I Spy*), 10 movies and thousands of performances as a stand-up comedian.

By now, you're probably somewhat familiar with Cosby's curriculum vitae: The eldest of three sons, he was born in Philadelphia on July 12, 1937. At Philly's Germantown High School, he was an excellent athlete (captain of the track and football teams) but a dreadful student. After his sophomore year, Cosby joined the Navy, saw the world and then saw the light: He enrolled in Navy correspondence courses, earned his high school diploma and then wangled a track scholarship to Temple University. Three years later, he again dropped out of school, this time because his weekend appearances at various

Greenwich Village nightspots had made him a hot comedy commodity. In 1963, he recorded his first comedy album, won a Grammy for it and has never looked back. He later received a degree from Temple and then earned a master's and a doctorate in education from the University of Massachusetts. Cosby's 242-page dissertation was titled "The Integration of Visual Media via Fat Albert and the Cosby Kids into the Elementary School Culminating as a Teacher Aid to Achieve Increased Learning." The net result is that the man known in showbiz circles as Cos is known in others as Dr. William H. Cosby Jr. And Fat Albert, who still lives inside his creator's head, is said to be very pleased.

To interview the 48-year-old performer, *Playboy* again teamed Cosby with freelancer Lawrence Linderman, who conducted the magazine's original *Playboy Interview* with him (and Linderman's first) in 1969. Linderman reports:

"I caught up with Bill a few weeks after *The Cosby Show* had gone into its second season of production. Cosby was spending the last days of summer doing two shows a night at tent sites in Cohasset, Massachusetts, and Baldwin, Rhode Island, both within shouting distance of his 265-acre estate near Amherst, Massachusetts. When we got together at Kimball's by the Sea, a snug little hotel in Cohasset Harbor, Cosby greeted me warmly, and I think both of us felt as if we'd seen each other only a few weeks before. Cosby hasn't changed much over the years: The only signs he shows of advancing middle age are a slight tinge of gray hair and the beginnings of a paunch, which he's busting his butt to eliminate. At our first meeting, we couldn't find the source of the tiny chimes that were sounding in the room until Bill realized the sound was coming from a pair of stop watches he'd just bought to time himself in 400-meter runs. (Once a track man, always a track man.)

"In any case, when all the tootlings were done with, Cosby whipped out one of the footlong Jamaican stogies he more or less chain smokes, and we got down to business. With the start of the new fall television season imminent, *The Cosby Show* provided the opening subject for our conversation."

PLAYBOY: The last time we spoke—in 1969—you were a hot young comedian. Since then, you've just about become a national institution. What does it feel like to be an American institution?

COSBY: Well, except for the fact that I was 16 pounds lighter 16 years ago, it feels good. It's *been* good. I remember 1969 very well. Couple of things have happened since. [*Grins through cigar smoke*] Right about then, I had four albums in the top 10 at the same time, and I don't think even Elvis Presley ever did that. Now, that was a high. Winning the Emmys was a high, then going on to do my TV specials. . . . I'll tell you, when I was growing up in a lower-economic neighborhood in Philadelphia, these were things I thought happened only to people on the radio.

PLAYBOY: For readers who may not know that there was such a thing as life before television, what do you mean by that?

COSBY: Oh, old radio programs, like *The Lux Radio Theater*. The announcer would say, "There goes Humphrey Bogart" or, "Sitting next to me is Edward G. Robinson." I'd picture those guys in my mind—I'm sure they weren't there—but that's how some of all *this* feels. I know the TV series has changed things for me, but up until it hit, I'd been very, very successful.

I consider myself a master of stand-up comedy, and I still really enjoy performing. I think even my commercials have been excellent, because I've done them only for products I believe in. But more than anything, I know how happy I am at home. My wife, Camille, and I are enjoying each other more and more, mostly because in the past eight or nine years, I've given up all of myself to her. I'm no longer holding anything back.

PLAYBOY: What part of you were you holding back?

COSBY: The part of me that was devoting more thought to my work than to my wife. That's a very selfish thing to do, and I think there are people who'll tell you quite openly that if they had to choose between their mate and their work, they'd choose their work. Well, eight or nine years ago, I realized that that was just silly, so I began releasing myself from my work—I'm not just talking about time now—and coming more and more together with my wife. And what happened was that I found myself falling deeper and deeper in love with her.

I think the fear of giving all of myself to Camille also had to do with a worry that perhaps someday she would leave me; I was afraid that if I gave myself to her completely and she left, I'd have no hope of recovering. I always figured that maybe I should save 11 or 12 percent of myself to get me through that day when she says, "Look, Bill, I met a man while you were on the road and he's a very nice guy." When I realized what I was thinking, I thought, Well, if it happens, it happens, and I'll deal with it then. But not now.

PLAYBOY: Despite all this success since we last spoke, there must have been moments that weren't as upbeat as all that. Wasn't there a time when Bill Cosby was in danger of going out of style?

COSBY: Oh, there was a point where the career—the performance, or comedy, career—began to have trouble. In the early 1970s, when the younger culture went into a kind of LSD period, a lot of legitimate show-biz people—Bill Cosby, Harry Belafonte, Andy Williams, even Johnny Mathis—began to feel like tumbleweed rolling through the back of the theaters. The economy was in a dip, our fans were becoming parents, the time seemed wrong. It was tough for a lot of us. I went to Las Vegas, worked Vegas. I worked conventions, one-nighters. . . .

PLAYBOY: But you were still a young man then, in your mid-30s.

COSBY: Yeah, but I was *talking* old. I was talking to audiences about my marriage, my kids—I was out of Fat Albert by then. I really didn't want to do "I'm a child" anymore; I was more interested in the behavior of a parent toward a child.

PLAYBOY: And the times finally caught up with you. It's being said that *The Cosby Show* may turn out to be the kind of comedic landmark that *All in the Family* was, so let's spend some time on it. Few industry insiders expected it to survive its first season, let alone become the most popular series on television. Have you been surprised by the show's success?

COSBY: Yes, it's gone way past what I expected. All I really wanted to do was satisfy people who'd understand what I was trying to give them—a series about a family that seemed as real as you could get within the confines of television, without using vulgar or abusive language. And I wanted to show kids that their mothers and fathers could be very, very firm people, almost dogmatic, yet you'd still love them because they have tomorrow's newspaper and what they're saying has to do with their love and concern for you.

PLAYBOY: Your show went to the top of the ratings virtually from the start. What do you think accounts for its popularity?

COSBY: Well, if you look at Cliff Huxtable, you see an overachiever who knows that American society tends to say that certain people can't do certain jobs because of their color or sex or religion. So people like Cliff work twice as hard to prove themselves. But the beautiful thing about

Cliff is that he's a man who truly loves his wife—all of her—and they both love their children. That's really why people watch the show—because of the family. When the show is over, I think people have the reaction I have to it: I smile and feel good.

PLAYBOY: Are you trying to educate viewers as much as entertain them?

COSBY: Oh, absolutely. You mentioned *All in the Family*. See, the difference between Cliff and Norman Lear's Archie Bunker is that I don't remember Archie ever apologizing for anything, and it's a point on our show that when Cliff or anybody else does something wrong, an apology is in order. For example, on a show we called "The Juicer," the kids get into trouble with Cliff after they mess with this food processor he's just bought. The kitchen ends up a mess, and each of the children is responsible for some part of what happened. But then the wife turns to Cliff and says, "Who left the machine plugged in in the first place?" So what we've got here is three people who blew it in terms of responsibility, and they're talking about it. Well, I *love* that.

Maybe I sound like someone who's trying to sell something to an audience, but I do have a track record in education: I started with *Sesame Street* three weeks after it went on the air, and from there I went to *The Electric Company* and to *Fat Albert* and to a series about a teacher named Chet Kincaid, which ran on ABC for two years.

PLAYBOY: The idea for this show supposedly originated with Brandon Tartikoff, president of NBC Entertainment, who saw you do a monolog about your children on *The Tonight Show*. Is that true?

COSBY: Yes, but the genesis of the show was more complicated than that. About three years ago, I decided I wanted to do a TV show that all my children could watch without my wife and I worrying about how it would affect them. I'd heard a lot of people say, "I don't want to let my children watch television," and I was feeling the same way. The situation comedies all seemed to get their laughs by using euphemisms for sexual parts of the body—lots of jokes about boobs and butts. And if there was a detective show on—and I'm not talking about the Tom Selleck show now—you'd see cars skidding on two wheels for half a block, or else some cat would be dropping to his knees with a .357 Magnum or sticking the gun in somebody's mouth. The language was getting tougher, the women were stripping down faster, and if you had a five-year-old daughter, she was watching men shooting bullets and drawing a lot of blood.

Let me jump way ahead of what we're discussing for a second, because I want to tell you about a very crazy moment for me. When NBC eventually went with *The Cosby Show*, they asked me to speak to a big crowd of advertising people who were being introduced to the network's '84-'85 lineup of shows. Well, I start to talk to them about why I wanted to do another TV show, and on a screen right behind me, NBC is running film clips of its new shows, and I tell you, if they ran clips of seven cop stories, six of them had the cars on two wheels, the guy busting into the room with a big gun and somebody in a bathtub about to be blasted. I'm there looking at this stuff and thinking, My own network is the one I'm trying to kill off. I really *did* set out to change all that.

PLAYBOY: Did Tartikoff get in touch with you about your monolog?

COSBY: No, but word of his idea reached Marcy Carsey and Tom Werner, two young producers, and they set up a meeting with me. We agreed very quickly on the basics of the show: The mother and father would both be working, they'd love each other very much and they'd have four children living in their New York apartment. But whenever the children show up—well, as Frank Gifford says, that's when the wheels come off. We were in complete agreement on everything until I mentioned the guy's occupation.

PLAYBOY: They didn't want a doctor?

COSBY: No, I wanted the guy to be a *chauffeur*. Marcy went crazy when I said that. She told me she couldn't see me as a chauffeur, and I said, "Hey, chauffeurs make good money. The guy will own his own car, meaning he'll be free to be at home at all kinds of weird hours—especially when his wife is working."

PLAYBOY: Aren't you glad you ran into Marcy Carsey?

COSBY: [*Laughs*] No, no, I'm not! And you should have heard the arguments we had when I decided I wanted my wife on the show to be a plumber or a carpenter!

Well, I was arguing long and hard with Marcy and Tom, but I was standing tall. I think I could have gotten them to go along with me. But then I changed my mind.

PLAYBOY: Why?

COSBY: Because Camille, my wife of 22 years, said to me, "You will not be a chauffeur." I said, "Why not?" And Camille said, "Because *I* am not going to be a carpenter." I asked her, "What's the problem here? Is there something wrong with being a chauffeur or a carpenter?" And she said, "Bill, of course there's nothing wrong with those occupations—I'd be stupid if I thought that. But nobody is going to believe that *you're* a chauffeur. Your image has always been Temple University, college, grad school. Nobody's going to believe it when you put on a uniform and stand beside a car and start polishing it. And people are going to laugh in your face when they see *me* with a hammer!" Well, I gave up on the idea right then and there.

PLAYBOY: Let's see if we have this right: You changed your mind because your wife felt that your TV wife's occupation—and yours—wouldn't square with the real image?

COSBY: Oh, no, I changed my mind not only because I absolutely trust Camille but also because at that point in the discussion, she had gotten upset with me. My wife doesn't get upset about casual things, but now she was *really* upset; she was asking me to go visit a psychiatrist and bring back a note. Case closed. I went back and told Tom and Marcy they were right, and we changed Cliff's occupation. Then they went up to Tartikoff with it and, boom, money came in and we did the show.

PLAYBOY: Who decided that Cliff Huxtable would be an obstetrician?

COSBY: I did. I wanted to be able to talk to women who were about to give birth and make them feel comfortable. I also wanted to talk to their husbands and put a few messages out every now and then.

PLAYBOY: Such as?

COSBY: That fathering a child isn't about being a *macho* man, and if you think it is, you're making a terrible mistake. It's about becoming a parent.

PLAYBOY: Do you think you've succeeded in putting out those messages?

COSBY: Oh, sure. In one episode last season, a new husband comes into Cliff's office and says, "I'm the man, the head of the household. Women should be kept barefoot and pregnant." Cliff tells the guy that being a parent has nothing to do with that kind of concept of manhood. And he really straightens him out by telling him that neither he nor his wife will be in charge of the house—their children will. But this is an example of why I say I always felt the Huxtables' jobs have very little to do with the show. It's the behavior, the dealing with the children, the dealing with the wife that makes it work.

PLAYBOY: But just as Cliff's profession gives him the opportunity to make certain points, doesn't his wife do the same thing in her capacity as a lawyer?

COSBY: Yes, but I don't think what she has to say emanates from a set of law offices. What I'm after is what happens to an individual. I'm not going after a broad social turnaround tomorrow. How can I put it? [*Pauses*] Look, I think I have faced these situations enough to say that if I threw a message out hard and heavy, I'd lose viewers. But if the message is subtle, people who want to find it will find it; and if they want to make changes, they will.

PLAYBOY: Which message do you mean?

COSBY: Any of them. Take the black female lawyer who's been in a firm for seven years and is hoping for a promotion. Generally, if you're black and female in a white-male firm that you've been fortunate enough to get into, well, when you're looking for that promotion and you don't get it, you're out. But if I put that on the show, my experience tells me no changes will come of it. So she got the promotion.

PLAYBOY: Since it obviously doesn't always work that way in real life, can't you be accused of giving viewers—especially in the example you just mentioned—a sugar-coated version of reality?

COSBY: It's my position and feeling that if I put a situation that's behaviorally negative on the show—let's say Claire deserves the promotion and doesn't get it—then I'll be putting some lawyers on the defensive. And what's the result? They'll say, "Listen, I don't want to hear this." If somebody doesn't want to give you something, they're going to continue not to give it to you, regardless of what you say. And if they find you doing something they don't like, they will at that point explain they were *about* to give it to you, but now that you've done something they don't like, they *won't* give it to you. It's my Uncle Jack theory.

PLAYBOY: Care to tell us more about it?

COSBY: Well, I had an uncle Jack who owned a bicycle shop. The man knew that I loved bikes, and I'd go down to his shop on North Broad Street in Philadelphia and just salivate at the sight of all those bicycles. I was 12 years old and my uncle Jack knew how much I wanted a bike, but he'd never given me one. He let me ride bikes inside the shop, and one day I ran into his glass showcase and cracked it. Uncle Jack said to me, "Bill, I was going to give you a bike, but since you just broke my showcase, forget about it."

Well, at the age of 12, I just said to myself, "Uncle Jack wasn't going to give me a bike anyway." That was a valuable lesson to learn.

PLAYBOY: And that has shaped your approach to dealing with social issues?

COSBY: Absolutely. By letting Claire get her promotion, I feel that when the show is rerun and rerun, there will be lawyers out there who'll see it and who'll maybe give a black, white or Asian female the promotion those women may deserve. We always try to put out a positive, and all the people on that show are very positive. The result is that we won't have lawyers looking at the show and saying, "Don't tell me the rotten guy who turned Claire down is *me!*" They'll want to be smart, like the lawyer who gave her the promotion.

PLAYBOY: If we follow your reasoning, then, is it fair to say that *The Cosby Show* avoids presenting *any* rotten characters?

COSBY: I really try not to. I'd rather have people we all recognize and who, in their own way, are funny. For instance, this year, the Huxtables are making improvements in their house, and we're introducing a contractor who'll be on the show maybe five times. I love the character. The contractor comes in to look at the work Cliff wants done, and he tells me the three things contractors *always* tell you: "I don't know how long it's going to take. I don't know what it's going to cost. And I just don't know when I'm going to get started, Dr. Huxtable." I think people will look at him working in the Huxtables' house—with cloths set up and dust rising and the kids flying around—and say, "Yeah, that's happened to us."

PLAYBOY: You've already mentioned the overlap your wife felt between your real family and your TV family: Do the Huxtables have four daughters and one son because Bill Cosby is the father of four daughters and one son?

COSBY: Oh, sure. What's funny is that in the beginning, we all agreed that the Huxtables would have four children. We had excluded the character of my real daughter who's away at college. It wasn't until after we did the first show that I felt that my oldest daughter was missing—I really wanted her to be part of that family in terms of my ideas. Sondra Huxtable, who's played by Sabrina LeBeauf, a very fine actress, is not our oldest girl, Erica. But in terms of having that family work, in terms of what I know, I *needed* an oldest daughter away at college. My only regret now is that we don't give Sabrina enough work. At the writers' meetings, I'll say, "Now, look, somebody remind me that we've got to bring Sondra home. I want to see her."

PLAYBOY: Do the Cosby children ever get upset because their father is duplicating or extending some of their own foibles on national television?

COSBY: No, because in my stand-up comedy work, the children have already seen me talking about them and naming them and embellishing what they've said or done, and they've always been cool about it. Sometimes they even enjoy coming back to me and saying, "Oh, look, Dad, please, I don't want people to think I'm like *that.*"

PLAYBOY: Some of the stories are straight out of real life, though, without embellishment, aren't they?

COSBY: Oh, yeah. There's a story I tell about my son, Ennis, walking around looking real thoughtful one day when he was 14. The boy obviously was working up the nerve to ask me for something big—a father *knows* that look. He finally came up to me and said, "Dad, I was talking to my friends, and they think that when I'm 16 and old enough to drive, I should have my own car."

"Fine. You've got wonderful friends," I told him. "I think it's terrific that they want to buy you a car."

The boy looks at me in shock. "No, Dad, they want *you* to buy the car."

This does not come as a shock to me. "What kind of car did you have in mind?" I ask.

"Gee, Dad, I think it would really be nice to have a Corvette."

Can't fault the boy's taste in cars. I say to him, "Look, son, a Corvette costs about $25,000, and I can afford to buy you one. I'd *like* to buy you a Corvette—but not when you don't do your homework and you bring home Ds on your report card. So I'll make you a deal: For the next two years, you make every effort to fulfill your potential in school, and even though Corvettes will then cost about $50,000, I'll buy you one. And I won't even care if you *do* bring home Ds. If your teachers tell me you tried as hard as you could, and that you talked to them every time you had a problem with your work, well, if a D was the best you could do, I can't ask any more of you. Just give a 100 percent effort in school for the next two years, and you've got yourself a Corvette."

My son gets very quiet. Finally, he looks up at me and says, "Dad, what do you think about a Volkswagen?" Young Ennis, by the way, is now 6' 3" tall.

PLAYBOY: Do you ever get out on a basketball court with him?

COSBY: No way. Ennis is much too quick and too strong for me. Listen, I run in a competition for older guys called the Masters, and if I can't beat men my own age—which I can't—what would I be doing going up against a 16-year-old kid? Ennis is a good athlete, but he's a gentleman athlete. He's not from the days of yesteryear, when you stayed out on the court for 17 hours even if the temperature reached 103 degrees. I mean, Ennis has *sense.*

PLAYBOY: More than you had as a child?

COSBY: No question. You know what my problem used to be—among others? Embarrassment when I found out that someone else was right and I was wrong. I'll give you an example: When I was about 12, my grandfather said to me, "Don't play football until you're 21 years old." Now, this was a man I loved and respected. I said, "Why, Granddad?" He said, "Because your bones won't heal until you're 21."

Very quietly, I dismissed him. He was not a high school–educated man. This was a hard-working steel driver, Samuel Russell Cosby, but I said to myself, "This man is trying to stop me from doing something I want to do." So I played football in junior high, I played it on the street, I played it in high school. Got on the football team at Philadelphia Central High School. First game, I jumped over a guy and cracked my humerus—my shoulder. They put a cast on it and I was out for the season.

So I'm on the sofa in our house in the Richard Allen Projects, and my grandfather comes all the way from his house in Germantown on the trolley car. He always would come over to tell me a story and give me 50 cents—the story *before* the money. He was a very wise man. So this day, he looks down at me and says—well, it's what he *didn't* say. He didn't say, "I told you so." He just told me to take care of my shoulder—and I've never felt worse, more embarrassed. His mere presence—

PLAYBOY: What passed between the two of you at that moment?

COSBY: Fifty cents. [*Laughs*]

PLAYBOY: Getting back to the Huxtables and the Cosbys, do you ever feel you're the head of two families?

COSBY: Very much so. But I don't get my children and wife confused with the people I work with. They're family in the same way Bob Culp and I were family when we worked on *I Spy* and still are. The people on *The Cosby Show* are people I love and care for, and I have things I want for the TV children. But when the day's over, I don't have any problems with them. And I know that Phylicia is family in the sense that she could be my younger sister. I have a deep respect and love for her.

PLAYBOY: You had final say on casting *The Cosby Show*. Why did you choose her to play your wife?

COSBY: Phylicia knew how to look at a kid when you put all the guns on the table and say, "You go upstairs to your *room*," and the kid knows that if he doesn't do it, he's going to find himself walking on hot coals without his shoes on. Marcy and Dick brought me the three finalists for every role, and Phylicia won flat-out. In dealing with children, some mothers yell and nothing is happening except the sound of a woman yelling. Phylicia was able to say "Case closed" just with her eyes.

Lisa Bonet, who plays Denise, was also an obvious winner. Lisa was just what I wanted for Denise—a fashion-conscious teenager who's hip but who appears to be a little off-center and might just decide to become Greta Garbo. She's not on drugs and isn't supposed to look like she is, but I wanted Denise Huxtable to seem a little spaced-out, and Lisa has that quality.

Tempestt Bledsoe, who plays 12-year-old Vanessa, was clearly the best in her category. Last year, she was the gossip and the child with the wisecracks. This year, she's discovering boys, letting her jersey flop off one shoulder and, when not checking herself out in the mirror, is always on the phone.

PLAYBOY: Which was the toughest role to cast?

COSBY: Theo, the son. When the three finalists for the part read for me, the boys all had a similar way of reacting to the parent telling them to do something: They sucked their teeth and rolled their eyes before answering. I said the same thing to all three separately: "Do you have a father?" "Yes, sir." "If you said something to your father that way, what do you think would happen to you?" They all gave a sheepish smile and said they'd either wind up going through a wall or doing a crash landing out on the street. So I asked them to talk to me the way they would to their fathers, and we had the three boys go back into the hall. When Malcolm-Jamal Warner came back, I loved what he did. The moves were right; he was talking to his *dad*. He's a very flexible young actor. There was another boy I liked, and I almost asked if I could have two sons. At that point, I knew we were going to have four kids in the house, and I wasn't too sure I wanted one of them to be a six-year-old girl.

PLAYBOY: Why not?

COSBY: I told Marcy we'd be there shooting for the rest of our lives if we had a little kid. Now, Marcy was the one who wanted the teeny-weeny, and when little Keshia Knight Pulliam came in—I mean, you can't argue about whether or not she's a beautiful little girl, because, of course, she is. But I really didn't think I wanted to work with someone so young. After meeting Keshia, I said, "Okay, she's very, very bright and she'll be able to handle it."

Well, now when people talk to me on the street or on airplanes, they all tell me they could just *bite* that little girl—I mean, Keshia's more than earned her keep. Getting her was a very smart decision on Marcy's part, because when you look over the Huxtable family, there's a kid for just about every age group.

PLAYBOY: Do you feel any pressure about maintaining your top ranking?

COSBY: The pressure in television is to stay in the top 20. You fight to stay alive each week, and you do a lot of hoping. And meanwhile, you've got a show to put together and then perform, and en route to doing that, you watch the numbers. It's almost as if each week, you're a person looking back to see how you lived. You know, right now, it may look like I'm the boss, but the ratings dictate who's the boss, and when the numbers drop, you get a visit from the network SS men.

PLAYBOY: Who are those horrible people and what tortures do they inflict?

COSBY: Well, they're executives who seem to get younger and younger every year, and they say things like, "We think you ought to try doing it *our* way," which is not what you want to do. I've been there before. If and when the rating erosion occurs, you weigh what they say, and if it's worth anything, you try to comply. This is a very cold business, and if you don't look at it that way, you can get hurt. For instance, *The Jeffersons* was on for 10 years, and suddenly the network said, "You've been on long enough; that's it." Well, 10 years is a tremendous amount of time to keep a show going on network television, but I think the actors were really upset when CBS let them go.

PLAYBOY: What did you think of *The Jeffersons*?

COSBY: I felt that it taught most of America about a different kind of sound. The characters' speech was Southern, and its rhythms were different from what you'd find on *I Love Lucy*, for instance. But maybe not so different from what you can still hear on *The Honeymooners*, because Ralph Kramden, even though he wasn't from the South, was a lower-economic street guy. *The Jeffersons* got a lot of Americans who watch TV accustomed to that sound, just as Flip Wilson and Redd Foxx had done. Then Richard Pryor came along with *The Richard Pryor Show*, which didn't last long—

PLAYBOY: That's the one where he said he wanted to appear nude and the network canceled it, right?

COSBY: Yeah, but it had impact. It worked on a sociopolitical level, as well as on an educated street level, which means you could be sitting in the Russian Tea Room, having *blinis* and having graduated from Temple University, and enjoy it right down to your roots.

PLAYBOY: You and Pryor met in the Village when you were both coming up, right?

COSBY: Yeah. He was at the Cafe Wha? and I was at the Gaslight.

PLAYBOY: Why did it take so much longer for him to make it?

COSBY: They wanted only one at a time.

PLAYBOY: And for then, that was you.

COSBY: Well, I came up at a time when Dick Gregory was doing very tough political humor, and I admired him so much I started out doing the same thing. But then I decided I had to break away from that; I felt that if Americans were going to judge people as individuals, you didn't have to hammer people over the head. So if I played the hungry i in San Francisco and then the Apollo in Harlem, I didn't go to the Apollo and load up on antiwhite material, nor did I load up on you-black-people-better-get-yourself-together talk. I did the same show at both places and people reacted the same way in both places; they laughed.

PLAYBOY: People often compare your comedy work with Pryor's and Eddie Murphy's. What's most obvious is the difference between their use of profanity and your avoidance of it. Has that been a calculated decision on your part?

COSBY: No, it's just that I've never been comfortable with profanity. During the early 1970s, there was a time when I used profanity onstage for about six months. I was trying to get the audience to understand the language between a father and a son, and it involved a lot of cursing. I did a bit that showed my father cursing me and I found that the audience . . . just was *not ready* for me to curse onstage. So I cut it out, and I had to find another way of doing that piece without using curse words.

Now, I happen to think that Richard's way of using four-letter words and 12-letter curse words has nothing to do with Eddie Murphy's way of using 77-letter curse words.

PLAYBOY: So you don't find Pryor's humor offensive?

COSBY: Richard to me is like Lenny Bruce, and I think a lot of what he does and says is to try to get people to understand different kinds of behavior. Richard has also developed some characters that I absolutely admire, such as Mudbone and the wino in a crap game—I've known those people. I've seen them, I grew up around them and they were wonderful. Those are not embarrassing characters. Pryor also has a brilliant study of a man getting drunk and coming home and wanting to punch out his wife but being too loaded to do anything but pass out. All of these things are pertinent to human behavior.

Now, I wish I could explain Richard when it came to physically abusing himself, but I can't, because I don't know behaviorally where Richard is or was then.

PLAYBOY: You seem ambivalent in your feelings toward Eddie Murphy. What do you think of the choices he's made thus far?

COSBY: Listen, Eddie Murphy is a young man who is extremely, extremely intelligent. In terms of performing and self-editing, Eddie Murphy has made a choice. He knows what's right, he knows what's wrong, he knows what will upset people and what will not upset people. He has decided he'll say what he wants to say, and if it upsets some people, fine—but he's going to say it, anyway. Now, I don't happen to think of Eddie as a stand-up comedian. One of the reasons there are only a few stand-up comedians, like Billy Crystal and Jay Leno, around is that when somebody gets hot, they go into movies—and Eddie Murphy packs people into theaters. The question, perhaps, then comes down to this: Is Eddie Murphy, with his street language, harmful?

When Murphy broke into movies in *48 HRS.*, I agreed with Pauline Kael of *The New Yorker*, who raved about the young man. I did not agree with the total about-face she did on Murphy in *Beverly Hills Cop*. Same fellow, right?

PLAYBOY: How did you feel when Murphy impersonated you on *Saturday Night Live* as a kind of pompous, cigar-waving Bob Hope figure?

COSBY: I didn't mind it. I think there are always these positions younger people take, coming into a field, looking at older people and thinking, Hey, you're not that good; I can be better. That's how you get pupils to surpass their teachers.

PLAYBOY: So, overall, you like Murphy's brand of humor.

COSBY: I like his movies—his *movies*. They make me laugh. They make a *lot* of people laugh. That's not an easy thing to do, which is why I have a problem with the entire entertainment industry and its rejection of comedians. People in the industry will admit that comedy is a tough business. They will also admit that you have to be very intelligent to be able to get people to laugh. Well, if we weigh and measure the importance of making an audience laugh and the good feeling people get from that, why does the record industry always make sure it won't even *announce* who won best comedy album on the Grammy telecast? And I think it's just flat-out dumb for the movie industry not to nominate funny actors like Steve Martin for Academy Awards. Academy Award nominations almost always go to actors who are deeply serious and who are in serious movies. Of course, a lot of those movies are funny anyway.

PLAYBOY: Are you grousing because you've made 10 movies and have yet to be nominated for an Academy Award?

COSBY: Absolutely, absolutely not! Whatever chance I ever had to be nominated was when I was part of the big cast—Maggie Smith, Michael Caine, Alan Alda, Jane Fonda, Richard Pryor and me—in *California Suite*. The producer of that movie, Ray Stark, called me and told me he was taking out ads and trying to get everybody nominated, and I told him I wasn't interested. It's very difficult to tell producers that.

PLAYBOY: Why did you?

COSBY: For the same reason I told the Emmy people that I didn't want to be nominated for *The Cosby Show*: I remember the years with Bob Culp on *I Spy*, being up against my buddy and hoping that I'd be the one chosen . . . for *what*? Well, because it's the highest award you can get from the television academy. Okay, I won Emmys three years running, and then I started hoping my television specials would be chosen for an Emmy over somebody else's television specials. But I wasn't *making* television specials in hopes that mine would be chosen over somebody else's. I'm not doing this situation comedy in order to compete with Bob Newhart and Robert Guillaume.

As far as that possible Academy Award nomination, hey, I knew that Ray Stark was talking to me about money, because if you're just nominated—you don't have to win—you'll be more in demand and you'll be offered more money the next picture you act in. Meanwhile, I have to tell you my performance in *California Suite* was not very good. I really didn't understand about a third of what I was doing in that movie.

PLAYBOY: What was the problem?

COSBY: Doc [Neil] Simon's lines don't knock me out; but then again, I'm not an actor, I'm a stand-up comedian. I like a flow from one line to another, and I just couldn't make the connections between Simon's lines. That had nothing to do with Doc's being white and Jewish. It just had to do with me—and Pryor, too, I think—not being a trained actor. If they'd done our segment with black actors like James Earl Jones, Cleavon Little, Clarence Williams III or Al Freeman Jr.—fellas who know their way around Chekhov and Ibsen and who also know their way around the complexities of a character—well, the thing would have come off better. But I still enjoyed working with Richard and I enjoyed the physical parts of our piece—the fight and the tennis match.

PLAYBOY: Despite your successful collaboration with Sidney Poitier in *Uptown Saturday Night*, *Let's Do It Again* and *A Piece of the Action*, movies have never really been your medium. Has that been a source of disappointment?

COSBY: No, because I never cared about being a movie star. To me, that was a gimme—you want to give it to me, fine, I'll take it. That's not to say we don't all have fantasies about becoming movie stars: "Oh, I'm *so* glad you liked my last film. Yes, right now my agent's sifting *through* a pile of offers. Of *course* I know that Marlon wants to work with me, but I won't even consider it unless we find the right director." In reality, the TV series is exactly what I enjoy doing.

PLAYBOY: You also once said that jazz was an important part of your life and that you learned a lot about comedy by watching jazz musicians perform. Still true?

COSBY: Yeah. I started consciously listening to jazz and loving it when I was 11 years old and bought my first pair of drumsticks. I'm a self-taught drummer, and sometimes, friends of mine like Dizzy Gillespie and Jimmy Smith will let me sit in with them. They do that as a favor to me, because it's no great thrill for them to have this incompetent up there with them—if I was *really* their friend, I'd stay in the audience, where I belong. Anyway, in the 1950s, Philadelphia had a lot of small jazz clubs, and when I was 16, I'd go listen to musicians like Art Blakey and the Jazz Messengers, Charlie Parker, Dizzy Gillespie, Max Roach, Charlie Mingus and Bud Powell. I once heard a jazz band play "The Joint Is Jumping" and "Cottontail" and then discovered that those two songs are really versions of "I Got Rhythm." So I began listening more and more to the piano players and bass players going through intricate chord changes, and I'd also watch the next soloist thinking about what he was going to play when it was *his* turn. When I started doing comedy, I began structuring my work the same way jazz musicians do; to me, a joke is a tune that has a beginning, a middle and an end. I'm the soloist, and my chord changes are the punch lines that make people laugh.

PLAYBOY: Can you play a little for us?

COSBY: Sure. Here's a very simple joke: You walk into a room to get something, and when you get there, you forgot why you came in. You stand there trying to remember what you were looking for, and then you leave the room. Now, that's all there is to this particular tune. I start out very simply, but en route to the room or standing in it or coming out of it, I can play any chord change I want—as long as it's funny. I can go into the room, look around and have no idea what I'm looking for, and then one of my kids will come in and say, "Gee, Dad, did you forget what you were looking for *again*? Boy, your mind's really *going*." That's one chord change, or I can talk to myself and say something like, "I'll recognize what I'm looking for when I see it." I may follow that up with another chord change: "Well, how do I *know* I'll recognize what I'm looking for when I see it?" I can play that tune any way I want to, which is how a jazz musician works.

PLAYBOY: You're also now writing a book about how to be a father. Do you consider yourself an expert on raising children?

COSBY: Ask me anything, I've got the answer. You know, when I first became a parent, I had certain ideas about how I was going to control the children, and they all boiled down to this: Children just need love. Well, some years later, you find yourself talking to your child, who is of high intelligence, and saying, "No, you cannot drive the car until you get a learner's permit." And then, 10 minutes later, you see your car being driven down the street by the same child you just told not to drive it. When the child gets back and gets out of the car, you have the following conversation: "Was that *you* driving the car?" "Yes." "Why?" "Well, I just wanted to see if I could do it." "But didn't I tell you *not* to drive it?" "Yes." "Well, if I told you not to drive the car, why were you driving it?" "I don't know." Well, to me, that's brain damage. *All* children have that kind of brain damage. Parents should prepare themselves to face that fact.

PLAYBOY: Is there anything you can do about it?

COSBY: Not much. Which is why you wind up doing a lot of yelling. There have been times when I've felt like a football coach in the locker room at halftime, and here we are, 16 points down against a team we're favored to beat by three touchdowns. And there *I* am, saying to this team, "Listen, if we win this game, we can go to the *Super Bowl!*" And I'm looking at a team that just won't wake up, though I know what they can do if they start to play. So now I'm kicking the benches, because I realize I might as well be talking to the walls, and I probably *am.*

If you're a father, you get to be very familiar with that situation. I don't know how many times I wanted one of the kids to go in a certain direction and the child wanted to go in another direction that I knew was no good for the kid, so I gave maybe my 55th reading on why the child should go in the direction *I* was pointing to. And there I am, putting in love, investing in presents, resorting to outright bribery in the form of cold cash and even invoking racial pride. I mean, I'm telling my daughter that black America is waiting for her, that she cannot disappoint Harriet Tubman—I'm giving it my best shot. And when I'm finally done, my little girl turns to me and says, "Gee, Dad, I don't think I want to do that."

PLAYBOY: Have you ever lost your temper and physically lashed out at your children?

COSBY: I was physical with my son just once, *very* physical, but not because I lost my temper. I just didn't see any other way of getting him to make a change, so along with being physical with him, I begged him to understand that I truly, truly loved him and that he had to understand that what I'd asked him to do was best for him. And I really wouldn't—and didn't—leave until he understood that. I stayed and poured out what was in my heart until he accepted the fact that I did the physical thing because I finally didn't see where talking to him had done any good. And that I meant for him to do *exactly* what I said and that I wanted him to understand he had no choice in this particular matter. And my son made a change.

Now, I don't want anyone to think I'm advocating physical punishment, because that doesn't always work, either. When I was a kid, I don't know how many beatings I got for different things. It was still a matter of my priorities versus those of my parents and what I thought I could get away with.

PLAYBOY: Have you run into situations where, as your children have gotten older, there's simply no dissuading them from a course of action you oppose?

COSBY: Yes, that's happened. We live in an academic environment, and Camille and I feel that formal education is the best way to go for our kids, but one of our children—who's entitled to privacy on this—has told us, "I really don't want to learn the technical aspects of anything; I just want to be out on my own." Obviously, this child has a better idea. So we let the child go. No one's getting kicked out of the house, and we're not pulling away the safety net. We have phone numbers, and the person is to call any time there's any trouble. But we're also saying, "This is your idea, and you're going to have to earn the right to be on your own. You get no money from us toward your support." In other words, the kid's really out there. It's not one of those things where the parents say, "Okay, go do it," and then they get a call and the child says, "Gee, folks, I've got this phone bill to pay and I need a car." We're telling this child, "You have to function on your own if you want to live the lifestyle you've chosen for yourself."

All our children have met a lot of black Americans who have succeeded, who have achieved and who are highly educated. The choice this child has made seems to be, "Listen, there's a lot of fun to be had out there." And it's disheartening. However, when I look at my own life and some of the choices I made when I was young—you just never know.

PLAYBOY: Do you think you may be too demanding, expecting perfection from others?

COSBY: Oh, I know that everything's not perfect. I mean, I see how people love the Huxtable television family, and then I turn around and look at South Africa and hear my government saying, "Well, we've got to take it easy," and I *know* everything's not perfect. To have a man like Jerry Falwell invoking the name of Jesus and talking about spending $1 million to strengthen South Africa's segregationist government—believe me, I know everything's *far* from perfect.

PLAYBOY: How do you feel about U.S. policy toward South Africa?

COSBY: I'm actually embarrassed as an American that our government—the one that's in office now—has done so little to change the situation there. Can't we be enough of a big brother to South Africa to take our younger brother very gently around the shoulders and say, "How do you feel?" Not necessarily, "Little brother, you're wrong," but at least say, "Take a look at us. Democracy isn't as bad as you think." Instead, we go over and dance with that brother and we give a clear message to the world that the United States is pro-apartheid. I was shocked that a representative of the Reagan Administration went on TV to chastise Bishop Tutu for not attending a meeting with President Botha, who had basically said, "I don't care what anybody else says or thinks, apartheid will remain the law of this land—but you can come to my meeting, Bishop Tutu." Once again, we got my uncle Jack working. And what isn't he going to give the black people of South Africa? Look at America's doctrine of democracy, and then read what the South African government says an individual can and cannot say and where black South Africans can and cannot live, and then read about how people who oppose the government—who simply *disagree* with it—are imprisoned. If black South Africans want democracy, uncle Jack will be glad to tell them why he has decided not to give it to them—it's because they had the nerve to ask for it.

PLAYBOY: What would you like President Reagan to do about South Africa?

COSBY: Why hasn't he seen to it that somebody in the government has stood up and said, "The Reagan Administration believes that this apartheid, this killing, is *wrong*, and you've got to clean up your act"? I am waiting for *somebody* in the government of the United States of America, the land of opportunity, to say to its little brother South Africa, "You gotta stop this. *Period.* Forget that you're making us look bad—morally, you *have* to *stop* this!"

PLAYBOY: What do you believe is going to happen in South Africa?

COSBY: I think that in our first *Interview*, I made a statement about the U.S. in which I said that black Americans would never again sit still for segregation or discrimination. And now, in 1985, my statement is that black South Africans have reached that same moment in time. If the white South African government decides to kill and go to war, there will be a war. But that government will not be able to hold on to the country *without* a war. Too many black South Africans are now saying, "If I have to live as a third-class citizen under the rule of apartheid, if this is to be my life, then I don't want to live." There's no turning back for the blacks of South Africa. Now, I'm not saying or thinking that South African blacks are going to slaughter South African whites and run them all out of the country and then say, "This is *our* land." I'm only telling you that those people will no longer tolerate apartheid. All they want is to live like human beings.

PLAYBOY: When you spoke about race relations in the U.S. 16 years ago, you were very pessimistic about the future. What are your feelings about the subject today?

COSBY: The same, and it isn't just blacks and whites—it's about what's happening among all people in the U.S. More and more in this country, we're not able to say the word American for everybody who lives here. Even the movie industry—maybe *especially* the movie industry—commits almost blatant crimes with some of the films it puts out. In *Year of the Dragon*, one white man walks into Chinatown and decimates the place. This again reminds everybody who's nonwhite that he can be mistreated—and we're still talking about Americans. For God's sake, if you grew up when I did and you were black, when you went to the movies and saw *Tarzan*, you were told that you could just drop a white baby out of a plane and by the time he was 16, he'd be running the entire jungle. This year, if you're black, you can go see a cult film popular with kids—and one of the dumbest pictures ever made—*The Gods Must Be Crazy*, which shows that if you just drop a Coke bottle out of an airplane, you can pretty much shake up an entire African culture. [*Laughs sarcastically*] Black people certainly are primitive, aren't they? If you want proof, send in a white filmmaker.

PLAYBOY: Let's close on your career. With everything going so well for you, why have some reporters written that this latest burst of success has made you difficult, arrogant? What's that all about?

COSBY: It's all about when I say no. It's all about how I look at someone when he knows he's said something dumb and I won't help him out of the hole. It's not that I pile the dirt on top of him and smash the shovel down, but I guess I let people know when I think a question or a statement is rude or dumb or whatever. A woman from *TV Guide* recently interviews me and wants to do amateur psychoanalysis. A photographer from the *Los Angeles Times* poses me this way and that way for what seems like an hour, and I finally tell her I think I've done what she wants. They're going to tell people I was arrogant.

PLAYBOY: How do you feel when you're accused of not being outspoken enough in your show on matters of race and politics?

COSBY: It depends on the person making the attack. If it's just some neoliberal who feels I should be a martyr—you know, the kind who says I should take my show, tell everything like it really is and get canceled in three weeks—that person has no idea what life is all about. And neoliberals have a great deal of racism in their hearts. Why else would they tell you to go out and get your brains blown out?

PLAYBOY: Who are these neoliberals—members of the press?

COSBY: That's what I'm talking about, the press.

PLAYBOY: Still, you've gotten a lot of very good press lately, most of it centered on the way you've become almost a national father figure—which means that the media will continue to ask you a lot of daddy questions. Do you have any parting advice on that topic?

COSBY: I'm doing a book on being a father. It'll be out around Father's Day.

PLAYBOY: You've already discussed the subject with us, and the book wouldn't preclude some remarks from you on the subject, would it?

COSBY: It might. The publishers have paid me an awful lot of money. And since this is only one brain I've got. . . .

PLAYBOY: Come on, Bill. This is the *Playboy Interview*—some of our readers are fathers, and even more are moving into that time of life.

COSBY: Yeah, I think that the subjects we've talked about are interesting—especially for *Playboy*—because what you have here is a guy saying that he's given all of himself to his wife and children. I think that may turn some lights on.

PLAYBOY: So we'll press you: What's your parting advice to people who'll soon be parents?

COSBY: Well, I speak to my son and daughters about heroes, people whom we look up to for various reasons. What is it we worship about a person? What is it that makes that person a hero to you? And if it is that the person is perfect, then you really haven't done an honest job on yourself, because people are not perfect. Edwin Moses is a great track star who this year was arrested for possession of marijuana and soliciting a prostitute. The TV networks picked up on it, and then came all these discussions about "What are our heroes coming to?" Now, I felt sorry for Edwin, but then I also felt, Well, if it's true, am I going to be *angry* with him and not think that he is a great athlete anymore? I told my children what Edwin was charged with, and I said, "I still want you to look at Edwin Moses as a hero." They said, "Well, Dad, how can we after he's done this?" I said, "Even if he's found guilty, are we going to trash what this man has done, which is to win 109 races in a row?" We became fans because he's a man who worked eight to 10 hours a day, punishing himself to get in shape to achieve his dream. We all said, "What a great athlete; what a great man dedicated to achieving his potential." *That's* what we can say about Edwin Moses. We've got to examine who and what a hero is and how far we, the fans, go in putting these people up on pedestals. They're not perfect, but then again, neither are we.

March 1974

GROUCHO MARX

A candid conversation with Minna Marx's third—and funniest—son

The hottest attraction to play New York's Carnegie Hall during 1972 was a frail 82-year-old man who used to be master of ceremonies on a television quiz show, and who before that was a movie star, and before that a vaudeville comedian and before that a baby. Although his Carnegie Hall concert consisted merely of reminiscences, a few songs and an occasional film clip, the capacity audience—the majority of them teenagers, many wearing painted mustaches and eyebrows, false noses and wire-rimmed glasses—was ecstatic. Three thousand people (among them his brother Zeppo) were turned away from this one-night stand by Julius Henry Marx. Subsequent sales of the recorded version of the concert, *An Evening with Groucho,* only confirm that the veteran comedian is one of America's most durable attractions.

Julius and his brothers Leonard, Arthur, Milton and Herbert—later to become famous as Chico, Harpo, Gummo and Zeppo—were sons of an Alsatian tailor who prided himself on his ability to size up a customer without a tape measure. According to Groucho, these appraisals were "about as accurate as Chamberlain's predictions about Hitler." Fortunately for his sons, Sam Marx was better at choosing a wife than at choosing a profession. A strong, astute woman, Minna Schoenberg Marx was the archetypal stage mother, and her untiring efforts launched her sons on what turned out to be legendary careers.

Showbiz ran in Minna's family. Her parents, who shared the small Marx flat in New York's German Yorkville district, had been professional entertainers in Germany before immigrating to the United

States. Minna's father was a magician-ventriloquist; her mother yodeled and accompanied the act on a harp. (It was this very harp that was found in a closet years later by Harpo, who took from it a name and a way of life.) The best-known member of the family, though, was Groucho's uncle Al Shean—of Gallagher and Shean—who was the idol of the young Marx Brothers.

As children, Groucho and his brothers were far from rich, but they didn't know it. Heroic quantities of beans, potatoes and chowder were cooked in a huge pot that was also used for washing clothes (the food and their shirts were heavy on the starch), and Sam could convert leftovers into what Groucho remembers as "something fit for the gods, assuming there are any left." Good thing, too, since Minna hated cooking and preferred making the rounds of theatrical agents, hunting jobs for her sons. A booking often was clinched by an invitation to the Marx home for one of Sam's concoctions.

Groucho actually began his career as a female impersonator (the mustache obviously came later), playing a singer in a small-time vaudeville troupe. With the onset of puberty and the subsequent change in his voice, he was left stranded by the troupe in Cripple Creek, Colorado, and you can't get more stranded than that. Though he'd never seen a horse, he wangled a job as a wagon driver until Minna could send him his train fare home. His next fling in show business ended just as abruptly in Waco, Texas, when the English-woman who had hired him to sing with her ran off with the married lion tamer who shared the bill. At 15, Groucho was already a stage veteran "between engagements." He found a job—cleaning actors' wigs, which he describes as a "hair-raising experience."

Undaunted, Minna organized an act called The Three Nightin-gales, featuring Groucho and Harpo (who couldn't sing at all) and a girl who couldn't sing on key but who did fit the bargain costume Minna had bought. The act became The Four Nightingales when Chico (pronounced Chick-o), who had been working as a lifeguard, had to be saved from drowning by another lifeguard. Finally—after the family moved to Chicago, when Groucho was in his late teens—Gummo was enlisted in the act, the girl was dropped and they became the Four Marx Brothers, adopting the stage names by which they have since been known, even to one another. They became one of the lead-ing comedy teams in vaudeville, touring on the prestigious Orpheum Circuit until World War I intervened. Harpo and Gummo joined the army, while Groucho and Chico made the rounds of military camps as entertainers. After the war, Gummo decided he'd had enough of show business and Zeppo, the youngest Marx, replaced him in the act. The Four Marx Brothers knocked around vaudeville for several more years until they were offered parts in an ailing musical comedy, *The Thrill Girl*. Rejuvenated as *I'll Say She Is*, it was so successful on tour that in 1924 it landed on Broadway. While being fitted for her opening-night dress, the indefatigable Minna broke her leg in a fall from a chair; characteristically, that didn't stop her. She was borne down the aisle to her front-row seat in triumph, on a stretcher. Her boys had arrived.

Though Groucho now describes *I'll Say She Is* as "a real stinker," it played on Broadway two years. Even bigger successes were *The Cocoanuts* and *Animal Crackers*, written by George S. Kaufman and Morris Ryskind. Paramount picked up the film rights to both and in 1929 signed the quartet to a five-picture contract. So the Marx Brothers went to Hollywood, where they made the films that have become classics all over the world. In 1933, Zeppo left the group and the three remaining brothers moved to MGM, which never recovered. Eight more zany Marx Brothers comedies were made over the next 14 years—during which Groucho twice announced his retirement from films. He came back, of course, but after 1949, all his roles were solo ones—minus the other Marxes.

From 1934 on, Groucho had been on radio, making guest appearances and doing his own programs. One of these was *Flywheel, Shyster and Flywheel*, in which he and Chico played comic lawyers. Then, in 1947, Groucho originated the legendary *You Bet Your Life* on radio; later he moved the quiz show to television, where it became one of the most successful series of all time. Groucho loved *You Bet Your Life*, which won several Emmy awards during its 14 years on the air; he still thinks it contains some of his best work. When the show finally went off in 1960, Groucho sensibly decided to retire; he could afford to and, after all, he was a ripe 69. But after several years of relative idleness, he got restless and—with a Marx Brothers revival burgeoning across the land—began to make the public appearances (mostly on TV talk shows) that led to his triumphant 1972 Carnegie Hall concert. Since then, he's suffered several strokes, at least one diagnosed heart attack and a bout with pneumonia. Somehow, he's always bounced back—most recently to do battle with publishers who have printed what Groucho says are fabrications purporting to be interviews. Lawsuits now pending ask for damages well into the millions of dollars.

To get a genuine interview with the indefatigable man behind the mustache, *Playboy* sent writer Charlotte Chandler to interview him. She reports:

"Groucho is still readily recognizable as his alter ego, Dr. Hugo Z. Hackenbush of *A Day at the Races* infamy. His distinctive voice is little changed; his serious expression is punctuated occasionally by dramatic movements of the famous eyebrows. Still verbally nimble, always on the attack against pretentiousness or pretensions, never at a loss for a word—or several—he remains the maestro of the illogical, of the deflated platitude and of *reductio ad absurdum*.

"Groucho is a gentleman, and a gentle man, yet he is the undisputed king of the sarcastic insult. He is a man of another time, but a man whose audience is now larger, younger and more enthusiastic than ever. The reputed chaser, always on the prowl for the not-so-elusive female, is in reality a staunch believer in the sanctity of marriage. Groucho has been married a total of 47 years—albeit to three women; he was divorced from all three.

"The interview took place over many weeks in varied locations, most often in Groucho's comfortable contemporary home in Beverly Hills—the house he built for his third wife, Eden. There he's surrounded by treasured possessions, including a 1915 playbill from the Orpheum Theater in Oakland; two framed *Time* covers, one featuring the Marx Brothers and the other Groucho alone; a collage depicting Groucho as *Blue Boy, Whistler's Mother* and others; an ancient hatrack festooned with berets, bowlers, straws and caps; the lectern he used in *You Bet Your Life*; the guitar that he still plays; and pictures of his parents, himself and his brothers as children.

"Some evenings we'd dine at Groucho's; the fare might be an elaborate roast or an indoor picnic from Nate and Al's Delicatessen. Other times we'd move on to Chasen's or the Beverly Hills Hotel, where in Groucho's honor the management for the first time in its history served clam chowder on a Saturday. Our meetings continued in New York, where Zabar's provided the herring in sour cream, smoked salmon, cream cheese, celery tonic and pumpernickel. So important is pumpernickel to Groucho that he measures the financial state of the nation by its current price. We talked over soufflé of fruits de mer and côte de boeuf at Lutèce. While watching the telecast of his taped appearance on *The Bill Cosby Show*, Groucho fortified himself with chocolate cake from Le Côte Basque. On occasion, we were joined by Erin Fleming, Groucho's attractive personal manager, who is also an actress specializing in Shakespeare and Shaw, but who could easily have played the Thelma Todd roles in the early Marx Brothers pictures. In real life, she plays Margaret Dumont to Groucho's Groucho. We also got together with Groucho's friend and intellectual ideal, CBS Vice-President Goddard Lieberson, and with Marx Brothers superfan and Groucho's superfriend, Woody Allen.

"For formal occasions, Groucho always wore a blue blazer over a turtleneck sweater in red, blue or white—and underneath that, a gray Tell 'Em Groucho Sent You T-shirt. In his lapel buttonhole was the Commander of Arts and Letters medal recently bestowed upon him by the French government at the Cannes Film Festival. Ever-present were the long cigars that have become his trademark; these he lit with one of his most prized souvenirs, a lighter engraved SRO to commemorate that sold-out concert at Carnegie Hall.

"Talking to Groucho was a delight, even though from the beginning he persisted in taking over the interview—as you will see."

MARX: I don't know what kind of an interview you're looking for. You want a silly interview? I don't know any jokes.

PLAYBOY: We could start by asking what question most interviewers ask you.

MARX: "Could Harpo talk?"

PLAYBOY: Maybe we'll ask that later. Why don't we begin instead by asking you the very first thing you remember?

MARX: You're asking me to remember almost a hundred years ago.

PLAYBOY: Well, then, what are your earliest childhood memories?

MARX: I remember riding on the back of a moving van. Gummo and I were back there; we must have been pretty young, because we didn't have our piano yet. And I remember playing stickball, which was a great challenge, because we played without a ball. We couldn't afford one. Anyway, we were surrounded by three breweries where we lived in New York City—Ruppert's, Ringer's and another one; when I went to school as a kid, I could always smell the malt. We used to go over to Park Avenue, where old man Ruppert lived in a big house with a fruit orchard, and we'd steal his apples and pears. There was a spiked fence about eight feet high, and dogs. We might have been dog meat, but we were very young, and we sure liked those apples and pears. I also remember the iceman delivering ice; you'd holler out the window to tell him how much you wanted. We had no icebox; we were very poor. While the iceman was delivering the ice, we'd get in his wagon and break off some ice. Ever since then, I've been great at breaking the ice.

PLAYBOY: How poor were you?

MARX: So poor that when somebody knocked on the door, we all hid. We were paying $27 a month rent and there were 10 of us. The five brothers, my father and mother, my grandmother and grandfather and an adopted sister. There were 10 of us and one toilet.

PLAYBOY: Did you want to be an actor when you were a kid?

MARX: No, I wanted to be a writer. But I became an actor because we were very poor and there were four brothers, so—

PLAYBOY: You said there were five of you.

MARX: That's true, but what's the difference? Anyway, I decided to be in show business.

PLAYBOY: Why?

MARX: Because I had an uncle in show business who was making $200 a week, and I wasn't making anything.

PLAYBOY: Did you want to be rich?

MARX: I always wanted to be rich. I still want to be rich. Why, years ago, I came to Los Angeles without a nickel in my pocket. Now I *have* a nickel in my pocket. Unfortunately, the nickel today isn't worth what it used to be. Do you know what this country needs? A seven-cent nickel. We've been using the five-cent nickel since 1492. So why not give the seven-cent nickel a chance? If that works out, next year we could have an eight-cent nickel. And so on.

PLAYBOY: You should have been an economist.

MARX: Then I wouldn't have been rich.

PLAYBOY: When you were still poor, what did you think being rich meant?

MARX: I used to think being rich meant having a lot of money. Now I think it means having a *lot* of money.

PLAYBOY: Do you have a lot or a *lot*?

MARX: Somewhere in between.

PLAYBOY: Does your money come just from income or have you also made some good investments?

MARX: I've always watched the stock market. Especially when it's going up. Do you know property values have increased 1000 percent since 1929?

PLAYBOY: No, we didn't. Were you hurt by the crash?

MARX: Yeah, I was wiped out. I had $200,000, which I'd saved over a period of many years playing small-time vaudeville, and I lost it in two days when the market crashed. My old friend Max Gordon phoned me at my home in Great Neck. His real name is Saltpeter, but he calls himself Max Gordon. And he called me up one morning and he said, "Marx, the jig is up." And hung up. I don't take his calls anymore.

PLAYBOY: You mentioned an uncle in show business.

MARX: Al Shean. He was an actor in vaudeville. He had originally been a pants presser on the East Side. I don't think he was a very good pants presser, because as soon as he got his job as a presser, he formed a singing quartet and the fellow who ran the factory threw all four of 'em out. He was always forming quartets and getting fired.

PLAYBOY: Tell us about your parents.

MARX: Well, my mother came from Germany, my father came from France. When he met my mother, neither one could understand a word the other was saying, so they got married. They spoke German, because my mother was the stronger of the two. My father wasn't very well educated. Neither was my mother, but she was brighter. She lived long enough to see us successful on Broadway.

PLAYBOY: Was your mother as important as we've heard in influencing you to go on the stage?

MARX: Of course. And as soon as she could, she got the others to go along. That's how we became the Marx Brothers. She used to book us herself. She thought she ought to look young, so she wore a corset and a blonde wig when she went to see agents. She was probably around 50 then, and everybody knew it was a wig. When she was at somebody's house playing cards, she'd get tired of wearing the corset, take it off and wrap it up in a newspaper with the strings hanging out.

PLAYBOY: She was from a theatrical family, wasn't she?

MARX: My grandmother played the harp and yodeled. My grandfather was a ventriloquist and a magician.

PLAYBOY: How about your father?

MARX: He was a tailor from Strasbourg, the worst ever. All his customers were easily recognized: One trouser leg was shorter than the other.

PLAYBOY: Did your father ever fool around on your mother?

MARX: He must have. There were five boys.

PLAYBOY: We mean with other women.

MARX: Not until my mother died. Then he got himself another girl.

PLAYBOY: Right away?

MARX: Well, not at the funeral.

PLAYBOY: Who were your idols when you were young?

MARX: I used to have a girl in Montreal.

PLAYBOY: Was she an idol?

MARX: She was idle a good deal, but she made a pretty good living, anyway. Does that answer your question?

PLAYBOY: No, so let's put it another way: Who did you like when you went to the theater?

MARX: President Roosevelt.

PLAYBOY: He wasn't on the stage.

MARX: Who said anything about the stage?

PLAYBOY: Did you have any girlfriends while you were growing up in New York?

MARX: Not until later, when we started traveling in small-time vaudeville. And even then, we really weren't in towns long enough to meet anybody.

PLAYBOY: So how did you meet girls?

MARX: We'd go to hook shops. We were a big hit in the hook shops.

PLAYBOY: How so?

MARX: We were entertainment!

PLAYBOY: You mean you'd go to a whorehouse and perform?

MARX: You can say that again. We also did our act. Harpo and Chico played the piano and I sang. The girls used to come to watch us at the theater—the madam and the girls—and if they liked us, they'd send a note backstage: "If you're not doing anything tonight after the show, why don't you come over and see us?" Sometimes we stayed all night. We were always after girls. We'd get into a town, and there was a hotel, and they had a piano on the mezzanine floor. Chico would start playing and there would be 20 dames there. Chico would pick out girls for us, too.

PLAYBOY: Did you meet any "nice" girls that way?

MARX: Gummo did once, in New Orleans; her father came up to him after the show and said, "You took my daughter out tonight. If you take her out again, you'll go back to New York in a box." Actors weren't very popular in those days. Except in hook shops.

PLAYBOY: What was your first physical relationship with a woman?

MARX: Going to bed.

PLAYBOY: We're going to have to be more careful how we phrase things: How did you lose your virginity?

MARX: In a hook shop in Montreal. I was 16 years old and I didn't know anything about girls. Before I left town, I had gonorrhea.

PLAYBOY: How did Chico lose *his* virginity?

MARX: To the first girl he met.

PLAYBOY: And Harpo?

MARX: Oh, Harpo didn't fool around much. He had a few dames. But Harpo only had three girls in his life that he was really stuck on, and they were all named Fleming.

PLAYBOY: You're now dating a girl named Fleming. How do you explain this coincidence?

MARX: It's no coincidence.

PLAYBOY: What kind of man was Harpo?

MARX: He was a short man. Even shorter when he was sitting down, which he always was, playing the goddamn harp. I hated the harp. But he was very serious about it. He was also serious about playing cards. And also that other game that's popular now. . . .

PLAYBOY: Backgammon?

MARX: Yes. He was very good at those games, although he wasn't educated. He used to make a lot of money. You know, he'd play with guys like George Kaufman and Alexander Woollcott and Herbert Swope, who ran the *New York World*, and people like that, and he usually won. He was a very smart cardplayer and good at all kinds of games.

PLAYBOY: He was also a great practical joker, wasn't he?

MARX: I don't know whether he was *great*. But I remember a good one he pulled in front of Tiffany's in New York. He went to Woolworth's and bought $5 or $6's worth of fake jewelry, then walked over to Tiffany's. He said he'd like to look at the jewelry, and he took it out into the street to look at it in the sunlight, and he did a phony stumble, and all the fake jewelry from his pocket flew all over the sidewalk. The cops came running.

PLAYBOY: Didn't you get involved with the law yourself when you "held up" the Morgan Guarantee Trust Company?

MARX: Oh, yeah. I was wearing a cap and I walked up to the . . . what do you call her?

PLAYBOY: Teller?

MARX: No, I didn't. She was with her husband. Anyhow, I said to the broad, "This is a stickup!" A lot of bells started ringing and inside of three minutes there were 20 uniformed policemen surrounding me. I pulled my cap off and said, "I'm Groucho Marx. Don't you know me?" Luckily, they did. Otherwise, I would've got shot.

PLAYBOY: There's a rumor that you and Harpo once went to a party naked.

MARX: It was when we were playing in *I'll Say She Is* and we were invited to a bachelor party for a friend of ours who was getting married. So Harpo and I got into the elevator and took off all our clothes and put them in suitcases. We were stark naked. But we got off at the wrong floor, where the bride was having a party for *her* friends. So we ran around naked until a waiter finally came with a couple of dishtowels—or, in my case, a bath towel.

PLAYBOY: Was Harpo a practical joker in Hollywood, too?

MARX: Yeah. He used to call up people and tell them the water tank was on the bum and they were gonna cut off all the water. He did it to me once.

PLAYBOY: Didn't you recognize his voice?

MARX: No. I filled all the buckets and pans with water. Then I filled all the bathtubs. He told me to leave everything filled, because it was going to be two or three days before the repairs would be made.

PLAYBOY: How could he fool you, his own brother?

MARX: I didn't usually recognize his voice, unless he asked me for money.

PLAYBOY: It used to be said that no girl was safe alone with your alter egos—Captain Jeffrey T. Spaulding, Rufus T. Firefly, Otis B. Driftwood or Hugo Z. Hackenbush. Is that still true?

MARX: You're too good for that crummy crowd, baby. If I were 15 years younger, no good-looking dame would get out of here alive.

PLAYBOY: Would a girl be in any danger today?

MARX: When a guy is 83, he should forget the whole thing. I know if I do it, it's going to be lousy, so why cheapen myself?

PLAYBOY: Doesn't this depress you?

MARX: No, it doesn't depress me. I don't miss sex. I know I can't do it properly anymore; if I could, I'd still be doing it. I've talked to a lot of guys who are 78, 79, and they *all* say it's hopeless. When you can't get it up anymore, you should quit. When a guy is 80 years old or thereabouts, he should read a book.

PLAYBOY: How do you account for your reputation as a lecher back when you were in your prime—at 65 or 70?

MARX: I was seething with charm. When my brothers and I were young, we were all looking for dames we could go to bed with. Nothing wrong with that. That's what they're for.

PLAYBOY: Don't you think they're good for anything else?

MARX: Yes. A lot of them can cook and a lot of them can take care of a house.

PLAYBOY: You don't seem to be a devout believer in women's liberation.

MARX: Well, I feel this way about it: I think if there's a war and a husband is enlisted, his wife should take a service job, too, not necessarily in the front lines shooting at the enemy, but there are so many things that a woman can do in an army. Since the man is risking his life, why shouldn't the woman be doing something? But I think they should have the same salary advantages as men.

PLAYBOY: Have you met any liberated women lately?

MARX: Erin Fleming. Erin is my idol. I told her if she ever quit me, I'd quit show business.

PLAYBOY: In what way is she liberated?

MARX: She does as she pleases. I don't follow her around. I wouldn't give a damn if she met a guy and wanted to go to bed with him. I'd say, "Go."

PLAYBOY: Would you want her to tell you about it?

MARX: In my particular case, I wouldn't care if she did. Because, like I say, I'm not interested in sex anymore.

PLAYBOY: When you still were, did you consider yourself a user of women?

MARX: God, no. I think a woman can be a wonderful companion. I *like* women! After all, my mother was one. I didn't find that out until a couple years ago.

PLAYBOY: You said your father was faithful to your mother. Do you believe in monogamy yourself?

MARX: I don't think man is basically a monogamous creature. It's natural for a married man to be interested in other women.

PLAYBOY: Isn't it just as natural for a married woman to be interested in other men?

MARX: Having affairs? It's not gonna be much of a marriage.

PLAYBOY: But it's all right for a man?

MARX: The man is the chaser of the two. The woman is subconsciously a chaser, but the man is—a man is a man. And if there's an attractive girl, he'll make a play for her. I think that's wonderful.

PLAYBOY: But not for a married woman?

MARX: I don't think it comes out even that way. I think the average woman, if she's married to a man she likes, won't necessarily cheat.

PLAYBOY: But if she did?

MARX: She should get a divorce and pay alimony.

PLAYBOY: Why couldn't they both keep the relationship going and have extra-marital affairs as well?

MARX: Well, then they shouldn't get married.

PLAYBOY: Why not, if they love each other?

MARX: How can he love her if they're both after other people? It would be better for two people like that to live together and not get married.

PLAYBOY: Feeling as you do, why did *you* get married?

MARX: With one of my wives, I asked myself that question for 16 years. But you know something? I didn't cheat on her once.

PLAYBOY: Why not?

MARX: I couldn't stop with just one.

PLAYBOY: Did you ever date rich women?

MARX: I could've married one and owned the biggest department store in Portland.

PLAYBOY: Why didn't you?

MARX: I didn't like her behavior in bed.

PLAYBOY: Was she too cold? Or inhibited?

MARX: On the contrary. She always wanted to go to bed. I think she was a nymph.

PLAYBOY: You're complaining?

MARX: I don't want a woman who knows more tricks than I do.

PLAYBOY: According to friends, you've never been romantically involved with a Jewish girl. Are you anti-Semitic?

MARX: No, it just always seemed to me that making love to a Jewish girl would be like making love to your sister.

PLAYBOY: Have you ever been a *victim* of anti-Semitism?

MARX: Oh, sure. Years ago, I decided to join a beach club on Long Island and we drove out to a place called the Sands Point Bath and Sun Club. I filled out the application and the head cheese of the place came over and told me we couldn't join because I was Jewish. So I said, "My son's only *half* Jewish. Would it be all right if he went in the water up to his knees?"

PLAYBOY: Getting back to women—

MARX: I've been trying to for years.

PLAYBOY: Have you ever had an interracial affair?

MARX: The whole first part of my life was spent sleeping with colored girls. They were chambermaids in the hotels we used to stay in. In those days, all hotels had black chambermaids. You'd give her a couple of bucks and take her in your room and lay her. That was very common.

PLAYBOY: How were they?

MARX: No different than a white girl. No, that's not true; some of 'em were even better. We couldn't get a white girl when we were in small-time vaudeville. They were afraid of actors. A lot of girls had been raped by actors. So we took what we could get, which was black chambermaids. But I remember doing a big act once with W. C. Fields and we had 20 girls in the show. They were all white and they were all friendly. I knew them by number rather than by name.

PLAYBOY: Who wrote your material when you started out?

MARX: I did. Except for Harpo, who didn't say anything.

PLAYBOY: Did you write for Zeppo, too?

MARX: I didn't have to. He was the funniest one of us. But he wasn't in the act that much. He was in more than Gummo, though, who went in the army during the first World War.

PLAYBOY: Why didn't he rejoin the act after the war?

MARX: He didn't want to be an actor. He went into the garment industry. I remember Gummo had a son named Bobby, and Bobby came home from school one day and his father said to him, "How was it in school today?" And Bobby said, "Well, the teacher asked all of us who our fathers were, and I told her, 'Groucho Marx.'" And Gummo said, "Why did you say that?" And Bobby said, "Who knows *you?*"

PLAYBOY: You said you didn't have to write lines for Harpo, since he didn't say anything. Did Harpo *ever* talk in a Marx Brothers act?

MARX: He talked a lot in a school act we used to do in vaudeville; he played a boy called Patsy Brannigan. In those days, if you did a school act, you usually had a Patsy Brannigan in the act. Patsy Brannigan was a kid with red hair and a funny nose. That's where Harpo got the idea for his wig. A fella had taught him a speech with a lot of big words in it and sometimes Harpo would dumbfound the audience by making this speech with all those big words. He didn't understand most of them, but he loved the speech.

PLAYBOY: What did Chico do in that act?

MARX: He helped Harpo. Harpo used to wear a funny hat. And I would say to Harpo, "Take dat ding off." I was a German comedian. Harpo would take the "ding" off and give it to Chico, and Chico would pass it to a guy who played a fag. Well, you asked; it was a pretty lousy act.

PLAYBOY: Did you get any laughs in those days?

MARX: Now and then. Especially when Zeppo came onstage and said, "Dad, the garbage man is here," and I said, "Tell him we don't want any." Another time Chico shook hands with me and said, "I would like to say good-bye to your wife," and I said, "Who wouldn't?"

PLAYBOY: How did you create the Groucho character?

MARX: When we were playing small-time vaudeville, I would try a line and if it got a laugh, I'd leave it in. If it didn't get a laugh, I'd take it out and write another line. Pretty soon I had a character.

PLAYBOY: How did the mustache originate?

MARX: The mustache came about while we were doing a show called *Home Again* at Keith's Flushing. My wife was having a baby at the time and I used to spend a lot of time in the hospital with her. One night I stayed too long and by the time I got to the theater, it was too late to paste on my mustache, so I just smeared on some grease paint. The audience didn't seem to mind, so I stuck with it. Or got stuck with it. Or got sticky with it.

PLAYBOY: How did you develop the Groucho walk?

MARX: I was just kidding around one day and I started to walk funny. The audience liked it, so I kept it in.

PLAYBOY: Did you always feel you were going to make the big time?

MARX: No. Chico did, and he did the least work in the act. He said, "We won't always be playing these dumps." And Chico got a guy who owned a coal mine and a pretzel factory to put up the money for us to become big time. Chico was a smooth character. He would be talking long distance on the phone to one dame and having his hat blown by another at the same time.

PLAYBOY: What was your first big success?

MARX: A play called *I'll Say She Is.* The money for it was put up by the pretzel-factory owner, who later got stuck on one of the girls in the chorus. It so happened that Harpo was laying this same girl at the time, but fortunately, he didn't find out. Anyway, the play was a smash in Philadelphia. It was a real stinker, but when we took it to New York, Alexander Woollcott gave it a good review.

PLAYBOY: What did your childhood friends think of your success on Broadway?

MARX: I had a friend in New York who lived on 93rd Street, where we lived. We always figured he was gonna be a Supreme Court Justice or something. Well, he became a lawyer, and he came to see *Animal Crackers* one day. He came to my dressing room afterward and he didn't mention anything about the show. So I said, "How'd you like it?" He said, "Don't you think you're kinda old to be jumping over furniture and making a fool of yourself in front of an audience?"

PLAYBOY: What was your reply?

MARX: I pointed out that I was making $1000 a week to make a fool of myself and that he was doing it for $150, and I asked him to empty the garbage on his way out.

PLAYBOY: You were soon making a lot more than $1000 a week in Hollywood. Did all that money—and your newfound fame in movies—attract a lot of women?

MARX: Well, it helped my brother Chico—who didn't need any help along those lines. But if *I* wanted to go to bed with a girl, I had to *marry* her.

PLAYBOY: Which stars would you have liked to make it with but didn't?

MARX: I'd have liked to have gone to bed with Jean Harlow. She was a beautiful broad. The fellow who married her was impotent and he killed himself. I would have done the same thing.

PLAYBOY: How about Carole Lombard?

MARX: She was a great dame. I loved Lombard. She was married to Gable at one time, you know. I met her on the street one day—I did a whole series of shows with her—and I said, "How are you and Gable getting along?" and she said, "He's the lousiest lay I ever had." That's the way she talked—the way a lot of men do. Very sexy dame. She was also a hell of an actress. She did a picture with Jack Benny, which Lubitsch directed. Benny was wonderful in it. It was called *To Be or Not to Be*. Lubitsch was the best director, I guess, in this country. There was nobody to equal him. He wanted to do a movie with us.

PLAYBOY: Why didn't you do it?

MARX: Well, we were tied up with Paramount making those five turkeys. I remember Lubitsch had an opening line that he tried out on me one day. It went like this: "You haf a girl in your betroom and she iss married. And her husband come home unexpectedly, just as a streetcar iss going through the betroom." And I said, "What's the joke?" My next line, he said, was, "Believe it or not, I was waiting for a streetcar." And then I was supposed to step out of the closet and onto the streetcar. He was a genius.

PLAYBOY: Speaking of geniuses, aren't you a friend of Orson Welles's?

MARX: Well, I've done a lot of shows with him. Comedy shows. He's a great straight man. He's also a great round man.

PLAYBOY: Weren't you also a friend of Humphrey Bogart's?

MARX: I was at his house all the time. He was a wonderful host. He'd have two or three shots of booze and get on his yacht to get away from Lauren Bacall. Not that he didn't like her. He just wanted to be around men. When I was around, could you blame him?

PLAYBOY: The Marx Brothers have also had a number of literary friends. Didn't you correspond with T. S. Eliot?

MARX: He wrote to me first. He said he was an admirer of mine and he would like a picture of me. So I sent him a picture. And he sent it back. He said, "I want a picture of you smoking a cigar." So I sent him one. Later he told me there were only three people he cared about: William Butler Yeats, Paul Valéry and Groucho Marx. He had those three pictures in his private office. When I went to visit him. I thought he wanted to talk about all those fancy books he had written, like *Murder in the Cathedral*. But he wanted to talk about the Marx Brothers. So naturally we became close friends and had a lot of correspondence. I spoke at his funeral.

PLAYBOY: What other writers have you known?

MARX: Ring Lardner used to come to my house in Great Neck and get drunk. If I had been him, I would have gotten drunk, too. He had four boys at home and couldn't get any writing done, so he used to go to the Pennsylvania Hotel in New York and take a room and pull the shades down, because there might have been somebody in another room across the alley from where his room was—and that's the only way he could write. He would stay there for a week or two and then he'd go back to Great Neck, where his four sons were.

PLAYBOY: How about F. Scott Fitzgerald?

MARX: *He* wasn't one of Lardner's sons.

PLAYBOY: Thanks for the information. We were wondering how well you knew him.

MARX: I knew him very well, because he was stuck on a dame named Sheilah Graham, who used to play a little tennis at my house.

PLAYBOY: You're not going to make any jokes about playing a love game with her, are you?

MARX: No, her serve was too big for me.

PLAYBOY: Who was the wittiest man you ever knew?

MARX: George S. Kaufman. I remember once he went to Philadelphia to see the tryout of a play one of the Bloomingdales was backing. They were the department-store people. After he saw the play, he said, "Close the play and keep the store open nights."

PLAYBOY: Why are theater and movies more serious today—or at least less funny—than they used to be?

MARX: There are no comedians left. Chaplin doesn't work anymore—he's too old and can't. Mae West isn't too old, but won't. Buster Keaton is dead. W. C. Fields is dead. Laurel and Hardy are dead. And Jerry Lewis hasn't made me laugh since he left Dean Martin. One of the reasons there are no comedians is that there's no more vaudeville. There is no place to train a comedian today. There's no place to be funny anymore. You've got just a few TV shows and nightclubs. There's no place for a comic to polish his act. That's what vaudeville provided.

PLAYBOY: You and Chaplin got together while he was over here for the 1972 Academy Awards. What did you talk about?

MARX: He just kept saying, "Keep warm. Keep warm." I think he's one year older than I am. He was worried that I wasn't keeping warm enough. I was saying, "Hi ya, Charlie, how are ya?" And all he said was, "Keep warm."

PLAYBOY: How did you and Chaplin first meet?

MARX: Well, my brothers and I were playing in Canada, and so was Chaplin. He was doing an act called *A Night at the Club*. It was a very funny act. I remember he had a big dowager in the act who used to sing, and while she was singing Chaplin was chewing on an apple and spitting the seeds in her face. This is the kind of comedy they had 60 years ago. Anyway, when we were in Winnipeg one day, my brothers went off in search of a poolroom to kill three hours before leaving for the coast. Since I didn't play pool, and I don't play cards, and I don't gamble, and I only smoke occasionally—just enough to cough—I took a walk and I passed this dump theater, the Sullivan-Considine. I heard the most tremendous roar of laughter, and I paid my 10 cents and went in and there was a little guy on the stage, and he was walking around kinda funny. It was Chaplin. It was the greatest act I'd ever seen. All pantomime. He had a shirt that he wore for the whole six weeks, 'cause he was only getting $25 a week and he didn't want to spend any money getting a clean shirt.

I went back to the hotel and told my brothers what a real comedian was, and I walked around funny like Chaplin, you know. Then the following week, I went backstage to visit him and tell him how wonderful he was, and that's how we got acquainted. Each week we would be in the same towns in Canada; I can't remember all the towns; this was a hell of a long time ago. We used to go to the whorehouses together, because there was no place for an actor to go in those towns, except if you were lucky, maybe you'd pick up a girl, but as a rule, you'd have to go to a hook shop. And then Chaplin and I got *very* well acquainted. Not together! I mean, I wasn't with him! I was *with* him, but not with a girl, I mean—

PLAYBOY: We understand. Had he made a movie yet?

MARX: No. He hadn't made anything. He was just doing this act.

PLAYBOY: Did he ever mention wanting to make movies?

MARX: No. It never occurred to him. He was a big hit in his act. Then, when we got to Seattle, there was Mack Sennett, who saw Chaplin in *A Night at the Club* and offered to sign him up. I talked to Chaplin afterward and I said, "I understand you were offered a job with Sennett and he offered you $200 a week." And he says, "I turned it down." I says, "You must be crazy! You turned down $200 a week for this lousy vaudeville act you're doing?" He says, "Nobody could be that good, so I turned him down." Chaplin went back to England after that. He was afraid.

PLAYBOY: Would *you* have accepted an offer from Sennett?

MARX: No. I was working with my brothers and they were busy shooting pool.

PLAYBOY: Seriously, do you think you would have been funny in silent films?

MARX: No. In the first place, Harpo didn't talk at all in the act. And Chico didn't talk if he could find a dame. So the only one that really talked was me. Anyway, I really wanted to be on Broadway at that time. Broadway was bigger than pictures in those days. Audiences paid $10 a ticket for *Cocoanuts* and *Animal Crackers* for the entire run. Anyway, getting back to Chaplin, six years passed, and we were now playing the Orpheum Circuit, and we got an invitation from Chaplin. He had bought the Mary Pickford home, he was so rich by this time from making pictures. So he invited us over for dinner. There was a butler in back of each chair, and there were solid-gold plates, and we had the most magnificent meal. He was a bigger star then than we were. Hell, he was the greatest thing in pictures.

PLAYBOY: How did you meet W. C. Fields?

MARX: We were on the bill together in Toledo. He was a tough guy. He was doing his juggling act, and there was a pool table on the stage, because he used to do funny stuff with a pool table, and Ed Wynn was also on the show. So Wynn used to get under the pool table, and while Fields was doing his stuff, Wynn would stick his head out and make funny faces. One day Fields caught him doing this and when Wynn stuck his head out from under the table, Fields was standing there with a pool cue and he hit Wynn on the head and knocked him unconscious. He was a funny guy, but he didn't want anybody to interfere with his act. Or to upstage him.

When we were playing together in Toledo, he walked off our show. He told the manager of the theater that he had "humpers on the carumpers." They were just words he was making up, but that's the way he was: He didn't want to follow us on the show. We did a big act with 30 people, and he was standing there alone on the stage with a cigar box, singing "Yankee-Doodle Went to Town," and the audience was walking out of the theater. So Fields quit the show and took the next train for New York. I knew him years later, when he worked in Hollywood. He used to hide in the bushes in front of his house and shoot at tourists with his BB gun.

PLAYBOY: Tell us about some of the other great comics you knew. How about Buster Keaton?

MARX: He used to put in gags for Harpo when we were at MGM.

PLAYBOY: In which films?

MARX: *A Night at the Opera, A Day at the Races, Go West.* He was washed up by then, but he was good for Harpo. Harpo was always looking for a good piece of business. He didn't talk, he didn't need lines, but he did need good business, and Keaton was a hell of a comic in silent films.

PLAYBOY: What kind of man was Keaton?

MARX: He was kind of eccentric. Near the end of his life, he bought a trailer and he would drive around Beverly Hills, stop the trailer, turn off the engine, take out a bridge table and have dinner in front of somebody's house. I guess everybody recognized it was Keaton, because nobody minded his eating his dinner in front of their house. It was a beautiful trailer.

PLAYBOY: It's common knowledge that you never got along well with Louis B. Mayer of MGM. Why?

MARX: Mayer took things too seriously. Nobody else took us seriously in Hollywood—just Mayer. One day he was having a conference with the censor about Lana Turner showing too much cleavage in her last film and Mayer was trying to convince the censor that MGM was a highly moral studio. So Harpo hired a stripper for the afternoon and chased her around the room while Mayer was talking to the censor. Another time we were sitting in Mayer's waiting room and after hours of waiting, we started a bonfire in his outer office. We'd done that to Thalberg years before. But Mayer didn't think it was funny.

PLAYBOY: We can't imagine why. Was he vindictive about it?

MARX: I think he wanted us to bomb. He didn't want us to take road tours and he refused to hire the best directors and writers; he gave us a lot of *schleppers* to work with, like the two German immigrants who wrote the ending to *A Day at the Races*. Mayer was cutting off his nose to spite his face. Now that I think about his nose, his face would have been better without it.

PLAYBOY: Do you have a favorite Marx Brothers film among those you did at MGM?

MARX: I liked *Duck Soup* and *Horse Feathers* and I liked parts of *Animal Crackers*. But I guess my favorite is *A Night at the Opera*.

PLAYBOY: Why?

MARX: It just has great scenes in it—great funny scenes. Like the scene in the stateroom where I'm meeting this lady, Mrs. Claypool, played by Margaret Dumont; I'm having a rendezvous with her. And when she arrives at my room, 14 people come out. I enjoyed *all* my romantic scenes with Margaret Dumont. She was a wonderful woman. She was the same off the stage as she was on it—always the stuffy, dignified matron. And the funny thing about her was she never understood the jokes. Seriously, she never knew what was going on. At the end of *Duck Soup*, we're alone in a small cottage and there's a war going on outside and Margaret says to me, "What are you doing, Rufus?" And I say, "I'm fighting for your honor, which is more than you ever did." Later she asked me what I meant by that.

PLAYBOY: After *A Night in Casablanca*, you made three pictures in a row without your brothers. They're not considered your best efforts, are they?

MARX: No, and neither are the pictures. After *Casablanca*, I made *Copacabana*, *A Girl in Every Port* and then *Double Dynamite*. That one was such a bomb it almost ruined the studio.

PLAYBOY: Which studio was it?

MARX: RKO. A fellow named Howard Hughes was running it then, and he's the one who came up with the title *Double Dynamite*. That was supposed to be a clever description of Jane Russell's breasts. With thinking like that, it's no wonder Hughes is a billionaire. He'd *have* to be a billionaire; otherwise, how could he make a living?

PLAYBOY: The last Marx Brothers film, *Love Happy*, was made in 1950, and that same year you began a whole new career with the television quiz show *You Bet Your Life*. Did you like doing that series?

MARX: You bet your life I did. It was some of the best stuff I ever did. I really had to think. I never worked so hard.

PLAYBOY: What was the meaning of the duck on your TV show and in your films?

MARX: Well, it's easier to crack a joke about a duck than an elephant.

PLAYBOY: Didn't you once appear in a television production of *The Mikado*?

MARX: Yes. I played Coco in *The Mikado* for NBC. That's how I got rid of my first wife.

PLAYBOY: By playing in *The Mikado*?

MARX: Yeah. Well, it's Gilbert and Sullivan, you know, and I love Gilbert and Sullivan, so I kept playing it at home, and she didn't quite understand it. She wasn't educated. Until I married her, I don't think she'd ever heard of Gilbert and Sullivan.

PLAYBOY: Where did *you* first hear of them?

MARX: When I was doing *Cocoanuts*, we had a fellow in the act who was what you'd call a straight man. His name was Basil Ruysdael. He had been in Gilbert and Sullivan operettas himself, and whenever we were backstage getting ready for a scene or something, he would start singing, "My object all sublime, I shall not . . . uh . . . to let the punishment fit the crime, the punishment fit the crime. And let each prisoner repent and willingly represent, a song of innocent merriment, of innocent merriment." I asked him, "What's that you're singing all the time?" "That's Gilbert and Sullivan," he told me. And I said, "Who the hell are they? A vaudeville team?" He said, "They were the greatest writers in England." That's how I got interested in them, and that's why I accepted that part in *The Mikado* when NBC offered it to me.

PLAYBOY: Are you sorry television has taken over so much of the movie industry?

MARX: No, because most of the movies today are lousy. I saw Barbra Streisand in *Up the Sandbox* recently. I thought it was terrible. They tell me there was some kind of symbolism, fantasy, in it, but by that time, I was in the toilet smoking a cigar. As people get older, they don't want to get in their car and go to a theater and stand in line to see it—even if it's a good picture. The average person hasn't got that much taste, either, so most people just turn on the television. It's much easier to just put on your bathrobe and look at a couple of lousy TV shows.

PLAYBOY: What was Hollywood like when you came out here?

MARX: Well, I was much younger.

PLAYBOY: We assumed that. When did you move out here?

MARX: We arrived here in 1930 from New York and immediately signed up with Paramount and did 12 pictures here.

PLAYBOY: Did you have wild times?

MARX: Not that I can remember, unfortunately.

PLAYBOY: From the newspapers of that time, it looks like the Marx Brothers tore the town apart.

MARX: We had fun. We were young. But I don't think the town has changed too much, except that there are fewer studios, because of television.

PLAYBOY: Would you be interested in playing in any more movies?

MARX: No. Not unless it was a great part and the hours were short and they held up cards so I wouldn't have to memorize everything.

PLAYBOY: John Cassavetes has said that you are the greatest actor who ever lived.

MARX: He was drunk.

PLAYBOY: Well, a lot of young, established actors admire the way you're able to play yourself on the screen.

MARX: I play *with* myself, too, but mostly off screen.

PLAYBOY: What would you do if you retired completely?

MARX: I'd get a massage occasionally and shave and take a walk. But I'm not gonna retire. I'd like to die right onstage. But I don't plan on dying at all.

PLAYBOY: Do you turn down many jobs?

MARX: Depends on the money. If a guy is worth almost a billion dollars—I'm talking about Bob Hope—and he offers me $1000 to go on his show, I consider it an insult. I wouldn't unwrap a cigar for $1000. When I did a show down here a couple of weeks ago, I got $10,000. For that kind of money, I not only unwrap a cigar but light it up and take a few puffs.

PLAYBOY: Would you ever do a show for free?

MARX: Yes. I'd do a show with the baseball announcer Vin Sculley, because he's given me so much enjoyment all my life listening to him describe baseball.

PLAYBOY: Who are your closest friends?

MARX: Nunnally Johnson, who was one of the top movie writers in this town: I knew him when I lived in Great Neck, and we've been friends ever since. And a fellow named Sheekman, who used to do a column for the Chicago *Times*. When I played Chicago, I offered to write a column for him because he had to do one every day. And when he came out here, I invited him to become one of the writers on our movies. Mostly, my friends are all roughly my age.

PLAYBOY: Who are your younger friends?

MARX: Well, there's Woody Allen, and Erin, and Goddard Lieberson, and Goody Ace. There are a few others that keep in touch with me, like Dick Cavett, Jack Nicholson and Elliott Gould. I have lunch with them occasionally, provided they pick up the check.

PLAYBOY: A friend of yours told us you sleep with your bedroom door locked. Why?

MARX: He's no friend of mine. But if you must know, I lock it when I'm all alone in the house.

PLAYBOY: Could that be because of your years in vaudeville, when you stayed in cheap hotels and locked your door so nobody would steal your money?

MARX: Could be. I remember in those days how I used to put the bureau up against the door. That was also during a phase of my life when I wanted to jump out the window. We were doing well in vaudeville by then, living in good hotels like the Statler in Cleveland or Detroit, but I was always afraid of jumping out the window.

PLAYBOY: Why?

MARX: I don't know. I guess it was a kind of nervous point in my life.

PLAYBOY: Were you depressed?

MARX: No. I'd seen some Boris Karloff movies and I was scared. I was very young then. I saw one Karloff picture and I took sleeping pills every night for about a month after that. It was the only way I could get to sleep.

PLAYBOY: Did you see a psychiatrist about it?

MARX: Yeah, but he said I was crazy, so I bit his leg and walked out.

PLAYBOY: What's your opinion of psychoanalysis?

MARX: It won't get it up if you're 83 years old, so what's the point of it?

PLAYBOY: But back then, you felt you were going a little crazy?

MARX: I was working very hard and I was single. And I had a wife who drank.

PLAYBOY: You were single and you had a wife?

MARX: So I'm a liar.

PLAYBOY: You were married to your first wife during your years in vaudeville, weren't you?

MARX: For part of them. We were married 21 years. She was so beautiful when I married her. She weighed about 109 then. The last time I saw her, she must have weighed 250.

PLAYBOY: This obviously wouldn't include marriage, but what's the most satisfying thing you've ever done?

MARX: I went to Germany, and while I was there, they showed me Hitler's grave and I danced on it. I was never that much of a dancer, but I was great that day!

PLAYBOY: How do you feel about being 83?

MARX: I'm still alive. That's about it. I can tell I'm still alive because I wake up in the morning. If I don't wake up, that means I'm dead. But talking about not knowing whether you're alive or dead, I remember once when I visited the offices of *The New York Times*, they showed me my obituary. It wasn't very good. I offered to punch it up for them, but they turned me down.

PLAYBOY: Have you observed any special diet over the years?

MARX: Well, since I turned 80, I've tried to limit my eating exclusively to food.

PLAYBOY: Do you drink?

MARX: The only drink I used to like is bourbon. Now I don't drink at all, except for an occasional shot of Maalox.

PLAYBOY: Have you ever tried marijuana?

MARX: One cigarette that Garson Kanin gave me. I took six puffs and I couldn't get to the other side of the room.

PLAYBOY: Do you think it should be legalized?

MARX: No, and I don't believe in booze, either. I didn't even have a drink until Prohibition. Then my father made wine in the cellar and killed all the rats.

PLAYBOY: What kind of cigars do you smoke?

MARX: This one comes from Havana. It costs $4. *Real* Havana, not from the Canary Islands.

PLAYBOY: What's it called?

MARX: Charley. Actually, this is the only cigar I have left that's genuine Havana. Bill Cosby gave them to me. Very few people can afford this cigar. Cosby can. I did a TV show for Cosby. It was all ad-libbed. We had a few cards to hold up, but they kept mixing them up. Cosby paid me off in cigars.

PLAYBOY: You've also made some talk-show appearances over the past couple of years.

MARX: Yeah. You get so little for being on a talk show, you're lucky if you can afford a five-pack of White Owls.

PLAYBOY: We remember, on at least one Cavett show, hearing you speak out against the amount of sex in movies today. Do you approve of film censorship?

MARX: Yes, I do. There are lots of children who go to movies. Besides, I don't like dirty pictures. I'm glad nobody took their clothes off in our movies. Can you imagine how ridiculous I'd have looked walking around naked with a cigar in my mouth?

PLAYBOY: There's a lot of explicitness on the stage these days, too. Have you seen any of the recent productions?

MARX: No. I wouldn't even go to see *Oh! Calcutta!* I had tickets to the opening night from Kenneth Tynan and I said, "I don't want to see it. I understand that what they're doing on the stage is what a lot of people do in bed."

PLAYBOY: Sleeping?

MARX: That's what I would have done in my seat if I'd have gone to see it.

PLAYBOY: Did you see *Hair*?

MARX: I saw half of it and walked out. Dick Cavett asked me if I'd seen it and I said no, and he wanted to know why not. I told him, "Well, I was gonna go see it, and then I called up the theater and I said, 'How much are the tickets?' They said the tickets were $11 apiece. I told them I'd call back, went in my bathroom, took off all my clothes and looked at myself in the full-length mirror. Then I called the theater and said, 'Forget it.'"

PLAYBOY: You said you saw half of it, and then you said you didn't see it at all. Which version are we to believe?

MARX: Both. I told you I'm a liar.

PLAYBOY: They say good liars make great storytellers. What's your favorite story?

MARX: Clean or dirty?

PLAYBOY: Just funny.

MARX: Well, a hooker picks up a guy. No. A married woman picks up a guy, takes him to her apartment and they go to bed. While they're doing it, the man says, "I've never had a woman like you. You're the most extraordinary woman in bed that I've ever heard of. You know, I'm not a religious man, but when I die, if there's such a thing as a hereafter, I'm going to come back and find you, no matter where you are in the whole world." And she says to him, "Well, if you do come back, try to come in the afternoons."

PLAYBOY: Do you have any more jokes?

MARX: No, except for this cheap cigar that Bill Cosby gave me. I'm suffocating.

PLAYBOY: Apart from cheap cigars, what annoys you most?

MARX: This interview.

PLAYBOY: Hang on, it's just about finished. Have you any regrets?

MARX: The fact that I *agreed* to this interview.

PLAYBOY: One last question: What would you do if you had your life to live all over again?

MARX: Try more positions.

WOODY ALLEN

A candid conversation with the bespectacled comedian, screenwriter-screwball, little-league lothario and self-styled superschlep

Sol Weinstein, debuting this month as a *Playboy* interviewer, has thrice regaled our readers—in serializations of *Loxfinger*, *Matzohball* and *On the Secret Service of His Majesty the Queen*—with the exploits of his seltzer-and-sour-cream superspy, Israel Bond. An ex-newspaperman, he drew on his deadline-at-dawn reportorial experience to beard this month's elusive subject in his New York den. Weinstein's dispatch—wired to *Playboy* collect—begins:

"In the cavernous attic of my ancestral estate, Twin Hangnails, in Levittown, Pennsylvania, the cameramen were set to begin filming my musical version of the notorious French novel *The Story of O*, retitled *Maim* for the Stateside market. Under the baton of Bobby Darin, the Marat/Sade Choir was running through the catchy score: *Who Whupped the Flesh Right Off o' Muh Back, Ma-a-aim?*; *A Floggy Day*; *Flagellation T. Cornpone*; and *You Should Always Hurt the One You Love*. Held in place by a devilish contrivance of barbed-wire clamps was the magnificent naked body quivering in anticipation of the knout. The lovely half-caste, Desirée Mandingo, fixed her fearful eyes on the cruel tip. 'Will it hurt, massa?'

"'Of course it'll hurt, dummy,' I said with some annoyance. 'But you knew what you were getting into when you signed to do the picture. Now, let's keep our bargain. Go on, whip me, whip me!'

"The lash rang out—so did the phone. For a second, I couldn't decide which had been more agonizing—the former's bite or the contumacious snap of the *Playboy* editor's command: 'Go interview Woody Allen; only keep it on a dead-serious level. *Playboy*'s readers have already gotten their quota of belly laughs from our interview with George Lincoln Rockwell.'

"Damn it! This ukase from the Playboy Building would play hob with my S.R.O. schedule of big-league projects. But I owed it to Hefner ('Ner,' as he is known to the inner circle), who, by publishing the condensed versions of my Israel Bond espionage masterworks, had lifted me from the mire of obscurity to my present lofty status as a semi-unknown. I barked at my wife: 'Bring me a bowl of Red Heart immediately, clear the decks for action and hold up on the following commitments: (a) my offer to co-author with Harry Kemelman *Monday the Rabbi Turned Buddhist*; (b) my campaign to have our own rabbi, Irving Fierverker, of Congregation Beth El, ousted because, though he is a holy, learned and fine man, he has failed to bring prestige to our synagogue by his unwillingness to solve a single murder; (c) my production of an LP, *William Buckley Reads the Poetry of the Firebrands of Watts*; (d) the telethon I was to host for the CH Foundation [Note: CH is a hush-hush disease not even the *Reader's Digest* dares talk about—Cerebral Hemorrhoids]; and my exposé for *Fact*, "What Were Masters and Johnson Really Doing While They Were *Supposed* to Be Observing Human Sexual Response?"

"Stalking the career of Heywood (Woody) Allen dictated a change of costume, so I slipped on my Oy Oy Seven trench coat and trench hat, which melded harmoniously with my chronic trench mouth, and touched the flame of my Zippo to my lips, inhaling the pungent scent of scorched flesh. Now, a lesser man would have asked Woody's press agent to ship over a ton of publicity material from which a fast, shallow, insincere 'puff' could have been punched out in two hours. But I am something more than a lesser man, so I told him, 'You keep the clippings, write the story, sign my name to it and send me *Playboy's* check by special-delivery airmail.' The fink hung up. This business is full of them.

"In its review of Woody's nutty mutilation of a Japanese spy flick, *What's Up, Tiger Lily?*, *Time* magazine had described the shriveled Socrates of Brooklyn as 'an anonymous little giggle merchant who looks like a slight defect in the wallpaper pattern,' a typical, lightweight *Time* simile concocted patently by a man who'd never seen Woody close up. A truer depiction, I thought, would be 'the product of a mad night of love between S.J. Perelman and a barn owl.' In any case, I wanted to see for myself, so I arranged my first session with

Allen at New York's Morosco Theater, where his first love-offering to Broadway, *Don't Drink the Water*, was in rehearsal.

"The press agent's uncooperative attitude had put me in something of a bind, however, and during the cab ride to the theater, I wondered aloud how I could ferret out the facts pertaining to the Allen saga. 'Oh,' said the bright-faced, crewcut cabby, 'you mean the Woody Allen who started as a teener batting out 25,000 jokes for a PR agency that used them to make its clients hilarious in print, became a top writer for Sid Caesar and Garry Moore and won the Gagwriter of the Year award from George Q. Lewis's Humor Society of America, then became a fledgling comedian at Greenwich Village bistros like the Bitter End, which, in turn, led to smash performances on *The Tonight Show* and *The Jack Paar Show*, a wild moneymaker of a screenplay, *What's New, Pussycat?*, a role in *Casino Royale* and the scripting of *Don't Drink the Water* and *What's Up, Tiger Lily? That* Woody Allen?'

"'You've been mildly helpful to me, cabby,' I replied. 'As a reward, I won't mug you.'

"I parked myself in the third row of the theater, my trained eye catching Lou Jacobi, Kay Medford and Anthony Roberts emoting on-stage, although it was difficult to pick up their dialog because of the roar of the greasepaint. When I did become acclimated acoustically, I found myself howling at the seemingly endless spate of crackling one-liners.

"'Gosh,' I observed on my way to Woody's dressing room, 'more than three decades have elapsed since Kaufman and Hart brought *Once in a Lifetime* to the Great White Way—and it still holds up.'

"'Yes,' bleated a petulant voice. 'But I wish they had the decency to rehearse my play.'

"The room was completely empty, and I wondered where the voice had come from. Then, after a minute of utter silence, a slight defect in the wallpaper pattern began to move. Making a mental note to renew my subscription to *Time*, I switched on my Webcor and pleaded with Allen to say anything that was on his mind.

"'Dandruff,' he croaked and started to crawl back into the wallpaper.

"'Woody, I'm a friendly sort, really. I got your albums, and I thought they were just melorooney, alligator.' A refreshing hipsterism would cement our relationship fast, I shrewdly reckoned.

"He wore a lavender smoking jacket that had once belonged to Laurence Harvey's dog, and a snug pair of Levi Strauss midafternoon walking jeanlets. He nervously drummed his fingers, which were genuine Slingerlands, against his red-thatched cranium. 'Be kind,' he moaned. 'I'm afraid of my shadow.'

"'From what I can see, you have no shadow,' I said jovially, in a bid to reassure the twitching lad.

"His uneasiness gone, Woody leaned against the dressing-room wall and began to whimper freely. This is the result."

PLAYBOY: By now, hundreds of thousands of people have seen your new Broadway play, Don't Drink the Water. Did you think it would be such a smash?

ALLEN: Not until some glaring faults were corrected in the Philadelphia tryout. We decided to open the curtains, light the stage and use actors.

PLAYBOY: In precis, what is its message to humanity?

ALLEN: An unequivocal admonition to refrain from imbibing H_2O.

PLAYBOY: We appreciate your candor. Why didn't you appear in it yourself?

ALLEN: Oh, I wanted to, heaven knows. I read for a part—but I didn't get it. And I even slept with the author.

PLAYBOY: How long did it take you to write it?

ALLEN: Four hours.

PLAYBOY: Why so long?

ALLEN: I couldn't concentrate for the first two and a half hours.

PLAYBOY: Aside from the basic concept, are there any lesser themes running through the play?

ALLEN: Yes. That people should make an effort to brush their teeth at least twice a day.

PLAYBOY: Con Gleem?

ALLEN: I'm not pushing any particular product. What matters is the consecrated act of brushing itself. It prevents cavities. If this play can prevent one single cavity, then I have fulfilled my obligation to American belles-lettres.

PLAYBOY: Are you planning a sequel to Don't Drink?

ALLEN: Actually, this play is the last part of a trilogy. Parts one and two I have no ideas for as yet. However, the best trilogies are those that run three-two-one, rather than in ascending order.

PLAYBOY: Remind us never to let you bet for us at Churchill Downs. Woody, you've just immersed yourself in the frantic, sinister world of James Bond, at least in Charles K. Feldman's version of 007, *Casino Royale*. How did you get involved in it?

ALLEN: Feldman asked me to. I would have accepted any acting role at that price—even a Greek chorus.

PLAYBOY: What was your contribution to the film?

ALLEN: Substantial—rape, looting and murder. As Sir James Bond's nephew, Little Jimmy Bond, who is sent off on assignment, I incinerate a few people, pull off some daring escapades, some romantic high jinks—the whole thing culminating in a terrific paycheck. My portrayal adds a new dimension of incredible cowardice hitherto lacking in these movies.

PLAYBOY: Do you identify personally with suave superspies like James Bond and Derek Flint?

ALLEN: No. But I did catch *Fantastic Voyage*, and I identified strongly with the germs.

PLAYBOY: We imagine you got to know London pretty well during the filming of *Casino Royale*. Is it really the switched-on city it's reputed to be?

ALLEN: Yes, yes! They have an all-night soft-drink stand.

PLAYBOY: What hip, fab, gear things did you do there?

ALLEN: I strolled about. I sat in a chair—twice. I went to a newsreel theater. I was sold pornographic dental X rays. And once a gypsy woman sidled up to me and unashamedly said the word "loins."

PLAYBOY: Did you run with the "in crowd"?

ALLEN: I had a very swinging group. We visited the tomb of Guy Fawkes and blew it up, hung out in Limehouse and hobnobbed in Whitechapel, where the Ripper does his mischief.

PLAYBOY: *Does?* Jack the Ripper is dead.

ALLEN: He's very much alive. I know this from personal experience. Years ago, I was taught how to dress in female garb by Irene Adler, whom I shall always consider to be *the* woman. While in London, I assumed the guise of an octogenarian trollop down to the last detail—rotting hoop skirt and bustle, cracked pancake makeup, and so on—and during one of my walks through shadowy Whitechapel, a black-cloaked man leaped out of a doorway and slashed at me with a razor, crying: "Saucy Jacky strikes again!" He was the spitting image of Basil Rathbone.

PLAYBOY: Did you buy any kicky Carnaby Street togs while you were in London?

ALLEN: Yes—a nifty sheet-metal suit and an all-crab-meat overcoat.

PLAYBOY: You shot *What's New, Pussycat?* on location in Paris. Are you happy with the way it turned out?

ALLEN: It turned out to be the greatest moneymaking film comedy of all time. All things considered, I thought it came off very well.

PLAYBOY: What part did you like best?

ALLEN: When Rommel gets defeated.

PLAYBOY: Don't you think *Pussycat* would have had more credibility if you, rather than Peter O'Toole, had won Romy Schneider at the end?

ALLEN: Yes—but we were going for a far-out, unbelievable ending.

PLAYBOY: Did O'Toole come up to your sexual standards?

ALLEN: He came close. But I have two or three moves he could never duplicate. Not unlike things you've seen Olympic high divers do.

PLAYBOY: It's rumored that you always contrive to be seen nude in every film you make. Is this true?

ALLEN: I *have* done a nude scene for every picture, but you can't tell, because I have Dacron flesh.

PLAYBOY: Let's have your frank opinion of your latest cinematic effort, *What's Up, Tiger Lily?*

ALLEN: It's an experimental film I was hired to work on. Originally it was a Japanese espionage vehicle. What I did was to cut out the Japanese dialog, write new dialog and put it into the mouths of the actors. What I wrote is completely contrary to what they're doing at the same time on the screen, so it comes off funny. Matter of fact, *Tiger Lily* was just voted one of the 10 most Japanese pictures of the year.

PLAYBOY: What new projects are on your drawing board?

ALLEN: I would like to shut myself up for a year and try to write a perfectly rhymed couplet. I'm also working on a way to transmute baser metals into gold. This, they tell me, is alchemy and was disproven years ago, but I don't believe their lies. I'm also creating interracial puppets, fasting as theater, nothing-happenings and organized nude string quartets. I am also tinkering with the idea of doing a musical version of the *Gilgamesh*, the Babylonian Bible. And after that, a no-character, off-Broadway drama, which I may call *Death of a Salesman* just to hypo the box office.

PLAYBOY: It sounds as if you're far too busy to relax with hobbies, such as the judo lessons you were allegedly taking some time ago.

ALLEN: With the help of judo, I have broken every major bone and organ in my body. Judo enables one to do that much quicker than any other form of self-defense. But I do have many intriguing hobbies. I collect stamp hinges, I play the comb, I threaten old ladies and I carve soap.

PLAYBOY: What kind of soap do you use?

ALLEN: I tried Lifebuoy initially, but Lifebuoy's a difficult medium to come to terms with. For essential purity, one should use Ivory.

PLAYBOY: What do you carve out of soap?

ALLEN: Soap dishes.

PLAYBOY: You used to play a pretty fair clarinet, too, we're told.

ALLEN: I still noodle around with it. I guess I could eke out a meager living as a clarinetist. But my real musical ambition is to be the first white bop harpist.

PLAYBOY: Wasn't there a jazz harpist named Corky Hale?

ALLEN: Well, I play the jew's harp. . . .

PLAYBOY: Let's backtrack a bit to your early years in show business, when you were writing jokes for Sammy Kaye, Guy Lombardo and Arthur Murray. Of them all, who did your material the most justice?

ALLEN: Oh, I'd say Sammy Kaye for the one-liners. Guy Lombardo for the longer, more philosophical routines. But Arthur Murray got the most mileage out of the material, because of what I'd call his "good look."

PLAYBOY: These were also the days when you were, shall we say, being phased out of New York University and City College of New York. Any regrets?

ALLEN: I wasn't exactly phased out. I was given a Section Eight, the only one ever awarded by a nonmilitary institution. My only regret is that I wasted as much time as I did in those places. The whole experience was like swirling in a grim, grisly pit of eels. When they called me before the board of deans to sever our connection, they said, among other things, that they didn't *like* being considered a grim, grisly pit of eels. They also called the police. To this day, I recall that just as the dean gave me the ax, he opened his raincoat and blushed. Queer duck.

PLAYBOY: Then came your break-in nights at various Greenwich Village bistros. Would you advise young comics to take the same route?

ALLEN: The Village still seems to be the place to get started. There's no other route. In those days I tried them all. I even auditioned at hootenannies. For many months I played a place called the Duplex at no salary and I had to supply my own cab fare and wardrobe. Things began looking up when I got a job at the Bitter End. I started at $75 a week and in just two years I was pulling down a fast $76 a week. Still no cab fare, though.

PLAYBOY: There's a story that the owner of the Bitter End used to send lovely models onstage during your shows to ease you through panicky moments by feeding you ice-cream sodas. Is that true?

ALLEN: Yes, but it is indicative of my maturity as both performer and human being that by the end of my engagement I had begun eschewing the ice-cream sodas and assaulting the models.

PLAYBOY: By now, do you think the public has accepted you as a star of the first magnitude and not just another pretty face?

ALLEN: I think so, although it has been very hard to overcome my uncommonly fine features in a society that puts such a premium on them. Anyone with an eye for aesthetics can see that just by scanning me.

PLAYBOY: What kind of people comprise your audiences?

ALLEN: Primarily left-handed people, single taxers, a liberal sprinkling of deviates, some Lutherans. The rest are Eskimos.

PLAYBOY: Do you think people of different social and economic milieu can appreciate the same jokes?

ALLEN: No. In order to appreciate the same jokes, you must be making the identical salary of a person appreciating the same jokes. And that includes deductions.

PLAYBOY: Is there a personal trap in being a comedian? That is, are you always expected to be funny?

ALLEN: Yes. But I fool people. I stand in the corner at parties and pretend to be an end table.

PLAYBOY: Do you feel there's any particular need for scatology in humor?

ALLEN: Definitely. When one of my monologs starts to flag, I always insert a wild, swinging Ella Fitzgerald riff. And the laughs come back again.

PLAYBOY: We meant obscenity in humor.

ALLEN: There's no particular need. If the material is funny, that's what counts. I could watch *nuns* do an act if they were funny. However, if you're dirty and funny, you run a greater risk than being clean and funny. Dirty and funny—you're a comic. Dirty and *unfunny*—you're a child molester.

PLAYBOY: If you hadn't been blessed with your comedic gift, what would you be doing now?

ALLEN: I imagine I'd be a bum. I don't believe in any sort of labor.

PLAYBOY: If you were really up against it, would you be willing to panhandle?

ALLEN: Since I can't interact socially, I couldn't take the emotional contact with the victim. Purse snatching would be far more suitable.

It's over quickly. No relationship. No guilt. Also, it's tax-free and a swell way to meet women. And you can sell the purses afterward.

PLAYBOY: What gives you the inspiration for this kind of far-out humor?

ALLEN: I smash my occipital area with a heavy mallet, then write down whatever comes. Everything good that I've ever written is the result of a sharp, searing blow.

PLAYBOY: A great deal of your comedy is self-deprecatory. In your heart of hearts, do you really think you're funny?

ALLEN: I think I'm a scream—but no one has confirmed it to me as yet.

PLAYBOY: One critic has suggested that your technique of turning personal misfortune into comedy helps you "get even with the world." Is he right?

ALLEN: No. I do it for the money. You can't get even with the world. It takes too long and too many lawyers.

PLAYBOY: Much of your subject matter is derived from your middle-class Jewish upbringing. How do you feel about Jewish humor?

ALLEN: There's a common misconception about my being Jewish. What it is, really, is that I'm not gentile. My father is hieroglyphic and therefore believes in mercy killing and free lunch. My mother is an orthodox paranoid and, while she doesn't believe in an afterlife, she doesn't believe in a present one, either. I, if the truth be known, am a devout pervert. We're a small sect who meet on crowded streetcars and worship in our own way.

PLAYBOY: You've said that your parents sneer at show business as an enterprise for "gypsies." Do they still want you to become a pharmacist?

ALLEN: Not anymore. They'd rather I got something on the docks—or prize fighting.

PLAYBOY: According to *Cahiers du Cinéma*, people laugh at you because you symbolize the little man who can't fit in with the dehumanizing world of technology. Are you still at odds with that world? It's been noted, for example, that you don't drive a car.

ALLEN: The National Safety Council this year presented me with a golden scroll for not operating a motor vehicle. They estimated that by my staying off our highways, 68,191 lives were saved.

PLAYBOY: While we're on the subject of your mechanical incompetence, you've also discoursed ruefully about your bedroom clock, which runs counterclockwise, and a tape recorder that talks back to you in a snotty, bored fashion: "I *know*, Woody, I *know*. . . ." Why do you think machines single you out for this kind of treatment?

ALLEN: There's a definite malevolence in all inanimate objects—like the pencil that breaks its point when I need it to sign something. It's willing to do that, to sacrifice itself, just to impede me. Have you ever stepped into a shower and noticed the deliberate sequence of ice-cold water, boiling water, ice-cold water again? Or the way taxicabs avoid you when you need one in a hurry? It's a conscious conspiracy. I think I'd like to write a paper on sinks.

PLAYBOY: Sinks?

ALLEN: There's evil in sinks. They have a decision-making ability no one knows about. In short, I have never known a noncommitted object. I know this theory of mine will erode the very roots of existentialism and incur the enmity of French intellectuals, but that's the way I feel.

PLAYBOY: Some of your funniest material has alluded to your psychotherapy. Has it been beneficial to you?

ALLEN: It did unblock my bank account. Though I must confess, I retain a tendency to run down the streets in undershorts, brandishing a meat cleaver.

PLAYBOY: What's your analyst's reaction to the spoofs you've done about him?

ALLEN: It's hard to say. He thinks he's a bathroom plunger. The whole thing has been eight years of unmitigated free association for him. Thus far, no breakthroughs for either of us.

PLAYBOY: Why not?

ALLEN: Because I don't believe he should know *everything*. Anybody can affect an analysis if he knows the facts. But I withhold strategic information, like the fact that I'm married, my fears, my sex, my occupation.

PLAYBOY: What does he think you do for a living?

ALLEN: He thinks I'm a quicklime salesman.

PLAYBOY: Who is your analyst, anyway?

ALLEN: A Croatian midget. Another reason I can't tell him everything is that he's probably in cahoots with his couch. You know how I feel about objects. I don't trust him *or* his couch.

PLAYBOY: What kind of financial arrangement do you have with him?

ALLEN: I get him broads.

PLAYBOY: You mentioned your fears. Is yielding to homosexual urges one of them?

ALLEN: Hardly. I have a lethal heterosexual potency that I supplement with budget-priced vitamins from shady mail-order houses. I'm naturally throbbing. I could walk into a crowded room and radiate sexuality.

PLAYBOY: Do you?

ALLEN: No, because I'm crowd-shy. However, I will occasionally do it by backing into an empty room.

PLAYBOY: This legendary shyness of yours—does it still plague you, for instance, when a stranger recognizes you on the street and gives you a cheery greeting?

ALLEN: I continue to be abnormally withdrawn. My reaction to such a salutation would be to blush and mutter.

PLAYBOY: What if he tried to prolong the conversation by saying something like, "I saw you on TV, and I thought you were great . . ." etc.?

ALLEN: I'd panic and deny being me. Then I'd try to force him into denying who *he* is. Then, as two impostors, we could seek new things in common, start afresh.

PLAYBOY: Some critiques of your material have suggested that your success is predicated on your failures. Yet we see before us a man with a lovely new wife, a man raking in the coin of the realm by the bushel from his plays, movies, acting roles, high-salaried nightclub gigs and writing for such publications as *The New Yorker* and this learned journal. You seem to be having more fun failing than most men have winning.

ALLEN: My life is still a series of small failures accruing to a monumental catastrophe. Given a fair opportunity, I can screw up any situation. While it may be true that the external trappings of my existence have changed, the basic problems remain.

PLAYBOY: What are they?

ALLEN: I'm still striking out with women—but it's a better class of women.

PLAYBOY: Are you still paying alimony on your first marriage?

ALLEN: We've an arrangement. We alternate. I pay her for a year; then she pays me for a year. The unfair thing is I'm paying for child support and we had no children.

PLAYBOY: Would you like to have children?

ALLEN: Eight or 12 little blonde girls. I love blonde girls.

PLAYBOY: Would you like them to go into show business when they grow up?

ALLEN: I'd like to see them either in a monstrous trampoline act or hustling drinks in Tijuana.

PLAYBOY: You and your new wife just moved into an apartment in New York. Tell us about it.

ALLEN: It's still in the process of being furnished. It looks like Mount Palomar. The living room is French Moroccan with a touch of Algerian

Resistance. The dining room is Aramaic; the sun parlor, Heavy Latin; the gym, Early Flemish. A stuffed Bedouin stands at the gateway to the umbrella closet. We eat off a mummy case. Our bedroom is under water, so we don't get as much sleep as we'd like. We can't hold our breath long enough to get our basic eight hours. Bags of cement lie about here and there, and clusters of garbage effectively arranged by our decorator, who's also lying about—effectively arranged by *his* decorator.

PLAYBOY: Would you call this a Playboy pad?

ALLEN: No, I'm not a Playboy-pad type. The items I described are all from my old one-room apartment, including the decorator.

PLAYBOY: Then you wouldn't like a round, revolving bed?

ALLEN: No, I'm not fond of circles. I'd like a bed shaped like the prime minister of Ghana.

PLAYBOY: What do you think of *The Playboy Philosophy?*

ALLEN: I think it consumes space that would be better used for nude pictures. Pack the magazines with "stuff" is *my* philosophy.

PLAYBOY: Woody, for all your sexual braggadocio, you've admitted that you're "no fun at orgies." Now that you've become a big star and hobnobbed with the worldly international set, would you revise that statement?

ALLEN: I've never been to an orgy, honestly. If I was invited to one, I'd be the guy they sent out for cold cuts. Anyway, I wouldn't care too much for the sight of strange naked men. However, I wouldn't mind *emceeing* an orgy.

PLAYBOY: How would you emcee an orgy?

ALLEN: Oh, I guess I'd just do my regular act. And I suppose they'd do *their* regular act, so it might work out.

PLAYBOY: We doubt it. You're said to be a nonparty type who prefers entertaining in a modest fashion at home. What would be your idea of a congenial evening? Would it be spent with fellow entertainers?

ALLEN: I'd rather spend it with one other person with whom I have absolutely nothing in common. The entire evening could be spent avoiding any sort of contact—mental or physical—and ducking issues, if necessary, by staying in the closet.

PLAYBOY: If you feel that way, why not refuse to answer the door when a guest arrives?

ALLEN: Oh, that would be rude. Unless, of course, I left a candy dish on the stoop.

PLAYBOY: When you're not throwing bacchanals, how do you spend your evenings at home?

ALLEN: Early evening is given to morbid introspection. After dinner it's watching *The Tonight Show* for diversion. From one to three A.M.—anguish and torment. From three to five A.M.—remorse and regret. Then a review of my life's mistakes, featuring the 10 outstanding blunders, 15 minutes of advanced anxiety, and so to bed.

PLAYBOY: Do you also have an organized schedule of nightmares?

ALLEN: No, I'm not an active sleeper. However, I have experienced dreams on rare occasions. In one, I am attacked by a cheese. In another, my body is dipped in a vat of feathers. In yet another, I make love to some moss formations. A fairly common one has me straying through an empty field, kissing rare minerals while my mother, symbolized by a penguin, smokes a Kool and wrestles the Harlem Globetrotters. During the filming of *Casino Royale*, I dreamed I was Ursula Andress's body stocking.

PLAYBOY: In your peregrinations, you've come in contact with some of the world's most fetching film goddesses. Who among them turns you on the most? Ursula?

ALLEN: No—Brigitte Bardot and Julie Christie. Bardot has everything—in spades. She doesn't have a defect, especially the defect of being too perfect.

PLAYBOY: And Julie?

ALLEN: She also has everything, but it's a different kind of everything.

PLAYBOY: Who's your third choice?

ALLEN: Margaret Hamilton, just the way she appeared in *The Wizard of Oz*, with contorted green face and riding a broom. She just *drips* S. A.

PLAYBOY: Aside from these three sex stars, what kind of girls turn you on?

ALLEN: Oh, tall, gelid, aloof Teutonic-Prussian girls. I adore Villagey-looking blondes. I like a girl who's arrogant, spoiled and dirty, but brilliant and beautiful.

PLAYBOY: How do you keep them in line?

ALLEN: I distribute ballpoint pens at Christmas. That keeps them faithful all year long.

PLAYBOY: We've noticed you constantly nibbling sweets throughout this interview. Does this compulsion have a sexual basis?

ALLEN: I'd rather nibble sweets than do anything else on earth. I'm a Hershey bar freak.

PLAYBOY: Has your wife been forced to disguise herself as a Milky Way or a Three Musketeers in order to . . . ?

ALLEN: She doesn't have to. My wife is very sexy.

PLAYBOY: Many stars have proclaimed the virtues of Wheaties as an aid to virility. What is your position on Wheaties?

ALLEN: I agree with Kierkegaard and the findings in his essay *On Wheaties*. Kierkegaard speaks for me on all major matters relating to breakfast cereals.

PLAYBOY: How do you get into shape for the love act?

ALLEN: Like any other act I do. I write it first. Then if I think it'll play, I do it.

PLAYBOY: We were referring to physical preparations.

ALLEN: I work out with the New York Rangers.

PLAYBOY: But they have a long off-season.

ALLEN: That's so. But I only have sexual intercourse during the fall and winter. Every once in a while, though, I barnstorm.

PLAYBOY: Could you possibly have any respect for a girl who wants you solely for your body?

ALLEN: My body is a miracle of engineering comparable to the aqueduct. I see no reason to fault a girl because she finds it unbearable to suppress an urge to taste nirvana.

PLAYBOY: While we're on the subject of physicality, to what extent do you think your success as a performer depends on your physical appearance?

ALLEN: Well, I feel I must *show up* before I can really do anything.

PLAYBOY: Our readers might be fascinated to learn just how big you are. Would you tell us?

ALLEN: I'm 5' 6" and fluctuate between 118 and 125 pounds. The exact poundage depends on certain shifts in the earth's crust. It's very involved.

PLAYBOY: What's your chest measurement?

ALLEN: Eight inches. Ten, expanded.

PLAYBOY: How do you keep your body in such superb physical condition?

ALLEN: Every now and then I have a representative of a metallurgical cartel come and give me an acid bath. And I buff myself regularly with Ajax.

PLAYBOY: Do you oil your body before posing for pinup shots?

ALLEN: No, I secrete a natural grease. I sweat Vicks—an unusual phenomenon. On a sultry day I'm like a swamp.

PLAYBOY: Who requests these pinups?

ALLEN: Beggars, convicts, an occasional shut-in and the sort of unsavory types whose names appear regularly on the blotters of the morals squad.

PLAYBOY: You were once quoted as saying, "I'm an intellectual Cary Grant." Is that true?

ALLEN: I never said that. Some writer did in an interview. But I believe it. Hell, the mirror doesn't lie.

PLAYBOY: You also claim to exude an animal magnetism that women find irresistible. What's it like?

ALLEN: It's what I'd call "the new sex appeal." I'd link it to the Michael Caine or Belmondo look, not commercial or waxy. Women sense in me a willingness to be violent.

PLAYBOY: Do you come across female mashers often?

ALLEN: Yes, because I deliberately place myself in jam-packed subways and buses and try to look as bewitching as possible by wearing a cuddly sweater or cardigan. You'd be surprised how often it works.

PLAYBOY: You once said, "I could be mugged and three weeks later come up with something funny about it." Can you say that now?

ALLEN: I felt that way until I *was* mugged. The only thing I came up with was my lunch.

PLAYBOY: You look like you're still wearing the suit you were mugged in. What do you say to haberdashers who lament your rumpled appearance?

ALLEN: To be truthful, I have a supreme noninterest in clothing. My favorite item of apparel is my Hathaway hair shirt, which I use to mortify myself over a fantastic guilt I have, based on accepting a cupcake once when I didn't deserve it. When I do buy clothing, it's because it looks great on the dummy. I've even gone to parties with the clothes still on the dummy.

PLAYBOY: Were you a hit at these parties?

ALLEN: No, but the dummy scored heavily. I still possess brand-new clothing I purchased three years ago, unworn to this day. My apartment is a treasure house of unworn clothing.

PLAYBOY: How do you choose your *ensemble du jour*?

ALLEN: I'm a first-hanger man: If it's on the first hanger, I wear it. If the first hanger is empty, I wear the first hanger. In addition to my hair shirt, I adore my huge turtle shell. It's wonderful when the weather's cold and, besides, it protects me from my natural enemies, squid and barracuda. As for shoes, if I find a pair that fits, I wear them relentlessly. It's also more comfortable to wear them with the shoe trees inside. Gives me a seductive shuffle when I walk.

PLAYBOY: Upon rising, do you have a regimen for cleanliness?

ALLEN: The left side of me is cleaned compulsively—the left of my nose, mouth, chest, navel, etc. Everything on the right side I let remain steeping in my natural body oils.

PLAYBOY: You do this, presumably, to make yourself sexually irresistible. Yet we're told that you got an unlisted phone number when your career took its sensational upturn. Why?

ALLEN: When it was listed, some of my loyal adherents would call at all hours. But then I began to get crank calls, people shrieking that they were considering committing suicide.

PLAYBOY: How did you handle them?

ALLEN: I'd try to be soothing and suggest various ways. But I myself am not suicidal. I have an animal fear of death.

PLAYBOY: Still, if you had to choose, how would you prefer to go?

ALLEN: Smothered by the flesh of Italian actresses.

PLAYBOY: Besides receiving the crank calls, have you ever gotten any hate mail?

ALLEN: Once in a while. It generally comes in two categories—either unsigned or from my family. And every so often I get a sexual proposition.

PLAYBOY: Do you turn them down?

ALLEN: It depends on the photo with the letter.

PLAYBOY: You certainly come off as a cool, jaded, worldly type. Are you?

ALLEN: My nerves are like ice water. Although I do have a propensity for throwing up under pressure, I'm basically very cool.

PLAYBOY: What procedures do you recommend in setting the stage for a seduction?

ALLEN: (1) Find a girl. This method will also work on a camel or a bacon rind, but a girl is probably the most satisfying. (2) Lean her against something soft—preferably another girl. (3) Put on the most seductive recording you can find of *Sheep May Safely Graze*. (4) Blow into her ear with a bellows. (5) Slip into something provocative, like a mink posing strap. (6) Assume a false name like Laslo or Helmut. (7) Impress her with your collection of post-impressionist chopped meat. (8) At the crucial moment, bring the New York Rangers out of the closet.

PLAYBOY: How do you tell a girl to be gentle at the moment of surrender?

ALLEN: I explain to her that (a) it won't hurt, and (b) it'll all be over in eight seconds.

PLAYBOY: Would you warn a girl, "Baby, I'm no good for you"?

ALLEN: I wouldn't have to. Rough going is written all over my face. A girl starts in with me, she knows what the score is. I carry an automatic and leave town fast. I also have a tendency to dribble—that hurts my chances sometimes.

PLAYBOY: Has it always been easy for you to get dates?

ALLEN: No, generally it's been hard. I'd rather not say how I met her, but I once dated a lady embalmer for five months. Neither one of us had any complaints.

PLAYBOY: In this connection, do you have any repellent personal habits or indulge in unspeakable acts of perversion that your PR men have tried to cover up?

ALLEN: I enjoy chewing gum already chewed by a midget. And sometimes I dress up in a nurse's uniform and talk bawdy.

PLAYBOY: Do you have any other secret vices?

ALLEN: Yes. Keeping 200 live Chinese in my bedroom at all times, prison food, eating out of tin plates—small, tasteless portions of beans, watery soup—and being pummeled by sadistic guards who look like Barton MacLane. I also love herbs, roots, locusts and larvae.

PLAYBOY: Are you on a nature-food kick?

ALLEN: Yes. The best thing is a good piece of timber—sequoia, if possible; if not, some of the hairier lichens. The best diet is fatty and cholesterol-rich, with gigantic amounts of sweets. Heavy smoking on top of all that builds the body. Exposure to radioactivity doesn't hurt, either.

PLAYBOY: What physical feats can you perform?

ALLEN: I can stand on my eye. I can sneeze backward. I can touch both ears together. I am able to lift large quantities of decayed matter. I both lie and make love pathologically.

PLAYBOY: Have you ever experimented with the mind-expanding drugs?

ALLEN: I take a chocolate-covered St. Joseph's baby aspirin now and then, and groove myself out of my skull. It's fantastic; it heightens my orgasm. I see colors more vividly, the veins in leaves, the birth of bacteria on Formica tabletops. Gradually I hope to up the dosage to two per trip.

PLAYBOY: So much for your predilections. Do you have any aversions?

ALLEN: I do not like turning rapidly to my left; I move right in a 270-degree arc until I'm facing left. I am fond of the Atlantic Ocean, but not the Pacific, which says nothing to me oceanwise. I have a psychological fear of dancing with a mailman. Had it since childhood. Oh, and a morbid phobia of breaded veal cutlets.

PLAYBOY: What else bugs you?

ALLEN: The fact that my jokes are constantly being purloined by other comedians.

PLAYBOY: Do they do your bits well?

ALLEN: They lack my command, authority and great natural warmth.

PLAYBOY: Are you feuding with anyone in the business?

ALLEN: One feud, a long-standing one with the nearsighted Mr. Magoo. No one will invite us to the same party.

PLAYBOY: Yes, we saw that in Winchell. Do your pet peeves include pets?

ALLEN: I don't find pets distasteful. If I could have any pet, it would be a clam. They're unusually affectionate, loyal and keep burglars away. They're quite responsive to commands, more so than dogs or chimps. Of all clams, cherrystones are the most dependable.

PLAYBOY: Let's talk about world affairs. What do you think of De Gaulle?

ALLEN: I don't trust anyone who speaks French that good.

PLAYBOY: How about LBJ and his crew?

ALLEN: He's got a ranch and one of those hats. Terrific!

PLAYBOY: Prayer in schools?

ALLEN: I'm in favor of it. There are no atheists during midterm exams.

PLAYBOY: How do you feel about the busing of schoolchildren?

ALLEN: I would just run over the more precocious ones.

PLAYBOY: Invasion of privacy?

ALLEN: My views on invasion of privacy must and will remain private. I deeply resent your boorish intrusiveness.

PLAYBOY: Black power?

ALLEN: I know nothing about chess.

PLAYBOY: The Red Guards?

ALLEN: Or checkers.

PLAYBOY: What's your draft status?

ALLEN: 4-P. In the event of war, I'm a hostage.

PLAYBOY: If you were 1-A, would you consider burning your draft card to avoid induction?

ALLEN: I regard the draft boards as I regard boards of education or any other inanimate objects—as sinister. As far as burning a card is concerned, I wouldn't be able to make a fire. I can't see feigning homosexuality; a stud like me wouldn't know how to begin. But if I did go into the army, my natural tendency would be to be a hero—if they gave out medals for desertion. Actually, I'm at work on an incredible secret weapon to use against the Viet Cong—an electronic beam that will give them postnasal drip.

PLAYBOY: Where do your sympathies lie in the debate between the Hawks and the Doves?

ALLEN: To be honest, my sympathies lie with myself. I have a terrific empathy with myself, tend to identify with myself more and more. Anyhow, I don't know who the Hawks and the Doves are, but when I find out, I'm going to ring their doorbells and run.

PLAYBOY: Lately, we've seen the emergence of an apocalyptic strain of comedy termed black humor. Have you had any particular vision of the apocalypse?

ALLEN: Death has visited me in the form of a shrouded figurine. I'm playing him gin rummy for my soul—at a penny a point, just to keep it interesting.

PLAYBOY: Are there any cultural trends you find pernicious?

ALLEN: I'm against evolution. The present progressive evolvement of the species toward higher forms is a dangerous trend that should be arrested—reversed, if possible. If I had my way, this Mr. Scopes of "monkey trial" fame would have been convicted.

PLAYBOY: Speaking of the monkey, do you frequent discotheques?

ALLEN: Quite often. My body generates a rhythm that can best be described as Indonesian. Once Sybil Christopher stopped frugging at Arthur to watch me with ill-concealed envy and hostility.

PLAYBOY: How do you feel about Mod fashions?

ALLEN: I like short dresses, but only on extremely fat girls with bulbous thighs, huge muscular calves and thick varicosed ankles.

PLAYBOY: What's your position on long hair for men?

ALLEN: I'd rather see a man in long hair than a pageboy.

PLAYBOY: For many young people, long hair seems to be a symbol of nonconformity and defiance of the establishment. How do you feel about student protest?

ALLEN: I'm all for it—and student riots, too.

PLAYBOY: How do you feel about "the new morality" on campus?

ALLEN: The present sexual revolution in the colleges has almost caused me to reregister. When I was in college, there was no all-out sexual revolution, just some sporadic guerrilla warfare. And I wasn't very good in ambushes.

PLAYBOY: What, in your eyes, is the major cultural contribution of the 20th century?

ALLEN: The movie version of *Act One*.

PLAYBOY: What would you place in a time capsule to represent the best of our age?

ALLEN: I would fill it with feathers. Plenty of feathers.

PLAYBOY: Master Heywood Allen, with your hit play, your movie scripts, your acting roles, your nightclub and concert engagements making your name a household word, you stand astride the entertainment world, as one critic has phrased it, like "a Colossus of Toads." Is all this enough for you, or do you have some greater mission in life?

ALLEN: Yes, to invent a better yo-yo and, even more important than that, to accumulate the world's biggest ball of tin foil.

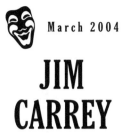

JIM CARREY

A candid conversation with Hollywood's most serious-minded funny guy about spirituality, drugs, denial and how The Truman Show *became reality*

With his head and his face bearing equal amounts of stubble, Jim Carrey arrives at his production company's office. He has just shaved his skull for a new role, and dressed in a black suit and white shirt he looks like a happy, prosperous monk. But the name on the door—Pit Bull Productions—reveals far more about Carrey's true nature.

Born in Toronto, Carrey had an uneventful childhood as the son of an accountant and a homemaker—until Dad lost his job and the family was left homeless and miserable. Carrey dropped out of school in 10th grade and worked at menial jobs to help out. He found better pay doing impressions on the stand-up comedy circuit. His harmless, permanently smiling persona translated to roles in such films as *Peggy Sue Got Married* and the short-lived TV series *The Duck Factory*.

The earlier hard times, however, had instilled anger and an edge in Carrey that eventually came out. Mindful that his father had been fired from a seemingly safe job, Carrey tossed out the mainstream act that had him opening for Rodney Dangerfield. He replaced it with a caustic, manic persona who went onstage without a set routine and punished his audience until it responded—sometimes with laughter, sometimes with debris. Keenen Ivory Wayans saw the edge as a strong match for his envelope-pushing Fox sketch show *In Living Color* and made Carrey the lone white male cast member in 1990.

Carrey scored a surprise hit as *Ace Ventura: Pet Detective* and followed that with *The Mask* in 1994, another blockbuster, which instantly drove his price from $500,000 to $7 million a film. When Robin Williams vacillated on playing the Riddler in *Batman Forever*,

Carrey jumped into the green suit and had his first global hit. Next: a record $20 million to star in the 1996 film *The Cable Guy*.

Hardly content to be a rich guy who makes faces and talks out of his ass, Carrey rolled the dice again. His edgy *Cable Guy* villain darkened the film's tone enough to horrify studio execs (and audiences, who stayed away in droves). Still, the performance helped Carrey take a step toward serious films. In *The Truman Show* he played the unwitting star of a 24-hours-a-day reality TV show. Carrey then played quirky comic Andy Kaufman in *Man on the Moon*.

The problem: Those serious turns seriously underperformed at the box office. In fact, 2001's *The Majestic* was enough of a bomb for people to start writing Carrey's career epitaph. The death notices were shelved when Carrey put on his funny hat again and delivered last year's top-grossing comedy, *Bruce Almighty*. What's an ambitious megastar to do? For Carrey the answer is to take the serious route yet again in his new film, *Eternal Sunshine of the Spotless Mind*, a surreal drama about memory erasing that was written by Charlie Kaufman, architect of *Being John Malkovich* and *Adaptation*.

Michael Fleming sat down with Carrey just as he began working on the role of Count Olaf, signature villain in the film *Lemony Snicket's A Series of Unfortunate Events*, an adaptation of Daniel Handler's kidbook series. The twice-divorced (most recently from actress Lauren Holly), now single Carrey was clearly getting into character. He seemed tightly coiled, partly because he doesn't like doing interviews and partly because he had decided to explain certain aspects of his personal life that he'd never talked about before—and he wasn't sure how his fans might react.

PLAYBOY: You've been working around the clock on your new film, and you've just shaved your head. Are you feeling overwhelmed?

CARREY: Not today. I just came off the beach in Malibu, near my house. It was the most beautiful day, except for that inevitable paparazzi triangulation.

PLAYBOY: Your *Truman Show* character has no privacy. Now, with the paparazzi following you, the same has happened to you.

CARREY: This country is getting us ready for *The Truman Show*. It's happening. I feel a little scared and sad. They're slowly desensitizing us to where there's a video camera on every street corner. Shows on TV are getting more like, "Ha! What a stupid guy, that Joe Schmo or whoever he is."

PLAYBOY: *The Truman Show* seemed cautionary in 1998 but now seems prophetic. On *The Joe Schmo Show* everybody was an actor except the unaware contestant. *Joe Millionaire*'s contestants were duped into falling in love with a phony millionaire.

CARREY: It's all unbelievably cruel. I believe in making fun of things that deserve to be made fun of—lies, arrogance. These are things you want to rip down as a comedian. But when you take a guy who's a good-hearted human and you just go "Woo, woo, woo" behind his head, it's cruel.

PLAYBOY: Even though they gave him a hundred grand?

CARREY: A hundred grand means nothing. What are you buying—his humiliation and misery? It feels as if we're just desensitizing people to the point where it will be all right to take a baby and do whatever you want with it. Or to kill somebody on camera.

PLAYBOY: Meanwhile, celebrities get more and more coverage. How do you feel when you see an E! show consisting totally of people like yourself being stalked by the paparazzi?

CARREY: Unacceptable. Way over the edge, man. That channel is now eating its young.

PLAYBOY: What do you say when they ask for an interview?

CARREY: I don't do it.

PLAYBOY: What about the argument that it's the price of being rich and famous?

CARREY: I don't think that argument holds water. We should respect the people who entertain us and make us feel good—unless I'm acting like an idiot, which I'm not. I know they justify it in their heads, but it can't make them feel good. Unless they're drunk or stoned and completely fogging over their feelings, I know that in their private moments, when they're lying in bed staring at the ceiling, they can't feel good about it. Taking is taking and giving is giving. Period. There will be a reckoning in their lives.

PLAYBOY: What do you mean?

CARREY: There will be some kind of unexplainable disease, something that happens in your life that makes you go, "Why me?" And I'm here to tell you, it's because of the choices you made.

PLAYBOY: So you believe in karma?

CARREY: Absolutely, without a doubt. But this isn't karma; this is the truth eating you alive. You can justify things all you want, but every human being knows the truth. To follow someone around with your lens like a little sneak—it hurts your spirit on this planet.

PLAYBOY: Do you feel this strongly because you see yourself as a victim?

CARREY: I just feel it as a human being. I'm always looking at myself. I'm in no way perfect, but I'm always challenging myself to try to be better—in what I eat and what I read. I've always thought that a higher level is possible, and I'm always looking for it.

PLAYBOY: When you played a guy with a split personality in Me, Myself & Irene, advocacy groups complained that you belittled the mentally ill. Isn't everyone guilty of insensitivity, even you?

CARREY: I wasn't trying to be insensitive at all. To me it was like a cartoon. I don't want anybody to be hurt by what I do. If that in some way hurt somebody, I'd feel terrible. But it wasn't intentional. Maybe that's the difference: I was being funny.

PLAYBOY: Do you understand the appeal of E! and other celebrity coverage?

CARREY: I'm not completely innocent here. I've indulged in it too. I watch those shows sometimes, but I know it's a disease. It's leading us down the wrong road, man.

PLAYBOY: You've done more than watch these shows. Before Man on the Moon came out, the media reported that, in character as Andy Kaufman, you got into a fight with Andy's wrestling nemesis, Jerry Lawler. Wasn't that a calculated press stunt to boost awareness for a movie that needed visibility?

CARREY: I'm not really allowed to tell you what happened, so either way I'm screwed. I think an interesting by-product was seeing how little had to happen to put the media into high gear—helicopters flying over the building, top story across the country. I sat in a hotel room watching and said, "Andy lives."

PLAYBOY: You talk about the entertainment media as if it were pornography.

CARREY: I don't know what my attitude toward porn is. I've studied a lot of Taoism. It talks about trying to find a higher place and not wasting your sexual essence, how these Chinese guys live to be 120 because they don't waste their essence. They might have sex, but they don't waste it all the time. I guess if you're going to squander your chi, the pages of Playboy are as good a place as any.

PLAYBOY: Squander your chi?

CARREY: There's a quote for you: Go ahead and squander your chi. But I guarantee you heaven isn't in Miss March's pussy. Sure, it looks good; it feels good. I have nothing against it.

PLAYBOY: Wait—are you telling us you're celibate?

CARREY: Oh, no. I don't believe in that. I do believe in staying in balance. I'm not celibate, and I do masturbate. But not like a fiend. I believe in moderation. I think there's an energy source. It's like anything else: You can't eat cake all day long or you waste your energy. And you get gray, lose vitality. And I'm really good at sex.

PLAYBOY: You are?

CARREY: Nah, I just thought I'd put that out there.

PLAYBOY: If heaven isn't sex, where is it?

CARREY: Heaven is on the other side of that feeling you get when you're sitting on the couch and you get up and make a triple-decker sandwich. It's on the other side of that, when you *don't* make the sandwich. It's about sacrifice.

PLAYBOY: So it's about not indulging.

CARREY: It's about giving up the things that basically keep you from feeling. That's what I believe, anyway. I'm always asking, "What am I going to give up next?" Because I want to feel. It's been my drive since I was a little kid, actually.

PLAYBOY: Name something you gave up that gave you comfort.

CARREY: I don't eat wheat, I don't eat dairy, I don't smoke cigarettes, I don't smoke pot. All these things I've enjoyed. I live very sparingly.

PLAYBOY: It sounds a little monastic.

CARREY: It is, a little bit. But I'm an experiment, you know? That's how I see life. I'm not trying to put myself higher than anybody or anything like that. But I am my own experiment, and I love that. Physical health to me is my hobby. Psychology and spiritual life fascinate me to no end. When everybody wants to go to a rave, I like nothing better than to go home and read my books and say some prayers and meditate and try to break through. I'm always trying to break through.

PLAYBOY: For how long have you been abstaining from these creature comforts?

CARREY: I have been struggling to do it my entire life.

PLAYBOY: But you're a wealthy movie star—you're in a position to deny yourself comforts. Most people don't have that many comforts to begin with. They have overdue bills and abusive bosses.

CARREY: That's denial, man. That's like obese people lobbying to call their situation a disease. I don't believe it. God bless obese people, but they've got work to do.

PLAYBOY: So you've given up pot, too?

CARREY: I think people underestimate the power of things like marijuana, the addictive quality. It's not that the substance itself is addictive; it's the stimulation of the pleasure center of your brain. It becomes an easy way out, an instant vacation. That's addictive. I know people who have been stoned every day of their lives, for 50 years. They seem fine, but they are not getting to a higher level.

PLAYBOY: Like who?

CARREY: I hung out at the Comedy Store with Richard Pryor and people who struggled when they wanted to do it straight. I stood in a parking lot one night with Richard when he said, "I don't remember. I don't remember 40 years. I don't feel like I did it." And of course he did it. But that's the trick. You can do it without that stuff. You don't need it if creativity becomes your high.

PLAYBOY: You're telling us that when you're in your big house alone you don't sometimes think, Screw it, I'm going to eat a gallon of ice cream?

CARREY: I have moments. But mostly I stay on my thing. I might have one day a week when I go off and have a glass of wine. I'm not completely dogmatic. But I keep honing this thing, this experiment. I fear that 90 percent of people are going to look at this and think, He's turning into a head case. I'm not. This is about my not wanting anything halfway.

PLAYBOY: You must have splurged somewhere.

CARREY: I've never been really decadent. Honestly, I don't put a lot of onus on the things in my life. I have things. I try to keep my life fairly simple. I have a plane, and that's an incredible luxury. But it mainly saves me so much stress because I travel so much.

PLAYBOY: Your own plane? That's a big comfort. How does that save stress?

CARREY: Not having to deal with the airports and the paparazzi, all that is involved with an airport. It's a worthwhile investment in my peace of mind. I'm all about keeping myself in a healthy place so that I can go the duration, man. I want to make it to 120 years old. I've got a date to run a 10k on the Great Wall of China when I'm 90.

PLAYBOY: Some people might say that this is just a fad—that during the next round of interviews for a movie you'll be pounding a Big Mac and supersizing.

CARREY: Or drunk at the Oscars, holding my genitals? I'd never say never, but if I was doing that at McDonald's, I'd just get back on my thing. I always have. Each time I go off and have one of those moments, it's a shorter span of time before I get back on my game. I don't promise anybody that I'm perfect. This is just my experiment.

PLAYBOY: Do your friends think, Gosh, Jim, you're not as much fun to hang with since you've turned into this Amish guy?

CARREY: I'm not as much fun for somebody who just wants to get wasted. I'm too confrontational to be around. But I don't judge people. You want to get wasted? I'll pass it to you. Here you go. You're your own judge. I don't want to judge anybody.

PLAYBOY: You came up alongside comics who became stars and were overcome by excess. After John Belushi became a movie star, people around him wouldn't let him have a bad moment even if it meant feeding him drugs.

CARREY: That's bullshit. It was his fault. John Belushi was a strong-willed motherfucker who'd kick your ass if you told him how to live. This is the mistake people make. Why couldn't someone talk to Elvis? Well, good luck. You were out the door if you did. It's this habit we have of shirking our responsibility to ourselves.

PLAYBOY: Many comics, such as Sam Kinison, seemed to work best when they were standing on the edge of a precipice.

CARREY: Sam was in total denial. He created a beast he couldn't get away from. I'm not saying that's ultimately what happened to him. But I know his struggle. He was always going back and forth. He'd come up to me and go, "Hey, Jim! We're drug-free Christians, man." We'd laugh because I was always trying to be straight and healthy. Then he'd go on *Howard Stern*, and Howard would say, "You know, you're not funny when you're not stoned." And he'd be right back doing it again. And this is the trouble—when you create the beast, you've got to *be* the beast, you know? I've got enough of a beast in me, man.

PLAYBOY: You are a perfectionist. Does this come at a high personal cost?

CARREY: Sometimes I hate it. Sometimes I don't want to do it. Especially things like this. I twist for three days before I sit down and talk to somebody like you. How do I try to speak my truth in an interview like this, to describe this trip that I'm on, without coming off like a self-important asshole?

PLAYBOY: You just say what's on your mind and take your chances. People will respond, or they won't.

CARREY: I'm trying to make sure that I'm a lion who likes to act like a monkey and not a monkey who likes to act like a lion. Don't ask me to explain it.

PLAYBOY: You shaved your head for *Lemony Snicket*. Why not put on a skin wig?

CARREY: I don't mind being a bit of a freak while I'm doing a movie. It gives me an excuse. It keeps life interesting. It scares me a little bit sometimes, because it puts me in a certain place that bangs up against where I want to be in my life spiritually. When you try to live a good life, one of the things you don't concentrate on is "How will I be self-loathing today? How will I hate God's creation?"

PLAYBOY: Did taking on the roles of Andy Kaufman and his alter ego, Tony Clifton, take a toll?

CARREY: Oddly enough, that one energized me. I was so lost in that character that I wasn't myself. I looked at it like this: Let's not be an actor doing Andy Kaufman's life story. Let's be Andy Kaufman coming back from the dead to do his life story. When I came out of it, it was as if I'd had a vacation from being Jim Carrey. I didn't think as I think, I didn't act as I act, I didn't make choices as Jim Carrey. I had gone off the planet. It was probably how you feel when you die—you just go, "Ahhh, what a rest."

PLAYBOY: It's remarkable that you could lose yourself so completely.

CARREY: It was actually spooky at the end. I had to sit for about three weeks and ask, "What do I believe again?" I lost track of my own likes and dislikes. I do know that it's possible to program your brain. It really is. I've done it my whole life. Everything I have is because of a constant kind of brainwashing that I've done to myself.

PLAYBOY: You have been prescient. You wrote a postdated $10 million check to yourself when you were poor, and when the date came up you had the money to cover it. You told yourself you were going to be one of the five biggest actors in Hollywood, that every major director would someday want to work with you.

CARREY: *Is* working with me.

PLAYBOY: So you consider this approach to be pretty successful?

CARREY: The whole thing is all good brainwashing. Not "I'm going to do this," but rather "I *am* doing this." I've always said it in the present moment, as if it already exists. I may not be connected to it yet, but it exists. When people ask me about an Oscar, I try to be polite about it. But I've already won it. In my head I've won Best Actor.

PLAYBOY: For which role?

CARREY: I don't know what the role is. I want that to surprise me. I'm not being arrogant. I don't have some sense of entitlement. It's just that I've experienced it already. I just work this way.

PLAYBOY: Does that block out fear?

CARREY: It just seems to program the computer. If it's God's will as well, then it'll happen and connect with my thought. If it's not, it won't.

PLAYBOY: What goals are you programming now?

CARREY: I have four more things in my wallet right now.

PLAYBOY: What are they?

CARREY: I can't tell you.

PLAYBOY: Come on, give us one.

CARREY: No. That's between me and God.

PLAYBOY: Are they professional or personal?

CARREY: They're career things, they're life things, they're spiritual things— they're everything.

PLAYBOY: You're not gearing for a run for governor of California, are you?

CARREY: Let's hope not. No, everybody would be in a lot of trouble if I did. I may do it in the movies, just so I can say what I need to say.

PLAYBOY: You come from Canada but have talked about becoming a dual citizen so you can vote.

CARREY: I'm in the process.

PLAYBOY: Would you have voted for Arnold Schwarzenegger?

CARREY: I like Arnold. I have no idea how qualified he is. The whole power of celebrity in this country scares me, the idea that we trust this guy and feel we know him because he's in a movie. If he mentions his frigging movies one more time in one of his speeches, I'm going to vomit. Dude, you're a politician now—speak about the issues. There is something dark and evil going on in the Republican Party that's just too frightening to get into.

PLAYBOY: Care to elaborate?

CARREY: I love this country. I came here from Canada with huge dreams, and America gave me everything I ever imagined and more. But I think we're in a lot of trouble. There's a lot of stuff that's going to hurt us. We might wake up one day and go, "Wait, *we're* the bad guy?" We've got to be careful.

PLAYBOY: You mean the invasion of Iraq?

CARREY: I mean everything. Our business overseas. How we treat each other. Insensitivity to people, to other races and countries. God knows I feel for our soldiers. It breaks my heart that people are dying, and I appreciate that they protect us. But I wonder how far that $87 billion might have gone in showing goodwill to the rest of the world had we taken it and said, "How can we help you?" We might have won the hearts and minds of the Arab people.

I just hope Bush and those behind him have their hearts in the right place. We're there now. We have to see it through. If their hearts aren't in the right place and this is about oil, there's no bunker thick enough or deep enough to get away from God's bunker buster. I also believe we should stop writing cute messages on bombs. It isn't funny—it's cruel, and it doesn't do the soldiers any good. If we're going to write anything on a bomb, it should be "God bless whoever this lands on and may God forgive us all, on both sides."

PLAYBOY: Let's change the subject. When you started out as a stand-up comic, what was your goal?

CARREY: When I started I wanted to please my mom and dad.

PLAYBOY: Yet you abruptly scrapped your mainstream act as an impressionist and replaced it with something much edgier and more unpredictable.

CARREY: Oh, I'd have a war with the audience some nights. I'd go to war.

PLAYBOY: Why?

CARREY: I just felt like it was my mood at the time and it was dishonest to give them anything else. So I would go to the Comedy Store and pull the guns out and start firing.

PLAYBOY: Did you have a plan when you took the stage?

CARREY: Sometimes I had no plan at all. I went up six months in a row and told myself that I wouldn't repeat a word I'd said the night before. Every night was like death. I was bleeding with sweat before I'd go onstage, because I wouldn't allow myself to repeat a joke or a line. I went up there with nothing.

PLAYBOY: What was the reaction?

CARREY: The comics thought it was incredible. They were all lined up at the back of the room going, "Do you know what he's doing?" Kinison would say, "You're not going to save any of that shit, man? That was funny shit." And I'd go, "Nope. Not gonna do it." It was brutal, and two thirds of the time it was absolute shit. I got chairs thrown at me, and I got in fights.

PLAYBOY: You had the added pressure of supporting your parents and siblings. That must have been tough.

CARREY: Well, yeah. It was hard when I threw my impression act out completely.

PLAYBOY: Why do it then?

CARREY: Because when you juggle for five minutes, they call you a juggler. That's it. Now, since I've developed other things, I can bring an impression back—in *Bruce Almighty* I do Clint Eastwood. It's fun, but it's not who I am.

PLAYBOY: Who guided you when you made that transition?

CARREY: My dad was really instrumental in the creative decisions I made. He was a jazzman, an orchestra leader.

PLAYBOY: Your father was also an accountant who lost his job. Did that show you the downside of playing it safe?

CARREY: For him it was a combination of fear and responsibility. He was a very, very good man. But I used to think my dad was a coward.

PLAYBOY: Why?

CARREY: Because he was such a nice guy to everybody, and he got run over in life. He got fired when he was 50, and no one wanted him anymore. He was always the guy who would give you the shirt off his back, and I used to look at that and go, "That's not honest. It's not entirely honest to be the nice guy all the time."

PLAYBOY: Did you ever say that to him?

CARREY: Not really, no. It was who he was. He loved people and showed me nothing but love, and I could never look at that in a bad way. But you learn from your parents. What I learned was not just to give everybody everything they want. They don't know what they want. And they'll eat you up and spit you out without even meaning to.

PLAYBOY: What's the alternative?

CARREY: If I got into a place where I felt pigeonholed, I would do the opposite until everyone forgot what I used to do. That came from seeing how it turns out when you pander to people. You're asking to be kicked in the teeth.

PLAYBOY: You first made good money doing impressions as Rodney Dangerfield's opening act. Audiences liked you.

CARREY: I saw where it was going. I saw it leading to Vegas and opening for people. Or if you're Rich Little, you become the Impressionist Guy. God bless him, but it was not good for me. This soul is too big to be housed by that.

PLAYBOY: Dangerfield took you under his wing. What did you learn from him?

CARREY: More than anything, he supported my creative whims. When I stopped doing impressions and started spiking my hair and doing weird things, he still hired me. He'd stand off to the side and laugh, and when I came off he'd say, "Man, those people think you're from another fucking planet." He's an incredible character. And he treated my father like gold, which was very important to me.

PLAYBOY: You've drawn clear lines about not discussing whom you date. Did you get burned?

CARREY: You do learn that if you're telling the truth it's going to piss somebody off. But the press knows. They know that the celebrities who stand in front of the paparazzi are, you know, half going, "Just be cool. It's okay. This serves a purpose. It gets the publicity out," and half going, "These are the fucking people who follow me around! What am I doing?"

PLAYBOY: The attention defines some entertainers.

CARREY: Yeah, there definitely are people out there who would do anything to get some publicity. I'm not qualified to speak for everybody. I'm kind of in rarified air. The main thing is, I just don't believe in meanness.

PLAYBOY: Comedy is sometimes mean.

CARREY: Sometimes I trip into it as a comic, but I have trouble reconciling that, too. Try to find a comic who isn't angry when he's 70. Why is George Carlin pissed off? He's brilliant. But the man is so angry it's getting unnerving. It's like he practically doesn't want to live on this planet anymore. I try to understand why that's happening, because I don't want that. I want to be a loving human being. I want to look at the world with joy and gratitude and see the things that are good about life.

PLAYBOY: Your newest movie is *Eternal Sunshine of the Spotless Mind*, which is about a couple who have their relationship erased from their brains. Why did you do it?

CARREY: What drew me is the idea that everybody has someone they'd rather erase: "Gosh, if I could just suck that out of my brain and my heart and never deal with it again, it'd be fantastic." Everybody identifies with that, has some relationship that hurts so bad that they just wish they could make the ghosts go away. You can't, of course.

PLAYBOY: The hardships you and your family endured after your father lost his job have been well chronicled. Would you erase that pain?

CARREY: Well, there was only one time when I felt something really horrible was going on. That was when we were all doing the job at Titan Wheels [a tire manufacturer]. The whole family was working. My dad was doing the night shift, and I was doing afternoons and going to school in the daytime. I saw it changing us, making us hateful and bigoted. I empathize with kids who go to school and can't understand or don't want to understand what the teacher is saying. I was so angry then, I just wanted to bash someone's head in.

PLAYBOY: Seriously?

CARREY: Yeah. I used to carry a bat on my cleaning cart. This factory was half Jamaican and half Indian—you know, Sikhs. Everybody had daggers and knives, and it was like a race war going on. I was in the middle of it.

PLAYBOY: What did they do to make you so angry?

CARREY: They'd taunt me. They'd pile their chicken bones two feet high in the corner of the cafeteria because they knew I'd have to clean it up. Or they'd take a shit in the sink. Constantly trying to push my buttons to the point where I walked around with a cleaning cart and a baseball bat, just waiting for my opportunity to crack a skull. It was bad. I wanted to hurt somebody. I was caught up in anger. So I get how that feels. I understand.

PLAYBOY: Would you be who you are now without those experiences?

CARREY: It definitely gave me an edge. And I don't think anybody is interesting on-screen unless they have an edge of some kind. There's a reason Russell Crowe is popular, besides being an excellent actor. The guy is an edgy dude. And all of us kind of live vicariously through guys who can bust some heads for us. I think an edge is interesting to watch. To have that, you've got to risk.

PLAYBOY: In Living Color gave you your start, but it wasn't Saturday Night Live. Would you rather have done SNL?

CARREY: I never made it in the normal way everybody makes it. I tried out for Saturday Night Live. The day I auditioned I went over to NBC, and as I'm getting ready I'm going, "Am I meant to do this?" I got out of my car, and an NBC page was standing on the ledge on the 10th floor of the NBC building, trying to work up the nerve to kill himself. And I just went, "This isn't going to happen. This is not going to happen today." Because I read the universe all the time and generally get my answers real quick.

PLAYBOY: That could be taken as some kind of sign.

CARREY: Yeah, and all these news crews were coming out of the building. And this guy was shuffling toward the edge, trying to decide whether to kill himself or not.

PLAYBOY: Did he?

CARREY: I don't know. I never heard. I went in. So the whole time I was in there I was thinking, Is he dead? Did he die? But I never watched the news. I forgot about it. That's how desensitized I was. It was all about whether I was getting on the show or not.

PLAYBOY: On In Living Color you were known as the white guy. Did you have any idea who'd be the biggest success? Surely it wasn't going to be the Fly Girl named Jennifer Lopez.

CARREY: God bless her, man. She went for it. That's a driven woman. Unbelievable how well she has done. Incredible. But she's paying for it big-time, too. I didn't really have any notions about it, honestly. Sometimes I'd talk with Damon Wayans, who by year three had started getting opportunities and was on the way out of the show. He was tired a lot of the time, and I'd say to him, "But this is it, man! We made it already." I was aware that this was a rung on the ladder, but I wanted to enjoy it. What if it wasn't? What if this was as high as I was going? So I worked it to the very last show. Probably a little desperately.

PLAYBOY: You've convincingly beaten the crap out of yourself in *Liar Liar* and *Me, Myself & Irene*. Does it hurt?

CARREY: I hurt myself on *Me, Myself & Irene*. I'd sprained my ankle during rehearsals in the scene where Renée kicks me in the mouth and sends me over the fence. So for the rest of the film, when I'm running after the car, jumping on the car and doing all this stuff—it's all with a sprained ankle. I still have scarring on my bones. I don't generally hurt myself that much, but there were a lot of bumps and bruises on that movie. And I was in hell in that Grinch costume, too. It was like knives were stuck in my eyes.

PLAYBOY: Because of the thick, colored contact lenses?

CARREY: Yes. It was just the worst situation comfortwise you could possibly imagine. But still, when they said "Action!" I was free, you know? There's something about that suspended life moment. When they say "Action!" I'm free.

PLAYBOY: You grew up loving Jimmy Stewart and played a role he would have taken in *The Majestic*. It didn't do well.

CARREY: It was a beautiful movie. I think what it missed was some humor. If you're going to do a hats-off to Frank Capra, you've got to have the part when the gymnasium floor opens up and everybody falls in the pool and he's stepping on her robe and she's naked, jumping behind a bush. This film took itself a little too seriously. Too sentimental. It's odd when people go, "Well, how do you feel that this failed?" I never see it as failure. How can it be? This was 500 people working for four months. We turned on a town and gave them significance. I learned to be a better actor and met Martin Landau. Andy Kaufman? A frigging triumph! I don't think it was meant to do a lot of business, because Andy didn't do a lot of business. We were true to him and polarized the same people.

PLAYBOY: What about *The Cable Guy*?

CARREY: Huge success! It has become this weird cult movie. So much focus was put on the money I made, and people came gunning for it. It's not Shakespeare, but there's some funny shit in that movie, man. It was dark. The mistake the movie company made was to tell people it wasn't dark. The audience got surprised. It's a dark, psychological, in-your-face comedy. I felt I'd done something fairly brave and that we had huge laughs doing it.

PLAYBOY: You aren't big on sequels. Did it bother you when New Line cast a look-alike for *Dumb and Dumberer*, a widely panned *Dumb and Dumber* prequel?

CARREY: Yes, it did. It was an odd kind of compliment and an odd, creepy thing to do, to dress somebody up and try to pass him off as me. That shouldn't happen until you're dead, right? I felt for that guy. He did a good impression.

PLAYBOY: Would you coax your 16-year-old daughter to go into show business?

CARREY: No one coaxed would ever fucking make it. If she has a burning desire beyond belief to make it in this business, she'll do it. No one can make it otherwise. No way. There are too many fucking humiliating things. She's going to be accused of nepotism. But she has talent, and that will prove her or not prove her. She's really a smart girl with a beautiful voice. She'll make it if she commits.

PLAYBOY: Having been forced to leave school for financial reasons, are you a stickler about her getting a degree?

CARREY: I want her to. I feel there's some kind of solace that comes with finishing things. I don't think about it so much anymore. I left halfway through 10th grade, but I read and I have a hunger for information and knowledge. Psychology has always fascinated me. One reason I love acting is that you always have to figure out where a character came from, what his parents did to him, what happened here. It's like being a psychologist of some sort.

PLAYBOY: You've been married twice; now you live alone. Do you miss having somebody around?

CARREY: It's less about that than about wanting to be real with somebody. I want to love somebody without walking around in a secret turmoil and feeling like I've been made to be something I'm not. Somebody I can be nakedly honest with—that's who is going to win my love.

PLAYBOY: Given your current level of fame, how do you date a woman and know if she's responding to you and not to your stardom?

CARREY: Sooner or later the monster shows its face.

PLAYBOY: How do you know?

CARREY: I think we're all innately psychic. We're like dogs, man. We smell it. Sometimes we deny it, but we know it. We know when somebody loves us because they love us. I'm pretty sharp.

PLAYBOY: Do you still go into relationships with an open mind, or are you cynical?

CARREY: The scariest thing for me is to change my mind and possibly hurt somebody. I don't think about *being* hurt as much as I think about possibly waking up one day and wanting something else and hurting that person. That's the fear, I guess. I want to have a lifelong love; I just don't know if that's real anymore.

PLAYBOY: Maybe you'd be a better husband now because you are less needy.

CARREY: I wasn't needy. I was perhaps not as tolerant as I could be. Perhaps I just picked people who were not good candidates to begin with, who weren't necessarily a good match.

PLAYBOY: Given your spirituality and your desire for dramatic roles, are you still a comic at heart?

CARREY: It is difficult because I've trained myself to be this comedic mind. That entails looking at something and deciding what's funny about it. What's funny about anything is what's wrong with it. So you're judging what's wrong with something or someone all the time, every day of your life. Down the line, that's got to take a toll. You can't end up being a happy guy if you spend every minute of your life going, "President Bush—what a fucker!" You may think that from time to time—and I certainly do—but I also don't believe that he necessarily thinks he's doing something wrong. Some people can look at life and go, "That's the beautiful thing, that's the beautiful thing. Hey, there's a beautiful thing." And that's where I'm trying to put myself.

 January 1982

GEORGE CARLIN

A candid conversation with the brilliant—and still rebellious— comedian about his new life after years of inactivity and a crippling cocaine habit

It began in 1970 on a typical September night in Las Vegas, as the early show went on at Howard Hughes's Frontier Hotel. The men and the mink-draped women in the theater appeared equally prosperous and provincial. A sign at the theater entrance read, Welcome, Award-Winning Salesmen.

The opening act that night was a 32-year-old comedian named George Carlin. Although most had never heard of him, a few members of the audience remembered seeing him on John Davidson's summer replacement TV series—a conventional stand-up performer who did cute voices and jokes about his New York childhood. Vegas regulars knew Carlin better: He'd been an opening act at the Frontier for three years, was a reliable pro who earned $12,500 a week.

On that night, when Carlin glared out at the audience with what appeared to be a combination of loathing and resolve, most people either didn't notice or thought he'd forgotten his contact lenses. When he opened with a dissertation on the number of ways to say "Shit," the audience fell silent. Carlin's next routine was about Vietnam, and that's when people started walking out. Before he'd finished a piece on American business ethics, half the room was empty and the others remained only to heckle him. At a few tables, angry men were restrained from rushing the stage.

In one night, the big-money, mainstream–show business career Carlin had worked 10 years to build was over. He went back to where he'd started—to the small clubs and coffeehouses, working for nothing; and with the help of unemployment compensation, he did the routines that had gotten him thrown out of Las Vegas. But the folk and college audiences loved them. Carlin's dazzling wordplay was lauded by critics, who compared him to H. L. Mencken and Alexander Woollcott, and his withering attacks on religion, big business and the Vietnam war made him a counterculture hero. Between 1971 and 1976, Carlin toured constantly and recorded five albums.

Then, as suddenly as his meteoric "second career" had begun, it ended. At the height of his popularity and income, Carlin took himself out of action. For the next five years, except for an occasional stint as guest host of *The Tonight Show*—where he'd appear competent but uncomfortable—Carlin left his public wondering what had happened. There were rumors of a drug problem and personal problems; a couple of years ago, word began circulating that he had suffered a heart attack.

But in November 1981, a brand-new Carlin album—his first in seven years—was released, quickly followed by the announcement that he had signed a multiyear cable-TV contract with Home Box Office and was writing a book and a movie. As abruptly and mysteriously as he'd disappeared, he returned.

Carlin was born in New York City in 1937 and when he was two months old, his parents separated. He was raised by a working mother, by the other street kids in his "white Harlem" neighborhood, by New York's parochial school system and by the radio. At the age of five, he decided to become a radio announcer, a comedian and an actor.

Always a "discipline problem," Carlin quit high school to join the Air Force, where he was court-martialed twice and eventually discharged 11 months early. But by then he'd become a disc jockey at an off-base radio station, and the long-range career plan he had laid out for himself at the age of five was begun.

In 1960, Carlin teamed with a young newscaster named Jack Burns and began doing a comedy act at small clubs and folk rooms. Within months, Burns and Carlin were "discovered" by Lenny Bruce and Mort Sahl. Although the team broke up in 1962, Carlin's career continued its ascent. By the late 1960s, he'd appeared on many TV shows, co-starred in a network show and had established himself as one of the top opening acts in Las Vegas. Unknown to Carlin throughout this "straight comic" period was a prediction made by Bruce: George Carlin would one day assume Bruce's throne as king of the social comics.

Then, on that September night in Las Vegas, Carlin abandoned the straight comedy he did so well, but no longer believed in, and finally made good on Bruce's prophecy. And, ironically, that change made him even more successful than he'd been before. But there were problems, most of them stemming from Carlin's obsessive involvement with cocaine. Finally, in 1976, with his 15-year marriage, his 13-year-old daughter and his own 25-year history of drug abuse closing in on him, Carlin, for the second time in his life, reined in a galloping career that had somehow gotten away from him.

Years of therapy followed. Then a heart attack. Finally, at the age of 44, Carlin emerged straight and sober, with his health and family intact. We sent New York journalist Sam Merrill (whose previous *Playboy Interviews* have included those with Ed Asner, Roy Scheider, Karl Hess, Joseph Heller and Roone Arledge) to visit Carlin as he prepared to launch what he himself has called his "third career." Merrill reports:

"The electronic gates of Carlin's Brentwood home swung back and I cruised up the driveway. Numerous dogs and cats—each with its own unique and somewhat bizarre charm, none a purebred—wandered past. There were three cars in the driveway: Carlin's BMW, his wife's Mercedes and a 1948 Plymouth, an old bomb. Behind the cars, Carlin was shooting baskets. I pointed to the Plymouth and asked if he were a collector. 'Naw, some guy left it here last spring and hasn't been back since.'

"After shooting a few hoops together, we entered his office—a small building between the house and the garage—pulled up a couple of chairs and, before I could ask my first question, Carlin said, 'I've been thinking about this interview and, I don't know, I'm afraid I'm not going to have very much to say.'

"He was right in one sense—Carlin rarely tells biographical anecdotes for their own sake. He is much more interested in what he is thinking than in what he is doing; the events of his life are related only as background to his impressions and opinions. But he is a man with a carefully thought-out opinion on almost everything. So instead of a biography, what emerged was a complex and often comical internal monolog in the voice of the Carlin character speaking. Every time he related his own thoughts, he did so in the voice of the side of himself dominant at that moment: the Irish street kid, the ludicrously self-important performer, the dope fiend, the wide-eyed observer of life. It all poured out with incredible ease. Although most *Playboy Interview* subjects find it helpful to vary the scenery from one session to another, Carlin and I did seven sessions over two weeks totaling 15 hours of tape in those same two chairs. It's the interior landscape that interests him, and his windows to that panorama are always open."

PLAYBOY: Back in the early 1960s, when you were still a disc jockey and just beginning to do comedy in small clubs, Lenny Bruce supposedly selected you as his heir—

CARLIN: Apparently, Lenny told that to a lot of people. But he never said it to me and I didn't hear it until years later. Which is probably fortunate. It's difficult enough for a young person to put his soul on the line in front of a lot of drunken people without having *that* hanging over his head, too.

PLAYBOY: Because of what Bruce said about you, are you now overly sensitive about being compared to him?

CARLIN: Yes, and those comparisons are unfair to both of us. Look, I was a fan of Lenny's. He made me laugh, sure, but more often he made me say, "Fuckin' A; why didn't I think of that?" He opened up channels in my head. His genius was the unique ability to investigate hypocrisy and expose social inequities in a street rap that was really a form of poetry. I believe myself to be a worthwhile and inventive performer in my own right. But I'm not in a league with Lenny, certainly not in terms of social commentary. So when people give me this bullshit, "Well, I guess you're sort of . . . uh . . . imitating Lenny Bruce," I just say, "Oh, fuck. I don't want to hear it." I want to be known for what I do best.

PLAYBOY: Nevertheless, throughout the early to mid-1970s, with a five-year run of albums and packed auditoriums for an act that viciously ridiculed every nook and cranny of "the establishment," you really did seem to be fulfilling Lenny's prophecy. Then it stopped abruptly about five years ago. No more albums; no more college tours. Why?

CARLIN: I've just now completed a five-year period that can perhaps best be called a breathing spell. A time of getting my health back and gathering my strength. That time also included incredible cocaine abuse, a heart attack and my wife's recovery from both alcoholism and cocaine abuse.

PLAYBOY: It's comforting to hear you talk about that breathing spell in the past tense.

CARLIN: My wife, Brenda, and I are both clean and sober now. I've been doing a lot of writing. By the time this interview appears, my first album in seven years will be out. I'm also working on a series of Home Box Office specials, a book and a motion picture. It's the American view that everything has to keep climbing: productivity, profits, even comedy. No time for reflection. No time to contract before another expansion. No time to grow up. No time to fuck up. No time to learn from your mistakes. But that notion goes against nature, which is cyclical. And I hope I'm now beginning a new cycle of energy and creativity. If so, it'll really be my third career. The first was as a straight comic in the 1960s. The second was as a counterculture performer in the 1970s. The third will be . . . well, that's for others to judge.

PLAYBOY: When and how did you get into drugs?

CARLIN: In my neighborhood—West 121st Street in New York, "white Harlem"—there were only two drugs: smack and marijuana. By the time I was 13, some friends and I were using marijuana fairly regularly. The *Reefer Madness* myth was still very strong then, but I'd been into jazz and those lyrics included so many casual references to pot that it was completely demystified for me. Heroin, forget it. In my neighborhood, I could see what heroin did firsthand and I was definitely afraid of that number.

PLAYBOY: How do you define fairly regular marijuana use?

CARLIN: Oh, I was a stonehead for 30 years. I'd wake up in the morning and if I couldn't decide whether I wanted a joint or not, I'd smoke a joint to figure it out. And I stayed high all day long. When people asked me, "Do you get high to go onstage?" I could never understand the question. I mean, I'd been high since eight that morning. Going onstage had nothing to do with it.

PLAYBOY: Are you still a stonehead?

CARLIN: To my surprise, my marijuana use has been tapering off steadily. As we speak, I haven't had a joint in two months.

PLAYBOY: You imply that this has been an unplanned withdrawal.

CARLIN: Completely. The enjoyment has been diminishing. Now, there's no question that it's sort of fun to get high. Let's say I had a little baggie lying around the office. I'd get up, come over here, fuck around, shuffle a few papers, and all the while I'd be thinking about that pot. I'd say to myself, "Well, whatever I'm going to do today, it's obviously going to be more fun if I have a hit or two." But I got to the point where taking those hits made me feel dumber than I'd felt before. I'd say to myself, "Man, you've been high for fucking 30 years and you don't want to be high anymore." [*Laughs*] I always have these little internal monologs. You'll get used to them. . . . I simply decided that dope wasn't worth the ritual.

PLAYBOY: So you were one of those ritualistic dopers.

CARLIN: The ritual was very important to me: cleaning the pot, rolling the pot—I was never a pipe or bong man. That's California stuff. I was an Eastern roller. My daughter had to teach me to use a water pipe, and I'd still fuck it up every time. To me, smoking pot meant sitting with a newspaper on my legs, rolling the seeds down, pulling the twigs out and finally producing a perfectly cylindrical, absolutely wonderful joint that you either locked at both ends or pinched off, or pinched at one end and left open at the other.

PLAYBOY: What was your technique?

CARLIN: We always locked in the East. I got to be a pincher later on.

PLAYBOY: Do you now find yourself lecturing others on the joys of sobriety?

CARLIN: No, never. I don't want anyone who reads this to think it's a message to him. It's not. This is merely an accounting of what I have done.

PLAYBOY: Would it be fair to say that you're not sorry about your 30 years as a pothead but you're glad they're over?

CARLIN: Exactly. Grass probably helped me as much as it hurt me. Especially as a performer. When you're high, it's easy to kid yourself about how clever certain mediocre pieces of material are. But, on the other hand, pot opens windows and doors that you may not be able to get through any other way. Being a very bound-up, Irish Catholic tight-assholed person, I've often thought that whatever negative effects pot had on me, it probably saved me from being an alcoholic and a complete fucking brainless idiot by the time I was 25. So I'd say pot has been a break-even proposition for me.

PLAYBOY: Did you ever get into hallucinogens?

CARLIN: I did LSD and peyote in the late 1960s, before I got into cocaine. That was concurrent with my change from a straight comic to the album and counterculture period, and those drugs served their purpose. They helped open me up. You know, if a drug has anything going for it at all, it should be self-limiting. It should tell you when you've had enough. Acid and peyote were that way for me. Cocaine was different. It kept saying, "You *haven't* had enough." I became an abuser almost instantly.

PLAYBOY: Specifically, what was your pattern of cocaine abuse?

CARLIN: I'd go on runs, four and five days without sleep. Then I'd crash and sleep about 18 hours a day for seven to 10 days. Then it would take a few more weeks to get over a vague sort of depression. Then I'd be off on another run.

PLAYBOY: How did those runs start?

CARLIN: They began the moment I scored. I'd take a few hits at the guy's house. Then I'd take a few more hits. Then I'd put it away. But before I left his house, I'd take some more hits. And when I'd get in my car, before backing out of the driveway, I'd open it up again and take a few more hits. Then, while driving home, I'd somehow contrive to stop and go to the bathroom and take a few more hits. Later on, when it got *really* ridiculous, I used to snort in traffic.

PLAYBOY: While the car was moving?

CARLIN: Yeah. And the moment I copped, I immediately wrote off that night's sleep, because it was a foregone conclusion that I was not going to put half a gram away at midnight. And I never took reds or Quaaludes to balance out the coke. So when it got to be four in the morning and the gram was three quarters gone, I'd start wishing it was nine o'clock and hoping the guy got up early. But, of course, he didn't sleep either, so there was no sweat. During all those years, I was always looking forward to the next snort or the next guy I could score from.

PLAYBOY: You mentioned the fact that Brenda was also a cocaine abuser. How did that mutual interest affect your relationship?

CARLIN: The effect of the coke on our relationship was very sick. Now that it's over, those were actually funny times. Looking for each other's coke, hiding it, finding it, doing some, not telling the other. Then fighting over it.

PLAYBOY: You actually stole coke from each other?

CARLIN: It was the typical paranoid experience. As soon as I knew my hiding place, I thought the whole world knew it. I'd write clues to my hiding places in code, then forget the code and spend the rest of the day looking for my coke.

PLAYBOY: Along with the paranoia, many cocaine users experience a heightened compulsiveness.

CARLIN: Oh, yeah. Sometimes, when I was really loaded, I'd sit on the floor and sort out every nut and bolt in the house. It was just sheer insanity. And often there'd be speed in the cut, so I was a speed freak, too. There are an awful lot of things in the cut of street drugs that eventually make you sick. I reached a point where the skin around the edges of my fingernails used to hurt all the time. And it would peel away easily. Now, that must have been from some poison in the cut.

PLAYBOY: Yet you continued to go on those incredible runs. Why?

CARLIN: It was just a compulsion. In fact, I soon realized that the only thing I really enjoyed was the actual snorting.

PLAYBOY: You mean the initial rush?

CARLIN: No, the act of it. Putting out the line. Inhaling it. That seemed to be what I was looking for.

PLAYBOY: That ritual again.

CARLIN: Exactly. After every hit, I'd look at myself in the mirror and say, "You stupid motherfucker. You asshole." And then I'd reach for it again, because it was more fun to snort it than to be high. It was an adventure to find a bar I could go into and use the bathroom. To take it out of my sock and chop it up without anybody's hearing. The secretiveness. The stealth. Those were obviously the aspects of cocaine use I was addicted to.

PLAYBOY: Were you able to function socially during those periods?

CARLIN: I couldn't even get through a conversation without saying to myself, "How can I get away from this motherfucker and go do me some coke?" I was always saying things like, "Excuse me, but I still have those loose bowels. I'll be right back." Fortunately, along with the speed, there's usually a lot of laxative in the cut, so I was able to say that with some conviction.

PLAYBOY: Did the coke affect your performances?

CARLIN: Two things happened. The creative side of my career was harmed. When I'd sit down and write under the influence of coke, the ratio of pages kept to pages thrown out declined drastically. But onstage, when rapping about a feeling I already owned, I would sometimes get a burst of eloquence. For an entertainer, part of the thing you do is just style. And the coke did help me get into great runs of pure form. But when I listen to those tapes now, the real cocaine shows; there's just nothing special about their content.

PLAYBOY: Were any of your albums recorded during a heavy cocaine run?

CARLIN: The *Class Clown* album was done totally sober. I'd realized what a hell I'd made for myself and I cleaned up completely for three months. You can hear the clarity of my thinking and of my speech on that album. But by the next one, *Occupation: Foole*, I was right back into the trip again. I'm more frantic, more breathless. You can hear how sick I am. If you want to see a cokehead, just look at the pictures on the *Occupation:*

Foole album. The angles of my body show you an awful lot. I started doing coke to feel open, but by that time, the hole had opened so wide that I'd fallen through. The body language in those photos tells you everything.

PLAYBOY: You're talking about astonishing quantities of a very expensive drug. Especially with both you and Brenda abusing it so heavily. How much money did you spend on coke during those years?

CARLIN: I never knew or cared. Of course, it was a lot. A fortune. But when I hear people tell me exactly how much they spend on coke, I think, Shit, man. They care more about the money than the drug. I was making a lot of money then. One hundred, maybe 110 dates a year at $10,000 a date, plus the albums. The money was sailing in and sailing out and somehow it all just about worked. But in terms of coke, the only money I ever thought about was that dollar bill I had stuck up my nose.

PLAYBOY: How did it end?

CARLIN: It ended suddenly for Brenda, more slowly for me. My runs began getting shorter and less pleasurable. I'd feel bad after only one day, or only a few hours, instead of four or five days. And I began to want to stop. One of the proudest moments of my life was at a rock-and-roll theater in New Jersey. A guy actually put some coke under my nose and I was able to say, "No, thanks," and turn my head away. I still had periods after that when I slipped back a little, but when that happened, I knew something inside me had taken hold. I was going to get well.

PLAYBOY: And for Brenda?

CARLIN: Because she had a drinking problem along with the coke, she had to hit bottom first. Most alcoholics do. And for her, bottom was an automobile accident that almost landed her in jail.

PLAYBOY: Was anyone hurt?

CARLIN: No. She just drove through a hotel lobby. Now, *that's* bottoming out.

PLAYBOY: Yes, but it's also pretty funny.

CARLIN: Not to me. It was my car.

PLAYBOY: Then what happened?

CARLIN: Brenda went into therapy and I soon joined her. First we put the drugs behind us, then we began serious work on our relationship. And, in time, we got well together.

PLAYBOY: Did you have affairs?

CARLIN: No.

PLAYBOY: Encounters?

CARLIN: Only during our worst period of drug abuse. The coke made me incredibly horny.

PLAYBOY: During your college-concert years, did you have many groupies?

CARLIN: Anyone who's onstage is going to attract a certain number of misguided people. But I was never very interested in groupies. Instead of thinking about the sex, I'd always think about the clap and the crabs those people have.

PLAYBOY: How are comedian groupies different from rock-star groupies? Are they smarter? Funnier?

CARLIN: The women who line up at a comic's dressing-room door are not what you'd call your class groupies. I mean, there are some decent star fuckers, but they all want to fuck musicians and movie actors. To be a comedian fucker is like being a juggler fucker. Can you imagine a girl who wants to fuck only the opening act? It's like watching an animal trainer and then wanting to fuck the chimp.

PLAYBOY: You had an auto accident yourself recently. A bad one, though, fortunately, no one was hurt.

CARLIN: Only the car and my nose were totaled.

PLAYBOY: This is a delicate question, but—

CARLIN: No, I was clean and sober. A tire blew at the wrong time and I lost it. That's all.

PLAYBOY: Are you sure that's all?

CARLIN: Actually, I suspect there really was more to my accident than bad luck. I think it was God's way of punishing my nose.

PLAYBOY: Just when you finally got clear of coke, you had a heart attack. What sort of heart attack was it?

CARLIN: My left descending septal branch artery decided to close without consultation with any of my other organs. It happened on Saint Patrick's Day, 1978. I woke up that morning and my jaw muscles were tight and achy. I thought it was from the way I slept, so I took three Tylenols. But the pills didn't go down right, or didn't seem to. It felt like they'd lodged in my esophagus. I was driving my daughter Kelly to school and the jaw ache and this feeling of a lump in my chest continued. And that's when it hit me, Jesus, I'm having a heart attack. So I got Kelly to school and went straight to my doctor. It didn't show up on the EKG right away, but because of my symptoms, he put me in the hospital for tests. They don't take any chances with comedians. The blood sample confirmed the heart attack and the angiogram supplied the details. I loved the angiogram. They stick a thing in your thigh and it goes all the way up to your heart. Isn't that a thrill? Well, at least the nurse scored thigh.

PLAYBOY: Had you suffered any previous heart problems?

CARLIN: I've always had irregular heartbeats. They're called PVCs—premature ventricular contractions. A lot of people have them, that feeling your heart almost stops for a moment, then starts again. I had a lot of PVCs in intensive care and they became life-threatening.

PLAYBOY: Both you and Richard Pryor suffered heart attacks after years of cocaine abuse. Did any of your doctors suggest that the coke had actually brought on the attack?

CARLIN: I suspect it might have. Sometimes, after I'd gone at the coke like one of those snow plows moving up First Avenue, I'd think my heart was over on the dresser, pounding, and I was watching it. I asked some of the doctors who drifted through the intensive-care unit what kind of effect total cocaine abuse has on the heart and they said things like, "Well, there's not enough valid information. . . ." That kind of answer. But I consider the coke a major cause. Of course, you could also make the argument that because cocaine speeds up the heart, it's good for you.

PLAYBOY: A drug-induced aerobic exercise? That's a unique theory.

CARLIN: But not a very good one. I'll tell you this: When I was really coked up, those PVCs were much more dramatic and more frequent than they are now. Each episode was so apparent. It would go, "*DOONG, DOONG, DOONG-DUCK-DUCK . . . DUCK-DUCK . . . DUCK-DUCK-DUCK . . . DUCK-DOONG, DOONG.*" And I'd go, "Whoa, Jim. Let's go lie down."

PLAYBOY: What were your worst episodes during those years of cocaine abuse and heart irregularities?

CARLIN: It's worst when you combine coke and fucking with an irregular heartbeat. That's when you *really* feel like you're on the edge.

PLAYBOY: You've been on the edge—of a stage, anyway—since you were a child. As a fatherless Irish street kid from the Upper West Side, it's at least a twist on the typical show-business background. Was there any particular incident or influence in your childhood that sparked your ambition to become a performer?

CARLIN: By the age of six or seven, I was already doing voices and faces, making my friends and my mother laugh. Then I saw Danny Kaye in a movie, and he was doing voices and faces on that big, big screen and making whole audiences laugh. It was just an instant hookup.

PLAYBOY: So you were always funny.

CARLIN: First I was a mimic. Practically from the moment I began talking, I did impersonations of the people in my neighborhood—the storekeepers, the policemen, my teachers. I always knew I could hold people's attention and make them laugh every 30 or 40 seconds, and I got approval and attention for that, so the behavior was reinforced. Later, that became an important skill on the street corner.

PLAYBOY: Did you know your father?

CARLIN: My father and mother separated when I was two months old. Although he lived until I was eight, I literally didn't know him. My mother had been a secretary, and after she and my father split, she went back to work for an advertising executive. So my older brother and I were "latch-door kids." We went home for lunch and after school by ourselves.

PLAYBOY: Were you a lonely child?

CARLIN: My mother didn't get home until about seven most nights and, yes, there was a sense of being very alone after school. She gave me all the proper guidance and influences, but physically, she just couldn't be there. So I became a radio nut. I loved the afternoon serials, and I got into jazz through the radio. I had a subscription to *Down Beat* when I was 12. And I'd spend a lot of time in front of the mirror, miming records.

In my fifth-grade yearbook—it's right up there on the top shelf—the last page says, "What about your future?" and under my name, it says, "When I grow up, I would like to be either an actor, a radio announcer, an impersonator or a comedian." By the way, another item on that shelf up there, next to the fifth-grade yearbook, is a Dodgers program autographed by all my heroes. Being a Dodgers fan led to my first Air Force court-martial, but that's another story.

PLAYBOY: Which we'll get to later . . . But for now, we're doing today's interview session in the little office next to your house, and it's a fascinating work space: two desks, a typewriter, a lot of recording and video equipment, books, records, tapes, files, all kinds of signs on the walls. Yet despite the clutter, there's an almost archival feeling of order.

CARLIN: My books and records are arranged according to subject, and within each subject, they're alphabetical by author or artist. The music tapes are alphabetical and the performance tapes are in chronological order.

PLAYBOY: Is that something you did on one of your coke runs after all the nuts and bolts were sorted?

CARLIN: There are two types of people: One strives to control his environment, the other strives not to let his environment control him. I like to control my environment, because I feel if I have my physical space in order, then I'm free to dream. So there is some compulsion involved. But the dividend I get is the freedom to be totally disorderly in my dreamworld.

PLAYBOY: What about all these hundreds of signs you have on the walls? Although they're all very interesting and funny, they're also obviously stolen.

CARLIN: I guess that makes me part vandal, part museum curator.

PLAYBOY: Do you enjoy stealing?

CARLIN: I think it keeps the child alive in me. There's a thrill when you steal something in plain view of other people. When you drop a newspaper over a sign and walk away with it, or take something off a wall and the sound of the glue ripping makes people turn around. Your heart is racing, it's a rush.

PLAYBOY: The one in the bathroom is marvelous: The MacLaine Hotel Commemorative Nixon Visit, 1968. And Nixon signed it at the bottom.

CARLIN: Yeah; as soon as I saw it in the hotel lobby, I said, "*That's* going." I guess they'll be after me now.

PLAYBOY: In your routines, you return constantly, almost obsessively, to your parochial education. Did you ever attend public high school in New York?

CARLIN: I went to George Washington High School for six months before my 16th birthday, when I could legally quit. That was an even worse experience than the Catholic schools. I mean, they were still teaching fractions. But mostly, I played hooky. I had one 63-day streak.

PLAYBOY: That's quite a streak.

CARLIN: Yeah, and I didn't count weekends or holidays.

PLAYBOY: Would you describe yourself as a problem student?

CARLIN: I was a discipline problem, and I never did homework.

PLAYBOY: What sort of trouble did you get into?

CARLIN: When I was in seventh grade, I was caught stealing money from the visiting team's locker room during a basketball game. So I was sent to The Brothers. That's what they called this parochial school up in Goshen, New York. I was supposed to get closer supervision there and more "masculine influence," whatever that means. But I was thrown out for telling a couple of really lame kids on the playground that I had heroin.

PLAYBOY: Did you?

CARLIN: It was just a joke, but back I went to my old school, where all the kids I'd been with for eight years were about to graduate. But the sisters wanted me to repeat the whole term; so I went to the principal and pleaded with her to allow me to graduate with my class. She finally agreed on the condition that I write the graduation play. It was called *How Do You Spend Your Leisure Time?* Catchy title, huh? But, once again, I was rewarded for my cleverness, my show-business skills.

PLAYBOY: Even before adolescence, the essential themes of your adult life and work were pretty clearly laid out: humor, rebellion and drug use.

CARLIN: And the patterns became even more vivid at Cardinal Hayes High School. That's when I began failing subjects and running away from home for days at a time.

PLAYBOY: What, exactly, were you running away from?

CARLIN: My mother and her plans for my future. She had it all worked out. I would attend a nice college, then get a job in advertising. "You'll be one of those smart-looking fellows in their Madison Avenue suits." She was in advertising and had become friendly with all those assholes from G.M., Procter & Gamble, General Foods. She'd rattle off their names like a litany of deities. And they really were almost like gods to her, gods she tried to foist off on me, along with the gods of the Catholic Church. And I rebelled against her and her values and her plans for my future at every opportunity.

PLAYBOY: That must have made for a tranquil home.

CARLIN: The older I got, the more apparent it became that my mother was losing control over me. She fought back fiercely with black moods, silent treatments and martyrdom. "You're letting me down." "How can you do this to me?" "You hang out with those bums on the corner till all hours. They'll never amount to anything. Water seeks its own level." And, of course, all she did was run my ass out of the house even quicker. The pressure was unbearable.

PLAYBOY: Later, during your college-concert years and on your early albums, that rebellion against your mother's values resurfaced. You were over 30 then. Were you still feeling that anger? Or were you just drawing on the memory of it to please your audience?

CARLIN: Oh, I was still feeling those angers . . . no, let's call them hatreds, because that's what they were. The rebellious mood of the country during those years allowed me to plug right back into my old hatreds. I could scream and holler, as I did on the albums, against religion, government, big business—all those assholes and their values. That hatred was very real.

PLAYBOY: Do you still feel hatred toward the establishment?

CARLIN: The visceral aspect of it is gone now. But I still hold all the values I held when I was screaming more. They just don't take a physical and psychological toll on me anymore. I'm not possessed by an us-versus-them mentality. Well, I still have my days when I'm answering the television with a little more hatred than necessary, when the "Fuck you, Dan Rather" comes out with a harder edge than it should. But that's much less frequent than it used to be. I think I'm getting well on that level.

PLAYBOY: When you came to L.A. in the early 1960s, it was a justifiable career move. But was it also another way of running away from your mother?

CARLIN: Yes.

PLAYBOY: Is your mother still alive?

CARLIN: Yeah, she's 85 now.

PLAYBOY: Will she read this interview?

CARLIN: Probably; but it really doesn't matter anymore. I've told her these things and I have what I used to call "the problem with my mother" out of my system now. Occasionally, she'll still push a few of the old buttons, but my anger lasts only a few seconds now, because I recognize them as old buttons. I tell her, "That doesn't work anymore," and we have a much better relationship. She even lives out here now. I no longer have to get away from her physically in order to escape the feelings that made me so unhappy in my teenage years.

PLAYBOY: Of all the values you rebelled against as a child, what was the one you most despised?

CARLIN: Religion. When the Catholics start laying their trip on you, you notice very early in life what a load of shit it is. The hypocrisy is just breathtakingly apparent, even to a child. But what I hated most was seeing those priests and brothers getting so much pleasure out of inflicting pain. I wondered what was wrong with them.

PLAYBOY: Do any other religions interest you?

CARLIN: None of the Christian religions do. They're all outer-directed. "Who can I convert?" "Let's go to this country and make them Christians." "Wear this." "Do that." "No, don't worship *that* way. Worship *this* way or I'll kill you—for the good of your soul, of course." Meanwhile, followers of Eastern religions are sitting in the middle of their minds, experiencing a bliss and a level of consciousness that Western man can't begin to approach. Christianity is all external, all material. Gold. War. Murder. The big churches operate, morally and economically, just like the big corporations. Yet they don't pay taxes. Let them pay their fair share, those fucking religions.

PLAYBOY: Can you see any good at all in Western religion?

CARLIN: The only good thing about Western religion is the music.

PLAYBOY: Do you pray?

CARLIN: I say things that can be defined as prayers. But I don't pray to a power or ask an entity to intercede in the earthly scheme, because I don't believe that happens. But if I see a really unfortunate person in the street, I do pray, yes, though I suppose it's really more like a mantra to ease my own sorrow.

PLAYBOY: You spent your adolescence running away from home, parochial school and the future your mother had mapped out for you. But until you hit 16, you really couldn't go anywhere. Did you take any *positive* action during those years to try to make your life a little freer and more satisfying?

CARLIN: I decided what I really wanted to do was go to the New York High School of Performing Arts, the school that was in the movie *Fame*. So I went down to 46th Street and laid my rap on this lady in the admissions office. "Hi, I'm George Carlin. I'm real funny. I do impressions. I'm gonna be an actor and a comedian and I'd love to come to your school." And she said, "Fine, but you'll have to repeat the last year and a half." I said, "Why?" And she said, "Well, you don't have any background in fencing and speech . . ." and she named about five things that I didn't know had anything to do with becoming a show-business legend. So I said, "Hey, okay, I'm gonna have to get back to you, lady," and I was gone.

PLAYBOY: And that's how you wound up at a public high school for your last six months, studying fractions and running up your streak?

CARLIN: Yeah. I couldn't go back to Cardinal Hayes. I mean, I *had* to get away from those priests and brothers, those maniacs.

PLAYBOY: Then, at 16, you quit school, bounced around for a year and joined the Air Force on your 17th birthday.

CARLIN: In those days, we avoided the draft by enlisting. Now, that's an interesting concept. . . . But I had a plan. See, I was engaged at that time, so I figured I'd join up, marry my girl, live off base, then use my GI Bill to go to disc-jockey school.

PLAYBOY: But you never did get married.

CARLIN: You get away from home for the first time and you're true to your girl for a while, and then you start realizing, Jeez, I'm horny. So we both started dating other people, and eventually we drifted apart.

PLAYBOY: You mentioned having a subscription to *Down Beat* when you were 12, and your record collection is incredible. Yet you don't talk about music very much in your act. Just how important is music in your life?

CARLIN: It used to be more important than it is now. I overdosed on music during my period of cocaine abuse. I'd be playing rock all the time to feed my speed head, until I finally burned out on it. Also, the music took a turn for the worse. Also, I began to get well. I needed peace of mind. I didn't need the fucking amplified levels of rock, and I've never needed heavy-metal music.

PLAYBOY: When you were following rock, how did your tastes run?

CARLIN: I always enjoyed people like John Prine, soloists who wrote their own songs and had a point of view. The bands I liked tended to be soft rock. I've always preferred the gentle approach as opposed to the strident approach.

PLAYBOY: The Beatles as opposed to the Stones?

CARLIN: There are things the Stones did that I couldn't ignore, but I've always listened to the Beatles four to one over the Stones.

PLAYBOY: What do you listen to now?

CARLIN: Classical music, mostly.

PLAYBOY: And when you were a child?

CARLIN: I loved the R&B bands, Budd Johnson and Earl Bostic. The hallway groups—you know, do-wop music. I loved black music that other whites weren't into, and I was jealous of that prerogative. One of the things that bugged me as a kid was when the white music industry moved in on that black music.

PLAYBOY: May we assume that you weren't a Bill Haley fan?

CARLIN: To me, Bill Haley was a horrible phenomenon. When I hear all this nostalgic shit about the 1950s, the image that comes to my mind is of a bunch of really lame white kids with fucked-up clothing dancing to Bill Haley and His Comets. That might have been America's 1950s, but it sure wasn't mine. My 1950s were hanging around Harlem, wearing conservative clothes—a vest, a four-button suit with no peg in the pants, wing tips, eyelet shirts, thin ties—walking like a black dude and smoking grass and going to parties and dancing so slow you'd hardly notice it.

PLAYBOY: Folk music must have gotten to you in the early 1960s.

CARLIN: There was a short period when folk music was of great interest to me. It seemed authentic—just like black music was. Most rock and roll struck me as inauthentic. It sounded like it was being created by an industry, not by a people.

PLAYBOY: Did you ever get into country music?

CARLIN: Oh, I *loved* real country music. Again, not the kind they manufacture in Nashville. I loved bluegrass and the real country people, you know, like Bill Monroe and Hank Williams.

PLAYBOY: What about today's country music?

CARLIN: There's still some with that real white man's working-class soul in it. I love those strains of stark reality: hopelessness, sorrow, broken love, death. Like authentic R&B, authentic country music speaks for a people, and the similarities and differences between the two forms have always fascinated me.

PLAYBOY: For example?

CARLIN: The very appearance of a black man singing R&B music is full of expression, full of a physical revelation of his feelings—sexual and otherwise. The body is never held back. The freedom that a black expresses by merely walking down the street is even more evident when he sings onstage. By contrast, the white Protestant Southern country man singing onstage barely moves his body. If he's playing the guitar, his fingers will move and his lips will move and one foot will tap—and that's all. He is a tight asshole and that's his hang-up. But the lyrics those two men will write are precisely the opposite. The black man sings in symbolic terms about jelly rolls and sugar pies, while the white man tells you exactly what's on his mind. "Ohhh, a truck ran over my baaa-by in the ro-o-o-ad." It's a marvelous paradox that tells us so much about those two cultures.

PLAYBOY: Getting back to your stint in the Air Force, somehow, it just doesn't seem as though signing up for military service was the best way for you to escape the regimentation of a parochial education.

CARLIN: That's true, and by the time my second court-martial rolled around, it had become fairly obvious to both me and the Pentagon that, as they say in a marriage, it just wasn't working out.

PLAYBOY: Your second court-martial?

CARLIN: Discipline has never been my strong suit. But, in the end, the Air Force was a great experience for me. I met a local DJ at an off-base party, began hanging around the station and eventually, when somebody got sick, I filled in. By the time I was discharged, I had my own show on KJOE, the number-one station in Shreveport, Louisiana.

PLAYBOY: When you weren't getting your show-business career off the ground, what were your military duties?

CARLIN: I was a radar, optics and computer mechanic on B-47s at a SAC base.

PLAYBOY: Interesting job for a future counterculture hero.

CARLIN: Yes, wasn't it? There I was, impeding the war machine just by showing up to work.

PLAYBOY: You said earlier that you smoked grass virtually every day of your life for 30 years. Even in the Air Force?

CARLIN: Sure. A friend used to mail it to me from New York—all cleaned and everything. I smoked right on the base all the time. People weren't familiar with the smell then. They thought it was some kind of cigar.

PLAYBOY: Tell us about your courts-martial.

CARLIN: The first one came the day after the Dodgers won the World Series in 1955. Our SAC unit was in England on a TDY, a sort of mobility drill that's supposed to be fairly serious business. But when Johnny Podres beat the Yankees in that seventh game, I went sailing into this little town off base, got drunk on cooking wine, then went back to the barracks with the intention of celebrating for the rest of the evening. When my tech sergeant expressed his displeasure at my actions—not to mention my noise level—I replied in a manner that he didn't consider in strict accordance with military protocol. I told him to go fuck himself. And to be honest, I don't think my salute was entirely up to standards, either. I didn't do any time for that one, but I did lose a stripe.

PLAYBOY: And your second court-martial?

CARLIN: That was more serious. We were having a simulated combat drill. The whole base was on alert and everybody pulled guard duty. So I was out there one night, and it was cold, you know. And I was tired. So I left my gun on the ground and went up into the crawlway of a B-47, smoked a joint and went to sleep. Fortunately, it was Christmas and I had a really benevolent judge, who said, "I should send you to jail for this, but I don't think any 18-year-old should spend the holidays in prison." So he let me off.

PLAYBOY: Then what happened to you?

CARLIN: Well, I had this DJ job in town, and the commander of my squadron figured I might be more valuable as a PR tool working full time at the radio station than short-circuiting nuclear bombers and telling everybody to go fuck himself. So he gave me an off-base work permit and took me off the flight line. Eventually, they pulled the permit and another stripe and mustered me out.

PLAYBOY: Which freed you to become a professional disc jockey.

CARLIN: Yeah. I worked in Boston, Shreveport again and Fort Worth—that's where I began to develop my voices.

PLAYBOY: Where did you meet Jack Burns, your first comedy partner?

CARLIN: In Boston. Jack was the morning DJ and we roomed together. We ad-libbed off each other and talked vaguely about doing a comedy act. But we split when I got the job in Fort Worth. Then, one night, Jack showed up in Texas in a car with four bald tires and said, "I'm on my way to Hollywood." This time, we did get an act together and began playing a coffeehouse in Fort Worth called The Celler. It wasn't a very good act, but people laughed. So we went to Hollywood.

PLAYBOY: Just like that?

CARLIN: It was crazy, but when we got to L.A., the first radio station we walked into was looking for a morning comedy team. Suddenly, there we were, in the second biggest market in the country, making $350 a week each—which at the time was a fortune—but after three months, we walked away from that to go into nightclubs full time. That was the fun of it. We really felt strongly about ourselves and were willing to take outrageous risks.

PLAYBOY: What was your first nightclub job?

CARLIN: A coffeehouse in Hollywood called Cosmo Alley. That's where Lenny Bruce and Mort Sahl saw us. We did skits and two-man situations about race and religion. Nothing memorable, but most comedy teams of that era did moron stuff. At least we were trying to say something.

PLAYBOY: What, exactly, did Bruce and Sahl do for you?

CARLIN: Lenny got us a contract with a major agency, which was incredible. I mean, we'd been comedians for a month and a half when we got booked into the Playboy Club circuit purely on the basis of Lenny's going to bat for us. And Mort got us into the hungry i in San Francisco. And because of those bookings, Burns and Carlin got work at a place called the Racquet Club in Dayton, Ohio, where the hostess was a young girl named Brenda Hosbrook. We dated every day I was there, wrote and called each other constantly afterward, and within a year, we were married.

PLAYBOY: You're not exactly a guy to agonize over important decisions.

CARLIN: Actually, it has always been a dreadful flaw in my character to stick with relationships and career plans far too long; but in those days, I was moving very quickly. And Brenda and I clicked on all levels right away.

PLAYBOY: What sort of love life did you have before meeting Brenda?

CARLIN: I did a lot of dating. . . . Well, dating may not be exactly the right word for it. Trying to get laid is a little more accurate. And please notice the word *trying*. I always wanted and enjoyed sex, but I never put much importance on scoring or having an athletic sex life. I guess I define myself more by my career and my commitment to a relationship than by my ability to have a lot of chicks or achieve 10 orgasms in an evening.

PLAYBOY: Would you describe yourself as a very sexual person who doesn't consider sex very important?

CARLIN: No, sex is important to me. I just never lead with my dick.

PLAYBOY: You and Brenda got married and lived the life of a road comic. Where was your home base?

CARLIN: Nowhere. For the first year and a half, we lived in a Dodge Dart.

PLAYBOY: Despite your success, Burns and Carlin broke up in 1962. Why?

CARLIN: We didn't work very hard and the act wasn't growing. I think that was mostly my fault, because after we split up, Jack became a tireless writer with Avery Schreiber and with Second City. I just never wanted to sit down and make up new routines, and I became a bit of a drawback to him. I guess I was subconsciously saving myself for my own act.

PLAYBOY: You saw your future as a single.

CARLIN: Definitely, and Jack always knew that.

PLAYBOY: Did you part on good terms?

CARLIN: Yes, and we've remained close friends for the past 20 years.

PLAYBOY: From 1962 until about 1970, you were a straight comic with a constantly ascending career. You continued working the Playboy Clubs, became a successful opening act in Las Vegas, then broke into TV. By your early 30s, you found yourself becoming rich and famous as a mainstream performer. But, as they say, were you happy?

CARLIN: I was happy about my success, but I was also frustrated, because I was sublimating the long-standing angers that I still hadn't begun to deal with. I mean, the nightclubs were full of businessmen, and I hated them madly. But I had to repress my hatred, and that took its toll. I had a number of angry confrontations, including one at a Las Vegas hotel and another at a Playboy Club, and found myself back at the coffeehouses, where I'd started. And the colleges. Before Vegas, I'd been a folk comic on Bleecker Street in New York and Wells Street in Chicago. So when I made my break in 1970, I said, "I gotta go back to those people. They'll understand me. They'll let me sing my song." And those audiences *did* make me feel comfortable. I fed on them. I got out all the anger I'd repressed in my teens and 20s. Looking back on it, I suspect that whole period from 1970 to 1976—the albums, the college tours, the cocaine—was all just a way of completing my adolescence. When I was *really* an adolescent, I was engaged and in the Air Force and making adult decisions. I never really got to finish the angry, screaming, rebellious part of my youth. Then, when I was in my 30s, the country seemed to go through its *own* adolescence. Anger and rebellion and drug experimentation and outrageous music and clothing—all the typical manifestations of adolescent behavior were suddenly present in American society, and I just fell right into it. The country's mood allowed me to finish that chapter of my own life.

PLAYBOY: Despite all the changes you've gone through, one aspect of your career has remained fairly constant: your *Tonight Show* appearances both as a guest and as a guest host.

CARLIN: *The Tonight Show* is one of the few things I do that makes me feel I'm really in show business. I used to feel that way on the old Ed Sullivan show. When the band played that theme, my stomach would drop and I'd say to myself, "Well, Ed didn't die, so you're definitely gonna have to go out there and do your monolog." I still feel that way when Ed McMahon announces me as guest host. It's exciting. Suddenly, I'm reminded that I really am part of that thing that was so glamorous when I was a kid—show business.

PLAYBOY: Most *Tonight Show* guests are mainstream-entertainment types—not the sort of folks we'd expect you to choose for five minutes of casual conversation. As a host, did you ever try to get the type of guests you'd really *enjoy* talking to?

CARLIN: The first time I hosted, I asked for Ralph Nader and Jane Fonda and was quickly told no. I asked why and they said, "Well, you know, we have advertisers who wouldn't be too thrilled with them." So I wound up with Dave Meggyesy. That was their sop to me—a radical football player.

PLAYBOY: But do you enjoy *The Tonight Show*?

CARLIN: Yes, and that's something I've found out about myself over the past four years—my getting-well period. As harmless and uncontroversial as those conversations are, there's a side of me that I used to deny that enjoys them. Now I let that side live, and entertain it when it needs to be nourished, and I still have my personal values.

PLAYBOY: But don't those personal values sometimes conflict with the overt commercialism of *The Tonight Show*?

CARLIN: I'd never read a commercial for them. I even have trouble doing the lead-ins. When I have to say, "Hey, Hi-Ho Paste Wax," I feel a little dopey.

PLAYBOY: Wasn't there a period in the early 1970s, when you were telling your club audiences to go fuck themselves, that Carson blackballed you from *The Tonight Show*?

CARLIN: Well, there was a period of about a year and a half when Carson wouldn't use me, but that was sort of my fault.

PLAYBOY: What happened?

CARLIN: The day before one of my scheduled appearances as a guest, I went in for my pre-interview with the talent coordinator. Now, this was just when I was beginning to go through my changes. My hair was long and I was wearing a tie-dyed T-shirt and sandals and rapping about Muhammad Ali, and at first she didn't even recognize me. I must have looked like I'd dropped all kinds of acid and they probably felt I wouldn't be reliable. So they bumped me off the next night's show and just stopped calling.

PLAYBOY: Did you try to reach Carson personally to explain the changes you were going through?

CARLIN: Sure. I went over there and visited him in the dressing room, but I was loaded up on snort and after listening to about 10 minutes of nonstop chatter, he very politely excused himself. He could see I was in trouble.

PLAYBOY: What got you back in Carson's good graces?

CARLIN: As I continued doing my new material on the albums and at colleges and coffeehouses, it became apparent that I was still a reliable, professional performer. So, eventually, *The Tonight Show* invited me back. And from then on, they paid my airfare, which they hadn't done before. I've always taken that as an apology.

PLAYBOY: Now that it's over, have you talked with Carson about that episode?

CARLIN: No, because I've always understood his position. See, it wasn't my politics that bothered him. It was me. He thought I'd become a maniac.

PLAYBOY: Do you like Carson?

CARLIN: I like the person who's interviewing me when I'm on the show, which is really the only way I know him. During the breaks, he usually leans over to share something private with me. Never anything that relates to the upcoming conversation. I love that. He seems always to be opening himself up, showing me he cares about me sitting here.

PLAYBOY: Your most famous piece of material from those album and coffeehouse years is *The Seven Words*. Of course, that piece had a lot to say about censorship, but its impact came from its shock value, a comedic tool you frequently use.

CARLIN: I don't like the phrase shock value. Surprise is essential in comedy, and if people are shocked by what I consider merely surprising, then that's *their* shock. But there is no joke without surprise. For example, if I say, "Isn't it amazing that most of the women who are against abortion are women you wouldn't want to fuck anyway?" it's much more effective than "Isn't it amazing that most of the women who are against abortion are women you wouldn't want to get pregnant anyway?" Although "get pregnant" is the logical phrase in that sentence, because I'm talking about abortion, not sex, the word fuck, because it's a surprise, gives the joke its light and power. If that word shocks you, it's your problem.

PLAYBOY: Was it that love of verbal surprise that caused you to write *The Seven Words*?

CARLIN: Definitely. And my love of language. That piece began when I sat down one day and made a list of all the curses I could think of. Then I honed the list by eliminating all the compound words except cocksucker and motherfucker. Finally, I had seven. Seven words I felt absolutely certain could never be used, even in the most learned conversation, on network television: shit, piss, fuck, cunt, cocksucker, motherfucker, tits. And over the years, I've written several routines around that list.

PLAYBOY: You became a part of American legal history when, because of an FCC action resulting from the airing of one of those routines, you were summoned for a command performance by the Supreme Court. How did that particular booking come about?

CARLIN: In 1973, WBAI-FM, a Pacifica Foundation radio station in New York, played an 11-minute version of *The Seven Words* as part of a program on language taboos. A gentleman from a group called Morals in Media—a forerunner of the Moral Majority—was driving around Long Island that day with his 13-year-old son and they listened to the whole thing.

PLAYBOY: Did anyone ever ask why he didn't turn the dial if he found the program objectionable?

CARLIN: Of course not. And when this guy complained to the FCC, that august body voted to censure WBAI, which is a serious mark against a station on its license-renewal application. So WBAI fought the censure and won in Federal district court. But that was the Nixon FCC, and they appealed the case to the Supreme Court.

PLAYBOY: How did you feel about that?

CARLIN: I felt like I was being called to the big principal's office in Washington. I mean, getting kicked out of school and kicked out of the choir and having a couple of courts-martial—those transgressions suddenly seemed like small potatoes. That these nine men had summoned me into their presence to question my conduct absolutely thrilled the perverse and rebellious side of my nature. I thought, Even if I just become a little footnote in the law books, I'll be a happy footnote forever.

PLAYBOY: How did the case turn out?

CARLIN: We lost. The Supreme Court found that the FCC *did* have the right to restrict a radio station from playing indecent material at a time when a child might be listening. The word obscene was kept out of the case, because obscenity is defined according to community standards. The word indecent has never been defined legally. And the Court never established how old a "child" is or exactly which hours a child might reasonably be expected to be listening. So the FCC still doesn't have the right of prior restraint.

PLAYBOY: In other words, there's still no official list of words you can't say—which is what your *Seven Words* piece was all about.

CARLIN: That was exactly my premise. All I want is a list. When I was a kid, nobody would tell me which words not to say. I had to go home and say them and get hit. As a result of the WBAI case, the Supreme Court has put the FCC in the same position as the parent. It can punish you after the fact, but it can't tell you beforehand exactly what the restricted areas are.

PLAYBOY: So American broadcasters continue to work in constant jeopardy—leading, of course, to self-censorship.

CARLIN: That's right. And they have to be extra careful with those two-way words. I mean, they can prick their finger, but they can't finger their prick.

PLAYBOY: That *Seven Words* case brought you together with Hollywood's left-wing establishment—another group of folks with whom you don't normally associate.

CARLIN: Norman Lear called me up and said they wanted to make me one of the ACLU's Persons of the Year or something, because of the *Seven Words* case—which I really didn't have that much to do with. WBAI was fighting all the battles and doing all the work and nobody was throwing testimonials for it. The ACLU was also honoring Lily Tomlin and Garry Trudeau that night. I mean, what the hell have two comics and a cartoonist really contributed to the cause of freedom in America? But that's Hollywood liberalism for you. And because my ego was obviously involved, I said, "Okay, that's cool, I'll go."

PLAYBOY: Who else was there?

CARLIN: The usual sad, stale Hollywood liberal crowd, these tired idealists. I don't have to name them. They're famous performers and you see them at every fucking rally. Only the button in their lapel changes.

PLAYBOY: Did you wear a tuxedo?

CARLIN: I wore a dark suit. That's as far as I go, even for the First Amendment.

PLAYBOY: In addition to being honored, did you perform at that function?

CARLIN: While all the other assholes were speaking, Lily Tomlin and I had fun just doing looks at each other across the table. She's great. But then I got up and actually performed *The Seven Words*. And as liberal as those people were supposed to be, and as interested as they were in the Supreme Court case, they just couldn't handle it.

PLAYBOY: You mean after all that, they didn't laugh?

CARLIN: Oh, they laughed, and at the end they applauded. But I've been a performer for a long time and I know when people are laughing from their guts, from the inside, and when their tuxedos are laughing.

PLAYBOY: Shouldn't a lifelong radical like you be more sympathetic toward liberal activists?

CARLIN: I have no patience for anyone who sits and mouths clichés. Everybody's got a fucking easy answer for all our problems. But there are no easy answers, because you can't change just one thing, you have to change everything. We've come that far in our destruction of this poor green planet. And I just feel removed from that.

PLAYBOY: Which leaves you open to the criticism that you're copping out.

CARLIN: I love that phrase: copping out. It actually means to admit guilt, not to get off the hook. And, yes, I do cop out. I cop out to not having glib and easy answers like all those wonderful professional crusaders.

PLAYBOY: Would you include Ralph Nader and Barry Commoner in that sweeping condemnation of American social activism?

CARLIN: I see them as giving heart to yet another generation of misguided idealists.

PLAYBOY: And is that so bad?

CARLIN: I think, strategically, it *is* bad. Because the function the crusaders and the investigative reporters really serve in this society is to show the true enemies of humanity—the people on top with the power—where their weak spots are. And then the establishment moves in quickly and silently with a little cement and covers up those holes. And the story goes away, and a few people are never heard from again, and the juggernaut rolls on—stronger than ever.

PLAYBOY: What about Watergate? That's at least one instance in which the investigative reporters broke the establishment.

CARLIN: Yes, Watergate. "The system worked." I believe that phrase now represents the official historical verdict on that glorious chapter of our history. Well, bullshit! The system worked because McCord left some tape on the lock. And what's the logical implication of *that* statement? Without the tape, the system *wouldn't* have worked. So fuck the system.

PLAYBOY: Do you vote?

CARLIN: No. We're led to believe we're free through the exercise of ineffective freedoms.

PLAYBOY: But some activists have helped the lives of some people—even without overhauling the system.

CARLIN: I know, I know. It's not that I'm unaware of the accomplishments of, say, Ralph Nader. He has made the lives of a small number of people a little better. But personally, emotionally, I'd rather divorce myself from the world than face the heartbreak of partial success. Because partial success implies overwhelming failure.

PLAYBOY: For a nonvoter, you hold some strong opinions about politics. Have you ever considered adding Will Rogers–style political humor to your act?

CARLIN: Will Rogers said, "I never met a man I didn't like." I say, "I never liked a man I didn't meet." And, although I never met him, I don't like Will Rogers much, either. He got away with an awful lot because people were more innocent then. His whole bit was that politicians stink, which is a poor substitute for humor.

PLAYBOY: Which comedians *do* you like?

CARLIN: So many brilliant comics have entertained and inspired me throughout my life that no list could ever be complete. The first, of course, was Danny Kaye. Then the Marx Brothers, Abbott and Costello, the Ritz Brothers. I don't know why the Ritz Brothers weren't more popular. It's my belief that Milton Berle and many other successful Jewish comics got their shtick from Harry Ritz. That man invented the moves for a whole generation. As a kid, I loved the radio comedians, especially Fred Allen. And I liked Jerry Lewis's early work. His abandon. That's what I've always admired. The ability to let go.

PLAYBOY: Were you a Steve Allen fan?

CARLIN: I loved his work on *The Tonight Show* in the 1950s. There was a certain power and impact to the phrases Allen used—"I certainly hope so and right in your mouth"—a crashing, cascading brilliance and an instinct for the jugular.

PLAYBOY: Who was the first comedian to influence you whose influence is still evident in your work?

CARLIN: Jonathan Winters. The voices, the characters—at least *I* see his influence on me. But he had something I lack: a window to insanity that he could climb through and really inhabit his characters. My characters just don't have the heights and depths that his do, but he's paid for his genius with several vacations in the Hoo-Hoo Hotel.

PLAYBOY: Does your love of abandon include an admiration for Don Rickles?

CARLIN: The first few times I saw Rickles, he amazed me with his brashness and willingness to cross lines. But I don't like the way he closes his act—by apologizing for what he does. It's insincere. A performer who kisses the audience's ass is full of shit.

PLAYBOY: One of your current projects is a motion picture you're writing. The two modern comics who've gone that route with the most success are Woody Allen and Mel Brooks. What do you think of their work?

CARLIN: In both Brooks and Allen, there's such an overriding theme of their own personal Jewishness that it's not always easy for a non-Jew to appreciate it all. But Brooks makes me laugh a lot—especially when he's being interviewed and giving instant answers to things. The *2,000 Year Old Man* killed me, just put me away. There are elements of overindulgence in his films that don't quite get to me, but the man himself has a brilliant comic mind. Woody Allen is irresistible: his beautiful observations and the wonderful way he toys with our psychological processes. And to have written so many fine scripts in such a brief period is really, to me, his most magnificent accomplishment. Twenty years ago, as a stand-up comic, Woody Allen wrote the following joke: "I was thrown out of NYU for cheating on a metaphysics exam. I looked into the soul of the boy next to me." If he'd done nothing else for the rest of his life, I'd still love Woody Allen for that one joke. He doesn't always make me roll down the aisle, but he always makes my mind laugh its ass off.

PLAYBOY: You and Richard Pryor started out together in the folk rooms of Greenwich Village, and except for his work as a movie actor, your careers have taken remarkably similar courses—right down to the cocaine and the heart attack. Do you see yourself as the white Richard Pryor? Or him as the black George Carlin?

CARLIN: In the early 1960s, Richie and I would frequently be on the same bill at the Café Au Go Go, and sometimes, while introducing each other, we'd do a few improvs between sets. There was always a rapport, and perhaps we share certain comic viewpoints, but I think Pryor is without peer. The thing he does better than anyone else is represent who he is, where he's been and who has been around him. He doesn't do whole characters in the sense that Lily and Jonathan do, but Richard does fantastic characterizations—an entire personality implied by just a line here, a gesture there. And his white guys *really* kill me. Richard is just a genius. He makes me laugh from the soles of my feet—that's S-O-L-E-S.

PLAYBOY: Does Steve Martin make you laugh?

CARLIN: I don't laugh as much as I do at some of the other people, but I like Steve Martin's mind. I like the attitude he brings to that arrow through his head. And I love the way he mocks the performer's situation and self-image—the way he does that phony asshole onstage.

PLAYBOY: Who else do you like?

CARLIN: Martin Mull. I can't even put my finger on exactly what about Martin I like, I just know that his jokes make me laugh very hard. They're unusual. The twist of his mind is refreshing. And his songs are great.

PLAYBOY: Have you noticed how many comedians keep going into their 70s and 80s? Do you think there's something about comedy that's good for the health?

CARLIN: I seriously have thought that there must be a therapeutic value to humor, a life force that's enhanced by laughter. Because it certainly is an observable phenomenon that comics just go on forever, though Freddie Prinze did fuck up the curve a little.

PLAYBOY: Do you consider it a professional obligation to rush out and see every hot new comic and every film comedy that's released?

CARLIN: On the contrary; I try *not* to see new comics—their acts or their films. Part of that is professional. I don't want to be influenced. But another part is fear and jealousy. I'm afraid to see how good they might be. I don't like that emotion, but it's part of me.

PLAYBOY: You never buy material, do you?

CARLIN: No, and again, this isn't a very flattering thing to say about myself, but I don't want anyone to think I need help. Now that I'm going to try to make movies, I have to open myself up to collaboration, because film is a collaborative art. And that's difficult for me. I have an extreme jealousy of authorship. . . . Folks, we've got a really twisted guy here.

PLAYBOY: You're said to be one of the most stolen-from comics in the business. What was the most blatant theft you can recall?

CARLIN: A comic I admire very much, Joan Rivers, did one of my pieces on *The Tonight Show* just recently. I couldn't believe it, because it was a bit I'd used regularly for years. I said, "When my mother was pregnant with me, she carried me very low. In fact, for the last few weeks, my feet were sticking out." And my follow-up, which Joan also used, was, "However, she did tell me it came in handy on stairs." Theft is one of the risks you run when you buy material, and I'll bet Joan bought that joke. . . . Now that I've said this in public, I guess I'll find out.

PLAYBOY: Any other examples?

CARLIN: Remember I said that Garry Trudeau was also honored at that ACLU dinner—along with Lily and me? One of the things I said that night was, "I'm into a new lifestyle that doesn't require my presence." Garry later used that line in an interview. Maybe he thought he heard himself say it.

PLAYBOY: In October 1975, you were the guest host on the first *Saturday Night Live* show. What sort of experience was that?

CARLIN: I was totally coked out that week, so my memories are imperfect. And there was so much tension around that nobody was giving off real life-signals. But I do remember being made to feel extremely welcome.

PLAYBOY: Was that tension more than the normal case of opening-night jitters?

CARLIN: There was the pressure of a live performance and the pressure of a new show—both of which are normal. But there was also a certain amount of tension between the technicians and these young, privileged, snotty, satirical kids who were getting this big break.

PLAYBOY: What was your first impression of the Not Ready for Prime Time Players?

CARLIN: I could see immediately that they were good comic performers and great sketch players. I had trouble personally on that show, because I don't consider myself an actor, and that includes sketch playing. I was so self-conscious and unsure that I eventually made them cancel a whole piece. I was supposed to play Alexander the Great at his high school reunion. I just felt so silly in that outfit and nothing in me could make me believe I was him. I guess I let a lot of people down, but acting has always been a problem for me.

PLAYBOY: Even without you in the sketches, that opening *Saturday Night Live* show had an incredible impact. Were you aware at the time of how strongly people would respond, both pro and con?

CARLIN: Oh, yeah. We even got Cardinal Cooke to call in before the show was over. I was particularly proud of that.

PLAYBOY: As we recall, you did a monolog about God that night.

CARLIN: Yes, and Cooke was so incensed he got right on the phone. All I said was that I'd been taught that I was made in God's image, but it looked more like we had made Him in our image. And if He was anything like me, He was far from perfect. Then I said I thought the whole idea of God's being perfect was out of the question. I mean, just look at His work. He can't make two leaves alike. Every mountain range is crooked. He can't even get two fingerprints the same. . . . And about that time, the phones lit up.

PLAYBOY: What did you think, overall, of *Saturday Night Live?*

CARLIN: The show made me laugh, but it didn't really take on a lot of issues. It *seemed* daring, and there were things that were sort of irreverent, but mostly they didn't present any alternate ideas, they just tore down. Which is a form of comedy I can live with but I don't love.

PLAYBOY: You mentioned your own inability to act. Are you now admiring an ability simply because it eludes you?

CARLIN: Maybe, but so far I haven't even been able to *try* to act. You see, I believe that ultimately, actors are escaping from themselves. I've spent the first 45 years of my life trying to figure out who I am and how best to expose myself to the world.

PLAYBOY: Is acting something you might like to get into someday?

CARLIN: If I can do what I'd like to do in comedy over the next 10 years—a couple of books, a couple of screenplays, some fun on cable, a few more albums—then I think it would be really magnificent, about the age of 55, to begin serious training as an actor. Between 55 and 70, I'd like to play small roles in out-of-the-way theaters, then get into films as an older character actor; show up for eight minutes in the bar scene, do my little shtick and disappear. Oh, I would revel in that kind of life, and I'm going to try for it.

PLAYBOY: Have you ever fantasized about living in another age?

CARLIN: If I had lived in Babylonian times, I probably would have chiseled my jokes in stone tablets and dragged them from house to house. In the Middle Ages, I'd have been that odd fellow standing in the middle of the square, telling stories. The townspeople would pass and say, "Every Friday he comes in and talks for an hour. We don't know why." I would have loved that.

PLAYBOY: In your performance fantasies, it almost doesn't matter whether or not people are listening to you, as long as you get to do your rap.

CARLIN: People become performers for many reasons. Some do it to get a lot of pussy—and that's a good reason. Some want a bigger car. Other guys want to travel. My reason has always been that I was screaming to let all this shit out of me.

PLAYBOY: Late at night, when the lights are out and the TV is off and Brenda is sleeping but you're not quite asleep yet—what do you think about? What goes through your mind?

CARLIN: I fly. I close my eyes and picture myself making the motions of treading water, and then I start floating over trees and houses and farms and fields that are crosshatched. It all rolls by just like in the penny arcade when you drive the car for a quarter. Occasionally, I'll throw in a lake or a river. Sometimes I let an animal run by. Maybe a dragon. One dragon, that's all. You don't want too many dragons in your fantasy.

PLAYBOY: Do you have any hobbies?

CARLIN: No.

PLAYBOY: No?

CARLIN: I have interests and I read a lot, mostly nonfiction, because I'm probably still trying to finish my education. But my primary avocations are to make my family and my household happy, to live inside my brain, to have funny thoughts and to write them down—for myself, mostly.

PLAYBOY: Do you think that desire to live within your own head derives from your lonely childhood?

CARLIN: Probably. My mother would always say of me, "He certainly knows how to entertain himself." So I don't seek a release or an escape in activities.

PLAYBOY: Do you deliberately avoid new activities because they might interfere with the life of your mind?

CARLIN: Yeah; I've never permitted myself to experience the joys of racquetball and I don't feel the loss.

PLAYBOY: But do you feel lonely?

CARLIN: I feel an aloneness, and I relish that. As much as I love my family, I enjoy it when the house is empty, because then I know I'm truly alone, as we all are on the planet, after all. You know, every atom in us is originally from a star. And during my moments of aloneness, I'm most mindful of that; that I'm just another group of matter randomly but wonderfully arranged. That's when I feel my immortality.

PLAYBOY: Your *im*mortality, as in afterlife?

CARLIN: Not in the Christian sense, but I do believe in the survivability of the human spirit. We were all part of a giant explosion once, and we've come a long way. The incredible distances of past and future time, the history of this whole fucking, vibrating, resonating mother mass—that's what I read and think about more than anything else.

PLAYBOY: Do you see much of a future for us?

CARLIN: I don't see much of a future for this planet. I think it's a cursed planet. The boundaries we've drawn between nations and the profit motive—those two factors—have, in my opinion, brought us to the point where almost nothing can stop the utter destruction of the environment and all our earthly life-support systems. Perhaps after a holocaust, the survivors can rebuild on a more spiritual level. Perhaps civilizations rose and failed many times on this planet before man arrived.

PLAYBOY: Your opinion of mankind is not exactly reverential.

CARLIN: Man in his finest state is a curious and investigative creature capable of the magic of creativity. In a book called *The Origin of Consciousness in the Breakdown of the Bicameral Mind*, Julian Jaynes argues that man didn't even reach what we call consciousness—that is, the ability to self-inspect—until about 1000 years before Christ; that *The Iliad* and *The Odyssey* were written by unconscious humans who had auditory hallucinations from the right side of their brains. Now, if we can come from a state of unconsciousness to consciousness in only 3000 years, imagine what other states we might reach given the time and the freedom to evolve.

PLAYBOY: Maybe we will get that freedom. American cultural influence pervades half the globe, and this *is* the home of the free.

CARLIN: The folks who settled the United States and migrated to it afterward have mostly been narrow-minded religious people, exploiters and frontier-justice types who shot first and asked questions later. We're not a freedom-loving people in the beautiful, spiritual sense. We have an inspiring Constitution, but we're a hardhearted people.

PLAYBOY: We've had a checkered past, at best, including slavery and the exploitation of immigrants and women. But we've made improvements on those fronts. Doesn't that give you hope?

CARLIN: No. When I see blacks and women wanting to gain their freedom so they can become corporation executives, I realize that the situation is hopeless. What's the good of having freedom if you then willingly go off and become a slave to an amoral institution? It's especially depressing to see blacks wanting to dive into the mainstream of American commercial life. They come from a magnificent African culture based on aesthetics, and now they all want to become fort builders like the vicious people who originally enslaved them.

PLAYBOY: You may despise the American corporate structure, which is unabashedly based on greed, but you're now despising it from a beautiful home in a beautiful neighborhood. Earlier today, you were despising it from inside a $35,000 BMW.

CARLIN: My money buys me the freedom not to be a member of the corporate structure. And I certainly don't feel guilty or hypocritical about that. The way our economy is set up, if you don't want to be a corporate moron and you don't want to be enfeebled in the streets, you must earn enough to know that you'll never have to go to *them* for money. And I've been able to do that without selling anything that injures the earth. I sell thoughts, laughs and ideas.

PLAYBOY: You never do commercials. Are you willing to condemn other performers who do?

CARLIN: It seems to me like a perversion of talent for an artist of any kind to further the corporate structure of America or the personal interests of the morons and thieves who run it.

PLAYBOY: Given your tough views about America, how do you feel about Soviet society?

CARLIN: I despise bullies in any guise. Russia offers very little freedom. Its economy is unsuccessful. It can't even get a harvest together. It *appears* to do its war machine well enough to get its geopolitical ends met, but I don't know how it'd fare if it actually had to fight a war. It would probably fuck that up, too. Russia just looks like a total failure to me.

PLAYBOY: Earlier, you referred to the U.S. Constitution as "inspiring." Do you endorse all of it—even the right to bear arms?

CARLIN: I have mixed feelings about that. I plan to get a gun if crime gets any worse. I believe my first duty is to survive. And I'm not just talking about criminals coming into my home. I once seriously considered getting a gun to protect myself from the police. If I need a weapon to continue living, I'll get one. And I'll use it.

PLAYBOY: But if violence in our society—

CARLIN: Look, I'm going to interrupt you: There are two ways to think about this existence we have. One of them is that it's Wednesday and it's three-fifteen and we're talking here in my home, and at four o'clock I have to leave for another meeting. Now, that's a reality. But there's another reality. We're in the solar system of a second-rate star, three quarters of the way out on a spiral arm of an average galaxy in a thing called the Local Group. And ours is only one of billions of galaxies, each of which has billions of stars. Some star systems are binary, and there could be a planet that revolves around a center of gravity between two binary stars. So you'd have two sunrises and two sunsets every day. One could be a red giant, the other a white dwarf; two different-sized, -shaped and -colored suns in the sky. And there might be other planets and comets. In other words, fuck Wednesday, fuck three-fifteen, fuck four o'clock, fuck the United States, fuck the Earth. It's all temporal bullshit. I like thinking about being out there and not thinking about the corporate structure, not worrying about freedom and not worrying about guns. I chose a life of ideas. That entertains me. That nourishes me. And that's why I run from this conversation.

PLAYBOY: Returning for a moment to the planet Earth, what have you done with all the money you've earned in your career?

CARLIN: A lot of it went up my nose. As for the rest, well, I won't invest in the stock market, so I've had various business managers—all of them now fired—who've gotten me into limited partnerships in real estate. I don't know how fair or unfair our rent policies are, because, again, I'm a limited partner. Really limited; limited not only by the definition of the agreement but also in terms of my own appreciation of business. I'm a *limited* partner. That's why they wanted me. They said, "This guy's limited. Let's get him into our fucking partnership."

PLAYBOY: Because those business managers are gone, may we presume that in the future you'll be doing other things with your money?

CARLIN: Land still seems relatively harmless, though it would be really nice if there were no ownership. One philosopher has rightly said that property is theft. But I'd like to use my future ownership of property to give something back. You've got to give back some of what you take out—especially when you take wealth out at an unnatural level, as entertainers do. So I think it would be fair and right to use some of my land and wealth for a drug-rehab center or an Indian school.

PLAYBOY: Is there anything you've said anywhere in this interview that you wish you could change?

CARLIN: No, but something I said will, I think, change me.

PLAYBOY: What's that?

CARLIN: I was thinking of that conversation we had about my outside interests and it occurred to me that I don't define myself by much more than my career. When I'm not actually doing my work, I'm planning it or thinking about it or reading things that on some level are transformed into performance fantasies. I have no active interests. I never go anywhere or do anything that transports me outside the boundaries of my mind. But because of this interview and the questions this interview has spawned among myselves—now, there's a frightening slip, "among myselves"—well, now I've begun thinking about getting into some extracareer activities.

PLAYBOY: Do you know what they'll be?

CARLIN: I think I'll join a softball team. Drinking beer on the bench with the guys. Shagging flies. Sliding headfirst into third base. . . . Wow, man, sounds great. I can't *wait* to sign up!

PLAYBOY: When will you do it?

CARLIN: In a year or two. I need to develop my reality picture first. Psychocybernetics. Dream something strong enough and it'll happen. . . . Ahhh, softball. I can taste the dust from the base line already . . . someday. . . .

 October 2005 ────────────────────────────

A candid conversation with the outspoken comic about his onstage meltdown, his stay in rehab, the state of the world and why he's not all that angry (really!)

Considering the number of brain cells George Carlin has barbecued over the years, we're astonished at how much firepower is left inside that head of his. As the comedian approaches 70, the lounge-lizard hair is grayer and the old ticker is faulty (he's had three heart attacks already), but his mind is eternally churning fresh ideas and raw insights, mainly about how completely fucked we humans really are.

Last December, just after losing his temper with an audience in Las Vegas, Carlin stopped sniping at the rest of us long enough to cast a cold eye on his own shortcomings—namely, prescription-drug and alcohol addictions. With his third comedy book, *When Will Jesus Bring the Pork Chops?* ascending the *New York Times* best-seller list, Carlin checked himself into Promises, an A-list detox facility in Malibu, where 30 days of therapy and soul-searching (along with an antidepressant or two) gave him the reboot he needed to end more than five straight decades of substance abuse. Now he's raging on the road again, sharpening his barbs at comedy clubs across America in preparation for his 13th HBO stand-up special, *Life Is Worth Losing*, to air live from New York's Beacon Theater on November 5. Although he's won four Grammys, has a wall of gold records and has sold more than two million books, Carlin has enough new material on his hard drive—some 2800 files' worth—for perhaps 70 more years of edgy comedy.

Still, Carlin will forever be known as the man who forced the Supreme Court to utter the words "shit," "piss," "fuck," "cunt," "cocksucker," "motherfucker" and "tits." In the landmark 1978 case FCC v. Pacifica Foundation, the Court ruled that Carlin's best-known routine, "Seven Words You Can Never Say on Television," was indecent and that the FCC could ban those choice expletives from radio and TV during hours when children might be listening.

Born in 1937, Carlin grew up on the edge of Harlem in New York City and was raised with his older brother by their single mother. He dropped out of high school at the age of 17 and joined the Air Force; he was court-martialed three times, once for taking a nap inside a parked B-47 bomber. He started his professional career as a disc jockey near the Air Force base in Shreveport, Louisiana and, after letting his hair grow in the decade that followed, became a comic voice of the burgeoning counterculture, with characters such as Al Sleet, the "hippie-dippie weatherman." In 1975, jacked out of his mind on cocaine, he hosted the first episode of a promising new TV program called *Saturday Night Live*.

Writer David Hochman (who last interviewed Donald Trump for *Playboy*) recently caught up with Carlin on the road in Las Vegas. Hochman's report: "Carlin called me seven times before the interview, partly because he was nervous but also because he was excited to finally have a lengthy format in which to discuss rehab, drug use, his marriage, his new girlfriend and the many problems of our time. We met in the Presidential Suite at the Stardust, but the old-school vibe creeped him out. So we ended up talking backstage and at the pristine condo he owns nearby. Wherever we were, one or two of his TVs were tuned silently to CNN.

"George's act was a little rusty, mainly because he was in rehab when he should have been rehearsing. But at the interview table he was electrifying, almost going into a trancelike state as he threw himself headlong into passionate rants. Not one idea escapes him. He keeps small Post-its everywhere, and as soon as something—a joke, a word, an absurdity—comes to him, he'll jot it down and then enter it into one of his four Apple computers. He even has an iPod dedicated exclusively to his recorded thoughts. And the man has hours and hours of thoughts."

PLAYBOY: The last time you were in Las Vegas you called your audience moronic, and someone shouted, "Stop degrading us!" What was going on?

CARLIN: While Vegas audiences can be wonderful when there's a younger crowd, 80 percent of the time you get these fucking overweight schlubs from the Mississippi Valley. And they're a fucking bother because they have no imagination and no appreciation for unusual, creative themes in comedy. They think everybody should be like what you see on television. They're fucking horrified when they hear some of my subjects. I said something about that. I said, "I can't wait to go back east, where the real audiences are," or something like that. I've said that to audiences before. Usually I say, "There are three types of people who come to my shows, and you're the third type, and it ain't fucking good, folks." The trouble is, a local gossip columnist was in the audience, and he used some sensational language to make a story out of it. Suddenly it became a fucking "meltdown."

PLAYBOY: Is that what pushed you into rehab?

CARLIN: Oh, I'd made that decision long before that night. [*laughs*] Here's the deal with me: I was 67, and I didn't like having a habit anymore. I got tired of running. I began smoking pot when I was 13, so technically I had a 54-year buzz. I stopped smoking pot 20 years ago, but that's when the Vicodin and wine took over. And the wine turned into a bottle-and-a-half-a-day deal, and I noticed the number of Vicodin creeping up to four, five a day. Mind you, that's nothing to brag about by rehab standards. Some of the guys in there were taking 50 Vikes a day and burning down their house and backing into police vans and shit. I felt almost unworthy. But it's your personal bottom that matters, and I definitely suffered the affliction every addict suffers. I just couldn't stop. The addiction had more power than I did, and that's the sign of a real problem. Plus, for me, there were just too many requirements: finding the drink, counting out the fucking pills to see how many days were left before the prescription ran out. "Okay, if I renew five days early, the insurance will cover it and the pharmacist won't say anything. So five days early, at four a day, that's 20 extra. Hey, I can have six today!"

PLAYBOY: Was there an intervention of some kind?

CARLIN: No. And I would have just translated friendly advice as nagging or interfering, or I'd have thought, Leave me alone; I know what I'm going to do about this. Besides, nobody knew the extent of my habit. I lied as you do when you're an addict or an alcoholic, and I deceived everyone, including the doctors I was getting the prescriptions from. The thing is, if I told the truth, the secret would have been out and I would have had to deal with it. So I bullshitted everyone and played down the amounts, the need, the effects.

PLAYBOY: What were the effects?

CARLIN: It was a slight opiate high. When I would wake up—and I'm not one of these fucking guys who just spring out of bed at full speed—I'd say, "Oh fuck. I have all this shit to do today," not always looking forward to it. So I would stumble around for a while, and then inevitably I would take a couple of Vicodins. About half an hour later I wouldn't feel any of that negativity. It was an absence of a certain downness. Then eight hours later I would take two more. At night I'd usually have a little bit of wine, say, before a show. But I certainly wasn't a wine connoisseur like that guy in *Sideways* or anything. I just wanted the buzz. I never drank enough to slur my speech or stagger, but the wine calmed me down; then a little more would help me fall asleep afterward.

PLAYBOY: You still play 150 club dates a year. Does a little Vicodin make a place like Akron or Scranton more tolerable?

CARLIN: The truth is, I feel better sober than I felt when I was using and feeling good. I never did a 12-step program before, and it was great to go someplace where for 30 days I was assured of not having anything near me, no temptations, and where I'd have a network of people who would pull me away from my addictions so I could put my wishes into play. But here's the biggest surprise: Sobriety is not a struggle for me. I don't have a yen and I don't have an urge. Intellectually, if I'm in the supermarket and I pass the wine section, I say, "Oh yeah, remember when you used to do that?" and I keep moving. The last thing in the world I would do is walk into some place and get a glass of wine, because what the fuck would be the reason? As they say in AA—it's clichéd now, but it's true—"One drink is too many, and a thousand are not enough."

And there's another cliché—AA's full of them because they serve a purpose—that goes, "When the train hits you, it's not the caboose that kills you; it's that first car every fucking time," which I thought was very wise. There would be no future in opening that door or those bottles again. For what reason? I feel wonderful now.

PLAYBOY: Did you ever worry that stopping drugs would screw with your creativity?

CARLIN: There comes a point when drugs start to hinder rather than help. A psychiatrist once very generously told me, "George, you're brilliant despite the fact that you use drugs." He said drugs were probably getting in my way. I believe that was true.

PLAYBOY: Cocaine was your drug of choice in the 1970s. How do you look back on those years now?

CARLIN: Well, if you're already anal and left-brained and fucked up with this tendency to be obsessive-compulsive, then the cocaine feeds that. I would organize everything. I once had all my screws and bolts and nuts and washers and nails on the floor of my garage and just sat there matching them all up. Or I'd sort through my fucking record collection. [talking fast] "Shall I arrange this by genre or by band name? What about soloists? Do they go separately? Well, Roger McGuinn has a separate album, but he was in the Byrds. But then he was also in Buffalo Springfield. Oh shit! But so were the guys from Crosby, Stills & Nash. Oh fuck me! Here's Neil Young! What the fuck do you do with fucking Neil Young?" [laughs] And next thing you know, you're outside cleaning the front lawn with a toothbrush. It was a fucking mess.

PLAYBOY: Yet here you are at 68, still kicking, still working and clean as a whistle. No harm, no foul, right?

CARLIN: Well, I'll tell you, people always say in these interviews, "Is there anything you regret or anything you would do differently?" I've always kind of defiantly said, "No, nothing." But now I know a little better. I think if I could magically go back and change a portion of my life, I would erase those five or six years of cocaine abuse, for a multitude of reasons. First, the cocaine made me ignore my finances and my business interests, which put me in a giant hole with the IRS and damaged my ability to have a reasonable net worth.

PLAYBOY: You owed close to $4 million in back taxes at one point, right?

CARLIN: It started at about a million and went to about $3 million. But it's the penalties and interest that kill you. Plus, there are always current taxes to pay. It never stops. I had a lien on my house for 20 years. So it was very difficult, and it was a character builder. The sad thing is, if I had had more presence of mind, I might not have let that happen.

PLAYBOY: In 1975, on a trip to Hawaii, your 11-year-old daughter, Kelly, made you and your wife, Brenda, sign a contract to stop snorting cocaine for the rest of the trip. Does it make you sad now to think of a child in that position?

CARLIN: It was a terrible fucking cruel, unthinking, unloving thing for any parent to have done, to put Kelly in that situation. That's my biggest regret in all this. If it hadn't been for the cocaine, I wouldn't have put Kelly through the trauma of her mother and father fighting like crazy and being on drugs and being maniacs in front of her. It was pretty awful. I had Kelly working with me on these sick strategies to deal with Brenda. After all, I was the more sober drunk. [laughs] Brenda would start drinking early, so we'd hide her car keys if it was after a certain hour—say, noon. Rehab wasn't an option back then, so you did what you could. One time I told Kelly, when she was probably too young to fully understand, "I may have to make believe to mom that I'm going to leave her. I don't want you to get scared. I'll just be right down the hill at that little hotel. Don't worry." Again, if it hadn't been for the cocaine, I think I would have dealt with Brenda directly, issued an ultimatum. But instead she had to hit bottom. She backed my BMW through the lobby of a hotel. That was as good a reason as any to get cleaned up, and she spent 22 years clean without a slip. But as I look back now, it put all that pressure on Kelly.

PLAYBOY: What's your relationship with your daughter like today?

CARLIN: Kelly is now in her early 40s. She's in a good marriage. She's a psychologist with a master's in Jungian depth psychology, and she will probably go for her Ph.D. She has worked through a lot in her own therapy, all of this scarring and damage. And she and I have put a lot of stuff on the table together to try to heal some of this, which we think we have. And we move on.

PLAYBOY: What impact did Brenda's death from cancer, in 1997, have on you?

CARLIN: Well, I didn't get terribly emotional about it. First of all, I'm very much a realist and a practical person, and Brenda had been sick for quite some time. If you have any imagination at all, you find yourself imagining outcomes. Even if a person you're with isn't sick, you occasionally think of what life without them would be like. But it was not pleasant by any means. She had been stabilized with chemotherapy, but then things took a rapid turn. They kept her alive an extra 12 or 18 hours, apparently just for me to get back in from the road. And by the time I got there it was gruesome. So it was no picnic, but my tears were fairly contained. I felt them—I cried and everything—but I didn't go to pieces from the whole experience. I had kind of rehearsed it in my mind.

PLAYBOY: And then, a year later, you had a new girlfriend.

CARLIN: Sally and I met at a bookstore. Her dog came over and chose me.

PLAYBOY: Dogs do have a keen sense of smell.

CARLIN: They must, because Sally is the love of my life. I must say that as solid and as good as I thought my marriage was with Brenda—and we kind of lived in détente after a while because she had been sober about 22 years and I was still drinking and whatnot—there wasn't a lot of emotional connection during those years. But when I met Sally lightning struck. That's not to denigrate Brenda or my relationship with her, but with Sally it's that teenagers-in-love thing all over again. We wear these Jupiter rings and call ourselves the king and queen of Jupiter. It's our planet and we reign over all things Jupiterian. It's all about Jupiter, baby! [laughs]

PLAYBOY: What do you now know about women that you wished you knew at, say, 20 or 25?

CARLIN: Mostly it has to do with communication. Never sit on your feelings. Those couples who never fight, they're the ones you have to watch out for. Something's got to give. If you're talking about picking up chicks, I was never a cunt man or a swordsman or any of those things. I was never the guy saying, "Oh boy, I'd like to fuck her." Certainly I would see women and *think* that. But I wasn't the guy who came to the party and immediately locked eyes with someone and then had her in the fucking coatroom the next 10 minutes. I'm Irish Catholic, so there's inhibition there. I didn't take the Catholic part very seriously as a kid, but you can't shake the Irish part too easily. And you know, Irish foreplay is "Brace yourself, Bridget."

PLAYBOY: But for the sake of oral history, can you recount your hottest groupie experience?

CARLIN: I was never really that guy. During my cocaine years I was a moron with my behavior when I was out on the road, because cocaine kicks up that sexual drive, and I did what a lot of people did at that time. But honestly I don't remember a whole lot. Even with the coke, sex had to be with someone I liked. She had to be someone I was attracted to, not just to her ass or something like that. So there was a degree of honor in it, albeit a very small degree.

PLAYBOY: How has the sexual landscape changed since then?

CARLIN: It's actually a weird time for sex. Sex is all over the place in this culture. It's wide open. Compared with the 1960s, when it was merely an aspect of youth culture—free love and all that—it's a virtual sexual carnival out there now. You've got the Internet, strip clubs, porn stars on the radio. Even regular television is all cleavage and legs and asses and hot policewomen on *CSI*. You go into any hotel and you can buy movies in which the mailman shows up with a big hard-on and suddenly he's fucking three women at a Tupperware party—and it all goes straight to your hotel bill.

PLAYBOY: Is that progress?

CARLIN: I'm not sure. It's commercialism, sales, cash in somebody's pocket, which is what this fucking country revolves around. But at the same time we have this supercharged religious and puritanical aspect of our culture. We are the most religious country in the world. Europe looks at us like we have dicks growing out of our foreheads. They can't understand what the fuck is wrong with us with all this religious bullshit. Let's leave actual spirituality over on the side; that's a different thing. You know, you get these people now who say, "I'm not religious. I'm spiritual." Fine. But religion in this country has become a complete distortion and exploitation of the spiritual urge. It's ruled by charlatans who tell us what God thinks about us. God doesn't like our bodies, and we shouldn't like them. Our bodies are sinful instruments, especially the sexual parts and the bathroom parts. Feel guilty, America. Be afraid, America. God wants you to be ashamed! And these opposing forces—the chaste and the unchaste, commerce and religion—battle it out.

PLAYBOY: And let's not forget politics.

CARLIN: That's where it gets interesting. Politics is where all this shit comes together to totally fuck over the little guy. Bear with me; this is a large point. You have the religious right steering this country now, led by its head fuck in the White House. And to keep these religious people happy, George Bush and the people he's put in power operate through various arms, including the FCC, which controls commercial television and radio. So Howard Stern will say "pussy" or Janet Jackson will flash her tit, and the FCC sends down a shitstorm: "That's indecent! God doesn't want you to look at that!" Now add in the business element and things get really crazy. Advertisers want to appear righteous and moral because they don't want to scare away customers. They certainly can't appear to be too loose with their sexual standards. Oh no. People don't want to think they're buying a tit with their bar of soap, right? Yet here's the big secret: The Republican machine—the people with the money, the people who own everything, the people who run these businesses—loves that there's sex all over the place, because it doesn't want people sitting around thinking about what's being done to them. It doesn't want people thinking about how bad they're getting fucked by a system that abandoned them a generation ago. It wants people distracted.

PLAYBOY: So instead of giving poor people tax breaks—

CARLIN: It gives them toys—three-wheeled all-terrain vehicles and snowboards and cell phones with cameras, anything to take their mind off what's being done to them, that they're being bent over and reamed up their asshole every day of the week. This fucking country is rigged against the little guy. It's been rigged against the little guy for a long time. So the machine tries to distract you. All this Howard Stern shit, all this Janet Jackson's tit shit, any shit at all that keeps people's mind off the real shit that's going on, has a function, serves a purpose.

PLAYBOY: So you see no worth in protecting family values?

CARLIN: I'm all for protecting the family—doing the right thing by people, doing good for the working poor and for children. But what these fucking religious right-wing Republican cocksucker fuckheads don't remember is that Jesus Christ—who they look to, Jesus Christ, who they trot out all the time—actually said, "Do something for these fucking poor, sick, hungry people. If they're sick, fix them. If they're fucking hungry, fucking feed them."

PLAYBOY: We take it you're paraphrasing Jesus.

CARLIN: Jesus would have fucking gone straight to these religious shit-heads and said, "Let's change this shit, people." He wouldn't have given a fucking tax break to cocksuckers like me and people with all kinds of money. And I'm just okay. What's happened with money in this country is sinful. *Billionaire* is a common word now. Not that I give a fuck if people are rich, but don't be giving a lot of shit back to them with tax breaks. Let them fucking help somebody who needs it. Isn't that the deal here? Isn't the deal humanity? Come on, people!

PLAYBOY: Jim Carrey once said you were his anti-role model because he didn't want to be so angry at your age. Aren't you tired of being angry?

CARLIN: Yes, he did say that in a *Playboy Interview*, and I saw it, and I'd correct him in the following manner: I like Jim a lot. He's extremely talented, and he's a good fucking human being. But he misread the thing as anger. It's not anger. Angry is getting into a fistfight, which I've never done. Angry is losing your temper and regretting it. People who have been around me for 20 minutes or 20 years will tell you they've never seen me angry. Now, I can get irritated like anyone else—in traffic, on a slow line in a store, at a dumb clerk. Hey, that's natural, especially when you're an efficient human being and you like things to go properly. But angry? Not me.

PLAYBOY: Then what is it? How do you classify your vitriol?

CARLIN: It's dissatisfaction and disappointment. I'm disappointed that my culture let me down. I feel betrayed by the people in this country. They're dumb. They're just fucking stupid. They don't know how to protect themselves and operate in their own interest. I'm telling you, my fucking species let me down a long time ago.

PLAYBOY: Is that why you haven't voted since 1972?

CARLIN: That's right, for George McGovern. It doesn't matter if anybody votes. Kerry wouldn't have been any different than Bush. One of the most interesting things in politics is that we always worry about censorship from the right because that's the standard formula, but suddenly it's barreling in from the left, too, from the campuses in the East and the intellectuals via political correctness. I think when you go out of your way to protect so-called minorities and disaffected people by altering the language used about them, by calling people "differently abled" or whatever shit it is, you're saying they're not strong enough to handle anything on their own. The left thinks it's protecting people, but it's actually insulting them, whether they're handicapped people or blacks or lesbians. But the bottom-line message is still the same, whether from the left or the right: "You can't handle life unless we, the white, paternalistic, educated, wealthy community, help you by altering the game plan." And that's just fucked.

PLAYBOY: Is there a politician you think could make a difference?

CARLIN: I'll tell you who's an interesting figure: Eliot Spitzer, the attorney general of New York. He's very articulate and bright, makes smart alliances and goes after the right targets. I'd love to see him rise nationally, but the politicians would figure out some way to destroy him. They'd say, "Well, his sister was a lesbian in Venezuela, and she contracted the syph and gave it to a nun who was in with the terrorists." I'm telling you, politicians do what they want. The people who own this country own the land that counts and control the corporations and all the sources of news and information. Big chemicals, big oil, big insurance, big accounting, big banking, energy—the rich control everything, and they bought the Senate and the House a long time ago. They bought the statehouses. They bought the city halls. The judges are in their back pockets. These people have convergent interests: How can we make more money and get things our way? Reduce government regulation. Reduce our taxes and increase the burden on the general fucking public regardless of its health or safety or well-being. It's property over people, and that's why I'm not getting in my car and driving to some fucking high school gym to punch a hole in a piece of paper.

PLAYBOY: Since the news seems to be skewed depending on which channel you watch or which newspaper, magazine or blog you read, how do you figure out what the truth is?

CARLIN: You can't, and that's why people have begun looking to the distorters for the truth—to Jon Stewart, who I love and think is brilliant, and to *The Onion*. But all news is distorted today. What's presented to us as news is a fabrication or at least a manipulation of reality. The problem with these fucking people—these network anchors or whatever—is that they need access. All these fucking people who cover Washington or anything a reporter covers need to know they can get interviews. You don't fuck up your access if you're one of these people. So you play a delicate game. You don't embarrass your sources; therefore, you don't reveal certain things. You don't ask hard questions, so you're compromised from the start.

PLAYBOY: Explain something to us, then. If this country is so averse to provocative viewpoints, why do your books consistently become best-sellers?

CARLIN: We're schizophrenic. Of course the Republicans would love to make this a complete theocracy and have America be a kind of Taliban state where they have strict control over behavior and whatever titillation there is in news, advertising or entertainment. But they can do only what they can do, and that leaves room for fuckers like me. That's why I love this place. I love this country. I love the things it has given me, and I don't mean a nice car. I'm not really wealthy by any means because I had a long struggle with the IRS that defeated that purpose. But I do well, and I love that. But I love more than that. I love that I get to talk like this. I think this is fucking great. And there will come a day when folks won't get to talk like this. You can see that on the horizon if certain things break certain ways.

PLAYBOY: Why not take to the airwaves with your ideas? Do you ever think about pulling a Howard Stern and doing a show on satellite radio?

CARLIN: Not really, because what would I say on the second day or in the second week or the third month? The celebrity platform has been badly abused, mostly by Hollywood people on the Leno show who say, "I'm really passionate about this fucking project." Who cares? But let me say a few words about Howard: Howard's great. Howard's doing the right thing. And Howard's going to make a fortune for himself—not that that's the important thing, but Howard has pioneered again. He's a smart and savvy guy who found a niche, a big important niche—a male following he knew how to play to. I always liked him, but I was never comfortable doing his show because I never fit there. I didn't have lurid stories to tell about my own life. If I had, I might have been a little antsy about telling them. I could never give his audience the kind of red meat it wants. But when I listen to Don Imus I hear a slightly more thoughtful discussion going on and guests who are interesting to me, not just people showing their knobs or talking about whacking off. Back in 1992, Imus saw a show I did at Carnegie Hall on HBO, *Jammin' in New York*, and he got on the air and gave it a great review. So I called to thank him, and I said, "You know, I do *Howard Stern* sometimes. I don't really fit in there, Don. Can I call in to your show every now and then?" He said, "Come on in anytime," and all that shit. So I started that relationship because I feel it's a better fit.

PLAYBOY: You never quite fulfilled your long-standing dream to become a movie actor. Your TV shows get canceled, and you get only bit parts. How frustrating has that been over the years?

CARLIN: Movies have been a nice sideline, but that's about it. I'm passionate about showing off, and I'm just fine doing that onstage and in my books. I'm a kid who quit school in ninth grade who needs to show people he's smart. I have this need to prove my brainpower. I'm long since past the real need; now it's just a habit. But I'm still the same little show-off who in fifth grade stood up in the class meeting and sang "Mañana," the Peggy Lee song, a cappella at Corpus Christi grammar school in New York City.

PLAYBOY: So that was your earliest comedy gig? What did the nuns think?

CARLIN: I was a good learner and a good student and I could answer any of the questions they asked, so the nuns left me alone. But in my spare time I'd look around and go, "Well, what the fuck. Hey, Joey, watch this." You become a fuckup, you know, by pushing and bending the rules all the time. You try to make the other guys laugh and you're disruptive. So that was my big sin. The sisters kind of winked at it, and I could see it was good to be yourself and have ideas. Soon my natural need to entertain took other forms, such as imitating famous people—Jimmy Cagney, Humphrey Bogart and Edward G. Robinson—making up routines and imitating commercials and newscasters and stuff.

PLAYBOY: Did that make you popular?

CARLIN: With the kids, yeah. With my mother, absolutely not. She couldn't stand it in the beginning. My behavior was always rewarded by two things: people's attention and approval. As a kid who was alone in his house a lot because of family circumstances, I needed attention and approval. I needed to know the world thought I was cute and clever and a smart kid. So I got that. It was an unspoken thing. I didn't put words like this together in my head; it just happened. Like a sunflower leaning toward the sun, I became approval-tropic. I started to bend that way.

PLAYBOY: You've said you don't remember your father, who died when you were eight. Any sense of how his death contributed to the person you are today?

CARLIN: My mother and father were separated many times before I was conceived. Two months after I was born my mother realized my father's drinking wasn't going to stop no matter what he said. He was also a bully, and he beat my older brother. My mother was spared because she had four brothers and her father was a policeman. Nevertheless, I spent much of my childhood in fear of his coming to our door. The routine was that my mother, my brother and I would be sitting at the kitchen table. If there was a knock on the door, my mother would stiffen up and fear would come over her face. She would mouth the words to me, "Go look under the door." So I would get down on my hands and knees and look under the door. If I saw a woman's shoes, I could say, "Who is it?" and open the door and get my mother. If I saw a man's shoes, I said nothing. I'd just walk back and whisper, "Man's shoes." And we'd just wait silently for the person to leave. I think that made me a realist, actually.

PLAYBOY: What did it mean to you when he died?

CARLIN: It didn't mean anything to me. I was coming home up the hill singing "Jingle Bells"—it was Christmastime—and I came up to the apartment. Mom sat me down and showed me the death notice, a simple, small notice from the *New York Journal American*. I read it and said, "Uh, yeah?" And she said, "Do you want to go to see him or go to the funeral?" I said no. My brother said, "Definitely not," because he hated the fuck. I didn't have any emotion because I never had any emotion about him to begin with, so his loss was just a nothing. I did know that it made my mother feel better, and we never had to worry about the door again.

PLAYBOY: In your last *Playboy Interview*, almost 24 years ago, you were pretty angry with your mother. Did you make peace with her before she died?

CARLIN: My mother always had a great sense of entitlement toward me, and we had a difficult relationship. I had to kick her out of L.A. twice. She thought she would just come to California and move in with me and be my lifetime houseguest. And that was not going to happen, because she was a troublemaker. She would get in between people. For instance, even though she never drank in her life she started becoming my wife's drinking buddy. She pitted one person against another, and she had some unpleasant parts to her personality, which were reflected in that 1981 interview. I didn't make peace with her, quote-unquote. But when she finally came to California I got her an apartment near the ocean in Santa Monica. She was melodramatic, and she would call and say, "I never hear from you. I never see you. You've dropped me out of your life." I had her in that place, and I was taking care of her, this and that. She had a little life and people around her there, but that wasn't enough. She wouldn't have been satisfied unless she was living in the room next to me. What's happened, with the passage of time since 1989 when she died, is that I look back at the fullness of her life, not at the parts that intruded on my peace of mind. After all, she raised two boys in New York City basically by herself through the end of the Depression and World War II. She earned what amounted to a man's salary in pretty good advertising jobs. And she was quite an individual, a very colorful woman. She was larger than life—melodramatic Mary, I call her—and the woman taught me how to command a room.

PLAYBOY: Did your mother ever come around to enjoying your comedy?

CARLIN: She came around in a single afternoon. Here's what happened: We lived on the same street as the church, and one afternoon some nuns came up to her after I'd appeared on the Johnny Carson show. They didn't hear anything dirty, but they knew the content. They said, "Oh, Mrs. Carlin, isn't it wonderful how George is getting so popular? He's doing so well." My mother, affecting the embarrassed good Catholic woman, said, "Oh yes, Sister, but you know, the awful language—" And they said to her, "No, Mrs. Carlin. You don't understand. He's using these words to teach something. He's making a social comment." And my mother said, "Then you're not upset?" "No, no, no, no, no." Well, let me tell you, once my mother knew the Church had let her off the hook, she was the proudest fucking mother of a star you ever saw.

PLAYBOY: You did *The Tonight Show* as guest and guest host more than 130 times during Johnny Carson's reign. What's your favorite memory?

CARLIN: One time I hosted, and I was full of cocaine. I had David Carradine on the program, and he was wearing some sort of diaphanous, half-Buddhist spiritual garb. He sat on that panel cross-legged, and I believe he was tripping on acid. My memory of it is this: I would ask him a question and he would answer the next question. I would say, "So how are you doing these days?" And he'd say, "Uh, my two brothers." Then I'd say, "So who was in this movie with you?" Or he'd say "a Chevrolet," and a question about a car would come into my head. I'm sure it was the coke playing tricks on me. In fact, I ran into David once and asked him about it, and he looked at me like I had a turd hanging out of my head.

PLAYBOY: Are you more of a Leno guy or a Letterman man these days?

CARLIN: The trouble with comedy is there's a lot of subjectivity. You love five people and hate five people. And you can't understand how the other person can't like a guy.

PLAYBOY: Come on, George. Jay or Dave?

CARLIN: I'd say I like Letterman a little better than Leno because he has that antishow thing going. He's kind of the non–TV host TV host. And he has a perversity and grouchiness I can relate to. I like Jay a lot, but it's tough. Johnny was the ideal model. He had a wonderful way about him. He had an impish quality people loved; he could kind of wink and get the laugh and still not take part in it. He was bright and quick. The world changed around him, but he never let the world change him. His show was a town square for America in a way that today's late-night shows can never be.

PLAYBOY: Which comedian makes you laugh these days?

CARLIN: Lewis Black. He has a great mind and a great way of presenting his dissatisfaction with things. Comedy is all about surprise—you get to thinking this is going to happen and instead that happens. That's funny. You're caught with your guard down and you laugh. I like Lewis's relentlessness. I love his overkill. I love the fucking sledgehammer. Lewis wields a mighty sledgehammer.

PLAYBOY: But most comedy today is pretty moronic, isn't it? Your generation had some great comedians, people who offered a view of life. Bill Cosby was cheerful and Richard Pryor was dark, but at least they gave you real views of the world. Today, people just do bits, quick reactions to things. How do you characterize the state of comedy today?

CARLIN: My comedy developed in the 1940s and 1950s, and the 1950s especially were a time when comedy stopped being safe and stopped focusing on "kids today" and "my wife's shopping habits." For the first time comedy became about saying no to authority. It was about individualism and people who had identities of their own and weren't just telling jokes—Lenny Bruce, Mort Sahl, Dick Gregory, Bob Newhart, Shelley Berman, Nichols and May. And there are a few more in there—Jonathan Winters and Lord Buckley, who wasn't a big figure but was very important to comedians. That evolved into Second City and the type of comedy that led to *Saturday Night Live*. Then the 1980s saw the comedy-club boom. People discovered they could take a fairly inexpensive storefront, put in cheap furniture and a bad sound system, pay the comics very little if anything, and then keep the whiskey money. These clubs exploited comedians in front of a hundred simple brick-wall backdrops, and it really hurt comedy. You had a lot of clubs, so you needed people to perform in them. You'd get these guys whose friends told them, "You, Joey, you're a fucking pisser. You ought to be a comedian." Then in the 1990s clubs became about getting somewhere else—how can I use this to get into the movies or land a sitcom? So your friend Joey was suddenly Harry the neighbor or the delivery boy in every sixth episode of some stupid sitcom. Which isn't to say great comedians didn't come up through the clubs. Letterman came out of them and so did Robin Williams and Jerry Seinfeld. But I think too many people were plucked from there and asked to do too much. I'm resentful that Eddie Murphy doesn't do stand-up anymore; he's a fucking brilliant stand-up. So is Steve Martin, one of my all-time heroes. But there's always hope for comedians. You know why? These comic fuckers live a long time. You notice how long fucking George Burns, Groucho Marx, Milton Berle and all these cocksuckers lived? I think it's because comedy gives you a way of renewing life energy. There's something about the release of tension that comes from being a comic, having a comic mind, that makes you live forever. Only the offbeat ones die young: John Belushi, Freddie Prinze, Andy Kaufman, Bill Hicks, Sam Kinison and now Mitch Hedberg, another great one. These people all had very different universes to offer us, and they've all been taken away.

PLAYBOY: Where's your comedy headed? What will the new cleaned-up George Carlin sound like?

CARLIN: Pretty much the same, but I'm always thinking of new shit. I have two more HBO shows I'd like to do. Then I have a Broadway idea about a stagestruck kid in Manhattan, namely me, who was on his own because his mother had to work. He had the run of the island. I'd love to do that. Then there's a fourth book coming. That will be more specialized ranting and raving about America and its government and crazy fucking people. And then you do today's work. Today's work always comes first.

PLAYBOY: Is there anything funny about getting older?

CARLIN: The older you are, the more noises you make. Standing up, sitting down—it's like you need a fucking lubricant. I agree with Bette Davis, who said, "Getting old is not for sissies." But it's just aging, so I say, "Fuck it." There were handicaps to being 10, there were handicaps to being 40, but the richness of memory, the richness of acquired and accumulated experience and wisdom, I won't trade that. At 68 I'm every age I ever was. I always think of that. I'm not just 68. I'm also 55 and 21 and three. Oh especially three.

PLAYBOY: In one routine you say, "God can't be perfect. Everything he makes dies." What do you want your tombstone to say?

CARLIN: I used to think it should say, "He was too hip for the room," meaning, of course, this earth. [laughs] But now I'm thinking something along the lines of "Geez, he was just here a minute ago."

PLAYBOY: How do you imagine heaven?

CARLIN: The best afterlife for me would be to be able to sit comfortably and watch the world on a kind of heavenly CNN—to be able to have my remote and say, "Okay, there's an uprising in Spain. Let's watch that." Or to watch China finally take over the fucking world. Because there's a billion of those motherfuckers, and they're going to eat our lunch. I would love to get the thousand-year view on the decline of the European birthrate or the Muslimization of Europe that's taking place or the explosion of Latin American culture in the western United States. Just sit back and watch. India and Pakistan each have nuclear weapons, and they fucking hate each other. I'm telling you, somebody is going to fuck somebody's sister and an atom bomb is going to fly. And I say fine. I just like the show. This world is a big theater-in-the-round as far as I'm concerned, and I'd love to watch it spin itself into oblivion. Tune in and watch the human adventure. It's a cursed, doomed species, but it's interesting as hell. That's what I want heaven to be. And if it's not like that, then fuck it. I'll just kill myself.

JON STEWART

*A candid conversation
with the smartass host of
The Daily Show about news
versus entertainment, the size of
Garry Shandling's ass and why
movies get sex all wrong*

Every evening, after the audience is locked and loaded but before taping begins, Jon Stewart bounds onto the set of *The Daily Show* to meet the people. He faces two sets of bleacher seats, cracks a few wry asides and takes questions from the crowd. Tonight a college student wants to know if Stewart will say the letters NYU on the show. Stewart mocks amazement.

"Why? If I do it for you I'll have to do it for everyone."

"Because I . . . I made a bet," the kid stammers.

Stewart is suddenly interested. "Oh? What's the bet?"

"I bet $10. If you say it I win."

Stewart mulls this over. "Will you give me half?" he asks. The kid seems hesitant, so Stewart adds, "Come on. I can't feed a family on cable money."

You can on the kind of cable money Stewart's making: an estimated $1.5 million a year for four years as the new front man of *The Daily Show with Jon Stewart*, Comedy Central's designated successor to *Politically Incorrect*. And according to the critics and fans, Stewart (who also helps write and guide the show) is worth every penny. Maybe that's why, late last year, in a *New York Observer* column "memo to David Letterman" lamenting *The Late Show*'s decline, Ron Rosenbaum wrote: "It started to go bad the moment your show stopped being about ridiculing big-ass, pompous television and started becoming big-ass, pompous television" and included an unexpected yet creative exit strategy: "Get Jon Stewart to replace you."

Not that Stewart is angling to move on. He has the greatest respect for Letterman, whose show helped launch Stewart's career, positioning him to have a talk show on MTV and, later, in syndication. And then there was the deal with Letterman's production company to host either a 1:30 A.M. talk show or to replace veteran Tom Snyder, for whom Stewart served as guest host, on *The Late Late Show With Tom Snyder*.

Are you keeping this all straight?

Stewart is a bright talent whose lightning-fast prowess with the ad-lib and wisecrack is savant-like. Since taking over *The Daily Show* from Craig Kilborn, he's seen the show's ratings improve (while Kilborn, who took over the Snyder show, seems badly miscast in his new role). Critics have raved about Stewart's self-effacing charm and smartass sensibility. That sensibility has been the secret to Stewart's success dating back to his days as talk show host on MTV. He doesn't try to be hip in the slightest, and yet he comes across as the hippest comic on television. It's no wonder that one critic called *The Daily Show* "the smartest thing on the air."

Jonathan Stewart Liebowitz, 37, grew up in the Trenton, New Jersey suburb of Lawrenceville, where he lived with his father, Donald, a physicist for RCA, and his mother, Marian, an educational consultant. The couple divorced in 1971, but otherwise Stewart's wonder years were typical for a young Jewish boy. He wondered: Would he "grow taller, get better looking, get laid"? Meanwhile, Stewart took refuge in *Mad* magazine, *The National Lampoon* and the defensive use of comedy to short-circuit any comments about his height, looks or religion.

At the College of William and Mary he got the answers to his questions (yes, yes and yes) and graduated with a B.S. in psychology, which he promptly put to use working as a bartender. His best drink: "A Whack in the Head—a mixture of Alabama Slammer and Long Island Iced Tea. Drink two and you're not getting up the stairs."

Stewart also worked for the state of New Jersey in various civic capacities and eased into a comfortable middle-class lifestyle that left him uncomfortable.

In 1987 he decided to pack his bag for New York City and test his secret ambition to do stand-up. His coming-of-age at the famed Bitter End was less than auspicious, but it still made him feel "better than anything else" he'd done. Even when another club owner told him that there were already too many Jewish comedians, Stewart didn't retreat to suburbia. He got a job hosting *Short Attention Span Theater* on Comedy Central in 1991. In 1993 he tried out with every other comedian to succeed Letterman on *Late Night;* Conan O'Brien got the job. Eventually, Stewart appeared on an HBO Young Comedians Special, then did the *Late Show with David Letterman.* That shot got MTV interested and he signed on to host the half-hour *Jon Stewart Show,* which debuted in September 1993. Paramount expanded the format to an hour and syndicated the show. Soon it was being replaced by *Roseanne* reruns, shifted to the 3:30 A.M. slot and was canceled in June 1995.

During the next few years Stewart turned up in unexpected places, including *The Larry Sanders Show,* where he often appeared as himself and was a creative consultant. He also launched a movie career (*Half Baked, Playing by Heart, The Faculty, Big Daddy*), hatched a production deal with Miramax Films and wrote a humor book titled *Naked Pictures of Famous People.* Rather than rely on the stand-up material he'd already mined in his 1996 HBO Comedy special, *Jon Stewart: Unleavened,* Stewart wrote essays skewering the conceits of popular culture. It was an immediate *New York Times* best-seller.

In January 1999, Stewart replaced the host of *The Daily Show* and hasn't looked back. "I'm very happy now," he says. Even if it doesn't get any better than *The Daily Show?* Yes, Stewart insists. "Let's just say that if it never gets any worse than this, then I've had one of the luckiest runs ever."

We asked Contributing Editor David Rensin, who last interviewed David Spade for us, to spend a few days with Stewart on the set of *The Daily Show.* Rensin reports:

"His office is littered with the detritus of celebrity: unopened champagne bottles, promo items, gift baskets and a biohazard container left by 'a guy who did flu shots. I wanted something to remember him by.' Jon's mind is similarly littered, but with the raw material of comedy-to-order. He could send up any topic instantly, especially when he detected an intentional (or unintentional) setup in my questions.

"For our second meeting, he asked if we could talk during the sixth New York Mets–Atlanta Braves Playoff game. We ordered in pizza and Cokes. 'This is going to be the best 12-year-old's pizza party you've ever had in your life,' Jon said. It was touch-and-go the whole game, and we would have watched the entire thing, but Jon kept calling his girlfriend to rave every time the Mets scored. Eventually he decided to catch the last few innings with her, and we said goodnight.

"The Mets lost, so I wanted to begin our next conversation on a cheery note."

PLAYBOY: Congratulations.

STEWART: Thanks. [*Pauses*] For what?

PLAYBOY: Isn't *The Daily Show* the longest you've ever held a job?

STEWART: That's true. I started January 11, 1999. How did you know?

PLAYBOY: This is *Playboy*. We know everything.

STEWART: We'll see.

PLAYBOY: Tell us about the time you destroyed thousands of dollars' worth of aquariums in what can loosely be described as a gymnastics accident.

STEWART: You *do* know [*smiles*]. First, the tanks were empty. No fish were harmed in that senseless tragedy. It was 1976 or 1977. My brother was an assistant manager at one of the first mega Woolworth's. He was a bit of a taskmaster, but good people. The main floor was filled with entertaining and wonderful items. I worked downstairs in the catacombs, with the stock shelves. To alleviate some of the boredom, we used to dive off the shelves. They were pretty high, but it was okay because this was back in the day of the beanbag chair. We'd pile them up and do whatever gymnastics routine we could imagine. Unfortunately, I hit a bag wrong and it shot across the room and wiped out thousands of dollars' worth of aquariums. Fortunately, I had the key to the incinerator. But, much to my chagrin, aquariums make a lot of noise when they burn. It drew the attention of some higher-ups and my brother had to fire me.

PLAYBOY: Too bad. You probably would have made manager by now.

STEWART: A major disappointment. But I sought professional help, improved my diving technique and haven't hit the bag wrong in years. I know it's one reason I've lasted so long with *The Daily Show*.

PLAYBOY: Describe *The Daily Show* to someone who's never seen it.

STEWART: It's a pulsating hour of drama. Actually, if someone's never seen it, chances are I won't be talking to them; I force people to watch a highlight reel before each and every introduction.

PLAYBOY: And then you walk into the room?

STEWART: Exactly. Then I say: "Do you watch the news? Do you think it's funny? We do, too." That's pretty much it.

PLAYBOY: What specifically is funny to you about the news?

STEWART: Not the news itself but how the news is delivered. The process of news. The parody is our bombastic graphics and the news song, the correspondents and their interaction with me. And by using the general structure of a news show, which we find inherently satirical, we've found a cheap way to get in 20 monolog-type jokes. Does that make any sense? [*Pauses*] Judges? Too bad: The East German says no.

PLAYBOY: Perhaps an example would help.

STEWART: Last night we had a bumper graphic that parodied how news programs tease viewers into watching the whole show: "10:11: Hero dog saves family. 10:13: Rapist on loose. 10:15: Do you know what's in ice cream? It could kill you. 10:17: Sports." Or look at the pomposity of *Dateline:* the grandiose set, the guy sitting in his chair, then getting up and the camera moving in that slow, sweeping way, as the host asks, "Would he escape from the ocean after eight days of drinking his own urine? When we return, the answer." Some news magazines will report on a murder trial while a ticker at the bottom of the screen counts people's phone-in votes for which side they think is right. "When we come back, the defense will present some evidence you won't believe!" It's gotten ridiculous. So we make fun of it.

PLAYBOY: On *The Daily Show* your interviews are only four minutes long. How do you prepare?

STEWART: Is it that clear that I don't? It's pretty standard stuff. Hank books the guests, does a pre-interview, then comes in with a dossier and we put up their picture. We do this in a secret basement room. We talk about their physical characteristics, their emotional characteristics. Has there been a breakdown? Drug allergies? Any notes from a doctor. Mental pressure points. Did you ever see Slim Goodbody? He wears a suit with the human organs on the outside for all to see. We usually go over that for each potential guest to see if we can find any weak areas. Once we come up with a game plan, Hank sends it out by code. I can't tell you much more because I'm already telling secrets.

PLAYBOY: In other words, you don't prepare at all.

STEWART: Hey, wait a minute! My goal is to be relatively spontaneous. The interview is really just a little something extra to throw into the show. It doesn't even have an angle, like when Kilborn did Five Questions. We just want it to be light and entertaining. We want to put our guests at ease. The key is to get them to go far enough to give the appearance of a heightened conversation that's not purely on the seller-buyer level. It's an easy gig. If it ran five minutes, I'd be concerned.

PLAYBOY: Have you ever taken on a guest over a disagreement with him?

STEWART: Not that I can recall, though that would be interesting. I've seen Chris Rock eviscerate people with common sense and wit while they sit there looking flummoxed. His interview with Representative J.C. Watts was one of the best I've seen. The Johnnie Cochran thing, too. We'd like to branch out into the political arena, but it's really hard to get anybody with a stake in politics to come on a network called Comedy Central. It's a fear of disgrace or embarrassment or humiliation. They know the rules of *Face the Nation* and *Meet the Press*, but nothing here is controlled.

PLAYBOY: Michael J. Fox was your first guest. Who would you like for your last guest?

STEWART: A 70-year-old Michael J. Fox.

PLAYBOY: Why is *The Daily Show* advertised as "the most important show ever"?

STEWART: It's a haven, an oasis of serenity and sanity. It's a new Statue of Liberty. It's a bully pulpit. We have an enormous effect on the population. The power is incredible. I hadn't planned to say anything about it, but we did a story about a peace accord in Kosovo, and the next day it happened. Coincidence? I don't think so. I liken myself to Oprah. When I plug a book, it flies off the shelves. Where would *Tuesdays with Morrie* have been were it not for our recommendation? Where would Stephen King be today? We saved his career.

PLAYBOY: Speaking of careers, though the press and public love you on *The Daily Show*, Jon Voight, when he was a guest, ribbed you good-naturedly about aiming higher. Did that bother you?

STEWART: No. I'm paid more money than I should be to come in, read the newspapers, write a bunch of jokes and work with an unbelievably talented group of people who make me laugh. It's better than being on a sitcom, where the show can be a big hit but your character has a terrible story line and nobody likes you.

PLAYBOY: Like Jeff Conaway on *Taxi*?

STEWART: Right. Everybody else goes off to these monster careers, but he ends up on *Babylon 5*. The last time I saw Jeff I was on the road, flipping channels in a hotel room. He and two strippers were learning how to do something in one of those flicks you pray for when it's late at night and the only thing on HBO is an old fight. It was some crazy titty movie. No dishonor in that, though.

PLAYBOY: In a recent *New York Times* story, Madeleine Smithberg, who helped create and runs your show, said that since Craig Kilborn left, the show "has lost the crystal-clear joke that it's a parody of the news." It wasn't a complaint, but what did she mean?

STEWART: They'd brought in an audience while Craig was there. An audience means you've given in to the fact that it is also a comedy show. When I came aboard I pushed that a little further. I don't say outright that we're doing jokes, but I ad-lib in a way that lets people at home know we're enjoying ourselves.

PLAYBOY: You seem more conspiratorial than Kilborn.

STEWART: That's my philosophy of television. If you're going to watch me, I might as well let you know I know you're watching. I don't think of this show as elitist.

PLAYBOY: Is TV bad for us?

STEWART: Here's what's really crazy: Everybody complains how the media are responsible for this or irresponsible about that. So the media hold forums to interview *the media* to find out what the problem is. I can't tell you how many times I've been asked on those shows, "Now you [comedians] push the limit and often offend people. How do you defend that?" Here's what I think of when somebody has the nerve to ask me what it's like to step over the line with a joke: What about a news program that shows a guy whose wife just got blown up in an accident? Right away they've got a camera at his house, in his face, and the correspondent asks, "How does it feel?" Then they show you the body. What answer will we get that's not some variation of "shitty"? What right do we have to know how that guy feels after losing his wife? There are times when I think, Man, this news guy would do a report from inside an open wound if he could.

PLAYBOY: They call it the public's right to know.

STEWART: That's true. But it's really the news functioning as entertainment. It shouldn't, but it does, because what the media really want—or need—is to create conflict. The hell with being informative; conflict is entertaining. If you scare people, if you use their fear against them, you can win. "Is your washing machine spreading dangerous bacteria to your children? Is a crazy rapist lurking in your supermarket? Uzi-wielding murderer on a rampage in local neighborhood! Film at 11."

PLAYBOY: Can the media reverse course or are we stuck with this national soap opera?

STEWART: I hope it's cyclical, but once you break through certain barriers, it's hard to reel that back in. The problem is the competitive nature of news. There's too much fear of being scooped. The news has always had a detrimental effect—Hearst did it during the Spanish-American War—but the march of technology has made it ubiquitous. And has exposed it. I remember after Columbine there was a press release about the network that claimed to have broken the story—as though how fast it broke was what really mattered. Fortunately, the network evening news isn't as slash-and-burn as what you see on a local level. The real disaster is the all-news channels. They have to fill 24 hours. They have enormous machines; tragedy and sensationalized material are their life raft. Without them, most of the time, they would drown in 24 hours of nothing. So: O.J., Menendez, Lewinsky, Columbine, JFK Jr., etc. They milk it.

PLAYBOY: Aren't they just trying to attract viewers?

STEWART: Yes. If TV thought that showing a naked girl jiggling car keys would do it—and they could get away with it—you'd see it tonight. TV news today subverts how I think news organizations should behave. Reporting news is a huge responsibility. It has to be taken more seriously. Bobcat Goldthwait had a great joke about the guy who videotaped the Rodney King beating. His joke was: "Put down the camera and help him!" He's right. News isn't a Discovery Channel documentary where you're not supposed to feed the apes because that would be messing with the journalistic credibility of your documentary. It's real life. News shows do, at times, affect the real news with their coverage.

An obvious example is when Bill Clinton, in his first 100 days, tried to do health care reform, among other things. But all we heard about was gays in the military. Was that his flagship issue? Did he say, "Health care reform? That can wait, as long as I get through my agenda of making sure that gay people are allowed into the military"? No, but that's how it came out because *that* was the most inflammatory story and the most conflict would come from it.

Same with the penis thing, the Lewinsky story. I still don't understand where the abuse of power was. You mean because he's an older guy and he's kind of her boss and she blew him? Like *that* abuse of power? Is that an abuse of the Constitution? Did he invoke some obscure article to get a blow job? The way it was characterized, you would have thought that getting a blow job from an intern was a crime against humanity, that even Adolf Eichmann would have said, "He did *what*? A blow job from an intern? Is he insane? My God. Think of the imbalance between their positions!" And there were the news media, over and over, trotting out the pomp and circumstance of "He lied to the American people." Don't they understand that we have memories? When Clarence Thomas was accused of sexual harassment, we could see that Republicans went out of their way to talk about how it wasn't important and how Democrats went out of their way to talk about the crucial nature of proving these claims: How could *any* man serve on the Supreme Court when he had mentioned pubic hair and Coke? Pubic hair and Coke? He's a judge! Judges aren't human! Then, a few years later, it switches around. Democrats are defending sexual harassment and Republicans are talking about the moral imperative of treating women as equals. Don't these people—news media and politicians alike—know that we sit home, watch this and go, "You only have situational ethics. You have no credibility with us."

PLAYBOY: So politicians are complicit in this?

STEWART: I think politicians look at these incidents with glee. They don't go, "Oh, I can help rid the country of perjury, lying and sexual misconduct." They think, I can use this to give my party an advantage.

PLAYBOY: What a surprise.

STEWART: Our elected officials hold themselves above the people and what's best. I don't believe for a second that Henry Hyde was appalled by Clinton's behavior. I don't believe Bob Barr was appalled by the conduct. Newt Gingrich? Newt Gingrich was fucking a woman—not his wife—while he was attacking the president for Lewinsky. It doesn't get any clearer than that. These guys are all just acting. You know that after Congress let out for the night they all went for a beer at some bar on the Potomac and giggled their fucking heads off. They're all in cahoots to keep their privileged places. Yet they and the media said, "Of course the American people care. Look at how the ratings go up." Big surprise: They were talking about the president's *dick*. Who's not going to watch that? "Hmm. Should I watch a rerun of *The Nanny* or a guy on TV talking about the president's dick and a cigar in a girl's vagina?"

PLAYBOY: For a guy the press has called "the Stravinsky of self-deprecation," you're pretty outspoken in print.

STEWART: It's how I feel [*sighs, exhausted*]. I also think I have to be outrageous here because I'm competing with naked women.

PLAYBOY: Seriously?

STEWART: Yeah. I'm not sure how long I can keep the readers from looking at the girl with no pants on, sitting on a llama. At some point you have to say something incredibly inflammatory, like "I fuck raccoons." Take Jesse Ventura's interview. It was tremendous. That was the key. I'm going for that little box with the bold print.

PLAYBOY: So what do you want as your quote?

STEWART: How about: "Please, please, just hang in there. Keep reading. You're only four pages away." I don't mind begging. "You can't masturbate forever. Everybody has to rest sometime. Don't hate yourself. We all do it. Just thank God you didn't flip to this page right before you came." You never want that image in your head: someone flipping the pages and seeing your picture at just that magic moment. That happened to me once with Gilbert Gottfried. Just as I was about to finish, I flipped the page and saw his face. It was like, "Oh boy, I got to work with this guy."

PLAYBOY: Does it bother you that, unlike Chris Rock or Dennis Miller, your voice is not the dominant sensibility of *The Daily Show*?

STEWART: My job is not to tell you what I think. My job is to tell you what I think is funny—which they do, too, by the way. If it's not funny it's not anything. Our show had its sensibility before I got here. But I also know that when I'm out there saying stuff on the air, I'd better be okay with it, so the editorial viewpoint is influenced by me. I like the balance. If the show's smart and funny, whether I have anything to do with it or not every night, I win.

PLAYBOY: Any advice from former host Craig Kilborn when you appeared as a guest during his final week?

STEWART: Not really. I congratulated him and tried to find out if I could use the bathroom. That sort of thing.

PLAYBOY: The feeling was that you, not Kilborn, would succeed Tom Snyder on *The Late Late Show* because you were under contract to the producers, David Letterman's company, Worldwide Pants. Instead, you replaced the guy who got the Snyder gig. What happened?

STEWART: My deal with Worldwide Pants was like a Vegas marriage. They were drunk, I was drunk. It seemed like a good idea at the time. Getting together was just an impulse thing. We both woke up the next morning, mouths a little dry, feeling a little cottony, eyes a little bloodshot. We looked at each other and went, "Man, you sure looked better last night when I was drunk." But not in a bad way. That's just how shit happens sometimes in this business.

PLAYBOY: Were you disappointed?

STEWART: No. I wasn't ready and Worldwide Pants wasn't ready. I don't think it was a priority for them to develop a show for me, which, originally, was talked about as for 1:30 in the morning. The whole thing was serendipity. I did a spot on Letterman's show; at the same time, I'd been offered the gig hosting NBC's *Later*, which Bob Costas and Greg Kinnear did. Letterman's people knew about it and said, "Hey, what would you think about . . . ?" I said, "You know, I'm sort of into this thing over at NBC." I think their reaction was, "Well, we don't want *them* to fuck this girl. We'd rather fuck her."

PLAYBOY: So you were seduced.

STEWART: I've got major admiration for Dave Letterman. To hear from him that he would somehow like to have his name associated with mine, in however peripheral a manner, was powerful candy. My sit-down with him was like an audience with the Pope. So even though a contract was signed and money exchanged hands, we committed without really committing. Thank God, because it never would have worked. A show of that magnitude, five nights a week, becomes your life. I've done it before, and not that successfully, even though I thought we did a nice job of it.

PLAYBOY: Were you concerned that doing *The Late Late Show* might look like failed-talk-show-host-can't-give-up?

STEWART: No. It's not as if I had a dartboard at home with my face next to Pat Sajak's and Rick Dees's.

PLAYBOY: What's the difference between Letterman on-screen and off-screen?

STEWART: On-screen is a performance. His interviews are like a sketch. He plays like he's actually interested in what I did for Thanksgiving and I play like something funny actually happened. Off camera, he's incredibly human. There is no game, no act. He was a very smart, funny man talking to me about his vision for late-night and his interest in me. I was impressed.

PLAYBOY: Did Letterman ever say that Snyder would soon retire, or that he wanted him to?

STEWART: That was never explicit.

PLAYBOY: Did you and Snyder ever talk about this when you guest-hosted *The Late Late Show?*

STEWART: We had one sort-of conversation in which I said, "Hey, I just want you to know I have the utmost respect."

PLAYBOY: Give us the short course on the fine art of sitting in.

STEWART: If there's a drawer that is locked, don't jimmy it with a butter knife. They'll know. Also, you can only pull that fill-up-the-vodka-bottle-with-water gag once.

PLAYBOY: You also tried out for the job that Conan O'Brien got.

STEWART: It was pre-MTV. I had no experience outside a couple of writing gigs and doing shows above the karaoke bar. I lived on the road, staying in comedy condos that had huge holes in the walls because the last comic there didn't have as pleasant a time as he'd expected. I tried out because the juxtaposition of my life with the idea of maybe replacing David Letterman on *Late Night* was so great I almost couldn't get my head around it. I thought of it as a lifeline. And the weird thing is that I got far enough in the auditions to believe for a second that I might get it. The audition was in a stand-up club. We each did 10 minutes. Among the "contestants" were Allan Havey, Drew Carey, Paul Provenza. It was like being in the Miss America finals. I knew I wasn't going to get it when, after two minutes, Lorne Michaels—who produces the show—stood up and said, "No!" That's when I thought, Oh, I should have turned the mike to "funny."

PLAYBOY: Do you now feel like you've had the last laugh?

STEWART: Not really. On the other hand, the prophecy I'd created for myself—one room without a bathroom, miserable old guy who will never love or be loved—didn't happen either. Some of us are optimists, some are pessimists. Some see the glass half full, some see the glass half empty. And some are sitting on shards of glass and trying to pick them out of their ass.

PLAYBOY: One magazine writer described you as the "celebrity equivalent of lint: He pops up in interesting and unlikely places." Another example of your waiting in the wings was when you appeared as yourself on the last season of *The Larry Sanders Show*, filling in for Larry. Rumors quickly circulated that you'd actually take over as faux host when Shandling left. Was that ever in the cards?

STEWART: That's the beauty of the show. They drew a bizarre line between fiction and reality. In reality, my becoming the host would be like saying, "Hey, Michelangelo's *David* could really use a mustache and mutton chops." It's like MASH and *After MASH*. Are people really interested in what Klinger and Radar are doing in Iowa?

PLAYBOY: How did you get involved with Garry Shandling?

STEWART: I met Garry through the personal ads in *The Advocate.* Or maybe it was through the 4-H circular. I can't remember. But his ad was charming and I thought we had a lot in common. Except his ass is bigger than mine. By the way, I've only eyeballed his ass. I don't know firsthand. You have to draw the line somewhere in a working relationship. Now when we hang out, it's not exactly dating because only light petting is involved.

PLAYBOY: How about the real story?

STEWART: When I hosted my own talk show, Garry did a walk-on for the last three minutes, the night Jeff Tambor played my sidekick. Of course, I knew who he was. I had a TV. I liked *It's Garry Shandling's Show* and his stand-up. I'd been aware of him for many years, from afar. The beauty of Garry is, when you think the joke is over, it's not over. Most of us run out of steam on punch lines. You get to that point where you've tagged your last tag and there's nowhere else to go. That's when Garry comes up with five more tags. I can't quite figure out how he does it; I just think his brain is wired more efficiently.

PLAYBOY: You're known for being lightning quick and dead-on yourself. Did you two ever trade professional secrets?

STEWART: No. I've spoken to some of his representatives and they have agreed with me, but I've never spoken to Garry directly. He was kept in a plastic bubble when we worked together.

PLAYBOY: Can comedians really be friends with other comedians? What's the rule?

STEWART: They have it up in the bathroom at the Improv, but I can't remember it. No, no, that's "Wash your hands before you leave." [*Pauses*] Most people have this impression that among comedians it's like *Diner*, a bunch of guys doing shtick over French fries; or that all we do is analyze comedy; or that we're all neurotic and crazy. Well, maybe that last bit is true. But some of the best conversations I've had with other comics at three A.M. sitting in a diner were *not* about comedy.

PLAYBOY: Are you the kind of guy you imagined becomes a comedian?

STEWART: Preconceived notions are invalid. With accountants the big gag is that they're boring. But I'm sure there's a hang-gliding accountant out there who knows how to play the drums and fucks like a champ. I'm sure there's an accountant somewhere who comes home late at night drunk, sticks his dick in the butter, laughs his ass off and goes, "If they only knew."

PLAYBOY: What's the most important thing to you about comedy?

STEWART: Nothing. It's silly. You want something important? Learn to take a guy's heart out of his chest, restart it and put it back in.

PLAYBOY: Isn't humor also curative? A way of enhancing the human spirit?

STEWART: Oh boy. Most comedians are incredibly cynical, and the last thing they're doing is enhancing the human spirit. [*Pauses*] Most are feeding their own gratuity machine, ingesting something they need and popping it out on the other side. If it happens to have a positive effect on people, that's great. But I believe very few comedians got into it because the children need to laugh. They do it to feed something in themselves. Somewhere in their brains a neuron fires happily and a need is eased, like a drug. It's almost self-medication.

PLAYBOY: Even so, the public gets something out of it.

STEWART: Yeah, but there's no Mother Teresa of comedy saying, "I'm going to go to Calcutta and live there for years in poverty and entertain the children." There are no development deals for martyrs. We're out there getting our swerve on.

PLAYBOY: Why did you want to become a comedian?

STEWART: Like most of the comedians I know, I was uncomfortable in other settings. Before I found comedy, nothing fit my receptors. But this felt right. As bad as I was when I started, it still felt better than anything else I'd ever done. It soothed a need, and that was good enough for me.

PLAYBOY: You did kids' puppet shows before stand-up; why didn't that feed the need?

STEWART: This is actually a great example that illustrates my point. Kids on the Block was a performance program in which half the puppets were disabled and half the puppets weren't. They interacted in a way that helped children understand people with disabilities and how to interact with them. It was a truly good and decent thing to do for people; an enlightened, wonderful performance. Yet I thought to myself, Fuck this. I need stand-up.

PLAYBOY: Like Larry Sanders, you wrote a book. But instead of an autobiography, yours has comic essays in which you take on Bill Gates, Hitler, the Kennedys, Hanson, Leonardo Da Vinci, chat rooms, Judaism, sitcoms, local news and more. What did you leave out?

STEWART: [*Laughs*] There was one piece called *Les Marlboros*. It was a parody of *Les Miserables* where the revolution was smokers versus nonsmokers. It actually included Jean Valjean, who didn't understand the whole thing, but he was French and he liked to smoke, so he decided to lead the band of rebels. It was long and boring.

PLAYBOY: What can't you wait to write about in the next book?

STEWART: As far as I can tell, in this country we can't keep a secret about anything. We even found out that Dick Morris was sucking the toes of a prostitute. So how come the guys protecting the truth about whether or not we've been visited by extraterrestrials have their shit together? I would love to figure out a way to write about the sciences. Cloning: We just hit six billion people and we're still working on a new way to make new people? It's fascinating that, with all the world's problems, scientists decided to make hard-on pills. I might write about how to make Viagra palatable. It could come in a gelatinous form, like Jell-O cubes, because we need to make it fun for kids, too! And I guess if you're 80, Jell-O is just easier to swallow. Pretty soon it'll be a Viagra patch. Or it'll be a pull cord somehow. It's this crazy idea that if we somehow keep old people fucking, everything's going to work itself out. It boggles my mind that that's where the money goes.

Violence is another interesting area, especially with kids who don't realize that everything they're so bummed out about now will turn around. My idea on solving that issue is to take high school kids on field trips. But not to planetariums and museums; take them to 20-year high school reunions. "See the fat guy over there? Bald? Crying in his beer? Captain of the football team." "That nerdy guy with the pocket protector? A billionaire." Giving them a sense of perspective would be good, and maybe we'd even come up with a cool T-shirt to give the kids.

PLAYBOY: Let's investigate your style. Thin ties or wide ties?

STEWART: You mean to wear? I wasn't sure. It's *Playboy*, so I figured at some point I'm going to have to throw in my sexual proclivities.

PLAYBOY: Better topic. Go ahead.

STEWART: *I fuck cheese!*

PLAYBOY: Anything else?

STEWART: In bed I always apologize. I take responsibility for a job poorly done. I like to end sex with, "I beg your pardon." Sometimes, if I've been doing a film, I'll say, "Check the gate." Or: "Sign this form and you can go. You can take something off craft services on your way out. We'll call you for the premiere."

PLAYBOY: When was the first time you had sex?

STEWART: What time is it? I guess I was 18. I was a freshman in college.

PLAYBOY: When was the first time you had good sex?

STEWART: Boy, I'm not good with dates. You mean sex with love, where there's actually emotion involved, other than fear?

PLAYBOY: Yes. When did fear leave your sexual routine?

STEWART: [*Whispers*] It was Christmas 1984. We hadn't had much snow that year and the potato crop had been good. We huddled around the hearth. [*Pauses*] I think for men the fear is never gone. While he may not be on your shoulder, he's certainly around: "All right, buddy. Don't get any ideas. I'm right here in the hall."

PLAYBOY: What are your turn-ons?

STEWART: People who ask me what my turn-ons are. Also, honesty and long hair.

PLAYBOY: And turn-offs?

STEWART: Short hair and lying. Makes sense, right? You never see: "Turn-on: Honest people. Turn-off: People who tell the truth." There's never that.

PLAYBOY: Tell us the truth: What was it like to kiss Gillian Anderson in *Playing by Heart?*

STEWART: I was upset. I blacked out and woke up with makeup on my face. That's all I remember about it, but I know the truth is out there. It's weird to kiss somebody you don't know in *that* way. It's not natural. I don't think anybody would tell you it's the most comfortable thing in the world.

PLAYBOY: So it was your first time?

STEWART: No, I kissed Jennifer Beals onscreen a few years ago. And I kissed Fran Drescher on *The Nanny*. Luckily, everyone was professional and nice about it. I've never had a situation where I did it and the woman turned to the director and said, "Uh, can we just get the stunt guy in here?"

PLAYBOY: Do you bring the kiss from home or do you act the kiss?

STEWART: I guess it's my personal kiss, but it's not like it's from home because it lacks the huge emotional thing. Also, a lot of what we're doing is impressions of what we think we're supposed to be doing. Remember those old 1940s movie kisses? *Those are kisses.* The-war-is-over, we're-in-Times-Square, I'm-wearing-a-uniform, you-look-pretty, I'm-gonna-smack-you-one-right-here, *bang!* kisses. They dip and do the thing.

PLAYBOY: But they don't even open their mouths.

STEWART: Right, but look at how they go for it. *Bang!* The new thing in kissing is the lean-in, the I-have-to-show-you-that-we're-just-coming-to-this. I don't recall that ever happening to me. It's usually far more awkward than that, and afterward you have to talk about it for six hours. In some ways we're doing an impression of what a Hollywood make-out scene is now. Have you ever watched soft-core movies on Cinemax? They're not having sex, they're doing an impression of what sex is. The girl sits on top and you raise your arms to cover her breasts, depending on if she signed a release about her nipples. It's fake sex. It's the impression of sex as we have come to know it through movies. It's sort of like comedians who do an impression of Jack Nicholson. It's actually an impression of a comic you saw doing a Jack Nicholson impression.

PLAYBOY: Which films moved you as a child?

STEWART: I can tell you the first two films I ever saw: *Ring of Bright Water* and *Yellow Submarine.* It was a back-to-back drive-in thing.

PLAYBOY: Did they influence your career?

STEWART: Well, it was a long time before I realized that the world wasn't animated. *Ring of Bright Water* is the most amazing movie. It was back in the old days when animal movies were supposed to end horribly. Now they have the kid weeping as he looks up to see the dog limping on three legs after traveling 2000 miles by train, with a smelly hobo, to come home. This movie is about a kid who had an otter. The otter helped the kid out of a tough jam and he and the otter were tight. So you think everything is okay; the kid's life is going to be good. Instead, he's walking along with his otter, moseying down this country road, when a farmer comes up and, in a split second, decapitates the otter with a shovel. Then the movie ends. It is the most bizarre thing I've ever seen. And the kid just looks at him like, What the fuck? It's sick. It's sadistic. I loved otters. [*Pauses*] Imagine a Disney movie today that got away with an ending like that. Mighty Joe Young shot through the head. At least they didn't roll the end credits on Bambi's dead mother: Bambi's an orphan, the fire is burning, see ya.

PLAYBOY: Let's break your life and career into *The Daily Show* segments. What are the headlines?

STEWART: Stewart's acne clears up just as back hair appears: will he ever win? Stewart scores seat at New Jersey bar, given tenure: will he accept it? Stewart hits the Bitter End, Robin Williams not shaking in boots.

PLAYBOY: Your first gig was there.

STEWART: I chose the Bitter End because of its vaunted history of comedic performances; also it was within walking distance. I thought of Woody Allen in front of the brick wall, spinning yarns, and Cosby and Richard Pryor. Then I remembered that that was 20 years earlier. It had become

Doors cover bands. I went onstage and after only two minutes received my first "You're an asshole!"

PLAYBOY: Your reply?

STEWART: Well, I'm known for my rakish comebacks. I believe I said, "Nuh-uh" and let him take it from there. It was raining as I was leaving, and I remember thinking, What a lovely literate metaphor for my career right now.

PLAYBOY: What kept you going?

STEWART: The combination of rejection and laughter. They didn't laugh 10 times, but they laughed once and I gambled that I could get them to do it again. I also realized that stand-up was about getting your face beat in, and I might as well get used to it. Comedy became like a new girlfriend. I'd wake up at four in the morning, and instead of a hard-on, I had an idea, and I wrote it down. Ninety-eight percent of them were garbage, but I was in love.

But there was no epiphany after a 28-hour cocaine binge, as I sat there, staring at my sweaty self in the mirror, thinking, *No one gets out of here alive!* It happened over two years. I was living a comfortable life: I made fine money working for the state of New Jersey. I had a car. I had a house. I played on the liquor store's softball team. That could have lasted 40 years.

PLAYBOY: Sounds like you were Jon Bon Jovi in that Ed Burns movie *No Looking Back.*

STEWART: You know what? I think I might be telling you that plot. I'm sorry. No: I didn't grow up around there at all. Wait! Hold on a second. No: I was an Army kid. No, that's *Three Kings.*

PLAYBOY: What did you do for the state of New Jersey?

STEWART: I was a contingency planner for emergencies. I happened to be a bit of a whiz at the then-new Lotus 1-2-3, so I had to make charts of centers for psychiatric treatment and how many extra beds they might have, just in case we were attacked by Pennsylvania and took some casualties. At what point could we set up a triage center and where would we find an extra minivan? I was responsible for our level of readiness in 1985. Let me tell you: We had a lot of canned goods. We were ready. It took me six months.

They were about to re-up me for another 40 years in Jersey, and before I signed the papers, I thought, You know what? I'm 23. If I leave, no one's going to miss me. I don't have kids, I don't have a girlfriend. I don't have anything that I've always romanticized having, so now's the time. I didn't want to be 30 years old and doing the same thing. I thought, I can always be one of the bitter guys in my town, so why not go to New York and fail and come back? It's not like they won't save a seat for me. I checked out in a week and a half. I'd never told my friends or my family what I wanted to do, so to them it was like a bombshell. I walked in and said, "I'm selling my car and moving up to New York to become a stand-up comedian." They looked at me like I had the three nipples I have.

PLAYBOY: Do you still love New Jersey?

STEWART: New Jersey is tremendous. Everyone's got New Jersey wrong. What we've done in New Jersey is create the world's largest, smelliest scarecrow, and we've kept people away from it for years just by saying, "Where's the point that the most people who aren't really dedicated to this state will see?" It's the Turnpike, because the majority of people are going to be hitting the airport or heading from New York down south or up north. If we create an area of what appears to be pure, toxic genetic-mutation soup right along that road, everyone who drives by is going to go, "Holy shit!" But it's a scarecrow. It exists solely for the purpose of driving others away.

PLAYBOY: Next segment: What's the correspondent's piece?

STEWART: We would visit the mosquito-catching program I was part of when I was 18. I used to go down to a Jersey Pine Barrens in a state car. We'd bring the little critters back to Trenton for encephalitis testing. We didn't pull their genitals off. My job was solely to catch them, knock them out with chloroform, sort them male-female, and bring all the females back.

PLAYBOY: How about "In Other News"?

STEWART: Stewart discovers alcohol and Tom Waits; Waits decides he doesn't want to be found.

PLAYBOY: The celebrity interview?

STEWART: My father. We'd bring him on. After the interview he still doesn't believe I have my own show.

PLAYBOY: Describe that interview.

STEWART: It'd probably be one question and then three and a half minutes of him explaining the answer to me by writing and graphing it on a napkin. He was a physicist.

PLAYBOY: What one question have you always wanted to ask your dad?

STEWART: Ain't I doin' good, Pa? Ain't I? Then he would explain through graphs and charts why I'm not. It's a very precise equation calculation.

It's calculus, something I don't really understand. But I would get to keep the napkins, to back it up.

PLAYBOY: Does your father really think you're not doing well?

STEWART: Hey, hey. Don't think you're on to something here! No, I think he thinks it's fine—probably.

PLAYBOY: How old were you when your parents divorced?

STEWART: Ten or 11.

PLAYBOY: You saw him afterward?

STEWART: Oh yeah. Hey, pizza every Sunday, my friend. Or every other Sunday.

PLAYBOY: Do you have a good relationship with him?

STEWART: Uh . . . what do you mean? He hasn't broken up with me.

PLAYBOY: Did he try to explain the mysteries of the universe to you?

STEWART: Not that I remember. I was just happy, when I turned 17, to realize maybe the divorce wasn't my fault. I saw that one afterschool special where the kid thinks it's their fault, and I watched it with tears: "Yes, that's true." Then you realize, Oh, it's *not* my fault. In my hazy memory, I was thinking I had done something or gotten into some minor trouble before it happened. You sort of have the sense of, Oh, Christ, what have I done? But that's because kids are completely egocentric: I fucked up, therefore. . . .

PLAYBOY: Didn't your parents say, "Dear, it's not your fault"?

STEWART: I'm sure they did. But you're living in the world of hyperbole at that age. The drama itself was somehow comforting. It was the 1970s; *I'm OK–You're OK* had just come out but I don't think anybody had read it all the way through yet.

PLAYBOY: Okay. Now let's go to "This Just In."

STEWART: Stewart lands a regular job, may never have to buy clothes again. Then we do a moment of Zen.

PLAYBOY: What's yours?

STEWART: Probably footage of me watching one of my cats a few years ago take a shit right next to the litter box because I had been too lazy to actually clean it out. It was a brief message of her displeasure. She was the Felix Unger of cats: If it wasn't just right in the litter box, "I'm sorry, my friend, I'm going right on the floor next to it, just to show you."

PLAYBOY: Much of your humor is based on your being Jewish. You even called your HBO special *Unleavened*. Are Jews funnier?

STEWART: Than?

PLAYBOY: Gentiles.

STEWART: Any time you're a group that wants desperately for others to like you so they'll let you stick around, you have a tendency to be more amusing. When you're in charge there's really no need to be funny. The captain of the football team doesn't have to be funny. Water boy? He has to be a little amusing.

My comedy is all about anything that, when I was growing up, made me feel different or disenfranchised in any way. What is comedy other than: *Love me! We're not so bad. We don't really love the money. Love me!* Height, looks and religion became the cornerstones of what I talk about. They had to, because as a kid you learn preemptive-strike comedy. If I hit someone with a tremendous joke about how small and Jewish I am, they had nowhere to go. All they could do is punch me once and leave.

PLAYBOY: Were you the only Jew in your school?

STEWART: No. There were probably four or five, but Lawrenceville was not a predominantly Jewish area.

PLAYBOY: Did you feel ostracized?

STEWART: It's not like I walked into school and everyone turned their backs and shunned me [*laughs*]. It was just in my head. I felt different even if no one else noticed or cared. Most people were very nice to me. I got my share of ass-kickings and being made fun of, but it wasn't anything unusual. My parents divorced, but other people have gone through that as well. I'm not going to write *Jonathan's Ashes*. I didn't have a tragic childhood. It was okay, normal. But if you're looking for what informs my thought process, it was those feelings of inadequacy that were placed there *by me, for me*. They were grounded in reality, but one with far less importance than I gave it. In other words, it wasn't like *The Breakfast Club*, with Judd Nelson just fucking poking me in the chest every day. But in *my* head I was a weirdo.

PLAYBOY: Are you now at ease with your height, religion and looks?

STEWART: When I stopped thinking about them, all the problems they caused went away. There comes a point in your life where you go, "I guess I'm not going to be 6' tall—and I can't believe how important that used to be to me." I'm fine. If I can't reach a glass, I can just stand on a chair.

PLAYBOY: Jewish mysticism has been in the news lately. Have you given any thought yet to studying the Kabbalah?

STEWART: I'm letting Madonna get her feet wet, and if it seems okay, I'm jumping in. You know, nothing shakes my world more than giant celebrities who tell us about their spiritual awakenings.

PLAYBOY: Oh? Why?

STEWART: Because it's amazing to me that the journey to superstardom always culminates in, "Hey, we really all have to be nice to each other." Well, thank you! Of course you should be celebrated for coming to that conclusion!

All kidding aside, I can't believe that it's newsworthy when somebody of grand fame and wealth has an epiphany that maybe there's a larger world out there beyond their narcissism—and I'm not speaking of anyone in particular. It's as if a celebrity epiphany is somehow more valid than anyone else's and therefore that star is to be congratulated on their arduous spiritual journey. And guess what else? There is no grandeur in that epiphany. A celebrity's spiritual awakening is no different from or more important than one that happens to whomever is mopping up come in video booths on 42nd Street.

PLAYBOY: Sounds like business as usual.

STEWART: Of course, because in this business your status is elevated just for *not* shitting on people. You're celebrated as more than decent for acting *normally*. It makes me wonder: My God, what's going on behind that?

PLAYBOY: What do you think?

STEWART: The problem, I think, is people caring about all the things they shouldn't and not caring about all the things they should. It's that disparity that creates a fucking star temper tantrum when the tandoori chicken isn't orange enough. Any human being who has any sense of perspective would understand not to shit on the five-dollar-an-hour production assistant because he didn't understand that you said "spring rolls" and not "dumplings." To miss that point is just insanity.

Brett Butler is a great example of this. I've known Brett for a lot of years and she's an incredibly intelligent, funny woman. She flipped out—which I think she would admit to now—but they didn't call her on it until the show was no longer making them the kind of money that justified tolerating her behavior. There is no medal of honor for the people who pulled the plug on that show. They waited until it was economically feasible for them to do so before saying, "Hey, you can't treat people like this."

PLAYBOY: And that sort of stuff is common in Hollywood?

STEWART: It's common in the world. We are a global capitalistic conglomerate. Corporation Earth. Whatever drives that bottom line drives our behavior. The more you bring in, the more you are allowed to fuck up. It's as simple as that. When you stop bringing it in, people stop hanging around.

The random glorification can also lead to random vilification. That's the double-edged sword. People in that spotlight are more loved than they should be and more despised than they should be. That's why they're always complaining about being praised and then suddenly attacked.

PLAYBOY: If we were to help you package your philosophy and get a celebrity interested in it, should he or she be celebrated for "getting it"?

STEWART: No. And I shouldn't be either. It's like the notion that tacking up the Ten Commandments on a wall in a high school is going to help. Who doesn't already know "Thou shalt not kill"? Who is going to walk into a principal's office, look at the Commandments and go, "Thou shalt not kill? Are you fucking kidding me? When did that happen?" It's the same thing with the red ribbon for AIDS. It's a wonderful thought, but who's not aware of AIDS? It's people putting their hope in symbolism and bullshit and not in the actual work it takes to attain the kind of world you want. The problem is that people have to stop looking to others to tell them how to act and feel. People's internal barometers have to be dialed up a notch. [*Pauses*] I'm on the pulpit now, brotha! Tes-ti-fy! By the way, this is all one man's bullshit. I want to make that clear. I'm not out there beating the fucking sidewalk with my donation cup and a bell, trying to get money for this. It's my worldview and it has nothing to do with anybody else. Sure, I wish everyone thought this way, but they don't. And I'm not saying it's any more valid or interesting than anybody else's point of view. Everything comes with disclaimers. For instance, this philosophy is not valid in Tennessee. Or Alaska.

PLAYBOY: We should wrap this up. Describe the Jon Stewart the public never gets to see.

STEWART: Here's the weird thing: *This is my secret life.* You have no idea what's going on in my real life. I actually manage a Bennigan's. No one knows I'm here. That's the beauty of it. They don't get cable.

PLAYBOY: With which celebrity are you most often confused?

STEWART: By people who are drinking or not?

PLAYBOY: Drinking.

STEWART: Seinfeld.

PLAYBOY: Not drinking?

STEWART: The kid from *Married with Children.*

PLAYBOY: Why did you drop your last name, Liebowitz?

STEWART: It's hard to see your name in lights when you feel like there won't be enough lights to spell it.

PLAYBOY: This interview will appear in early 2000. Would you care to predict what will happen during the millennial celebrations?

STEWART: Hmm. I won't come out of my bunker until January 8, so many of those days will be something of a blur. However, when I do come out, through the smoldering ruins, I'll see the hand of a child holding a daisy and think, *We're going to be okay!* Then an animated bluebird will land on my shoulder and whisper something dirty and vaguely anti-Semitic in my ear.

PLAYBOY: What do you already miss about the last 1000 years?

STEWART: I guess the pace of it. The kindness we showed each other. The gentle tableau of a pie cooling on a sill while Ma stands out in the back and tries to figure out why the radar dish won't get the porno channel.

January 1980

STEVE MARTIN

A candid conversation with the immensely popular comedian about life and laughter and arrows through a prematurely gray head

Navin Johnson is The Jerk: a character of comedian Steve Martin's fertile imagination who began as a simple stage routine that has now turned into a movie that Universal is hoping will make Martin its answer to United Artists' Woody Allen and Warner Bros.' Mel Brooks. The idea is simple and funny: Martin stars as Navin, who was raised by a poor black family only to discover late in life that his skin would never turn dark. Setting out to make his fortune, he stumbles through a series of escapades and inadvertently invents a product called Opti-Grabs, which fastens to the bridge of one's glasses and keeps them from slipping. It makes him ridiculously rich, but not even wealth can make him smart.

After a poolside scene has been shot, Martin and director Carl Reiner go to watch it on instant video replay. Reiner thinks Steve can do better. He demonstrates for Martin, who listens obediently. Reiner, after all, has worked with the best—from Sid Caesar and George Burns to Mel Brooks—and Martin appreciates talent.

Martin's mother, standing offcamera, appreciates a porcelain rose Steve has given her, though she's unsure what to do with it. "Do you put it in a vase?" she asks Steve's girlfriend and co-star, Bernadette Peters. "I think it's best to keep it flat, like on a table," Bernadette says. Steve's father is also on the set, watching his son make his first movie. He looks at Steve's bare torso and comments on the mat of gray hair that covers his back and chest. "They always called him hairy," he says, "even when he was young."

Steve Martin, whose bizarre, often existential humor shot him to the forefront of American comedians a few years ago, has been called a lot of things besides hairy. His comedy has been labeled silly, brainless, Disneyesque and West Coast wacko. He has been known to lead entire audiences into the street after a show, ordering 600 hamburgers from a junk-food dive, only to change it to one order of fries to go. He has made the arrow through the head and the phrases "Excuuuse me!" and "I'm a *wild* and *crazy* guy" his trademarks.

At the Grammys (which he's won twice for his first two comedy albums), he has appeared without his trousers, and at the Oscars, without his head (he wore a dark stocking over it). At the American Booksellers' Convention, he appeared on the dais with James Baldwin and Ray Bradbury and received an enthusiastic ovation from the booksellers, who were applauding the fact that his book of short, zany stories, *Cruel Shoes*, which was critically killed, was at the time the country's number-one best-seller.

He recently completed an East Coast tour (which he is hoping will be the last tour he ever does), in which he stood before audiences ranging from 5000 to 20,000 people, pulling out old favorites (turning balloons into animals, singing his million-seller single "King Tut," showing his seven-minute film, *The Absent-Minded Waiter*) and adding new material. With his new album, *Comedy Is Not Pretty*, approaching gold (his first album, *Let's Get Small*, sold about one and a half million and his second, *A Wild and Crazy Guy*, sold about two and a half million), Martin is now concentrating his energies on the promotion of his first feature film, which he conceived and co-wrote.

Huge success has happened very fast and has made Martin very rich. (His manager and longtime friend, Bill McEuen, worked out advantageous career moves for Martin, including complete ownership of all his albums and properties. When Steve appears, he doesn't get a set fee, he works on a percentage of the gate—which can, at times, close in on $1 million for him in just a few days.)

Privately, Steve Martin is not a goofball, not wild and crazy, not even very funny. Born in Texas but raised in Garden Grove, California, he grew up an avid churchgoer (something he has forsaken as an adult) and a diligent worker (his parents like to tell how he once swept floors for a quarter when he was nine). At the age of 10, he was hired to sell guidebooks at Disneyland, and for the next eight years, he worked at the Magic Kingdom, demonstrating tricks at the magic shop, selling books and newspapers, and dropping in at the Golden Horseshoe Revue, where his idol, Wally Boag, delighted audiences five times a day (he's still there, in his 24th year, doing the same show) with balloon tricks and cracking cornball but perfectly timed jokes. Boag was Martin's inspiration. But it was at the Birdcage Theater at nearby Knott's Berry Farm where he was given the chance to do his magic act and comedy routines.

While there, he met a girl who convinced him that a college education was important, so he enrolled at California State, Long Beach, and studied philosophy for a few years. When that got too confusing, he tried theater arts at UCLA, where he took a TV writing course. He was also performing in Westwood at Ledbetter's (Randy Sparks was instrumental in giving him the chance to perform) and, by the time he was 21, he was hired to write comedy for *The Smothers Brothers* TV show and eventually made $1500 a week. He dropped out of college, but the pressure of writing funny regularly led to high anxiety and a near nervous breakdown.

When *The Smothers Brothers* was abruptly canceled, Martin got other jobs, writing for Sonny & Cher, Pat Paulsen, Glen Campbell, John Denver. But what he really wanted to do was perform his own material. His agents at William Morris said he'd never make it, which encouraged him to try (and to drop them once he proved them wrong). He started appearing at the Boarding House in San Francisco, as an opening act for the Nitty Gritty Dirt Band. In the late 1960s and early 1970s, he went on the road. Soon he was opening for the likes of Ann-Margret and Helen Reddy in Las Vegas. With a new agent, Marty Klein, he was booked on *The Tonight Show* and *Saturday Night Live*, which brought him the kind of audiences that change careers. To date, he has guest-hosted *The Tonight Show* numerous times and his appearances on *Saturday Night Live* have become classics.

In real life, Martin, who is 33 and prematurely gray, lives alone but steadily sees Bernadette Peters, whom he considers to be a stabilizing influence on his life. He was once linked with Linda Ronstadt for a brief time and he has lived with other women at different times. He likes to ski, play tennis, get massaged and work. He owns a solar-heated house in Aspen, another house in Beverly Hills and another in Santa Barbara. His primary obsession, outside his comedy, is collecting 19th century American art, which Contributing Editor Lawrence Grobel (whose *Playboy Interview* with Al Pacino appeared last month) discovered when he met with Martin at his apartment just off Sunset Strip. Grobel's report:

"The first thing I noticed was the paintings, which covered all the walls, and the boxes filled with art books, which covered most of the floor space. Steve claimed he doesn't even look at his paintings while they hang on these walls, because it's all temporary—he's waiting for his home in Beverly Hills to be remodeled—and he considers his current setting as storage.

"After describing some of the paintings, he sat down behind a large desk and we began our talk. I had visited the set of *The Jerk* a few times, and he was pleased that it was over with. He was also anxious about how it would be received, and prepared for the worst. Steve is a cynic and a worrier. He feels he is vulnerable to criticism and that he has been unfairly attacked recently.

"He showed me a short review of the film *Alien* that he had submitted to *The New Yorker* (which later rejected it—one can't move in too fast on Woody Allen's turf) and was interested in an opinion, an action generic to writers, who are constantly looking for feedback. During our talks, he would try out bits of new routines, play tapes he'd made and discuss properties he was considering for potential film projects.

"I flew to New Jersey to catch his concert act, but, unfortunately, saw him on an off night. The audience was not completely with him and he pulled out all his tricks in a desperate attempt to get the Big Laugh, which never came. The next day, I met him for lunch at the Carlyle Hotel in Manhattan and we discussed what had gone wrong. Afterward, he dropped some of the bits that weren't working, juggled some routines around and tightened up the act he had not wanted to do in the first place. (He recognizes that even Woody Allen did stand-up until he could make it just doing films, and that's the direction Martin is following.)

"Our last time together, we went to the Frick Collection on 70th Street off Fifth Avenue. It's one of Martin's favorite places and there are two particular paintings he likes to see. One is a melancholy, wistful Holbein portrait of Sir Thomas More and the other is a portrait of a lady, by T. Lawrence, whose pure-white skin reminded me of Bernadette Peters's.

"We parted on Madison Avenue. My last words were, 'See you on the cover.' Which seems an appropriate way to begin this interview."

PLAYBOY: Our cover shows you in character—a wild and crazy guy. Is this going to be an in-character interview?

MARTIN: It's hard for me to be funny for 14 days or however long we're going to do this. I can't disguise my true self that long. But I'll be funny when there's a question I don't want to answer.

PLAYBOY: We thought we'd start with your background and work our way up through your—

MARTIN: Nobody gives a shit about where I grew up and all that. That's boring. Even *I* don't give a shit. When I read an interview and it gets to the part where the person grew up, I turn the page.

PLAYBOY: What, then, interests you?

MARTIN: The only thing of interest to me is the future.

PLAYBOY: How do you see your future?

MARTIN: I have no idea. I don't even know what my plans are. So I can't talk about it.

PLAYBOY: Let's get this straight: You're bored with your past and you can't talk about your future. The present is probably too fleeting, so that leaves us with what? Sex?

MARTIN: Well . . . as long as I don't get into: Did I go to bed with Linda Ronstadt? Actually, I'm reluctant to talk about sex or my girlfriends or ex-girlfriends, because that's *really* your private life and you're affecting people who never thought they would be affected.

PLAYBOY: No past, no future, no sex. What about politics?

MARTIN: I'm not political, because I don't know what's going on. Get someone who knows politics to talk about it.

PLAYBOY: What you're saying is you don't have much to say.

MARTIN: In theory, you do an interview because you have great things to say. If I had great things to say, I'd say them onstage or in a movie, or somewhere else. In my work, I *disguise* what I have to say. That's what art is.

PLAYBOY: What do you mean?

MARTIN: You can't just say, "Life is not worth living." You have to write a novel that says life is not worth living. In an interview, you're talking directly; you're not an artist anymore.

PLAYBOY: You're forgetting that there is an art to conversation.

MARTIN: That's true. I've turned down all other requests for interviews because I want this one to have meaning.

PLAYBOY: Which will be quite a feat, since you've put so many restrictions on yourself.

MARTIN: The interviews I've done in the past are so redundant. Superficial. Either you give it all or you shouldn't give *any* of it.

PLAYBOY: Our feelings exactly. Should we stop now or continue?

MARTIN: Obviously, this is where I end up giving it all.

PLAYBOY: Terrific. Now—

MARTIN: Although there are some things I'm determined not to talk about.

PLAYBOY: Let's start over. You're a comedian. This is an interview. To hell with the restrictions. Now, who's the funniest person in America today?

MARTIN: Richard Pryor.

PLAYBOY: Have you ever asked anyone for an autograph?

MARTIN: Bobby Fischer. I followed him into a bathroom.

PLAYBOY: When you were a kid, what was your image of a man?

MARTIN: Guys who dressed in black and wore swords. Zorro.

PLAYBOY: Would you like to have kids of your own one day?

MARTIN: I don't want any kids. It's a lifetime job. People have kids and go off and do something else. Or they're too stupid to raise them. Every time you think that you might want to have kids, go to a restaurant and sit next to one. You just don't want one.

PLAYBOY: What's the most enjoyable thing you can have done to you without fearing the consequences?

MARTIN: Get a massage. It's the one thing that feels good that doesn't lead to trouble. If you smoke, you get cancer. If you eat desserts, you get fat. If you fuck, she gets pregnant or you get involved. A massage—you pay for it and it feels great. It's the one thing that doesn't have a bad consequence unless it loosens a clot that goes to your heart.

PLAYBOY: Did you ever go to bed with Linda Ronstadt?

MARTIN: I saw her for about three weeks one time. We were just friends. We never got in bed. We had a mutual affair without sex.

PLAYBOY: If you could choose how you could be remembered, what would that be?

MARTIN: There's one thing, specifically, I would have liked to have done. That was when the guy knocked eight million dominoes over on *The Tonight Show*. If it'd been me, I'd always be remembered for that thing.

PLAYBOY: Well, that about does it. You got anything you'd like to add?

MARTIN: What about comedy? I can talk about that.

PLAYBOY: Comedy? Oh—right, we forgot. What makes you think you can talk about that any more than sex or politics? After all, most politicians are comedians and most comics have sex.

MARTIN: Okay. Let's take the question: Why am I not political? One reason is purely aesthetic. There were too many political thinkers in the 1960s. There was too much political comedy. It was a cheap laugh. The world didn't need another political comedian. The world *still* doesn't need another serious person. There're too many people who are really good at it; they don't *need* me.

PLAYBOY: A Ralph Nader of comedy you're not.

MARTIN: As Ralph Nader is necessary, so am I necessary. Checks and balances. If everyone were Ralph Nader, we'd have no consumers; and if everyone were me, we'd have no champions. Choosing *not* to decide something is an existential decision. That's the way I feel about politics. Choosing *not* to be socially aware, choosing to be naive about it, is a statement.

PLAYBOY: Did you make that choice from the beginning?

MARTIN: When I was starting out, I intended to put meaning into my act, to be a social satirist, to say something about truth and beauty and everything. And then the Beatles came along and they started saying it—in their songs, with *Sgt. Pepper*. And I went, *shit*, they did what I had planned to do. They had put meaning into entertainment. So, at that point, I said, now I have to turn it the other way. That's what was the premise of my whole act during a time when it never could have succeeded. I was doing my act without meaning. Consciously avoiding politics.

PLAYBOY: Why, at that time, did you feel it couldn't succeed?

MARTIN: Because the 1960s *needed* a hard-hitting response. People were being killed. There was a real threat, people were going to war. So they had to say it, they didn't have time for satire. Satire was so easy then, because *everyone* knew what you were talking about. Everyone knew that you were supposed to laugh at a drug joke and to applaud a war joke and anything you said about Nixon was all set up. But then everything became so *stupid*, like suddenly every idiot had something to say. They almost had no right to say it, because they weren't artists. And the songs were stupid. Bob Dylan, the Beatles, they were real masters of the form—then for six years afterward, you had guys singing these drug songs, "Blow my mind" . . . it was just very trite.

PLAYBOY: You've taken quite a leap. For an asocial, nonpolitical comic, that is.

MARTIN: The last time I voted was for McGovern. Or was it McCarthy? McGovern. Okay. He was defeated so badly, I thought it was the stupidest thing I'd ever been involved in. That's exactly why I don't talk about politics, because it's so futile. You can only close your doors and think about your own life. You don't live in America, you live in Hollywood.

PLAYBOY: How do you see what *you* were doing at the time?

MARTIN: I was freeing myself and representing people who didn't have to be socially or politically conscious. When you vote for McGovern and you're defeated by a landslide, that's insignificant. You're powerless, it was a waste of a day, a waste of registering. My act symbolized the need to turn away from the phony responsibility, when it was hip to have an opinion. Where one time to protest the Vietnam war was a necessity, it suddenly became hip. You had people growing their hair who never should have grown their hair long. And then Watergate—that was past the point of our being able to do something about it. The next thing was that it was okay to create your own world or your own country in your head.

PLAYBOY: And your timing was right?

MARTIN: The timing was *so* right. I see myself as a success of timing, having the right act at the right time, when everybody was sort of starting to think that way. That's why I was a phenomenon rather than just another comedian. We were in the midst of the 1960s when I was starting to formulate this idea. I'd say, "Someday this consciousness will grow tiresome." It's like impressionism: a master movement, a great movement; but no matter how great it was, someday it was going to grow tired. That's what I felt in the 1960s. This was a master movement and I was into it. I knew that someday we'd have to change, just out of boredom, and that's what I was formulating. Almost getting ready for it, in retrospect. I felt like I was the avant-garde. And three years ago, I *was* the avant-garde.

PLAYBOY: It sounds very calculated. Let's see if we can focus on this master movement. What *does* your comedy deal with?

MARTIN: I'm dealing with a very personal side of a human being's brain, that little tiny area that tells him if this is funny or not. The best way to hit that is to never determine that for him. That's what I believe is the reason my comedy worked, ultimately. It became a private joke among friends. My first, initial, original thought in comedy was, If I say a joke that has a punch line and they don't laugh, then I'm screwed. If I just start talking funny-type things and never give them a punch line, eventually their tension is going to grow so much that they will start laughing on their own, they'll start choosing things to be funny, which is the strongest kind of humor. *They* have determined what is funny, not me. The laugh I like to get is, "What? I don't know why I'm laughing."

Laughter is the most peculiar emotional response of all. It doesn't relate even to joy, as tears relate to sadness and terror. But laughter is really a spontaneous act. It doesn't even mean you're happy. It's a very strange commodity—laughter. To be supplying that to people. I used to stand up there and act like I could not care *less* if this got a laugh. I'd take out the jokes and do those nonsense things. One of the first jokes I'd say was, "Now, the nose-on-the-microphone routine." And I'd put my nose on the microphone and go, "Thank you." Which is all very simple and childlike, looking back, but that was the premise that I first started operating on. At that time, if they didn't laugh, you had to believe it was *their* fault, they didn't get it.

PLAYBOY: What you're saying is that you were at the forefront in taking us from the social 1960s to the silly 1970s?

MARTIN: I've been criticized for being on the brainless side, which is the furthest thing from the truth in my head. Silliness. It's so way off, I don't have to defend that. Comedy has always been brainless, superficially. Are Laurel and Hardy brainless? I don't think so. What I say onstage relates more to psychoanalysis. It relates to human beings, to individuals.

PLAYBOY: Do you see yourself more as a harbinger of the "me" decade?

MARTIN: I hate to hear it referred to as a narcissistic point of view, because that means love of yourself. That's only turning inward without a reason. Not for love of yourself, just for its own sake.

PLAYBOY: For the sake of this interview, let's look at some real issues and get your views of them. Okay with you?

MARTIN: Okay; this might help me in my routines.

PLAYBOY: What do you think about the problems in the Middle East?

MARTIN: I've always heard there was trouble over there, but I went there personally and there was no trouble at all in the Middle East. I went to Tennessee, East Virginia, Maryland, and I'm happy to say there's no trouble.

PLAYBOY: That's certainly good to hear. Let's move closer to home. Where do you stand on the ERA issue?

MARTIN: I just can't figure out all this turmoil over the Earned Run Average.

PLAYBOY: All right, one more: Are there any causes you support?

MARTIN: I wanted to get involved in a cause now that I have the time. Celebrities have an obligation to have a cause to live for. I didn't know what I wanted to live for, so I put all the causes in a hat and I just chose one. It was gay rights. So I joined it and worked for it, but then I quit.

PLAYBOY: Why?

MARTIN: I'll tell you why. Because that organization is infiltrated with *homosexuals!*

PLAYBOY: And now you have nothing to live for?

MARTIN: This brings to mind *Manhattan*, the scene where Woody Allen is fooling with his Dictaphone, talking about the reasons to live. It was the most daring thing I've seen in modern filmmaking, where a guy *numbers*, *enumerates* the things that are worth living for. I don't care what he said, I admired the fact that those were his personal things. And except for a couple of food things, they were *all* artistic things—Mozart, performing artists, Groucho.

PLAYBOY: What's your greatest pleasure in life?

MARTIN: My greatest pleasure is conversation. And wit. The most fun game in life is exploring your own wit and intelligence and feeding off someone else's. All it takes is a little bit of your own intelligence and a lot of intelligence from the people around you. It's like, choose your friends. If you hang around with slobs, you'll be a slob.

PLAYBOY: Who are some of those people?

MARTIN: There's a clique in New York that's so much fun: Mike Nichols, Candice Bergen, Paul Simon, Carrie Fisher, those people. Real intelligent, witty, fun. On this coast, I know Carl Reiner, Mel Brooks, Dom DeLuise—which can be the most hysterical evening you'll ever have. And their wives.

PLAYBOY: Do you try out new material for these people?

MARTIN: Oh, yeah, I'll try out with people I'm with, like Carl, because I'm around him a lot now, or an art-dealer friend, Terry DeLapp, or Bernadette [Peters].

PLAYBOY: Can you give us an example of how your friends may influence your material?

MARTIN: A new bit in my act is something I was doing at Terry's house. We'd get together and he loves big-band music of the 1940s, so he'd put this on and I'd start dancing to it. You know, silly. And his wife would just die laughing. The more she'd laugh, the more I'd do it. Then I'd think, God, it'd be great, I'm going to be standing onstage doing my act, then have this big band, Benny Goodman's *Stompin' at the Savoy* come on and I'll go, "What's going on here? What *is* this music?" Then I'll start my toe slightly tapping and then I'll do my dance until it gets real big. In the middle of it, I'll turn on a strobe light and stand perfectly still for 30 seconds.

PLAYBOY: That sounds like a variation of your *Happy Feet*. Where did that one come from?

MARTIN: The genesis of that was I wanted a routine where I look like I'm being controlled by something else. I was going to look up at the sky and start dancing and go, "Leave me alone, leave me alone, leave me alone." And that evolved into *Happy Feet*. The audiences didn't get it when I looked up and said, "Leave me alone." They didn't understand the setup, but the dance got laughs. So I just dropped the setup. It's funny, just the way it looks, with your arms and feet flying. But there's also a little more sophisticated concept: like, does this happen to you often? Is it something everyone gets?

PLAYBOY: Sort of like your line about farting when someone smokes?

MARTIN: Bill McEuen, my manager, made that up. He said it at a dinner table one night. He overheard someone say, "Mind if I smoke?" He said "No; mind if I fart?" My eyes lit up and I said, *Gold!* I got up and wrote it down. It became a staple of my act for a long time. "Mind if I fart?" It would get a big laugh anywhere. It was a little sanctuary for me. It's like once I'm experimenting out there, I can always go to this and it will be pretty safe.

PLAYBOY: Like your *King Tut* bit. Did that come to you after seeing the exhibition?

MARTIN: Yeah. I went to the art museum and thought it was a shameful exploitation of King Tut. So I said, What's the stupidest melody I can think of? What're the dumbest lyrics? That's where "King Tut" came from.

PLAYBOY: Are new routines constantly popping into your head?

MARTIN: I thought of one this morning, for a TV special or something. You see me with a bow and arrow, then you cut to one of those big targets made out of hay. I shoot the arrow and the next scene is I've got the target on the dinner table. I've got to write that down.

PLAYBOY: While you do that, are there any routines that you feel are funny but that don't go over?

MARTIN: There was a routine that I always had confidence in. The Jackie Onassis bit. Where I meet Jackie Onassis for lunch and she turns out to be a pig, eating with her hands, unbelievably bad table manners. They didn't go for it in 1970; I guess she was too sacred. But then about two years ago, I put it back and it started getting laughs. It's on the third album.

PLAYBOY: Which is *Comedy Is Not Pretty*. Why isn't it?

MARTIN: That's a line I ad-libbed one night. I did the joke about my girlfriend who came to me and said, "I don't think you respect me as a woman." I said, "What are you talking about? You are the best hog I have ever had." The audience just laughs and they go boo. So I said, "Hey, wait a minute, comedy is not pretty." That's where the title came from. I like everything about that album.

PLAYBOY: Each of your three albums seems to get a little further out. Is that intentional?

MARTIN: There was a method in the release of those records. I couldn't put those new bits on the first record. In *Let's Get Small*, I had to put the bits that made the most irrational sense, that were concrete, that were self-contained and clean. I don't mean language-wise, I'm talking about the clean lines of the routine that flow from piece to piece. On the second record, we went with material that was probably a little further out. The last record is the most challenging.

PLAYBOY: Didn't you have some problems with the second album, *A Wild and Crazy Guy*, and a distributor because of the language?

MARTIN: It was a problem. You go on *The Tonight Show* and you don't say fuck. Then the parents go and say, "He's great for little Billy, 'cause he doesn't say fuck," and they buy the album and it says fuck. As much as I realize that parents went out and bought their kids my album and it says fuck on it, I can't rescind, I can't say I apologize. The only thing I apologize for is it doesn't say on the record: "By the way, this says fuck on it." That's fair. Tell them what they're buying ahead of time. But you don't change it, that's censorship. Records and movies are great sanctuaries to be away from censorship. It's not like I suddenly went out and said, "Well, now I'm going to say fuck." I've been saying it in my act since I was 19. It used to be worse.

PLAYBOY: While the reviews of your first album seemed mostly favorable, you were cut up a bit for the second album. A *Rolling Stone* critic wrote that "clean, apolitical comedy is one thing, while cartoonish mediocrity that wholeheartedly supports a decade's social clichés instead of deflating them is another."

MARTIN: That comment is very interesting in that he's acknowledged that I've elevated mediocrity to a place of importance. That is really the secret of my act. But it's done intentionally. He doesn't regard it as satire when, in truth, it's very satirical. It's like he missed the last point of my act.

PLAYBOY: Did he also miss when he compared your "smug, emasculated, rancid showbiz condescension" to Milton Berle's push-anything-for-a-laugh excess?

MARTIN: The point has been missed again. It's not, for instance, that the arrow through the head is funny, it's that someone *thinks* the arrow through the head is funny. It so happens that the nose glasses *are* funny, but my point was, it's gone beyond the glasses; it's the *putting on* of the nose glasses that is funny. I'd love to answer with such a sword that it cuts up that criticism, but I'm vulnerable to it. It's true, in a way, if you don't really examine what I'm doing, if you just stop there. But kids like my act because I'm wearing nose glasses. Adults like my act because there's a guy who thinks putting on nose glasses is funny.

PLAYBOY: Would that analogy apply to your coming out to deliver a Grammy award on national TV without your pants?

MARTIN: That was logical because it had a payoff that made total sense. It wasn't a person who was dropping his pants for a laugh—that's the Milton Berle approach. My approach was that I thought it would look funny first of all. But I had to have more than that. I had to say it was because my pants didn't show up. After the bit's over, the thought the audience may have is of me standing back there going, "I don't have my pants, they're not here yet, they're supposed to be back from the cleaners. Well, I'll just have to go on like this." To me, that's the best part of the joke. The subtext. The thinking that the audience has to supply to figure out why I went out without my pants on. Although, I must say that my first thought was, I'll go out with no pants.

PLAYBOY: Good old Uncle Miltie.

MARTIN: You know what it is? It's making fun of the situation. All these awards and people in tuxedos and it's making fun of it. I did that with the Billboard Award show, where I went out and said, "This is the most coveted award in the business, we should understand the sanctity of this award." And I pulled out a cheese sandwich wrapped in wax paper and ate the sandwich while I gave the award.

PLAYBOY: Do you believe in awards?

MARTIN: Only the fun side of them. I don't like to feel like I'm in a race or a contest, and that's what it becomes. It's like Miss America. You've got 45 losers is what you've got. The history of awards is they're usually wrong. The people who really take them seriously are the people who want them and the people who refuse them.

PLAYBOY: When you were up for a Grammy, did your heart beat steadily?

MARTIN: I must say my heart pounded a little fast when the thing came up. That's just the thrill of being there. The Grammys are the stupidest comedy award ever.

PLAYBOY: The Oscars will probably mean something else to you this year, now that you're the star and one of the writers of your first film, *The Jerk*. Actually, make that the first *feature* film, because you did write and star in a seven-minute short with Buck Henry called *The Absent-Minded Waiter*. Since that is shown, for the most part, at your concerts, what is it about?

MARTIN: It was a sketch I wrote about 10 years ago. It took me about an hour. Submitted it for TV. Turned down. Went on to other TV shows. Submitted it. Turned down every time. Then, on the new *Smothers Brothers Show* a couple of years ago, we did it and it went over great. Then, in our deal with Paramount [Paramount dropped its option to *The Jerk*], one of the ideas that [producer] David Picker had was to make a short that would promote my face to the moviegoing public. So when my movie came out, I would be a movie star, in a sense.

PLAYBOY: And you just happened to have something you wanted to do.

MARTIN: I thought this was the safest thing to do. I worked over the script with Carl Gottlieb, who directed it. It takes seven minutes. I'll tell you what it's about. A couple—Buck Henry and Terri Garr—go to a restaurant and ask the maître d' for my table. Buck Henry says, "You're not going to believe this; you're going to see the most absentminded waiter *ever*." And she says, "So what? Why did you bring me here?" I come and say, "Here's your water," and pour the water on the table and then set down the glasses. There's water all over them now. Then I say, "Can I take your order?" Buck orders. I turn to Terri, "May I take your order?" She orders. I turn back to Buck, "May I take your order?" Buck orders again. I go to Terri, "May I take your order? Okay. What would you like to drink? Two martinis? Fine. What would you like? Martini? Okay. And what would you like? Okay, two martinis. And a martini." I come back and bring them six martinis. After the drinks, I bring the desserts. Buck says, "We haven't got our main course yet." So I say, "Oh, that chef, he's always forgetting," and go back and bring them the main course, but it's all screwed up. A lard omelet and a Truly Maple Surprise. Meanwhile, Terri Garr is going, "Why did you bring me here, this is our one night out, why here?" Buck says, "Don't worry, just stick with me." Finally, she says, "That's it, I'm so pissed off, I'm never going to come here again, and I'm just as mad at you." Then I come in and I go, "And here's your change . . . $10, $20, $30, $40, $50, $60, $70, $80, $90, $100, $200, $300, $400, $500, $1000, $2000, $3000, $10,000. Thank you and come again." And I walk away. They start giggling. Buck starts lighting up the money. I come back and go, "May I help you?" Terri goes, "Yes. Two. For dinner." And they sit down and go through the whole thing again. It *is* funny. I've seen it play 500 times on my concert dates and it just works great. I'm really proud of it. I'm proud that I made something that is *funny*. Not any other reason, just funny.

PLAYBOY: Is that how you feel about *The Jerk*?

MARTIN: I think it came out great, very funny. We congratulate ourselves a lot, in that it's a picture that has never been made before. That's the one thing we're most proud of is that, really, you don't know what's going to happen next in the picture.

PLAYBOY: Whose idea was *The Jerk*?

MARTIN: The script was basically my idea: A guy is raised by a poor black family but realizes at some point that he's actually white—and a bum. Then he gets rich off the dumbest thing in the world. That story always fascinated me, about the guy who invented the hooks on your pants who made a million billion dollars. Then the story appeared about the guy who invented a plastic gasket, a millionaire living in Palm Springs, and he's still got his gas-station shirt on. So that's all I had. The rest was vignettes. That's probably why it needed two rewrites. Carl Gottlieb and I worked for six weeks on the first version.

PLAYBOY: What was Carl Reiner's contribution?

MARTIN: Carl Reiner added wisdom. And structure and character. He made it better. In fact, it would have been a lousy movie without him.

PLAYBOY: His son is also in the picture, isn't he?

MARTIN: One of my favorite scenes is with Rob Reiner. I'm hitchhiking in front of my house. It's night, I've been standing there for eight hours. Finally, a car comes and he pulls over. He says, "I'm going down to that fence," which is, like, 10 feet away. I go, "Okay." I get in and I say, "What's your name?" And he goes, "Well, here we are." I say, "Thanks for the company," and he drives off.

PLAYBOY: Is it wrong to assume that you're now in a position in which anything you want to do will get done?

MARTIN: I feel that right now. I don't have to sell. I can walk in and say, "I've got an idea for a movie about a clock that gets shit on." "Sounds good, Steve, baby." After the picture comes out, we'll have more power—or less. That's why it's critical right now for me to be thinking, because they'll say yes to anything. So I have to think what's good for me. My agent said, "Steve, you've got to read your scripts with care, because if you say you'll do it, the picture will be made. No matter how bad." It's like *Moment by Moment*. They had John Travolta and Lily Tomlin. *I'd* make that picture. How could it bomb? How could *The Fortune* bomb? It had Jack Nicholson and Warren Beatty and Mike Nichols directing.

PLAYBOY: And *The Jerk* has you, Bill Murray, Rob and Carl Reiner and Bernadette Peters. It's a pretty important film for her, isn't it?

MARTIN: Oh, yeah. This is the first part she's had that hasn't been a crazy woman. Her talent is unrevealed to the public. I think this movie will do more for her than for me. I really do. What I do in the picture is expected. What she's doing is a surprise.

PLAYBOY: Is she very anxious about it?

MARTIN: No, she's the most calm, easygoing person I've ever met. She really can take things or leave them. Her ego is not big. She doesn't read her reviews, let's put it that way.

PLAYBOY: Sounds like you're proud of her.

MARTIN: Yeah. People go nuts when they meet her. I feel proud of her when her talent is exposed. She'd be happy being an actress, but I think she wants to pursue performing, singing, records. She's a great singer; I think she can be one of the best—a real landmark singer. Because her voice is so controlled. It has an unusual quality to it.

PLAYBOY: Where did you meet her?

MARTIN: In Vegas one time when I was working there. I was with another girl, it was a celebrity softball game. We went out to a dinner afterward. Then I met her on *Hollywood Squares*. I was attracted to her, so I clowned around like a teenager. She was a square below me, so I'd throw things down. I was having fun. I had put up a venetian blind in my square, so I could close it. I put up a sign that said Closed and Open. Move the slats so I could look out. It was funny.

PLAYBOY: Sounds like you stayed in character in your attempts to woo her.

MARTIN: I got her phone number that night. Like I was in high school. And I started seeing her. She had just had an affair break up, six months earlier.

PLAYBOY: Would your parents like you to marry her?

MARTIN: Oh, they'd love it. They'd die for it. It doesn't occur to me. It only occurs in certain moments, and then you live to rue the day, as I seem to recall e. e. cummings said. No, I have no interest in it.

PLAYBOY: But if Bernadette wanted to get married, would you do it?

MARTIN: I'd certainly consider it. If it meant losing her or getting married, I'd consider it. But she's a woman who has lived all her life without getting married, too, so obviously, it's part of her makeup. She lives alone and we're two peas in a pod that way.

PLAYBOY: Why aren't you living together?

MARTIN: There's no way we can live together right now. When my new house gets off the ground, we'll see. We've talked about it.

PLAYBOY: Have you ever lived with anyone?

MARTIN: Yeah. I lived with three different girls. The longest was a couple of years; but I'm against talking about sex. I don't think it's essential to my personality. It's purient, per, pru, perient, *prurient* in regards to me. If you're asking Roman Polanski that, then it might relate to *his* personality. It's private with me. You have to choose to whom you reveal your past. Maybe there's something I don't want Bernadette to know, because it's pointless and it may throw a wrench in something. Maybe there's something I don't want my mother to know. So why should I suddenly, for the nation, reveal something that I don't want my mother to know?

PLAYBOY: That's an understandable position. However, being on the road for all those years, surely you were exposed to a lot of wild and crazy temptations.

MARTIN: That's something I don't want to talk about.

PLAYBOY: Because of your mother or Bernadette?

MARTIN: I have a different life now. That part of my life is five years ago, so anything I say about that doesn't apply to now. Because I don't get into those situations anymore. I couldn't go for the one-night thing anymore. I couldn't wake up with a stranger. That whole thing—it was depressing. And I have to be rude to people who knock on the door here. You open it up and it's a 14-year-old girl. And you just have to say, "Wrong. You go away." Let me just say that it's as hard to get laid if you're Superman as it is . . . you know . . . it's harder! At whatever level you are in life, it's hard. It's just as nerve-racking.

PLAYBOY: Have you ever dressed up funny, put on nose glasses, before engaging in any kind of sexual congress?

MARTIN: I can't remember. Let's just say I've gotten laughs in bed. [*Laughs*]

PLAYBOY: Did you ever fantasize about certain women when you were a kid, some famous actress or singer?

MARTIN: It didn't have to be a big star for me to fantasize. It could have been the girl in the corner holding the spear. Rhonda Fleming, that's who I liked. For a long time, I was in love with Joni Mitchell. Never knew her, never met her, but she was really appealing to me. Linda, I was really taken with her.

PLAYBOY: Here we are again, back to Linda Ronstadt. Where did you meet her?

MARTIN: She was a singer and I was a comedian at the Troubadour. She was with the Stone Poneys. I saw her singing onstage and thought she was great. It was just before she had a hit with "Long, Long Time" or "Different Drum." I started hanging around with her and her friends, like the Eagles, before they made it, and Kris Kristofferson. We were both very changeable then. We were always thinking of the future, looking around the corner to see what else was coming. I'm a little more stable now, because Bernadette's pretty stable. Or very stable.

PLAYBOY: You mean you realized that the life of a rock star was not for you?

MARTIN: Yeah, I nixed that. I was into it for a while just because my friends were musicians, but the hard-core rock life—I realized I would kill myself if I did that.

PLAYBOY: Well, now that you're beginning to live the life of a movie star, are there any actresses you'd like to work with?

MARTIN: I'd love to act with Jane Fonda. And with Diane Keaton, but that's difficult, because I don't want to be a Woody Allen *schlepp*.

PLAYBOY: Have you ever met Woody?

MARTIN: No. He's just a real artist. I'd love to meet him, but I'd hate to go through the agony of meeting him over the dinner table or shaking hands with him at a party. Because he and I are both agonized at meeting people. If you said, "Steve, you've got to share Woody's apartment with him for four weeks," that would be better.

PLAYBOY: Do you know that he writes most of his short stories in bed?

MARTIN: That's probably a good place to do it. Maybe I'll ask him if I can get in his bed and try writing something. His stories are brilliant, some are unbelievable. He's a real writer, a guy who writes every day. He's really concerned with words and language when he writes those stories. What I write has nothing to do with what he writes. I'm a guy who thinks and makes a note and puts it in my act.

PLAYBOY: Or in your book. You do have a best-seller at the moment.

MARTIN: It's not comparable. On the one hand *Cruel Shoes* is a joke book. I'm not demeaning it, I think there's some pretty good stuff in there, but it doesn't take the form of a Woody Allen short story. His are extremely complex and beautiful. *Cruel Shoes* is like Erma Bombeck's *If Life Is a Bowl of Cherries*, which I presume is very light. I can't judge its quality. It's amusing, it's interesting, it goes from very light to very serious, but it's not J.P. Donleavy. And it's probably not as funny as some people would expect it to be.

PLAYBOY: Were you surprised it reached the top of the best-seller list?

MARTIN: That's all a fluke. That's a matter of timing. You know, it's beat out two diet books. I thought it would sell well, because my albums sell up to two and a half million copies, so why shouldn't the book, which is cheaper than an album? The book sold because it was by Steve Martin, a comedian. I know that. That doesn't bother me. It was never intended to be a great book. I like to think that along with buying the book, a little something else goes with it: a better understanding of what my comedy means. I think I'm probably most sensitive to the criticism that my comedy is brainless, when I know it's not. Hopefully, something like the book makes my comedy a larger world.

PLAYBOY: Not according to most of the critics, who didn't have very nice things to say about it.

MARTIN: I knew they were going to kill me, but I don't give a shit. It's just like doing *The Tonight Show*—you're exactly the same on every television set and you've got half the people who loved it and half who hated it. *Cruel Shoes* is like that. They say, "I loved this one," and another guy says, "I hated this one." There's no sense at all to it. I know what the book is, I don't need to be told. I know where the problems are. But they are criticizing things like the photographs or the length, which is totally ridiculous, because length has nothing to do with quality. Go review *The Waste Land* and then come back and tell me it's too short. Also, they are missing the point. They are taking intentional bad writing and criticizing it on a very superficial level. Some of the stuff is criticizable—nobody wants to read a poem by a comedian; maybe that was a mistake. Who knows? Fuck you.

PLAYBOY: You sound disturbed.

MARTIN: See, I've read eight million reviews of me, and in the past two years, I can see them start to change in attitude. In the beginning, I thought, Oh, boy, my first review, I'll read it. But I don't want to be influenced by a review. And I found that you *are* influenced. Reading a review is like being a naughty boy—you know you shouldn't, but you do it anyway.

PLAYBOY: Do you think part of the criticism has to do with the fact that you've made it so big?

MARTIN: The press's attitude goes in a cycle. Right now, I'm vulnerable to criticism because I'm at the top. It's now the thing to knock me down.

But you know what happens? They don't criticize me, they criticize the audience for liking me. It's weird, it's kind of a perverted way to criticize something. I have been misrepresented through criticism, which is the last way to understand something. Especially something intended to be aesthetic. If we're going to criticize, then we all have to stand next to Leonardo or Michelangelo or Mozart or Beethoven. And *anything* is going to look like shit next to that. So once you acknowledge that, then it's okay to go, "Well, I make little jokes."

PLAYBOY: What you're saying is that you feel a backlash.

MARTIN: I sat down two years ago and I said to my agent, they're going to love me; for a while, I'm going to be uncriticizable. They cannot criticize if there are 20,000 people there. Then the backlash will start. After the backlash is over, everybody'll mellow out and the truth will come out. And we don't know what the truth is.

PLAYBOY: It's rather ironic; here you are, at the very top of your profession, and you're sounding like an underdog.

MARTIN: I'm beginning to understand that the underdog syndrome is important. The insult is in some ways as good as the praise. Right now, I'm being insulted. I need bad reviews as much as good ones. Because every time you get a bad review, someone out there rushes to your defense. Someone more important than the reviewer: the comedy consumer.

PLAYBOY: Have you always gotten good career advice?

MARTIN: When I was with William Morris, I went in and told them I was leaving television writing to be a performer. They said, "Don't do it, you'll never make it." Which I loved. I love when they say you're not going to make it. That's like, Jesus Christ, I've seen that in 18 movies. They told the guy he wasn't going to make it and he did. That's all part of it. I almost felt like a third person watching it: Oh, finally somebody said I'm not going to make it. [*Laughs*] Rejection is part of your accomplishments.

PLAYBOY: You sound like a man who has a lot of confidence in himself.

MARTIN: Oh, yeah, I have a lot of confidence in my ability. In show business, if you don't think that you're going to make it, or if you don't think that you're great, you haven't got a chance. Because there's too much working against you. There's too much shit to go through for seven years unless you think you're great. You have to stand there and bomb for three years and think *they* don't get it. When I started out, it was the thrill of not getting laughs. The thrill of making them go, "What?" more than getting laughs. I thought, Well, the least I'm doing is blowing their minds.

PLAYBOY: What were some of the more outrageous things you used to do?

MARTIN: There *was* a time when I was truly a wild and crazy guy. Onstage and after the show. Like, I used to take the audience into the streets at the end, which I can't do now because of legal problems and because there're 15,000 people now. In Nashville once, the police stopped me because we had 300 people out on the street. The first time I ever did that, I was working a college, 150 seats, and the dressing room was on the stage. There was no way out except through the stage. I finished the show, went back in my dressing room and they were still sitting there. I came out and they were still there, so we sort of went outside and I had them all get in an empty swimming pool. I swam across the top of them.

At one club, I said, "Who's seen me before?" A guy raised his hand. I said, "Get up here and finish the act for me." And I'd go sit and he'd get up there. He'd stumble through some jokes and I'd applaud and say, "Hey, this guy's great." It was *real* loose and funny.

PLAYBOY: It also got a bit bizarre, didn't it?

MARTIN: Yeah. At the opening of my act at the Boarding House, the lights would go down, but I wouldn't go onstage. You'd just hear my voice saying, "They can't hear me, can they? I hate this audience. Why do I have to go out there? I hate doing this. What in the hell am I doing here?" Then I go on: "Hi, everybody!" Then I go off at the end of the show and I'd say, "They can't hear me, can they? What a bunch of assholes. Jesus Christ!"

Sometimes I'd end the show, go back, change my clothes and be walking out when I'd stop and start doing another act. Bill McEuen and I look back on it as the days when I was *really* funny. That's when we were doing comedy because we had nothing to lose.

PLAYBOY: It was also when you opened for the Nitty Gritty Dirt Band, whose audiences weren't too receptive to your style of comedy.

MARTIN: Yes. It was the days of beer and drugs. The audience was not into comedy, not into listening to someone talk, not into giving a performer any courtesy at all. Even to the band. No respect, almost. That's when I made a very important decision—that I was *only* going to headline; I'm never going to open another show. When you're opening, I don't care who you are, no one comes to see you. You have to put your name up. I don't care if you're Bozo the Clown, if you put Bozo on top at the Roxy and the Eagles below, half the people there will be there to see Bozo. That's psychology.

PLAYBOY: Before that decision, though, you worked a lot of hostile crowds. Did you ever get so angry that you just walked off?

MARTIN: It happened. I was an m.c. for a rock show outside New York. There were five bands. They introduced me and I walked on and there was no change in the din of the crowd. Finally, I gave them the finger and walked off. I've done that a couple of times: "Fuck you" and I walk off.

One time I was standing doing my show and these four 16-year-olds are in the front row, yelling, "Quaaludes! Quaaludes!" to the point where it was interrupting the show severely. I couldn't concentrate. No one else can hear them but me, because they're in the front row. They're just so excited about quaaludes that they have to call out the name. That's one of my great hatreds of performing live: the uncontrollable idiot in the audience who throws off a show. There are loudmouths who have timing and you can use it to your advantage and there are loudmouths who don't have any sense of timing and will call out anything at any moment. Which totally frustrates the flow of what you're doing.

PLAYBOY: It also allows you the opportunity to put them down, which usually goes over well.

MARTIN: Sometimes. Like when someone starts talking to me, I'll say, "Oh, I'll get my camera, this is great, I've never had a picture of an asshole before." Usually, I mimic them. Someone interrupts with, "Hey, Steve, how's it going?" And I'll say, "And the sad thing is he says that all the time, no matter where he is. He just happened to be here and it happened to fit in. But wherever he is, at restaurants, anywhere, he always goes, 'Hey, Steve how's it going?'" It pisses me off.

PLAYBOY: To the point that you want to stop performing live?

MARTIN: I've felt that way. I don't need this. I'm not doing a carnival here. It's harrowing to be in front of 20,000 people and someone's down at the foot of the stage, smacking the floor with a gift he has for me. And I'm supposed to be gracious—oh, wonderful, a T-shirt with writing on it or something. It just drives me nuts.

One time a guy wanted to give me a T-shirt. He wrapped it up in a beer can, full of beer, and then he suddenly threw it on the stage and the T-shirt flew off and the beer can hit me.

You don't know what's happening. You think you're being killed. It's frightening to have something thrown at you onstage. I had to leave the stage for that. The guy thought he was being nice, but it really freaks you out—your heart's pounding and you're flipped out. You can't see; all you know is that you're a target. It makes me afraid. The more it happens, the more you've got it in the back of your mind. Audiences are insane; it's like a new kind of weird mass hysteria.

PLAYBOY: We've talked about audiences on the coasts, but what about your impressions of Middle America?

MARTIN: I remember when we did those long-stretch tours in the Midwest, we'd say, Thank God we don't have a day off. Because what do you do in Podunk for a night? You get more depressed. The worst time is when you're sick—and you always get sick on the road. Or when you're nowhere. Nowhere is worse. There's not a movie, there's not a TV, or it's off at 10. There're no people in town.

PLAYBOY: What's the most nowhere place in America for you?

MARTIN: Terre Haute, Indiana. Very little main street. And literally not a restaurant with any good food. You'd go into whole towns where it's completely made of fast food. If you were looking for something to buy, just looking to amuse yourself by buying something, you'd walk down the street, there was nothing for sale. There was nothing of anything you'd want. They say you can always tell that you're somewhere when they have manure ads on TV. [Laughs]

PLAYBOY: Talking about those days now, are the memories amusing to you? Are they the "good old days"?

MARTIN: No. Because it was so hard and depressing and dreary. There's a real loneliness out there. That's why you meet waitresses. It's depressing at night. You feel so shitty in the morning and you can't figure it out. I couldn't put two and two together. Why am I depressed? I used to go home and I'd stink. It took me a month to figure out it was cigarette smoke. In my hair, my clothes. Your suitcase stinks and reeks and you don't have any money and you're living in the sleaziest hotel.

PLAYBOY: Is there anything going for you when you're on the road trying to make it?

MARTIN: The most thrilling thing is when the audience is not laughing but you've got the waitresses and the sound man and your manager laughing. Bill Cosby said once, "I was onstage and I wasn't getting laughs, but I saw the waitress laughing, so I knew I was going to make it." They've seen you several nights, now you're starting to make them laugh. A lot of comedy is that—getting used to someone.

PLAYBOY: Which is what people obviously did with you.

MARTIN: But when I was 29, 30, I said, "Well, this is it, it's not going to happen, I'm not growing." Then I went to the Boarding House and it was sold out on a weekend. That was enough to keep me going.

PLAYBOY: What would have happened to you had you not gotten the laughs?

MARTIN: I was going to go further out. Become an artist totally. Not be concerned with show business at all. There's nothing I really can do except this.

PLAYBOY: Besides the laughs, what's the greatest rush you get when performing?

MARTIN: There's a real thrill of timing. That's the greatest fun of all. When you're resting, waiting; you've got the next line in your head and you're just waiting for that little intimate moment. And you know it's right to say it, you know it's right to do this, to move your hands this way. Really flowing. Charged. Like a ballet. Only you're using everything. It's not just dance, it's words.

PLAYBOY: Have drugs ever aided your sense of timing and control?

MARTIN: I created a lot of my material when I was out of my mind. I learned how to play the banjo when I was stoned, because you can sit there for six hours and listen to shit and you think it's great. I wish it had an effect on me now like it did then, but it doesn't. It was making me lethargic.

PLAYBOY: Are fans always trying to lay drugs on you?

MARTIN: I'm really offended by people who come up and assume that you use cocaine or smoke dope and they're offering it to you. First, they're idiots, they're out of their minds. And I got so turned off from the audiences at the rock concerts that I said, "I can't be this stupid. I'm never going to end up like that idiot." I'm against the symptoms of the drug overdose, when a guy is totally stupid. It's like the same hostility that I feel toward an absolute drunk. I know there are mature users of drugs that are aids to them, and sometimes I envy that. It would be great to get stoned, but I'm afraid of it, for one thing. It's like LSD. I'd love to take LSD when I'm 60. When you've got nothing to lose.

PLAYBOY: In the days when you did get stoned, what kind of material were you writing?

MARTIN: A lot of sketches for television.

PLAYBOY: Did you find TV writing hazardous to your mental health?

MARTIN: Yes and no. Television was a great discipline for me. You didn't have time to say one piece of poetry, it had to be a joke. The greatest thing I learned was take out the crap. It's the greatest advice you can give anybody. Lose it. Take it out. X it. And I learned the structure; it was my own structure for writing jokes.

PLAYBOY: Was what you wrote often what actually appeared on the tube?

MARTIN: Once you write a piece and think it's funny, you hand it to a producer and he changes it. Then you hand it to the star and he changes it or doesn't rehearse it and fucks it up so badly. Then the director shoots it and he misses the joke. I can remember standing there, going, "Boy, are they screwing that." Then it goes to postproduction and they sweeten it till there's no jokes left, no humor, no spontaneity, no charm, no mystery. Sometimes the distance from the printed page to what you see on the screen is so far that the joke's been homogenized and disappeared.

PLAYBOY: You started writing for *The Smothers Brothers* at a very young age, didn't you?

MARTIN: I was 21 years old and suddenly somebody said, "Write for television." I'd never written *anything*. *The Smothers Brothers* decided that year to get rid of all their old writers, meaning old in years, and hire all young people, so they got me and Carl Gottlieb, Bob Einstein, John Hartford, Mason Williams and Rob Reiner, who was younger than I was. But I wasn't prepared emotionally to handle that challenge.

PLAYBOY: What do you mean?

MARTIN: I teamed up with Bob Einstein the first day. He is a great comedy writer for television. He played Officer Judy on the show. He used to make me laugh so hard I thought I was dying. I was going through my anxiety stage and I'd be having these anxiety attacks *laughing*, he was so funny.

PLAYBOY: What do you mean by anxiety attacks?

MARTIN: I was a little overwhelmed at that whole scene, being expected to write these hysterically funny bits. You never know if you're a good writer, you always have the next thing to write. It's like you're only as funny as your last joke. That was always the feeling on *The Smothers Brothers Show*. You wrote a great sketch this week, now what's next? I didn't know if I was capable. Even though it was proved, I didn't know what proof was then.

PLAYBOY: Did you finally crack from the pressure?

MARTIN: Yeah.

PLAYBOY: And that's when you went to a psychiatrist?

MARTIN: I was already seeing a shrink for the draft. I'm very practical about those things. I go, All right, I've got something, which was anxiety, so you read about it, find out what it is and what causes it, and once you understand it, it's not as fearful. And eventually, it leaves because you understand it.

PLAYBOY: Has anxiety left you?

MARTIN: That kind of anxiety—intense, don't know what's happening, physical reactions—that's pretty much gone.

PLAYBOY: Did you stop working when that happened?

MARTIN: No, I kept working. It bothered me for a long time, a couple of years. Like, I couldn't stay in a restaurant for more than five minutes or I couldn't go into public places. I couldn't go into a movie theater. I had to get out. I was fearful. The definition of anxiety is fear without an object. Fear without something threatening you. Or whatever is threatening you is so buried in your subconscious, you don't know what it is and you just have to escape. It's exactly the symptom you have that someone's charging you with a knife. Increased heartbeat. You're nervous. You don't know what you're going to do. Only someone's *not* charging you with a knife.

PLAYBOY: Did you take anything for that?

MARTIN: I used mild tranquilizers.

PLAYBOY: Do the symptoms return occasionally?

MARTIN: The only thing that bothers me now is when people look at me. It's just a matter of figuring out what the problem is now. Before, I was so optimistic all my life that I didn't realize I had a problem. And that's what causes it—you're dismissing these little intimations that you have. What's more fearful with anxiety is fear of the symptoms striking you again. That's the most frightening thing. Once you realize that the attack is harmless, you've made a big step. It's not a unique set of symptoms. I prepare myself: I say, "This is never going to work." That way, I've already failed. And if it succeeds, then it's a bonus.

PLAYBOY: You mentioned that you were already seeing a shrink because of the draft. Did your anxiety attacks keep you out of the Army?

MARTIN: Let's put it this way: I had migraine headaches about the time I was about to be drafted. I went to the library and found out the symptoms for migraines. I was making enough money at the time to go to a shrink for two years to establish it. But it so happens I never could have gone into the Army, anyway.

PLAYBOY: Why not?

MARTIN: Because of my antiwar stance, my inability to kill someone and my lust for life.

PLAYBOY: A lot of us felt that. None of those would have kept you out.

MARTIN: Let's put it this way: I would never have gone to Vietnam. I was prepared to leave the country.

PLAYBOY: Did you ever participate in any antiwar protests?

MARTIN: I don't like to go out in crowds, so I never showed up at marches. As a writer for the Smothers Brothers, we were doing a lot of antiwar commentary on TV. I felt I was serving through that show.

PLAYBOY: What happened to that show?

MARTIN: The Smothers Brothers were politically axed off CBS. I believe the government put pressure on CBS to get them off the air. Because the ratings were good, the show was good. They came up with a phony excuse; they said a show wasn't delivered on time.

PLAYBOY: One show?

MARTIN: Yeah. Like, two days late. And they canceled it. *The Smothers Brothers* were giving the government a lot of shit.

PLAYBOY: How did you react?

MARTIN: It confirmed my distrust of the government and of bureaucracy. Bureaucracy is the worst evil.

PLAYBOY: After *The Smothers Brothers*, you wrote for a number of other shows, including *Sonny & Cher* and *Glen Campbell*. That didn't last long, did it?

MARTIN: Bob Einstein and I wrote a lot of funny sketches for *Sonny & Cher*, and a lot of those monologs, which you always tried to get out of writing.

PLAYBOY: Why?

MARTIN: Because you're always stuck with the same thing, you always go out on the same short joke: a nose joke. The reason I went to that show is they told me I could perform. I was really determined to be a performer. I said, "As long as I'm going to be there, I may as well write, too." I started writing and never appeared. Oh, I played a head one time, served on a silver tray, that did one-liners.

PLAYBOY: And how long did you last with Glen Campbell?

MARTIN: I quit after 13 weeks. I realized I was wasting my time, I was making $1500 a week, which was a lot of money, but after *The Smothers Brothers*, where you were really encouraged to write hard-hitting satire, to then go and simply write comedy, it didn't appeal to me anymore. I wanted to perform.

PLAYBOY: Which you did soon after. How many shows did you do on TV?

MARTIN: I did a lot of Steve Allen shows. Probably 35 of those. I did Della Reese, Joey Bishop, Merv Griffin. I've been on TV a *lot*, probably 500 times. *The Tonight Show* at least 35 or 40 times. When I first did *The Tonight Show*, I thought, That's it. But it wasn't. I realized after I'd done the show 15 times, I got recognized only once in the street. Then the next 10 times they were going, "Oh, this guy." Then the next 10 times, it was "Steve something."

PLAYBOY: What's the craziest thing you've ever done on *The Tonight Show*?

MARTIN: I had a couple of bits I rather liked, a long time ago. One was a comedy act for dogs.

PLAYBOY: You told jokes for dogs?

MARTIN: Yeah. The other bit was reading the phone book to make people laugh. You always hear that Olivier could read the phone book and make people cry, so I figured without any props or gimmicks, I could make them laugh by reading the phone book. So I'd pick up a book and go: "Aaron Adams, 612 North Frederick Street." There wouldn't be a laugh. "Bill Bosack, 647 North Atlantic." No laughs. I took out my arrow and put it on. Then I'd read a sillier name. "Mary Ann Pinball, 62. . . ." By the end of the thing, I was waving toothpicks from my head and holding up rubber chickens and then, finally, I'd say, "Don't look at me, I didn't write this shit." I thought it was hysterical. But it was the last time I appeared with Johnny for a long while.

PLAYBOY: Because he didn't think you were funny?

MARTIN: Maybe my skills weren't developed enough to warrant a re-appearance. Which may have been true. Because I'd sit on the panel and I'd be uncomfortable and he'd be uncomfortable. So why should he waste time talking to me? But Carson has respect for the agony of comedy. Whatever his ego is, it's not egomania. Whatever he feels about you, if he hates you or likes you, he will always give you the break as a comedian. He also saves your ass. Sometimes my mind will sit there completely blank and he'll have something to talk about and you're going, "Thank you thank you thank you thank you."

PLAYBOY: Carson has commented on your comedy: "He has a likable comedic style . . . that's well done, but it can be limiting. He's been doing it for a while." What flashes through your mind when you hear Carson say that?

MARTIN: The thing that instantly comes to mind is: Is he right? I read that comment, and at the time, I had coming out a book, a movie and a record. All expansive material. It's not remaining the same. So I answered the question in my own head.

PLAYBOY: You don't fear becoming a cliché?

MARTIN: I fear *so much* becoming a cliché that I don't think it will happen to me. When my act started, I was a left turn from everything that was going on, and I had the courage then to do it. *Cruel Shoes* was a left turn from what I'd been doing. The third album was a left turn. And *The Jerk* is not so much a left turn, but it's me in a completely different environment. I intend to make more left turns.

PLAYBOY: Could one of them possibly be taking over *The Tonight Show* when Carson leaves?

MARTIN: No. It would put an end to what my goals are in show business, and that's to make funny movies. You can't make funny movies if you're working five days a week. Also, I could never host *The Tonight Show*, because I'd always be doing my own version of what Carson does, and anyone who does that is an imitator, which is so wrong it's unbelievable. The real thrill of hosting *The Tonight Show* is getting to go out and act *like* Johnny Carson. You sit at the panel and you try to come up with a witticism like Johnny would have, you try to make a look like Johnny would. That's the real truth. It's like a goal, somehow, in show business to be able to do what Johnny Carson does, as just sort of your catalog of things you do.

PLAYBOY: What about a TV series? Has that ever been a temptation?

MARTIN: About three years ago, I turned down an appearance on somebody's show. There was an option in there for a series. Whoa! I'd be fucked right now if I had an option for a series.

PLAYBOY: What if it turned into something like *Mork & Mindy*?

MARTIN: I'm not taking anything away from Robin Williams, because I think he's outstanding on that show. If I'd been in Robin Williams's position, I would have taken that show. Because he was less along at that time than I was at this other time. That's a way in. But now I just wouldn't want to do that weekly piece of shit. And it doesn't necessarily have to be a piece of shit, but the odds are it *will* be a piece of shit.

PLAYBOY: How do you feel about *Saturday Night Live*?

MARTIN: Oh, I love that. *Saturday Night* reaches my people. I work real well with Gilda [Radner] and with Aykroyd; the chemistry on-camera works. I haven't done that much with [John] Belushi. I love Murray.

PLAYBOY: Are they friends or is it strictly professional?

MARTIN: I feel some of them are friends. We get along real well, with mutual respect. They have their own lives that I'll never be a part of. It's hard to get to know Belushi. I get along with Aykroyd real well, but I know there's a point where I stop in his realm, his world. He's like I was 10 years ago. He's tuned in to certain things that you really can't share. I'm not going to take Danny to 21—although I've never been to 21—but he wouldn't enjoy that. One time I said to Danny, "Let's go to Saks Fifth Avenue and get some clothes." He said, "I'm not into clothes."

PLAYBOY: Who thought up the two Czech brothers routine?

MARTIN: My character was in my act, but he wasn't Czechoslovakian. Then Danny saw the act and he said, "Let's do Czechoslovakian, two Middle-European brothers." It was essentially his idea to put them together as brothers.

PLAYBOY: How long did it take to get the routine working?

MARTIN: Instant. We just started talking. We were laughing at rehearsal, we were laughing when we read it, we thought it was hysterical. Repetition sold it, I think.

PLAYBOY: Do you think you could put that kind of comedy into a film?

MARTIN: I'd like to do me, Belushi and Aykroyd as *The Three Caballeros*. [*Sings*] "We are three *caballeros*, three gay *caballeros*."

PLAYBOY: Could you get them to agree?

MARTIN: Nah. That's a long way off. I don't think we could ever get the three of us on mutual deals. You've got to commit yourself so totally—it's a year. Then you start thinking, Do I want to work with Belushi for a year?

PLAYBOY: When you first appeared on *Saturday Night Live*, your father wrote in a local newsletter that that show set back your career five years. Did that bother you?

MARTIN: Frankly, it irritated me. Instead of encouragement, you get an insult. They would have liked it if I had been an entertainer they could take home to Texas and show around, one who didn't say fuck. As it turns out, I do say fuck, so they can't take me completely back to Texas.

PLAYBOY: Your mother told a reporter that you should get some new writers. Does she know, now, that you write your own material?

MARTIN: I think she does. I don't bother to explain most of the time. It makes you a little angry or hurt sometimes. I keep telling them, "Don't do articles in the paper and don't publicize who you are." I fear that.

PLAYBOY: Why?

MARTIN: They got an obscene phone call one time about me. Some girl called them and said I was a faggot. That's evil. I was *really* upset. A sick person, to call someone's mother. And tell her all these lies. Just pure lies, and hate.

PLAYBOY: In some of your routines, you make jokes about your mother—borrowing $10, making her carry your barbells to the attic—but you've never joked about your father. How come?

MARTIN: I guess it's because the mother is so vulnerable. Like, the attitude of those routines is that I was so *sick* that I would do that to my mother. And you wouldn't do that to your father, because he was stronger.

PLAYBOY: Would you say you've always wanted to win your father's approval more than anyone else's?

MARTIN: Absolutely. You know, you're always trying to please your dad, to get approval from Daddy. Which is okay, because it motivates me. There's the symbolic father that I'm working for when I write a screenplay. I may want approval from Carl Reiner or from the producer. The symbolic father is my own knowledge of the greatness that exists in the world and in art, so maybe when I'm finished, I'm thinking, okay, T. S. Eliot, is this okay? That's why I'm always slightly ashamed of certain things that I do. I know they don't live up to the standard that's been set.

PLAYBOY: Getting back to your real father, do you think you've got his approval by now?

MARTIN: Oh, yeah, I have his approval now. My parents have become closer since I've been successful. Success has vindicated me, in a way. I can go back to them with pride and they can be proud.

PLAYBOY: Do they comprehend what's happened to you?

MARTIN: They don't understand the evil side of people. They haven't been at a concert when somebody grabs you and won't let go or you feel a little bit of that terror. They're oblivious to it. We'll go for a drive and my mother will say, "Let's stop here and get out. You walk on the street and we'll watch the people look at you." [*Laughs*]

PLAYBOY: What else have you given them, besides pride?

MARTIN: They have a house and I'm making the payments. But I want to throw them out and raise the rent.

PLAYBOY: How did they feel about you when you were a kid?

MARTIN: I think my parents would agree there wasn't much camaraderie in my family. Discipline was part of my growing up.

PLAYBOY: Did you and your family fight much?

MARTIN: Not fighting, no. Just kind of Orange County blasé.

PLAYBOY: Orange County and Disneyland apparently had a big influence on you, especially since you worked at the Magic Kingdom from your 10th to your 18th year. Is Disneyland where you learned to hate people?

MARTIN: I hated waiting on people. It drove me nuts. The stupidity. They used to ask me, "How much is that 25-cent thing?" I just made a vow that I was never going to work with the public on that kind of level again. *Boy*, I hated it!

PLAYBOY: Have you ever gone back there?

MARTIN: Yeah, and I've never forgiven Disneyland for what happened. I had really felt like a part of Disneyland from 1955 till I quit in 1963; it was a real part of my youth. I went back there one time with long hair and they wouldn't let me in. I felt, like "You assholes, you're really Fascists." After Walt Disney died, everything started changing.

PLAYBOY: When *Cruel Shoes* was published, Putnam put out a press release that said, "The Disneyland style of entertainment—clean, unbitter and somehow very free—influenced Martin throughout his development as an artist." Do you agree with that?

MARTIN: I don't think my comedy is totally unbitter. There's a lot of bitter cynicism in it.

PLAYBOY: What about one critic's remark that you're the John Denver of comedy?

MARTIN: I think they're implying that that's an insult. I'm not into est.

PLAYBOY: Do you consider yourself an Orange County conservative?

MARTIN: What does that mean? When I grew up, I was never taught racial prejudice. We never discussed "Jewish," "nigger." That never came up. So I walked out when I was 21 and I didn't know you weren't supposed to like Jews or blacks. It was news to me.

PLAYBOY: You've been described as the Great WASP Hope. Why do you suppose comedy has been dominated by minorities?

MARTIN: Jews are very smart people and comedy takes smartness. They are more outgoing people. WASPs are traditionally barbecues. Richard Pryor does it perfectly. Maybe that's why there have been two great black stand-up comedians: Cosby and Pryor. Their whole lifestyle was outgoing. They're always talking. The traditional WASP dinner table is everyone sits and eats and you're real quiet. But the WASPs in the country need a WASP. Let me rephrase that. I don't call myself a WASP, because that implies that I'm a Protestant. Or was. [*Laughs*] I don't take any racial pride in my WASP-ness. I don't even consider myself a WASP. That term is derogatory. It implies simplicity and propriety, and I don't think of myself like that. Do you know how many WASPs it takes to screw in a light bulb?

PLAYBOY: How many?

MARTIN: Three. One to screw in the light bulb, one to mix the martinis and one to turn on the SC game.

PLAYBOY: You commented before about Richard Pryor's doing the WASP perfectly. Are you that white man?

MARTIN: Yeah. But it doesn't inhibit me. My comedy is definitely linked to the white man.

PLAYBOY: Didn't you, your manager and a sound engineer take a train from L.A. to New Orleans, recording ad-lib bits for some future record called *White Man's Vacation?*

MARTIN: Yeah. We were nuts. It was never for a record, we had an idea to do documentary comedy, like a documentary film, only we were try-ing to make it funny. Some of it worked. Like, I had one idea to go to Juarez, to the shops, where if something's $20, you end up buying it for two. We actually recorded this. I said to a shop owner, "Tell me the price for that hat." "Four dollars." I said, "I'll give you six." The guy said, "No." I said, "I'll give you eight." He was lost. Finally, after $10, he goes, "Okay." I gave him $10. We did it a couple more times and then he had me: "Do you want to buy a comb? Do you want to buy . . . ?" It went on and on. The mikes were hidden, but the piece never came off on tape, we had some technical problems. *White Man's Vacation* is a five-minute piece we recorded on the train. We had a young black porter who was a little militant and it inspired us to do this piece one night. We turned out all the lights in this compartment and we sat there and drank wine and I ad-libbed the whole piece, where I played a militant black porter and Bill played the innocent white man on vacation. It was going to be on *Comedy Is Not Pretty,* but we decided to cut it from that record.

PLAYBOY: Why?

MARTIN: A lot of reasons. I've always been nervous about the language at the end—the way it was delivered. It is very hard. We just made a decision that we were going to make a record that is all dirty, put it all on one record. Besides, the piece didn't fit on the album. Would you like to hear it?

PLAYBOY: Why not? [*In his bedroom, Martin puts a tape on his stereo set. The sound of a train can be heard. Martin sets up the routine by talking of how wonderful it is to have an opportunity to talk to some of the porters who have worked on the trains for so long. Bill McEuen's voice comes in, asking straight questions. Martin's voice changes to a high-pitched, twangy, militant black man's. Questioning the service, McEuen asks if it's a first-class-service car. Martin, in character, answers: "That's right. Then we got the superfirst class and the ultrasupersonic first class. In other words, you's in the shits. You have got the shits service . . . . It is 36 hours between New Orleans and L.A.*

. . . and in your room, you can't flush a toilet that whole time. That is the kind of service you got, white boy." McEuen, as the white vacationer, asks what he's supposed to do. The porter answers, *"You just got to sit there and dig it."* McEuen asks if he can get off. The porter says, *"No way, man, you is in prison. Once you pay your money, we have got you. You may even die on this trip. If you don't die . . . you are going to get scurvy, because we ain't giving you any oranges or apples."* The porter then tries to excuse himself, because, *"I have to go up to the superdeluxe ultra-first-class and clean out their toilets with my tongue."* McEuen laughs. The porter says, *"You better laugh now, 'cause in about two hours, you aren't going to have any lips . . . . we are going to serve them to the white people up in the front cars."* As a last request, McEuen asks if the porter can unlock the bunk bed, to which the porter responds, *"You can take this and shove it in your goddamn motherfuckin' white ass, you shithole white man. I will come in there and take that bed, you asshole mutha."* McEuen says to forget it. The routine ends with the porter saying, *"No, man, listen, I want to serve you."*]

PLAYBOY: We can see why you're a little nervous about releasing that. It seems to get racist.

MARTIN: I don't think it's racist at all. It is just funny. Thin-skinned people are going to get uptight about it. The truth is, it puts down white people. It takes a militant-black point of view. I guess I will have to take some shit for it, though. But Richard Pryor does white people.

PLAYBOY: Do you see any similarities between you and Pryor?

MARTIN: Richard Pryor and I do two completely different things. He is a *great* stand-up comedian, a true artistic personality and the *smoothest* stand-up thinker. His performance is more stunning when you consider that he laid off for a long time, then came back with a completely new show. I mean, not one word from his old stuff. Pryor has consciously reduced the size of his theaters to 3500-, 5000-seaters. He came to me one time after he saw me in Chicago and he said, "I used to work at these big places, but it was like stealing. Half the people can't see you." He's right. I said, "Well, I'm just going to steal for another couple of months." I used to mention Richard Pryor and Lily Tomlin in the same breath and say, "That's it, that's comedy today." But now I tend to say Richard Pryor.

PLAYBOY: What happened to Lily?

MARTIN: Lily has the artist mentality, she'll always be in show business and her career will rise and fall, depending on how good her project is. She's the female Richard Pryor, although Richard's talent is more impetuous, more forceful, more satirical.

PLAYBOY: That's how you once felt about Lenny Bruce, isn't it?

MARTIN: I used to go to sleep listening to Bruce's records. I remember I first heard the name Lenny Bruce and they said he was dirty. I said, "Aw, it's just a trick, some comedian's out being dirty and it's a gag, it's a hook." Then I saw him on the news. He was speaking at Long Beach State, doing his bit about defending his act. He was being prosecuted at the time and he had to cop. He wrote down his act and had to go to the judge and do it. I thought, That's not dirty. Then I started listening to his records and I realized how great he was. He was a funny person, not a political person. Most of his records are just good, funny bits. A master, undisciplined. A dialectician. Bruce is like Richard Pryor to me. His punch line isn't *motherfucker*. He was firing this chorus girl: "All right, you're fired, pack up your cunt and get out of here." That's a good joke. That's not profane. He was talking like people talk. He naturally used language, naturally used profanity. Then, suddenly, he's put in a position to defend it. It's like wearing Bermuda shorts. You walk in and somebody goes, "What are those?" And you didn't even think about it. You go, "It's okay to wear Bermuda shorts, because it's hot out." You have to make up a reason. It's like me being in a position to have to defend not being political in my act. Huh? You know, just a minute, let me think up a reason.

PLAYBOY: Who are some of the comedians who tickle your funny bone?

MARTIN: Well, I grew up listening to Bruce, Nichols and May, Jack Benny, Red Skelton. Steve Allen was my great love, he was the fastest ad-libber in the West; there's nobody faster. I like Rodney Dangerfield. Andy Kaufman. Robin Williams on Mork & Mindy makes me laugh. Bill Cosby made me laugh. David Brenner, Henny Youngman. Don Rickles is funny. He's like scotch, it's an acquired taste. Sid Caesar makes me laugh. And Soupy Sales.

PLAYBOY: Soupy Sales?

MARTIN: I love him. I think the format of his show is fantastic. You don't see anybody, you see a hand, a puppet. It just strikes me as clever. The jokes are stupid and every 20th joke you laugh. And he doesn't care. I love the background of the crew laughing.

PLAYBOY: What about Monty Python?

MARTIN: Makes me fall down and laugh. I think that's the greatest comedy of our time.

PLAYBOY: Is there a West Coast and East Coast brand of comedy? *Newsweek*, for instance, called you the "ultimate West Coast wacko," as opposed to the "archetypal East Coast neurotic, Woody Allen."

MARTIN: I think my comedy's West Coast, whatever that means. If we were to define East Coast comedy, it's more psychoanalytical. We're all starting at the same point: We're all depressed. Now, the East Coast approach is to show your depression, investigate it, learn about it, talk about it. The West Coast's approach is to say, "We're not depressed." It's to *be* depressed and to cover it up and go along and act as though you're not depressed.

PLAYBOY: We asked you before about possible similarities to Pryor; what about similarities to Chevy Chase?

MARTIN: Yeah, we have similarities. But I don't think it's one guy stealing from another. It's coincidental, we're reacting to similar times. I liked to watch Chevy on *Saturday Night*, he was real likable, a charmer, very funny. In *Foul Play*, he was totally underdirected. He wasn't Chevy Chase, he was an actor. He was being kind to the director and playing his script, rather than being what Chevy is capable of doing.

PLAYBOY: Did you audition for that role?

MARTIN: I read for *Foul Play*.

PLAYBOY: Why did you say no?

MARTIN: I didn't say no. They said no.

PLAYBOY: Do you feel lucky?

MARTIN: Made me realize I don't want to do murder mysteries. [*Laughs*]

PLAYBOY: Back to some of your peers. What about George Carlin?

MARTIN: You have to give Carlin a lot of credit. He came along as the hip comedian, but he still made people laugh. He never lost his sense of humor. He is real funny. I started out when there were no comedians, except Carlin. But I was still working before Carlin came along, too, around '66, that's when I really started working, and there was nobody to aspire to. Looking back, I'm proud of that. I want to stand alone. It's a matter of pride. There's also a lot of ego in that opinion.

PLAYBOY: Do you think Andy Kaufman could have made it without your having paved the way, in a sense?

MARTIN: Kaufman's real funny, but he's not for everybody. When he read *The Great Gatsby* on *Saturday Night*, it had me on the floor. I feel like I am the link for the normal audience to understand Andy Kaufman. Andy is where I may have gone if this never worked. I feel like I made a step in the direction of that comedy. A contributor. Kaufman's got enough entertainment value to make his art watchable.

PLAYBOY: What about Martin Mull?

MARTIN: I *love* Martin Mull. He's a real talented cynic. He influenced me a lot. I worked with him in Atlanta and he was wearing business suits and Pierre Cardin shoes and I was wearing a suit with tennis shoes. I thought, Why do it half-assed? Then I got into the white suit, because I thought it was new and different. I realize now it was just another of those things that John Lennon did five years earlier.

PLAYBOY: Do you think that men are funnier than women?

MARTIN: Not necessarily. Lily Tomlin proved that women can be funny. The problem is that the women comedians are emulating men, and it doesn't work that way. Someone is going to come along and be a *woman* comedian. There've been as many funny women in movies as there have been men, or even more. Like Judy Holliday, Marilyn Monroe.

PLAYBOY: Rodney Dangerfield thinks it's more acceptable for a man to be a comedian than a woman.

MARTIN: It's true. The tradition of being a comedian is being hard sell. Having to really sell the material. And the female tradition is being soft and vulnerable. The two haven't met. Pretty soon they will. Because the tradition of women being soft and vulnerable will become less significant in people's minds once the old people die off. Also, someone will figure out they don't have to have the hard sell. It's now permissible for a woman to be a comedian.

PLAYBOY: But could a woman do your act? Could a woman be outrageous and dumb and get away with it?

MARTIN: Elaine May pulled it off. She played dumb and she played smart and she played pseudo-sophisticated in a style that really worked all the way. So it's already been done, it's just a matter of being done on a large scale.

PLAYBOY: What do you think of Carol Burnett?

MARTIN: Carl Reiner says she's the best sketch player who ever lived. I said, "Even better than Lucille Ball?" But Lucille Ball wasn't really a sketch player, she was working in one sketch every week.

PLAYBOY: So who's the queen of comedy to you?

MARTIN: Gilda Radner is the queen of the female comedians to me. Gilda has the future. Her talent is so deep. She should do movies. She made a great comment about comedy one time. She said comedy was having your pants down around your ankles.

PLAYBOY: One comic whom we haven't touched upon but who might be considered a predecessor of your brand of humor is Jerry Lewis. What do you think of him?

MARTIN: I think Jerry Lewis is a real comedy genius. The movies of the 1950s with Jerry Lewis are 90 percent masterpieces of comedy. He always got a little sentimental at some point, which always turned me off, but there were great jokes and he was really in control. I'm talking about the movies he did by himself, like *The Bellboy*, *The Errand Boy* and *The Nutty Professor*. Funny movies. Sometimes I'm onstage and I feel myself doing someone. It's that little moment when you say, "I got that from a Jerry Lewis movie. Or from Jack Benny."

PLAYBOY: What do you think happened to Lewis?

MARTIN: From what I hear, he got very difficult to work with. He was the lord and master of comedy. I can't speak against him, because his accomplishments affected me and what stopped his accomplishments didn't affect me. Jerry Lewis always greased his hair back. What would have happened if, when the 1960s came along, Jerry Lewis grew his hair long, combed it over with the dry look? Maybe he'd still be funny. Who knows?

PLAYBOY: Since you're speculating, we'd like to ask you about Freddie Prinze. Do you think you could have handled success at the age he had to, 22?

MARTIN: I'm so glad it didn't happen to me then, because I wouldn't have had the experience to back up the demands that have been made on me. If I had to go to Vegas, like he did, when I was 21, shit . . . *I'd* kill myself. That would have been a terrible pressure. I think the reason Freddie Prinze killed himself was because he had a gun in his hand. He never should have had a gun. That kind of thing should be outlawed. That's why I won't have a gun around here. Because I get depressed.

PLAYBOY: Would you say that the pressures of being a stand-up comedian are greater than most other areas of show business?

MARTIN: Stand-up comedy is the hardest job in show business. There's no music, you can't sing for three minutes, there's no room for failure. Missing a joke or a mistimed joke or a failed laugh reduces the audience's confidence in you. Now, they have to evaluate whether something is funny. That's why it's so difficult, because there's never a chance to fail. You're literally hanging on every word. Or being hung on every word.

PLAYBOY: What do you feel when you're out there performing?

MARTIN: Fear is the biggest thing I feel out there. There's no fun, it's all work onstage. And you are always in danger of losing control. Every second you're on, you're on trial. I think of it as an enemy. As a challenge.

PLAYBOY: Does that mean you don't want to perform live anymore?

MARTIN: Stand-up comedy is transient. History shows that you can stand up for so long; after that, you're asked to sit down. To me, the object was to get out of stand-up and go into movies. A movie, a record, television, they're always new. The stand-up is such a toush thing, there's a tendency to leave it the same because it works. I just can't leave it the same anymore, for my own head.

PLAYBOY: On the tour you recently completed, how much material was new?

MARTIN: About 75 percent, but people still think they have heard it before, which I knew would happen. Why should I make up a new act? It doesn't prove anything; it's going to be more of the same. I can't change it. I can't make it 100 percent different. It's impossible. So why even do it? After one show, I started getting very depressed. I could tell the show was slipping away. At points, I thought, This is ridiculous. Toward the end of the act, I thought, I can't believe I'm out here. I felt like the worst amateur in the world.

PLAYBOY: What has that taught you about success and failure?

MARTIN: That if you're struggling to do the best you possibly can all the time, you'll fail 50 percent of the time. See, success in comedy has to do with something other than how good you are.

PLAYBOY: When did you feel you'd finally made it?

MARTIN: To us comedians, the proof of when you're big is when you start drawing. My manager and I have in our heads the date when I first played the Dorothy Chandler Pavilion in Los Angeles. It was 1976 or '77. I thought they were *crazy* to book me there. It seated 3500 and the most I had played was 500. But it sold out. I had done *Saturday Night Live*, hosted *The Tonight Show* and then did the Dorothy Chandler Pavilion. But in terms of fame, Abe Vigoda is as famous as I am. He was seen by 20 million people every week for however long his series lasted. No one's more famous than TV stars. We're not talking about quality now, we're just talking about fame. There's still a lot of audience out there for me to reach yet. I think a lot of people never heard of me, because I haven't been on prime-time TV that much. Kids come up to me, their parents send them over, they say, "That's Steve Martin, get his autograph." The kid doesn't know, he comes over to the table and he asks Bill McEuen for his autograph. [*Laughs*] I know John Lennon couldn't walk down the street. I *can* walk down the street. I don't think I'm at the height of my career yet.

PLAYBOY: Still, there are things about being famous that you resent, such as people staring at you or telephoning you.

MARTIN: It's the loss of your mental privacy. Your last privacy. The biggest loss is that you can't go anywhere and be an observer. Or have fun like everybody else. You can't go to Disneyland. You can't go to a park. You can't go to the zoo, which I love. When you start to do this, you're not thinking about, Wait, I better not write this joke, because I might get so famous that I won't be able to walk down the street. All you're thinking about is writing the joke and getting a laugh. Even if I got out of the business now, it's with me for the rest of my life. Think of the people who are famous and who are bothered just as much as I am who aren't making money. Like Nixon. I mean, he's not making $100,000 a day. Or some minor political figure. Ralph Nader. He's got people coming and bothering him, and he's not making $100,000 a day. Think if I had to go through this for no reason.

PLAYBOY: But for a price, you are willing to put up with the hazards of fame.

MARTIN: Sure, I'll be famous for that kind of money.

PLAYBOY: What kind of money are we talking about?

MARTIN: I don't work on a guarantee, I work on a percentage. For a while, I was really pulling in a *lot* of money per night. There was a time when I earned $1 million in two weeks. I did two days at the Nassau Coliseum in New York and made about $840,000.

PLAYBOY: That *is* a lot of money. What did you do with it?

MARTIN: Started lighting it up. [*Laughs*] You can only get what you're going to draw. It's like Albert Brooks's joke about Neil Diamond, who'd do a concert and they'd give him the building. Recording stars are the richest people in show business. Think of Barry Manilow; he must be incredibly rich. The money never stops. Every half year, they must be sending him $3 million, $5 million.

PLAYBOY: Did your sudden wealth sour old relationships?

MARTIN: Yes. Money gets people more than anything. I know people who genuinely were disturbed by my success. And not exclusively show-business people. I mean old friends.

PLAYBOY: At least you've been up front about it—you've even incorporated your love of money into your act.

MARTIN: I had one joke where I say, "I love bread." All it was was a lead-in to a routine. Then I read it quoted, "Steve loves money, loves bread." It was just a joke. It's like saying, "Steve gives his cat a bath with his tongue."

PLAYBOY: Are you saying you *don't* love money?

MARTIN: I don't *love* it, no. It's a sales tool. My manager may say that to somebody to get more money.

PLAYBOY: How are your record and movie deals constructed?

MARTIN: Bill's biggest contribution to my career was that when we made it, we were totally independent, with not one contract signed to anybody. Not record companies, not agencies, not anything. Bill made the Warner Bros. deal, the record deal, the movie deal, all the big deals. Marty Klein, my agent, was really responsible for personal appearances, a lot of top television. He got me on *The Tonight Show*, on *Saturday Night*. Those were his critical contributions.

PLAYBOY: And didn't you and McEuen buy Klein a Rolls-Royce?

MARTIN: Marty had always kidded that "Someday you'll buy me a Rolls-Royce." So, since he had really helped our careers, we did. That was our joke.

PLAYBOY: Do you give money to any charities?

MARTIN: I don't believe in organized charity. I mistrust them. I always think the funds are being misspent. I like the small kind of charity. I think it's the best value for your dollar. [*Laughs*]

PLAYBOY: You own five cars, three houses, an apartment . . . for a guy who tells jokes, you're not hurting. What's the most extravagant thing you've ever done?

MARTIN: In '72, I was in London and I bought a $1000 watch. I was probably making $30,000 a year, but it didn't matter if I was making $1 million, it was overcoming the psychology of buying a $1000 watch. Another extravagant moment was when I bought my first painting. I think it was $800. The greatest thing with money for me is paintings. And relief from the phone bill. Carl Gottlieb told me you can never have enough money if you collect art. People like me are an art dealer's dream.

PLAYBOY: How many Early American paintings do you own?

MARTIN: More than 40. I'm buying rapidly with caution. I can't be fooled. I always have the pictures looked at by experts.

PLAYBOY: Why did you choose Early American paintings to collect?

MARTIN: To learn that language. There was a *Doonesbury* cartoon that was fantastic, it really related. He's a rich kid, collecting stamps, and he says, "I've found this new hobby, collecting stamps. It's really thrilling." He picks up the phone and he calls the stamp shop. "Send me all the stamps from Nicaragua." Hangs up and says, "This is great."

PLAYBOY: Do you mind talking about your collection?

MARTIN: I'll talk about it, but let me preface it with saying I don't want to talk about it. I mean, I'm criticized for performing, for making records, for making movies, and I know one day I'm going to be criticized for my art collection. That's the one thing I feel I don't have to stick out. I don't have to have somebody write that this is a piece of shit, that this artist is lousy. So with that in mind, after I said "Fuck you" to all the people who are going to talk about it, I'll talk about it.

PLAYBOY: Why do you collect?

MARTIN: It occupies my time, my spare time, my energy. It's like going to the Bahamas.

PLAYBOY: Are you collecting as an investment?

MARTIN: I haven't made a fortune on these pictures. I look at it as a luxury, not an investment. People are very unfamiliar with the language of paintings.

PLAYBOY: What's the most you ever paid for a painting?

MARTIN: I don't like to talk about that stuff, because what seems reasonable to me, to most people is going to seem insane.

PLAYBOY: Would $150,000 be a good guess?

MARTIN: There're none that are more. But there are a lot that are less.

PLAYBOY: Could you pay $1 million for a painting?

MARTIN: It's not against my nature to do it. The price of paintings is the biggest example of existentialism there is. There's almost no explaining it. I mean, can a work on canvas be worth that much money? But they are, because people pay it. That's the only explanation. A painting is worth $1 million because someone will pay $1 million.

PLAYBOY: Do you have a favorite painting?

MARTIN: One of my favorites is the Rembrandt at the L.A. County Museum of Art: *Raising of Lazarus.* It's a pretty somber picture. You can see Lazarus sitting up, he's just been risen. And Christ is there, he's got his hand up and a look of surprise on his face, like he really did it. And Lazarus is amazed, he doesn't know where he is. It's just the most dramatic, beautiful thing I've ever seen.

PLAYBOY: Didn't you, around 10 years ago, actually have a show in a Los Angeles art gallery?

MARTIN: I did a whole show in '68 at a gallery in Los Angeles. It was essentially good jokes. I was intense about it, I meant it. I had an empty framed mirror on one side of the wall and the other side was blank and it was titled: *Infinite Reflections. Two Mirrors, One Invisible.* Then I had a rose in a vase: *Invisible Rose, Unfinished.* A lot of little puns and jokes.

PLAYBOY: You studied philosophy in college but came to the conclusion that performing was the better choice. How did you reach that decision?

MARTIN: After studying Wittgenstein and Sartre, I realized that the creative process is the only thing that can't totally be torn apart in philosophy. That it exists without rules, without problems of language and semantics. So I left philosophy for that reason. See, there are certain rules—you can't walk through a wall, you can't fly. Everything else is what you create. So the creation of your life is what it's all about. That's when I said I'll be an artist, I'll be in theater. It was the time to build my catalog of actions and accomplishments and creations.

PLAYBOY: Would you say that your studies in philosophy left you pretty cynical?

MARTIN: I would think so. Pretty cynical. Man is no better by nature than an animal until you do something to elevate yourself above that level. Honestly, I would rather save some animals' lives than some people's lives.

PLAYBOY: Speaking of animals, you're a cat man, aren't you?

MARTIN: I like cats because I don't have to take care of them that much. Dogs are like having a kid.

PLAYBOY: Someone once observed that you never show emotion, which is why you like cats.

MARTIN: It's false to say I've never shown my emotions toward anything. But I do like cats for that quality. Their ability to take it or leave it.

PLAYBOY: Do they protect you from burglars?

MARTIN: Yeah. Killer cats.

PLAYBOY: What's your biggest argument with the human race?

MARTIN: That people don't take pride in what they do. Businessmen and executives put out shit. They make shit. They sell shit. It's all crap. There's no pride in it.

PLAYBOY: Like junk food?

MARTIN: Those Saturday-morning commercials drive me nuts. "Wholesome goodness." You look at it and it's all sugar. Followed by corn sugar, vanilla sugar and every kind of sugar. Then it goes into chemicals.

PLAYBOY: Enough to turn one into a vegetarian, which you are, aren't you?

MARTIN: I once went on this Atkins diet, which is pure protein, pure meat. I got to hate meat so much that I thought, What do I really love? What I really love is cheese and vegetables and grilled-cheese sandwiches. That's what I turned to. I just cut meat out. I eat fish. I hate killing animals, but I love to kill fish.

PLAYBOY: Is it true you stopped taking vitamins because they started turning your hair brown?

MARTIN: Yeah. But since then, I reconsidered and I take some vitamins again.

PLAYBOY: When did your hair turn gray?

MARTIN: I got my first one when I was 15. It runs in the family. I've given two minutes of thought to my gray hair.

PLAYBOY: You gave a lot more thought to Somerset Maugham's book *The Razor's Edge*, which had a big influence on you when you read it. What was it that reached you?

MARTIN: The questioning of everything sacred. That was the first time I had ever heard that kind of thought.

PLAYBOY: Any other books really help you lately?

MARTIN: I'll tell you the best self-help book I've ever read: *How I Found Freedom in an Unfree World*, by Harry Browne. His tenets are complete honesty at all times, which is almost impossible. His point is that the only person who feels guilty in saying no is you.

PLAYBOY: Do you still have a lot of guilt to work out?

MARTIN: I think there are several years' worth of things to work out. I'm working out things constantly now. Finally getting off the road for a while and getting into a normal situation, where you're in the same bed every night and around the same friends all the time. I was working out a lot of things: the question of numbers, how they determine your validity; charts; how reviews affect you. How to regard your privacy. What to say in an interview. What I want to reveal about myself.

PLAYBOY: How do you think you've done so far?

MARTIN: I think I've said more than I wanted to say. I don't know if I'll even read this. I'll just get depressed, no matter how good it is. I feel like some asshole who's been asked questions of sophistication.

PLAYBOY: How shaky is your mental balance?

MARTIN: I feel very fragile mentally, sensitive to everything.

PLAYBOY: What makes you cry?

MARTIN: I was on the road about three years ago, making about $1000 a night. I was in New York at the St. Regis, watching TV, and this old comedy came on. It was, like, W. C. Fields. It was a shock to me, watching him be the buffoon. I just sat there and suddenly I started crying. I was all by myself in this room, weeping. I could've stopped myself, but there was no one around, so I didn't. This had never happened to me before. The next time, I was talking to my mother, recently, on the phone. It was just something like, "We really appreciate what you've done." That kind of thing. We were both sort of weeping. Two years ago,

I was driving to Aspen and I'd made cassette tapes of e. e. cummings's six records, called *Six Nonlectures*. He speaks very hypnotically, talking about the artist's responsibility, the artist's life, and his dedication was so strong and so beautiful and moving that it made me weep.

PLAYBOY: You're a very romantic person, aren't you?

MARTIN: I think so. Romantic in the capital-R, classical sense. In your youth, you are so romantic and your emotions are so strong about certain things that when they're finally crushed, like in your childhood love affairs, it's very hard to go back to being overtly romantic in your own life. Maybe that's why you turn to painting and music and literature instead of sailing to Tahiti on the pirates' boat.

PLAYBOY: How happy are you, even if you haven't gotten on that boat?

MARTIN: Happiness is so hard to define and foolish to define. Am I acting? That's the worst thing you can ask yourself. You can be happy suddenly. It can spring on you, not when you reach a plateau. You can be happy going backward or going down. You can be happy at the loss of something.

PLAYBOY: That's a pretty serious happiness.

MARTIN: If I could correct one thing about myself, it would be to exploit my creativity in a more jubilant way; to take everything with the old "Fuck you" attitude. It's the idea of not taking yourself seriously.

PLAYBOY: Not being afraid to blow it?

MARTIN: The only fear I have is of blowing it all. It's the old show-business story. You make it and you're a flash, and then you're sitting there with nothing left. I've always kidded I'd be a bum in the gutter. But that's not going to happen to me.

PLAYBOY: You said that low.

MARTIN: I'll say it high. *It's not going to happen to me!*

PLAYBOY: Well . . . *excu-u-use me!*

MARTIN: One thing I'd like to clear up about people imitating me. I read in reviews or interviews that I created these cliché or catch phrases. But no one sets out and says, "I think I'll think up a cliché." I never wanted to encourage it. It just started happening. I had to drop the "Excuse me" routine, because people knew it too well. Sometimes I still do it, but I try to twist it around a little. For a while, I was saying, "I don't say '*Excuse me*' anymore. And if you don't like it, well, *excuuuse me.*" It's like singing a hit song over and over. But I'm not premising my act on it anymore. I don't want to be identified with "Excuse me," because once "Excuse me" dies, then I go with it.

PLAYBOY: You don't want to go the way of the Hula Hoop or pet rocks?

MARTIN: I realize I'm a fad, so I don't get too excited. It's interesting to have made up a fad or to make up a saying.

PLAYBOY: Like the license plate in California that says Get Small?

MARTIN: I used to get pictures of people with their birth announcements and pictures of their kids with nose glasses announcing the birth of a wild and crazy guy. [*Laughs*]

PLAYBOY: Do you feel funny just before you go onstage? Lenny Bruce said that he threw up three times before he could go out there.

MARTIN: I don't feel funny until I hit the stage and get my first laugh. In fact, I *only* feel funny onstage. A person's work and who he is are two different things.

PLAYBOY: Many people don't know that about you.

MARTIN: They told me about a guy up in Philadelphia who has my personality to the point of psychopathy. He can't get out of it. He is in the hospital, he goes to a shrink. He talks like me.

PLAYBOY: It might help him to know what you're like offstage.

MARTIN: I really *am* two people!

PLAYBOY: The comedian and the quiet depressive. Actually, three: the musician. Where did you learn to play the banjo?

MARTIN: I was at a friend's house and I heard a record and said, I'm going to learn how to play that. As I said, I was stoned. It just slayed me. I used to slow records down to 16 and pick up the notes.

PLAYBOY: What's your favorite music?

MARTIN: I like classical guitar, bluegrass and Irish music. I'm eclectic when it comes to music. I don't have one pop record.

PLAYBOY: Now that you've become an actor, will you study acting?

MARTIN: No, I don't have the time or the inclination to practice. I say earn while you learn. [*Laughs*] I think I have enough natural experience to get by. I'm a beginning actor; experience will make me better.

PLAYBOY: What would you consider your greatest accomplishment to date?

MARTIN: *The Absent-Minded Waiter.* And the position I achieved in stand-up comedy. To me, that's a true accomplishment. I can look back on last summer and say, "I did the impossible. I did what one in a million do. Or one in 10 million do." Even for a moment, to be on top. That's all on top is, a moment, no matter who you are, even if you're Elvis, you're on top momentarily in terms of time. That's the thrill, to say, "Yeah, I was the biggest comedian in the world."

PLAYBOY: Earlier, you said you're not at the height of your career; now you're putting yourself in the past tense.

MARTIN: I never expected it to *last* a long time, because that kind of frenzy can't. It's almost like breathing a sigh of relief. Bob Newhart told me when he was the biggest comedian he kept wondering, Who's going to be next? And when Cosby came along, he said he went, Uhhh, thank God. That's the way I feel. It's like I can level out and let my talent come out rather than my ability to manipulate.

PLAYBOY: And where would you like that talent to lead?

MARTIN: I will be very happy if, when I'm 60, I can look back, having made 40 comedies, and say, "I was a funny person in this world."

PLAYBOY: And what would you say to young comedians from that vantage point?

MARTIN: Always take your wallet onstage with you.

 January 1993 ——————————————————————

A candid conversation with a former wild and crazy guy about his new life in movies, his old life in comedy and his favorite screen kiss—with John Candy

People still approach him on the street and ask for his autograph (they don't get it—he hands them a preprinted card instead). They plead with him to do the shtick they remember from his many appearances on *The Tonight Show* and *Saturday Night Live*.

Steve Martin refuses. Long gone are his days onstage in his trademark white suit with a fake arrow sticking through his head. The new Steve Martin plays an evangelist, an architect, a producer or a sentimental dad in hit Hollywood movies. The wild and crazy Steve Martin has given way to the mature and sedate Steve Martin, right?

Maybe yes, and maybe no. During Johnny Carson's final week hosting *The Tonight Show* last spring, Martin appeared in a turban in front of a tiny placard that announced one of his many alter egos, the Great Flydini. After reciting the requisite magic words and unzipping his pants, he conjured forth an egg, then a telephone, then a puppet singing like Pavarotti, all through his fly.

The Great Flydini, of course, is vintage Martin, a throwback to his earlier days of offbeat, zany comedy. His new movie, *Leap of Faith,* is strictly a dramatic role. Perhaps only Robin Williams has accomplished what Martin has—achieving fame as a stand-up comic and translating it into success as a serious actor. But Martin hasn't stopped there. He has also written some of his most successful movies, including *Roxanne* and *L.A. Story.*

His acting work is eclectic: He played romantic leads (in *Roxanne* and in 1992's *Housesitter*), earnest and endearing dads (in *Parenthood* and *Father of the Bride*) and semi-straight men (to John Candy in *Planes, Trains and Automobiles,* to Lily Tomlin in *All of Me* and to Michael Caine in *Dirty Rotten Scoundrels*). He stole the show in *Little Shop of Horrors* (in which he played a mad drill-wielding dentist) and *Grand Canyon* (in which he portrayed a movie producer whose artistic sensibilities were insulted when the blood and guts were cut from one of his films). In other movies he sang and danced (*Pennies from Heaven*) and read the weather (*L.A. Story*). Some were comedies with a bit of drama and others were dramas with some comedy.

Most of Martin's movies have done well at the box office and he has won numerous awards—though the Oscar has eluded him, even when he was rumored to be a shoo-in for best actor for *Roxanne.* *Time* called him "this decade's most charming and resourceful comic actor," and *Entertainment Weekly* estimated that audiences have spent three quarters of a billion dollars to see his movies.

As a child, Martin had no plans to become an actor. He was born in Waco, Texas, and raised in southern California, where his father worked as a real estate salesman. Fortune brought the family to live in Garden Grove, an Orange County suburb in the shadow of Disneyland, where the young Martin found work selling guidebooks and, later, hand buzzers and fake vomit in a gift shop.

As a college student at Cal State–Long Beach, Martin earned money performing at Knott's Berry Farm, where he did magic tricks and sang, accompanying himself on the banjo. But show business was just a hobby; Martin planned to teach philosophy after graduation.

Instead, a girlfriend helped him get his first Hollywood job, as a writer for *The Smothers Brothers Comedy Hour.* He wrote hundreds of skits, won an Emmy and went on to write for shows hosted by Sonny & Cher, Pat Paulsen and Glen Campbell.

Although his agent predicted he would fail as a performer, Martin left television writing to take his stand-up act on the road. Stand-up comedy was still in its dark ages then—it would be a few years before comedy clubs started springing up across the country—and Martin had little choice but to serve as the opener for such acts as the Nitty Gritty Dirt Band and Linda Ronstadt.

Those audiences, unfortunately, were not particularly receptive to comedy, so Martin made another career change. In 1975 he decided his days as an opening act were over and his days as a headliner should begin. He started touring small music clubs as a solo act, losing money and trying to establish his oddball brand of comedy with audiences around the country. His move paid off: Rave reviews in Miami and San Francisco gave his career a gigantic boost, and he was finally invited to appear on television talk shows, including *The Tonight Show*.

No one quite knew what to make of Martin. He wasn't political or topical along the lines of George Carlin, Lenny Bruce, Robert Klein or Richard Pryor. He did gags and one-liners with props (the fake arrow through his head, balloons). Much of his comedy was physical, in the tradition of Laurel and Hardy and the Marx Brothers.

Even Lorne Michaels, the executive producer of *Saturday Night Live*, was confused. "His act seemed too conventionally show business," Michaels said. "It was so new it looked old." At first, Michaels dismissed Martin as too unhip for *SNL*. But he later relented, and Martin became the show's most popular guest host. Soon, Martin was playing 20,000-seat arenas.

His comedy records sold millions and won Grammys, and he had a best-selling book in 1977, *Cruel Shoes*. A film he made (*The Absent-Minded Waiter*, which he showed during his concerts) was nominated for an Academy Award. He had become, as Carl Reiner said, "the first rock-star comedian."

As abruptly as he had started headlining, Martin quit stand-up for a movie career. In *The Jerk*, directed by Reiner, a friend from his *Smothers Brothers* days, he played the title role, the adopted son of a black sharecropper. Although the movie was trashed by reviewers, who called it sophomoric, *The New York Times*, in a TV listing for *The Jerk*, recently called it "a sophisticated comedy."

Since *The Jerk*, Martin has been in at least one movie a year. He has also had a run on Broadway in *Waiting for Godot*, opposite Robin

Williams, and has continued to pop up on *Saturday Night Live*, where his comedy seems as antic and silly as ever.

Offscreen, his life is quiet and busy. He met his wife of the past six years, Victoria Tennant, on the set of *All of Me*. The British-born actress, goddaughter of Laurence Olivier, was also his co-star in *L.A. Story*, which he wrote and co-produced. When he's not on location, he lives with Tennant in Beverly Hills. The couple also has an apartment in New York City.

Although Martin hates the glitz of Hollywood, he counts many fellow actors among his good friends. He is an avid art collector whose taste runs from a David Hockney portrait of Andy Warhol to works by Roy Lichtenstein and Stanton Macdonald-Wright. He says he's not political, though he and Victoria traveled to Saudi Arabia to meet with servicemen sent to fight the Gulf war.

In his 20th and latest movie, *Leap of Faith*, Martin portrays a con man evangelist managed by Debra Winger. It's a far cry from his first role in *The Jerk*, when he was the subject of an earlier *Playboy Interview*. In that interview, he wondered aloud if he was going to last.

Martin did more than last, he soared. Now, 13 years later, he has become one of the exclusive group of subjects that *Playboy* has interviewed twice (joining Fidel Castro, Robin Williams and Gore Vidal). Contributing editor David Sheff, who conducted last month's interview with Sharon Stone, was sent to Los Angeles to face off with Martin. Here is his report:

"Martin uses the restaurant at the Four Seasons Hotel in Beverly Hills as his living room for business meetings and interviews. It's a hotel that's teeming with movie stars. As Martin drove into the parking lot in his steel-blue BMW, Tom Cruise and Nicole Kidman were slipping into a Porsche and Sam Shepard was reclaiming his Jeep. Later, Ron Howard and Harvey Keitel wandered through the lobby.

"Martin was given the best table in the restaurant, and the waiter was unfazed when he ordered 'Just water,' since he had already eaten lunch.

"At first, Martin was anything but relaxed, though he eased up by our final session. Still, he fidgeted, folding his napkin, rocking in place and drumming his fingers on the linen tablecloth. Today, it seems as though Martin no longer feels he needs to hide behind a joke. Offstage, he doesn't try to be funny, at least not on cue. That's a significant change for him. He told *Playboy* in 1980, 'I'll be funny when there's a question I don't want to answer.' Instead, he spoke candidly, albeit cautiously, and chose his words carefully. There were many subjects he was reluctant to speak about—'because I don't have to,' he said. He usually relented, but it was often like pulling teeth—as if I were the demented dentist he played in *Little Shop of Horrors*.

PLAYBOY: Why are we here and not at your house?

MARTIN: I don't do interviews at home because I'm a private person. I don't want the house talked about or described. It's an intrusion into our lives.

PLAYBOY: Did something make you gun-shy?

MARTIN: I've always tried to separate my home life from my work. I did a few things early on when I was living in apartments, and I've done some things in my New York apartment, but the story becomes about art on the walls and bath towels. All the articles about Johnny Carson said that he survived with his dignity intact, as if that were a rare thing in Hollywood. Well, he almost never did interviews and he never showed his house in *Architectural Digest*. That's the way to do it.

PLAYBOY: But?

MARTIN: But you sort of get trapped.

PLAYBOY: How? It would seem that you are successful enough now to call the shots.

MARTIN: Incumbent on an actor who makes movies is publicizing the movies. You have to do it. It's something that you deal with, like autographs.

PLAYBOY: But you give out business cards instead of autographs.

MARTIN: It's a way to deal with it quickly and not to be rude. Most of the times that people ask for autographs, it's a way of proving that they saw you. I know this from when I asked for autographs. People always want to know, "What's he like? Did he say anything funny? Was he nice?" You have thirty seconds to be all those things. My card covers it all: It says that you found me nice, you found me funny and you found me charming and friendly.

PLAYBOY: Do some people get mad? Do they want more than a card?

MARTIN: No, they like it, though occasionally somebody yells at me.

PLAYBOY: Whose autographs have you asked for?

MARTIN: Bobby Fischer, Jerry Lewis and Earl Scruggs.

PLAYBOY: Were they funny, charming, nice and friendly?

MARTIN: All of those things.

PLAYBOY: Why did you want their autographs in particular?

MARTIN: Earl Scruggs was the first guy I ever heard play the five-string banjo, which motivated me to pick it up. Bobby Fischer was a legendary hero—I play chess a bit, too. I grew up watching Jerry Lewis.

PLAYBOY: It sounds as if you haven't much liked the trappings of celebrity.

MARTIN: At the same time, I wouldn't want to go back to the years of struggle. I recently visited Paris and it was perfect. You have enough fame to get into restaurants but not enough that you're constantly bothered.

PLAYBOY: Do you ever tell people to leave you alone?

MARTIN: Yeah, I do.

PLAYBOY: Do they get angry?

MARTIN: You can't please everybody. It really used to bother me to think that I had made somebody mad. Now I realize that it's inevitable, so I draw the line. That's why I don't talk about things that are personal to me.

PLAYBOY: Are you shocked at how personal the press can get? What have you thought about the Woody and Mia soap opera?

MARTIN: It feels as if it's so much their business that I'm opinionless.

PLAYBOY: Just the other day, at a press conference, you were asked if you were America's next Woody Allen and you said, "I haven't slept with one of Mia's daughters yet."

MARTIN: Yes, and I regret having said that. The fact is, I like them both.

PLAYBOY: Do you often stay home because you don't want to deal with the attention?

MARTIN: No. There are places we can go where we won't be bothered. It's like having a hump. You have it, so you deal with it. You sort of ask for it if you do this kind of career.

PLAYBOY: Particularly when you succeed in such visible media as stand-up, television and movies. Do you have a favorite of those?

MARTIN: Movies, because that's what I'm doing now.

PLAYBOY: How do you choose your movies?

MARTIN: A lot of people think we actually make decisions about what we want to do next. But it's really about what is offered. More often, you make choices by what comes to you at the time.

PLAYBOY: Can't you do whatever kind of movie you want to do?

MARTIN: It has to exist. Finding something that is well-written is extremely difficult.

PLAYBOY: Is that why you write scripts? Does that make you less dependent on what's available?

MARTIN: Yeah, but the ones I write are not career moves. They're, "I want to write this." Or, "I think this would be a good movie."

PLAYBOY: What is a career move?

MARTIN: When you say to yourself, "I want to do a drama with a showy role and I'm going to make sure that no one else shines in the movie." [*Laughs*] A *legitimate* career move is, "I want to show them that I can do more than pratfalls, so I'm going to do something that will show that." It usually doesn't work out that way, but you try anyway.

PLAYBOY: What's an example of a legitimate career move?

MARTIN: *Parenthood.* I wanted to show that I could play a real person.

PLAYBOY: You had never played a real person before that?

MARTIN: I had played a real person in *Planes, Trains and Automobiles,* but in *Parenthood* I was really a real person. Up until then, I think, the comedy was carrying the acting, not the other way around.

PLAYBOY: Meaning what?

MARTIN: Meaning that I didn't play characters as much as I did jokes and gags and gave looks.

PLAYBOY: How do you feel about those who think that your goofier roles are your finest?

MARTIN: I'm glad people like them. It's funny because they used to be considered stupid. I'm interested in what I'm doing now, comedy, but comedy within the confines of real characters.

PLAYBOY: Is it easier when you're in someone else's movie and reading someone else's lines?

MARTIN: Yes. I love doing scripts I didn't write because I am only a hired actor and I have only that one thing to worry about. If I write it, I have another whole set of problems.

PLAYBOY: Then why do you write?

MARTIN: It gives you something to do when you're off, for one thing. You don't want to just sit there. Mainly, I am a writer. I just am.

PLAYBOY: When you are in someone else's movie, do you change lines and come up with jokes, or do you stick to what's written?

MARTIN: It depends. *Grand Canyon* was a writer's script, written by Larry Kasdan. I didn't add a line. In a movie like that, you play the character as honestly as you can. In other movies you always try to think of jokes. That's what I'm good at. Maybe that's why they hire me.

PLAYBOY: In *Grand Canyon* you played a cynical Hollywood producer who has had a momentary lapse and has imagined making socially conscious movies. He comes to his senses and realizes that he would go on making what people want—insipid violence. Was he typical of the kinds of people you run across in Hollywood?

MARTIN: For all the talk about those people, I don't run into them much. I don't think I'd be around very long if I did.

PLAYBOY: Was your *Grand Canyon* character a caricature?

MARTIN: No, not at all. There are people with crass taste who know that violence sells. They also justify what they're doing. Victoria and I argue about them. I don't think they're evil. I think it's a question of style.

PLAYBOY: What is your wife's view?

MARTIN: She equates that behavior with some kind of moral flaw. But it's not murder, lying, cheating or stealing. You may not like it, but it's not a horrible thing. You hear all the time that good films are no longer being made. It's baloney. They say moviemakers care more about money than movies. They're right about that. Movies cost $25 or $30 million. How can you ask them not to care? It's a question of money and it always has been.

PLAYBOY: Did Robert Altman, in *The Player*, go too far in portraying the movie business's ruthlessness?

MARTIN: The movie business gets a lot of attention because of movie stars, and people tolerate bad behavior in movies more than they would in other businesses. In any business, one's power is defined by one's position. In advertising or banking, you know who you control. In the movie business, it's amorphous. The producer may have the power, or the star may, or the director or the studio—it changes. Since it is undefined, everyone vies for power. It's all about bluff, seeing what you can get away with. There is also this insecurity. No one can be completely confident, because even geniuses fail in this business. Except me. [*Laughs*]

PLAYBOY: Is everyone insecure?

MARTIN: The truth is that no one knows what they're doing in show business. A painting is one person's vision. In show business, you need this unpredictable animal called the audience. Ultimately, no one knows how to do it right every time. If we did, we'd always make hits. Our insecurities are such that we always put it on others—that they know. You begin to think you need these other people. If they happen to be behaving badly, you still think you need them. It gives people enormous power. All the time we hear, "So-and-so is the only one who can play this part." Once you start thinking that way, you're screwed.

PLAYBOY: Screwed how?

MARTIN: If you have been shooting a movie for three weeks and an actor or actress decides to show up late, you can't fire them. You've already shot three weeks. If somebody wants to behave badly—unless you want to reshoot the entire movie—you can't fire them.

PLAYBOY: Do actors, perhaps, have the most power of all?

MARTIN: It all depends. But one thing seems to be true: The worse the behavior, the smaller the talent.

PLAYBOY: And how easy are you to work with?

MARTIN: I've always been pretty easy. I come from television writing.

PLAYBOY: What makes TV writers so saintly?

MARTIN: Five guys sit in a room and shoot out ideas. It is friendly but brutal. Your ideas are shot down all the time. It humbles you.

PLAYBOY: In *The Player*, Altman suggested that the art is lost when moviemakers have to modify their movies depending on audience responses. Do you disagree?

MARTIN: I don't think you can ignore the audience. At the same time, you can't cut the picture for the audience.

PLAYBOY: At least that's not a wishy-washy answer.

MARTIN: [*Laughs*] I mean you can't just give an audience what it wants. An audience won't be fooled. It has to be challenged and surprised. On the other hand, testing is valuable because we have to be sure we're communicating what we want to communicate. If audiences don't get an important plot point, you've lost them. For comedy, it's really important to test. The great jokes—the ones we love the most—don't always work. When you screen a comedy for an audience, it's a new day. It's like starting over.

PLAYBOY: Why can't filmmakers trust themselves?

MARTIN: Maybe movies are too big. There are too many factors to consider. We just never know if we're seeing things objectively. Our best jokes fall flat.

PLAYBOY: What's one of your favorite jokes that didn't work?

MARTIN: In *The Jerk*, I play a gas station attendant. A carload of criminals comes in for gas and I don't want them to escape. So I tie their car to a fireplug, which in turn is attached to a church. The criminals drive away and the church rips in half. [*Laughs*] I thought, This is going to kill them. The movie came out and the audience watched the church being dragged down the road—there were chuckles, but it was no big thing.

PLAYBOY: Is it devastating when a joke doesn't work?

MARTIN: They don't all have to work. I think it was too big to get a laugh. The real laughs always come from something very small and surprising—although another one they didn't get in *The Jerk* is when I'm hitchhiking to St. Louis. My character's name is Navin Johnson. A guy pulls over in his car and asks, "St. Louis?" and I go, "Uh, no, Navin Johnson." I told the line to Carl Reiner [the movie's writer and director] and we laughed for 45 minutes. It's so stupid! But in the movie, it just kind of goes away.

PLAYBOY: If you're in a theater and you hear nothing at one of your favorite jokes—or worse, if you hear a groan—how do you feel?

MARTIN: It depends. What's really satisfying is when one person gets it. It's quiet except for someone laughing alone. There's usually something that strikes people, at least someone, as peculiar. In *Sophie's Choice*—

PLAYBOY: A very funny movie.

MARTIN: Well, no, but there is a great line. Struggling with the language, Sophie says, "Why don't you wear your cocksucker suit?" Ten minutes later I'm still laughing. By then it's embarrassing. People are looking at me.

PLAYBOY: You cited lines in *The Jerk* that didn't quite work. Do you view the movie as a failure?

MARTIN: No. It did what I was trying to do at the time. It put my comedy act into a movie. When I look at it now, I think I yelled through the entire movie. But I like it.

PLAYBOY: Which of your movies are your personal favorites?

MARTIN: I like the simple, elegant comedies that 10 years from now will come on channel five and you'll go, "Hey, that's funny." An example is *Dirty Rotten Scoundrels*, which did okay when it came out. But as time went on, more and more people came up to me—they rented it or saw it on TV. *Planes, Trains and Automobiles* is another one. So is *Roxanne*. It did fine when it came out. As time goes on, you can see it again and it holds up.

PLAYBOY: Are you good at anticipating the reaction to a movie?

MARTIN: Yes, although the thing that has changed is the number of sources of criticism. There are a million reviewers now. There are the TV shows, big papers, small papers, 12 cable channels. You used to get a clean sweep—all bad or all good. Now you can't. Now there's a bell curve because there are so many opinions, from stupid opinions to brilliant ones.

PLAYBOY: The stupid ones being the negative reviews, the brilliant ones praising you?

MARTIN: Exactly.

PLAYBOY: Is your confidence level such that you know when something's good, no matter what the reviewers say?

MARTIN: No. But I realize that their opinion isn't the final opinion. The final opinion comes five or 10 years later. Is the movie still around? Are people watching it? Or did it come and go? I picked up *The New York Times* the other day and was so pleased to see that *The Jerk*, which was vilified when it came out—it got 99 percent bad reviews—was described as an "eccentric, sophisticated comedy." It was moronic. Now it's sophisticated.

PLAYBOY: Do you have a special place in your heart for *Roxanne*, the first movie you wrote on your own?

MARTIN: Yeah, because it was a real struggle to write it. I was very fearful of it.

PLAYBOY: Fearful of what?

MARTIN: It was my first solo screenplay and, in addition, I was taking on a classic. It took me a while to write it—four or five years. There was a great deal of self-doubt.

PLAYBOY: Why tackle *Cyrano de Bergerac?*

MARTIN: It's very emotional and the humor comes out of the emotions. Nothing is better. As you're getting a joke, you're crying.

PLAYBOY: Did you view it as a risky idea? Wasn't it like remaking *Gone with the Wind?*

MARTIN: I didn't know if I was capable of doing it. The humor had to be updated because of the nineteenth century references—stuff about the Greek gods, for instance, who no one pays much attention to anymore. At the worst, though, I knew it was a place for some good one-liners.

PLAYBOY: Was it tough to persuade a studio to make the movie?

MARTIN: I told the first executive I saw that it was an update of *Cyrano de Bergerac* and he asked, "What's *Cyrano de Bergerac?*" I had to pitch *Cyrano*, which is sort of like pitching *Romeo and Juliet*. The second studio I went to was Columbia, where I saw Guy McElwaine, who was then the president. I told him it was an update of *Cyrano de Bergerac* and he stood up, went to the window and began reciting lines from the play. He gave me the go-ahead.

PLAYBOY: Were you a fan of the other *Cyrano* movies?

MARTIN: I liked Gérard Depardieu's *Cyrano*. The Jose Ferrer *Cyrano* was fabulous. He won an Oscar for it. I met him and told him how great

I thought the performance was and he said, "All I remember is how bad I was."

PLAYBOY: Are you generous when you view your movies?

MARTIN: No. I can't stand to look at myself.

PLAYBOY: Never?

MARTIN: Occasionally. But it has to come as a surprise, like flipping through the channels and suddenly you see a moment and say, "Hey, that was okay."

PLAYBOY: You also wrote L.A. Story by yourself. How much does the movie show of your real life?

MARTIN: My life kind of looks like that. Those houses and the restaurants are places I would find myself. It's funny that it ended up being considered this L.A. movie when I really set out just to make a love story that happened to be set in L.A.

PLAYBOY: But much of the humor is about L.A. Where else could freeway signs spout spiritual riddles?

MARTIN: That's true. It's a fun city to make fun of. It's not hard to do.

PLAYBOY: Because it was a love story starring you and your wife, people said the movie was an homage to Victoria. One reviewer called it a love letter to her.

MARTIN: That would be awful if it was. I don't want to spend $17 million of someone else's money on an homage to my wife. I'll do that at home with a box of candy. You could take another actress and put her in there and tell the same story. The movie was an allegory about romance—how it feels. It happened to star my wife. I wanted to movieize that state.

PLAYBOY: As opposed to the state of love?

MARTIN: Yes. They're very different. This is about the first blush of romance. As opposed to L.A. Story II, which, if there were one—don't worry, there won't be—would be The Married Years. After romance is love: trust and knowing the person. You love for different reasons.

PLAYBOY: At which stage is your relationship with Victoria?

MARTIN: Definitely a love story. I never really had long-term, steady girlfriends until Victoria. It's really because of Victoria that I understood what it meant to be married.

PLAYBOY: What does it mean?

MARTIN: I can't describe it specifically, but it is more about an attitude. We're a couple forever. I came from the philosophy that it lasts as long as it lasts. As soon as you accept the vision that it is going to work forever, it can. I once went to a psychiatrist who said that your emotions follow your intentions. If your intent is to last forever, your emotions go that way. Once I saw that, I could see that it can last forever. As our marriage goes on, I like her more and more and admire her more and more. Romance is about a feeling and marriage is about so much more: the intellectual, the compassionate, the friendship. It has to do with a way of life, too, a circle of friends. Part of the deal is that you strive to be together as much as possible. We've been together for eight years and we recently took a vacation in which we spent seven weeks essentially in one room. And it was great. It was, like, better than ever. [*Laughs*] I'd better be careful. People say, "We have this perfect marriage," and two weeks later they're divorced.

PLAYBOY: But not you?

MARTIN: Not us.

PLAYBOY: You said that *L.A. Story* wasn't about Los Angeles—it was just set there. But Victoria said that L.A. is unmistakably you—"like Baltimore is unmistakably Barry Levinson or New York is unmistakably Woody Allen." What do you think?

MARTIN: I guess I'm thought of as a West Coast comedian. My style seems to warrant that label. There's probably something California in me.

PLAYBOY: What are the California things?

MARTIN: I don't know. Lack of ethnicity. I have no accent.

PLAYBOY: You made another Los Angeles movie, Larry Kasdan's *Grand Canyon.*

MARTIN: When I read the script, I told Larry that it was *L.A. Story: The Dark Side.*

PLAYBOY: The film was prophetic.

MARTIN: When the movie was first screened, people complained that it didn't present L.A. in a nice light. It was spooky how much it revealed.

PLAYBOY: Since the riots, are the worlds portrayed in the movies more opposed?

MARTIN: I don't think so. That's the problem. L.A. is not where I live. I live in West Hollywood, Beverly Hills and Santa Monica. It's a different place.

PLAYBOY: Did the riots blur the lines?

MARTIN: The problems are definitely encroaching. In that way the riots were good because they made us look. There will be action. But as to understanding that part of town, I'm too well off and too happy even to have a comment, even to pretend to understand it.

PLAYBOY: That may be honest, but it's a limited view. The message in *Grand Canyon* was that you can make a difference in other people's lives.

MARTIN: It was and you can, but the problems are enormous. First is to understand that all our talking about it doesn't do anything.

PLAYBOY: Do you get involved? Have you done political benefits?

MARTIN: Politics really doesn't interest me. Except to get mad.

PLAYBOY: Do you get really mad?

MARTIN: I do.

PLAYBOY: What makes you maddest?

MARTIN: Politicians who have an answer for everything. When I was in college, studying philosophy, I had an answer for everything. People get that way in their religion, too. You can ask a Christian, "If Adam and Eve were the first people on earth and they had three sons, where did everybody else come from?" and they'll give you an answer. Well, all those answers don't begin to touch the real problems. That makes me mad. The problems are bigger and different from the quick answers we are given.

PLAYBOY: If you don't work for candidates, how about for causes?

MARTIN: I haven't done a lot, but I will do more as I get older, when there's more time. I've done benefits, though.

PLAYBOY: In 1982, you said you were going to vote for George McGovern. Have your politics changed since then?

MARTIN: Everything that's happened to me could be predicted. As I get older, I get more conservative. I'm certainly not on the right, but on issues such as taxes I don't know where I am. I've always been a Democrat, but I don't even know what that means anymore. Gore Vidal said we don't have a two-party system, it's a one-party system with different factions. I think it's true.

PLAYBOY: You made a strong political statement when you visited the Persian Gulf before the war.

MARTIN: It wasn't a political trip. It was humanitarian. If there was a political motivation, then I'm saying I'm for war. Being an old 1960s guy I can't say that. Still, I know that it was hot out there. The soldiers needed some people to tell them that we were thinking about them. I wanted to see some of them and show them that they were not estranged from the country.

PLAYBOY: You have said that you never would have fought in Vietnam— you would have gone to Canada. Was part of your motivation to go to the Gulf guilt over your position during Vietnam?

MARTIN: It's better to talk about after Vietnam. The vets came home and were hated. It seemed wrong. The war wasn't their fault. Even if you were against the Gulf war, you couldn't take it out on the soldiers. That's why I felt good about going.

PLAYBOY: What was the experience like?

MARTIN: It was incredible to one day be walking down the streets of New York and the next flying in an open helicopter over a camel train. You land and it's not pretend.

PLAYBOY: Press reports said the State Department stopped you from performing.

MARTIN: No. There were several reasons I didn't perform. I didn't have anything to perform and the Saudis were very nervous. They don't know what entertainers mean. The main thing was that they didn't want to collect 10,000 people in one place. It would have been very dangerous. Instead, I flew to places where they had a little stage set up. Sometimes I just signed autographs and posed for pictures.

PLAYBOY: Were you there when the fighting began?

MARTIN: No. It was still chilling, though. We were instructed in how to mix in Saudi Arabian society. Never expose the bottom of your foot. Never look at a man's wife or talk about a man's wife. Victoria and I were in a car and she had taken her army fatigue jacket off and was wearing a T-shirt. A guard stopped us and went crazy. He screamed, "Women shouldn't be dressed like that." It was a whole ordeal to get back to the base.

PLAYBOY: Do you feel good about having gone there?

MARTIN: Absolutely. It was an incredible experience. You can't just go from movie to movie.

PLAYBOY: When you look back on your life, do you see where your sense of comedy came from?

MARTIN: No, I don't. I was just always interested in it.

PLAYBOY: What brought your parents to California from Texas?

MARTIN: This was the promised land. Texas was too hot and humid.

PLAYBOY: So when did you think about performing?

MARTIN: All I know is that I always loved comedy, whether it was on TV or in magic shows or movies. Milton Berle. Laurel and Hardy. Jerry Lewis. Jack Benny. There are lots of names. Steve Allen. Lenny Bruce. I loved anybody who made me laugh. They made me want to do it.

PLAYBOY: Are they your most important influences?

MARTIN: They all are. And Buster Keaton, Jackie Gleason, Chaplin.

PLAYBOY: Did you have a favorite?

MARTIN: Cary Grant, I guess. He was such a delectable comedian because it all seemed so effortless.

PLAYBOY: Do you think of him when you act in movies?

MARTIN: Sometimes. He's an ideal. I would never hope to be that good. I love what he did in *Arsenic and Old Lace*. He was just very big, very broad. His smoothest stuff is really broad. Big, goofy takes.

PLAYBOY: Do you ever wonder what would have been different had your family not moved west?

MARTIN: I do. It was one of those twists of fate. I wouldn't have had the proximity to show business or the outlets. It's impossible to think of what I would have been.

PLAYBOY: Does a lot of the drive to perform have to do with the recognition?

MARTIN: I've never been able to analyze that part of it. The main thing I think about is making the thing, the performance or the movie or whatever it is. All that other stuff is subconscious.

PLAYBOY: What was your first act at Knott's Berry Farm?

MARTIN: We did a play and then they had what they called olio acts, a singer or comedian would do four or five minutes. I was going to college at the time. I planned to be a professor and all that. I was very serious about it.

PLAYBOY: Was your interest in philosophy theoretical or personal?

MARTIN: It started out as personal and became academic because you realize that the personal thing will never be answered.

PLAYBOY: What personal things were you trying to answer?

MARTIN: I was just looking to the future. When you get into college, you realize the world is a lot bigger than you thought it was. Particularly in the 1960s.

PLAYBOY: Were you involved in the student movement?

MARTIN: Yeah, although I wasn't that involved. I was on its side, let's put it that way. It didn't quite hit Long Beach, where I went to school.

PLAYBOY: Was your college life serious or more in the tradition of *Animal House*?

MARTIN: Very serious. One or two friends. Small, enclosed, not part of the social scene at all. I missed The Beatles. I wasn't listening to the music. I just studied and on evenings and weekends worked at Knott's Berry Farm.

PLAYBOY: What diverted you from a career as a philosophy professor?

MARTIN: I realized I would never know if I could have been a performer if I didn't try it. My girlfriend at the time was a dancer on the *Smothers Brothers* show. We met and fell in love in college. She gave some of the material I'd written in college to Mason Williams, who was the head writer. They went for it. It was a miracle because the material wasn't that good. They just wanted writers under 30 because of the 1960s thing. I just happened to be in the right place at the right time.

PLAYBOY: How brutal is TV writing?

MARTIN: Actually it was a great job. I wrote with about five other writers. Sparks flew. I love collaborating.

PLAYBOY: But you do it less and less.

MARTIN: The only reason I don't collaborate on my scripts anymore is that I don't want to have a meeting. I want to work when I want to. Still, it was great.

PLAYBOY: Do you have people you bounce things off of now?

MARTIN: It's different each time. Frank Oz. Carl Reiner. We spark off each other. We share this odd thing of appreciating each other's twisted visions. Carl came up with one of my favorite lines. He just said it one day and I said, "That's too fabulous." I called him about five years later and said the line would go perfect in *L.A. Story* and asked him if I could use it.

PLAYBOY: What was the line?

MARTIN: "I could never be a woman because I'd just sit around the house all day and play with my breasts."

PLAYBOY: We remember another great joke about breasts in that movie.

MARTIN: I was filming a sex scene with Sarah Jessica Parker and I didn't have a line. It was just a basic sex scene. I thought, There's something wrong here. It looks like Steve Martin is feeling up Sarah Jessica Parker. It needs something. So I came up with the line. I had him feel her up and ask, "Hey, what's wrong with your breasts?" She said, "They're real." You never know where it comes from. I was so happy when I found the line. It made the scene.

PLAYBOY: Most of the sex in your movies is fairly discreet and subtle. Does that reflect your sensibility?

MARTIN: I think that there's something nice about watching Richard Gere and Kim Basinger having sex, but there's not something nice about watching Groucho Marx and somebody else having sex.

PLAYBOY: You see yourself as Groucho?

MARTIN: I've never been known as a sexy star. I feel kind of silly humping on-screen. Also, something bothers me about it: the idea that if I did a heavy sex scene, it would be Steve Martin doing it.

PLAYBOY: As opposed to?

MARTIN: As opposed to the character. Bernadette Peters said it to me first: "I'm not going to do a nude scene because when you take off your blouse you're not the character anymore, you're Bernadette Peters with her blouse off."

PLAYBOY: Do you object when other actors do it?

MARTIN: Definitely not. Believe me, I'd love to be in a great sexy scene or have a fabulous screen kiss. But the movie has to engender it and I'm not in those kinds of movies.

PLAYBOY: In *The Man with Two Brains*, Kathleen Turner let you suck her finger. Did you at least enjoy that?

MARTIN: It was all very pleasant. But if we were doing that scene now, she'd have to wear a little finger condom.

PLAYBOY: When you have to climb into a bed and make out with a relative stranger, is it the same as acting any other part of a script?

MARTIN: It's different because it's more tense. You're kissing someone you hardly know. Victoria had a scene once on her first day of shooting a movie in Berlin or somewhere like that. She flew in and the male actor flew in, they came onto the set at noon and had to do a sex scene against a wall. So yes, it's weird. Victoria says that Michael Caine has a great attitude about it. If he has to do a sex scene, he gets in bed with his boots on, shoots in some mouth spray and says, "Okay, ready." He uses humor to diffuse the tension.

PLAYBOY: Who has been your favorite movie kiss?

MARTIN: John Candy.

PLAYBOY: Of course! Now that you've brought it up, let's talk about romance. Did lots of women throw themselves at you when you were on the road?

MARTIN: It didn't happen. It always happened to the other guys, I guess. I've always been a loner type, so that never bothered me. The fact is, when you're finally a big enough star, you become very isolated. I suppose the people who want to throw themselves at you can't get to you. Also there was something very unsexy about groupies.

PLAYBOY: So we can assume you didn't go on the road to meet women. Why did you leave your life as a TV writer?

MARTIN: I just knew I had to quit writing for television and go on the road. I was a bit frustrated because I'd write the material and they'd kill it. I wanted to be able to show my work and not have it go through a committee. I decided to go on the road.

PLAYBOY: As a stand-up comedian.

MARTIN: Yes. So I did it and lost money on every performance. I was working as an opening act for bands like the Nitty Gritty Dirt Band.

They were great but the audiences were rock-and-roll audiences and not friendly to comedy. That's when I decided to headline, even if it meant a big drop in income and the risk that nobody would show up.

PLAYBOY: What made you think you could get away with it?

MARTIN: All I knew is that I could have opened for a million bands and nothing would have ever changed. I would open and be killing the audience—*killing* them—and the singer would come on and would do fine. In the review the singer would get three quarters of the column and I'd get one sentence. You have to be the headliner to get the attention. So I went to Florida and got into a club and got a rave review. It was the first time I was ever singled out as an entity. I worked in a few other clubs around the country when I started to get some rave reviews. It just started to happen.

PLAYBOY: You were part of the wave that brought stand-up comedy into the mainstream. Now there are comedy clubs everywhere.

MARTIN: The Comedy Store came into existence after I had my success. I played music clubs. I think it would be very rough out there now. God, to find something original. . . .

PLAYBOY: On the other hand, there's an audience that goes to comedy clubs to laugh. When you were playing music clubs, audiences didn't always know what you were trying to do up there.

MARTIN: I think of that as an advantage. They didn't know what to expect. If I was going out there now, I'd perform anywhere except comedy clubs. It becomes too homogenized. You should be like Andy Kaufman, off by yourself going nuts. At least it's different from what everyone else is doing.

PLAYBOY: In those early years, who was doing it besides you?

MARTIN: George Carlin, Robert Klein, Richard Pryor and Lily Tomlin. Robin Williams came a little after me—at least with his success.

PLAYBOY: What changed so that comedy became such a big business?

MARTIN: It was a practical question. They could put on a show with only one guy. There didn't need to be a band or sets. The background was a wall. For me it was great because I didn't have to audition. Once I auditioned for a TV show and couldn't stand leaving it in someone else's hands. With stand-up—or whatever it was that I was doing—it was up to the audience, not to a producer or a writer or somebody else.

PLAYBOY: Carrie Fisher said that Robin Williams, onstage, was possessed, manic, while you were more in control, more disciplined. Is that accurate?

MARTIN: There was a time when all this was being developed that I was very undisciplined. It was about freeing yourself and finding new things. There was a time when the act was very spontaneous. You can't come up with two, three or four hours of material being rigid. You know, there's this thing about Robin being spontaneous, but he had material, too. It all looks spontaneous. That was the point. There was a time when I was walking out in the audience, picking up objects and ad-libbing, not knowing where I was going. I used to do 40 minutes after the show was over, in the audience or out in the street.

PLAYBOY: Did you ever die onstage?

MARTIN: About three times I did a joke and then, 20 minutes later, I did it again. I just forgot. I remember driving through Utah at night with some friends. We stopped in the middle of the desert and just sat there. Without the roar of the car and the conversation, a wave of silence came over us. It was shocking. That's what it was like when I did the joke the second time. It just dies. All this silence hits you.

PLAYBOY: How do you view your stand-up days?

MARTIN: It was hard work but that was the funniest I ever was. I was new, the audience hadn't quite gotten it yet. You could still blow their minds.

PLAYBOY: Was that the goal—to blow their minds?

MARTIN: Any way you could.

PLAYBOY: Are you nostalgic for it?

MARTIN: Not at all. I don't like talking about it because I'd rather have the memory as a good one than look back and realize that it wasn't so good after all. At the time, you feel good about it because that's what show business is: getting hot, getting cold, getting hot again, getting cold, getting hot. But there's nothing quite like getting hot for the first time.

PLAYBOY: How does stand-up compare with acting?

MARTIN: In the movie business, you can be subject to variables. They might not like the movie. Doing stand-up the variables are drunks yelling through your show. You might not even have the chance to get it right.

PLAYBOY: There's no buffer between you and an audience when you're doing stand-up. If they don't like your stand-up, they don't like you.

MARTIN: No, that isn't it. With stand-up, I had to go to Detroit, to Baltimore. With movies, the movie goes to Detroit, to Baltimore. I stay home. It stays the same. You did it as best as you could and it doesn't change from night to night.

PLAYBOY: Is there a quantifiable difference in the kinds of expression in both forms?

MARTIN: In movies it's richer. First, I was sick of doing the same thing every night. But also, the range of emotions is greater for me in the movies. Larger stories can be told. With stand-up, I felt as if I didn't have anything else to say. My early act had a definite point of view. It had a feeling of new. I don't have any of that in me.

PLAYBOY: Is stand-up comedy a young man's game?

MARTIN: For me. But I don't mean to be minimizing those days. I feel like I resurrected a kind of comedy, even a kind of fun. I believe I was the first to be doing anticomedy, when the joke is nonsense and it is how outrageous you can get.

PLAYBOY: When was the first time you did your stand-up on television?

MARTIN: Oh, I did all the TV shows—Steve Allen, Della Reese, Merv Griffin, Virginia Graham. I lived on those shows—not financially, but I was always billed, "as seen on the *Steve Allen Show.*"

PLAYBOY: Do you remember your first time on *The Tonight Show?*

MARTIN: Yes. I did a magic act. I did a magic act the last time I was on, too. The Great Flydini.

PLAYBOY: In which you materialize objects from the fly of your pants. Was it emotional for you when Carson retired?

MARTIN: It was. There was a sense of passing. I was on the show so many times that I found myself sitting on the panel conversing, in a sense, as a peer. There was a feeling of accomplishment and disbelief.

PLAYBOY: Were you nervous?

MARTIN: The first time I was because it all came down to this. In a weird sense I felt that same feeling the last time I was on the show. Flydini is a very difficult act to perform. I had to practice for three days. There's always a chance you will blow it when you're out there.

PLAYBOY: What could happen?

MARTIN: Everything could fall apart inside your pants. When it came time for the show in Carson's last week, I came out and was nervous for about a minute and then you have a job to do.

PLAYBOY: What do you think is going to happen with *The Tonight Show?*

MARTIN: I don't know. There will never be anyone like Carson. He influenced a lot of us. His timing is precise. All comedians praise him because he is so good at setting us up for our bits. It truly was an end to an era.

PLAYBOY: Did you ever want to be the new host?

MARTIN: I had a fantasy 15 years ago, but not now.

PLAYBOY: What do you think of Jay Leno?

MARTIN: I think he'll do great. He does a good job.

PLAYBOY: You also reached a huge audience from appearances on *Saturday Night Live*. What do you remember most about that time?

MARTIN: It was very exciting. No matter how petty this sounds, you feel as if you're in the avant-garde for that little while. It was the coming together of two avant-gardes, myself and the show. It was good times.

PLAYBOY: What are your favorite moments when you look back to your time on *SNL*?

MARTIN: I like some of the monologs I did with Bill Murray. He's the fastest ad-lib I ever saw. I was doing a monolog and I called him up out of the audience. We rehearsed it, and on the air I asked him something I had never said in rehearsal: "Have you ever been on TV before?" He said, "Once at a ball game in a long shot." I enjoyed working with him and with Gilda Radner. There were a lot of high points. Working with Dan Aykroyd was one.

PLAYBOY: Did you know John Belushi well?

MARTIN: Vaguely, not well. He was a big personality. Before he died, just after he finished *Continental Divide*, he was at my house in Beverly Hills. He said, "I just did this movie and it's like a whole new acting thing for me. Now I see where I want to go."

PLAYBOY: Meaning?

MARTIN: He had a vision that he could become an actor beyond his stand-up and *SNL*. He realized he really had a future. And then he died.

PLAYBOY: Was it devastating?

MARTIN: Devastating? No, because I wasn't that close to him. It seemed so much a part of the mystique and persona. I remember seeing him standing in the middle of a street in New York. He was directing traffic, shouting, trying to get a taxi, and you could tell he was doing it for show, because he thought he should. He was living the myth. That was my impression.

PLAYBOY: Did his death cause you to reevaluate your own life?

MARTIN: I had nothing to do with that kind of lifestyle.

PLAYBOY: Never?

MARTIN: No. I never got close.

PLAYBOY: You never had to learn about drugs and alcohol the hard way?

MARTIN: No. When I was about 20, I smoked some marijuana. That was about it. I think some personalities are just addictive. John felt like it was his duty to do it. I have no sense of that. I noticed the difference in the times that I allowed myself to drink and the times I didn't. There was a big difference in my energy and how I slept. Those guys were doing it all the time. It had to take a toll.

PLAYBOY: So you have what might be called a nonaddictive personality?

MARTIN: I wouldn't call myself nonaddictive. I'm obsessive.

PLAYBOY: Was it a conscious decision to stop doing stand-up and start making films?

MARTIN: I just decided to do it. I still had some stand-up bookings, but I knew that there was only one way to go as a stand-up and that was down.

PLAYBOY: Many stand-up comedians fail when they try to get into the movies.

MARTIN: I guess I had enough residual power from stand-up that I could do those five or six films that it takes to learn your craft. I thought it would be an easy transition, but it wasn't.

PLAYBOY: What did you have to learn?

MARTIN: Movie comedy. It is very different from stand-up.

PLAYBOY: How so?

MARTIN: I can't describe it because it's subconscious. It's more about acting. In the early movies, the comedy was way more important than the acting. Then, as I got older and I learned more, it was about learning to let the acting support the comedy. But all this is bullshit. I don't know what I'm talking about. I'm just saying that something happens that makes you better.

PLAYBOY: When *Roxanne* came out, there was a lot of talk that you might win an Academy Award. Did you care about that?

MARTIN: It's hard to answer. No decision is ever made in my life for the Academy. I wasn't expecting anything because I'm not Academy material. Being Academy material is like a hurricane. It just happens. It has its own course. There's nothing you can do to affect it.

PLAYBOY: Have you been overlooked because of your roots in comedy?

MARTIN: Yes. I came from silly stand-up. But then, as with *Roxanne*, people start talking, "Oh, it's a cinch"—the *L.A. Times* said it was a shoo-in—it becomes kind of puzzling.

PLAYBOY: Do you think the bias against comedy is changing a bit?

MARTIN: Well, it certainly changed for Robin Williams. I mean, he's very nominatable.

PLAYBOY: What made that happen?

MARTIN: I don't know. He did a remarkable thing. He turned his film career completely around. He once commented that he used to get scripts with my fingerprints on them. He doesn't anymore. He turned it around through drama, though, not comedies. *Good Morning, Vietnam,* which was sort of both, and *Awakenings* and *The Fisher King.*

PLAYBOY: Both of your careers were built around comedy. Is there more at stake when you do dramas, as you do when you play a preacher in *Leap of Faith?* Are you intimidated by dramas?

MARTIN: Not at all. I have had enough drama in the movies I've done, starting with *Planes, Trains and Automobiles* and *Roxanne. Leap of Faith* is a drama, though there is some showy stuff. I'm a con artist evangelist. When you're preaching and yelling and singing and dancing and all that, it's very much a show. I'm not asking the audience to sit there while I do *Hamlet.*

PLAYBOY: There's still a question of how far to go—how crazy a preacher to be.

MARTIN: Yes, but it's a dramatic question. It's not a comedic question. In this case, I didn't have to go bigger than the character. Evangelists go pretty big on their own.

PLAYBOY: Is your character modeled after any evangelist? Maybe Jimmy Swaggart or Jim Bakker?

MARTIN: Swaggart and Bakker were con men but they were also sincere. This guy's not sincere at all.

PLAYBOY: There were reports of trouble on the set—the producer was fired and your agent was canned for not taking better care of you.

MARTIN: I saw that report and it was unfortunate since it wasn't true. The producer left because he had a dispute with the studio over money. My agent left the agency because of long-standing problems. None of it had anything to do with me.

PLAYBOY: Tom Smothers said that when you stop being funny, you reveal very little about yourself. Is it true?

MARTIN: Was he talking about me or about comedians in general?

PLAYBOY: You.

MARTIN: Yeah, I think that's probably true. You go through a time when you become famous and the demands are constant. Then everyone starts to get offended about what you're not doing. When they get around you, they stand and look at you, waiting for you to do that thing that they know. When it happens once or twice, it's fine, but when it's constant, you start to get mad and you actively withhold that thing to show to yourself that you're not a puppet.

PLAYBOY: How about when you're not around fans who want you to perform for them? How about when you are on your own, with friends.

MARTIN: Perhaps. I have a quiet side and it can certainly appear. I have no idea what generates it. It's not depression. It's a kind of shyness or maybe insecurity. Around my friends I never feel that way. Not my really close friends. But they number, like, four.

PLAYBOY: Who are your best friends?

MARTIN: Marty Short. Chevy Chase. Lorne Michaels. Paul Simon. Kevin Kline. Some of the people you meet in show business are just so fantastic. It's great when you meet someone who's clever, creative and on the same wavelength.

PLAYBOY: Is that why so many of your friends are also actors?

MARTIN: They're just the kind of people you meet. I met most of them in movies. There are Rick Moranis, Larry and Meg Kasdan, Frank Oz. Tom Hanks—he's a very, very funny guy. I had dinner the other night with him and Ron Howard and their families. They're the people in comedy I like to hang around with. Their comedy is different from what they do on-screen. It's more sarcastic or satiric. Marty Short, for example, can do an impression of an assistant director he just worked with. You've never met him, but it's hysterically funny. Glenne Headly has that ability, too. You know who else? Phoebe Cates and Kevin Kline. Chevy and Marty Short and I hang out a lot since we got to be good friends while doing *Three Amigos*. In real life they are some of the funniest people there are.

PLAYBOY: Would a dinner conversation among the three of you sound like the dialog from a movie?

MARTIN: It would be much hipper.

PLAYBOY: Is there a sort of comedy cocksmanship when you're together, with each trying to outdo the others with cleverness?

MARTIN: In the circles I run in it's not about outdoing the other guy, it's about building on the other guy and then he builds on you. That's when it's best. It's just about being funny. It's like the comedy god entered the room and you want to see how far you can go with him.

PLAYBOY: Do you have to be careful not to lose touch with ordinary life when you're rich and famous?

MARTIN: We have our problems, too, and they're just as real as anybody else's problems and, for the most part, they're probably the same. Maybe you don't have to worry about paying a bill, but we're not stupid and we can figure out what it would be like not to be able to pay a bill.

I saw *The Last Boy Scout* on laser disc. It's very ugly. It's about a family falling apart. The wife is having an affair and the husband is a detective who's always at work. The daughter is just plain repellent. Her language is horrible. Toward the end of the movie she supplies the gun to her dad to blow away the people. Early on, the wife is trying to get a rise out of her husband and she says something like, "You don't care about me. Why don't you just say, 'Sarah, fuck you. I'll spit in your face if I ever catch you with another man again.'" By the end of the movie, this has become the love theme. When he says to her, "Fuck you, I'll spit in your face if I ever see you with another man," she melts.

I'm thinking, Is there a world out there I don't know about? Is that the way a lot of people are in this ugly, ugly world? Well, I don't know about those problems. I know about the problems in *Parenthood*.

PLAYBOY: But you have no children.

MARTIN: Well, I know those kinds of people, so I understand them.

PLAYBOY: Do you want kids?

MARTIN: It's not something I talk about.

PLAYBOY: You once said that any time you get the urge to have children, all you have to do is spend some time with one.

MARTIN: Yes, but since then lots of my friends have had children. I have seen what it means to people. So who knows? But I don't want to go into it.

PLAYBOY: Let's talk about your art collection then. That's safer.

MARTIN: I don't talk about that, either. Talking about personal parts of your life cheapens them, I think. I collect art but I'd rather not talk about it.

PLAYBOY: Was roller-skating through the Los Angeles County Museum of Art in *L.A. Story* a boyhood fantasy?

MARTIN: It was wonderful but very scary, too. The floor is very slippery and you don't want to crash into any of those paintings.

PLAYBOY: You donated an enormous canvas to the museum, didn't you?

MARTIN: It's not something I want to talk about.

PLAYBOY: Excuuuuuuse us.

MARTIN: [*Smiles*]

PLAYBOY: How does it feel to have your lines—such as that one—find their way into the vernacular?

MARTIN: It's sort of funny but it's not anything to be really proud of. It's pop.

PLAYBOY: Where did some of them come from? How about that one: "Well, excuuuuuuse me"?

MARTIN: When I was 15, I worked at this shop in Disneyland. A woman there from New Orleans always said, "Well, excuse me for livin'." It came from that. It was never meant to be a catchphrase. The routine was always about getting mad over nothing. For instance, I'd get mad at the spotlight operator because he went to a blue spot when it was supposed to be a white spot. It always made me laugh when entertainers were so self-important that they freak out over these things.

PLAYBOY: How about the "wild and crazy guy" line?

MARTIN: It all started with the idea of playing a folk hero that was completely contrary to the way I look. The folk hero was a rambling man—you know, "Lord, I was born a ramblin' man," from the song. It struck me as funny because of the contrast—somebody who considered himself wild, but who was anything but. One of the *SNL* writers took the line from my act and used it in his sketch for Danny [Aykroyd] and me. I think the idea was Danny's. That's how the Czech brothers became the two wild and crazy guys. After millions of nights ad-libbing onstage, some things stick.

PLAYBOY: Your wife said you have spent years living down that phrase. Are you ever wild and crazy anymore?

MARTIN: Hanging around with friends, never because people want me to be.

PLAYBOY: Is it difficult being Steve Martin, as opposed to another famous person, because people expect you to be funny?

MARTIN: Yes, although I don't give in to it. Worse than that is that people laugh at things you say that aren't meant to be funny at all. And yeah, a lot of people want me to, like, go back and do routines I did when I was 20. They want me to be the wild and crazy guy. People point their cameras and say, "Act crazy." But hey, what do they want from me? I'm 46, you know.

PLAYBOY: At 46, you're playing the father of the bride. Was it a jolt to find that you're no longer cast as the groom?

MARTIN: There's that moment where you go, "I can't play a *father!*" and you start counting and you realize, "Oh. I guess I can." I think one of the secrets of maturing in the movie business is knowing when something is over and something new is beginning.

PLAYBOY: Is there a bittersweet aspect to the idea of maturing?

MARTIN: No, it feels good. About the stuff in the past? I did it. There's a certain satisfaction in making it through all those years and still being around, knowing that you were not a flash in the pan.

PLAYBOY: Was that a big fear?

MARTIN: When you're a sudden hit like I was, the first thing that enters your head is, When's it going to be over?

PLAYBOY: Have you joined those people in show business who, in spite of good years and bad years, won't go away?

MARTIN: Well, maybe. I never like to take things for granted, but I feel way more at peace with that question. It doesn't now depend on your latest hit or flop.

PLAYBOY: Many of your recent movies, such as *Father of the Bride* and last summer's *Housesitter*, came on quietly yet earned more than the so-called big movies. What is it about them?

MARTIN: They deliver. They're nice. Certain audiences feel too sophisticated and will never like them. But otherwise, it's hard not to like those movies, unless you've got a chip on your shoulder. I've been happy with them. I am happy to realize I'm now a young older leading man. It's nice to know you can be funny, even at 46.

ROBIN WILLIAMS

A candid conversation with the lightning-quick comedian and actor about his roles as Mork, Popeye and Garp—and the elusive person behind them

Four years ago, an unknown, offbeat comic named Robin Williams starred in the first installment of TV's *Mork & Mindy,* and after two weeks, the ABC sitcom became one of TV's top-10-rated programs—and Williams was being hailed as the medium's brightest young star. As Mork from the planet Ork, Williams portrayed a zany, engaging extraterrestrial whose rapid-fire ripostes were the series' strongest asset. Ably supported by actress Pam Dawber, who played his girlfriend (and then his wife), Williams made mincemeat of TV's tidy demographics, for he somehow appealed as much to adults as to children. Although the industry had anticipated a warmed-over remake of *My Favorite Martian, Mork & Mindy* turned into a showcase for one of the most remarkable talents TV has ever presented. Within a very short time, indeed, the show's 55 million weekly viewers were delighting themselves (and driving everyone else batty) by greeting one another with their Orkan hero's best-known phrase, "Nano nano."

Mork & Mindy rose to the top of the Nielsen heap, but Williams didn't even briefly stop honing his high-energy nightclub act. After putting in a full day at Paramount, where *Mork & Mindy* was filmed, Williams would take a short break and then rush off to perform without pay at several Los Angeles comedy clubs. Money was no problem: From a reported initial salary of $15,000 per episode, Williams had been raised to $30,000 after *Mork & Mindy*'s first season and by 1981 was said to be earning more than $50,000 for each installment.

As a nightclub comic, Williams is unlike his TV persona. Eager to put as much distance as he could between himself and Mork, the funky performer often began his act by asking people at the front tables to move back a bit, whereupon he grabbed his crotch and announced, "I'd like to show all of you something I'm really very proud of." After that, Williams unleashed such comedy creations as Beverly Hills blues singer Benign Neglect ("Woke up the other day, Ran out of Perrier"), the Reverend Earnest Angry ("Remember, you can fool some of the people some of the time and jerk the rest off") and Russian lounge entertainer Nicky Lenin ("I would like to begin by doing some basic Soviet suppressions"). A brilliant impressionist, Williams became Bette Davis playing Quasimodo, Jacques Cousteau doing a commercial for Union Oil, Lord Oliver selling Ripple wine and Mr. Rogers greeting America's tots with, "Let's put Mr. Hamster in the microwave oven, okay? Pop goes the weasel!" As if all that weren't enough, Williams then acted out all the parts of an imagined Japanese horror movie titled *Attack of the Killer Vibrators* before presenting his original one-man ballet, *Death of a Sperm*. It was ingenious, high-powered stuff, and in 1979, when Williams recorded *Reality . . . What a Concept* (his only comedy LP thus far), the album quickly went platinum by racking up sales of more than one million.

In what seemed like the blink of an eye, Williams had become America's undisputed young king of comedy, and TV, record and nightclub reviewers felt no compunctions about comparing him to everyone from Sid Caesar and Jonathan Winters to Danny Kaye and Marcel Marceau. When Williams was picked by producer Robert Evans to star in the movie version of *Popeye*, most show-business observers believed that the 5'8" performer would quickly emerge as *the* new screen star of his generation.

At that point, however, a funny thing happened to Williams's career: It began to fall apart. *Mork & Mindy*'s ratings began to plummet in the 1979-1980 season. Then, *Popeye* premiered in December 1980. Williams received lukewarm reviews and the movie itself turned out to be a turkey. ABC canceled *Mork & Mindy* this past April. Williams's second movie, *The World According to Garp*, was released in July, and although they didn't put down his acting ability, most critics agreed with *Playboy*'s Bruce Williamson: "Good as he is," Williamson noted, "this still isn't *the* breakthrough role to suit his unique talent." Many of Williams's fans began to ask themselves an unspoken question: Was their boy's rocket-like rise to the top about to flame out as spectacularly as it had begun?

The comic himself didn't think so. Born in Chicago in July 1952, Williams, the son of a Ford Motor Company vice-president, grew up in the ritzy Detroit suburb of Bloomfield Hills. Just before Williams entered his senior year of high school, his father retired and moved the family to Marin County, California. After graduating from Redwood High, Williams studied at two California colleges and then won an acting scholarship to Juilliard in New York City. After spending nearly three years there, he returned to San Francisco, where he began putting together a stand-up comedy act that won him a following there. In 1976, he moved to Los Angeles in quest of bigger things, and within six months, he was signed by producer George Schlatter to become a regular on NBC's ill-fated 1977 revival of *Laugh-In*. By the following year, Williams had won his role in *Mork & Mindy*, and the rest, as they say, is showbiz history.

Playboy assigned Lawrence Linderman to follow Williams around California. His report:

"Robin Williams and his wife, Valerie, live a peripatetic life. They have two residences in the L.A. area (a home in one of the canyons and an apartment in Hollywood), an apartment in San Francisco and a ranch in the Northern California wine country. I live just outside Sonoma, and I bumped into Williams there when Tommy Smothers, who owns a nearby vineyard, took him to Marioni's, the town's leading hangout. The word for Williams is charming. He's polite, amiable and funny, and also caught up, I think, in puzzling out how to hold on to aspects of his personality that he wants to share with no one but himself and his wife. (Valerie, incidentally, is one terrific lady.) Williams told me he was trying to spend as many weekends as he could at his recently purchased spread in neighboring Napa County; that was where he wanted to begin our interview. Several weeks later, I met him there one afternoon when he was watching a telecast of *On the Waterfront*. Want to know who Robin Williams is? In the last 10 minutes of the movie—when Marlon Brando's Terry Malloy is getting the shit kicked out of him by Lee J. Cobb's Johnny Friendly and his hoods—I glanced over and noticed that Robin had a hand over his face, which didn't at all conceal the tears that were streaming down his cheeks. I don't think I've ever interviewed a more sensitive guy. Or a gentler one, for that matter.

During the following weeks, I saw Williams frequently in L.A., and before our interview was done, I caught his nightclub act at San Francisco's Boarding House. In place of his lineup of various characters, Williams now does what amounts to total improvisation that blends burlesque, satire, mime, impressions and occasional stand-up comedy with such blinding speed that it's almost impossible to define his act in normal terms. One moment, he is a Brooklyn bruiser doing a number on those Falkin' Islands; the next, he's doing a takeoff on *Quest for Fire;* the next, he's improvising on subjects shouted to him by the audience. Williams uses a career's worth of premises in a single show, darting in and out of them like a manic postman on his appointed rounds. There's really no one else who does what Williams does.

In any case, when we finally began our interview, *Mork & Mindy* had just been canceled, and that provided the opening subject for our conversation."

PLAYBOY: Let's start with your television work, which is how most people have come to know you. ABC announced earlier this year that it was canceling *Mork & Mindy.* Why did the show's ratings slip so badly during the past couple of years?

WILLIAMS: I think the stories just got too complex and we got away from the simplicity of the character. *Mork & Mindy* originally worked because it was about this cheerful little man from outer space doing very simple things—"Mork buys bread" or "Mork deals with racism." Mork and Mindy were both very straitlaced and the charm of the show, I think, was in having Pam Dawber deal with me in normal, everyday situations—to which I would react in bizarre ways. The show began with very human roots, and Pam was responsible for a lot of that; she's a fine actress and a friend, and there was a wonderful exchange of humanity between us. I think people really connected with the characters we played, and in our first year, the series was exactly what it was designed to be: a situation comedy. When you think of, say, *The Honeymooners,* you know who Ralph Kramden was and you know who Norton was; they were at their best in everyday situations, and the simpler the better. If the stories ever became too complex—which is what happened to *Mork & Mindy*—there still would have been some funny things going on, but the show wouldn't have been nearly as effective. I didn't want to see *Mork & Mindy* bastardized that way, but it was.

PLAYBOY: Why did it happen?

WILLIAMS: The network got cocky. Television is like a game of chess, and guys at the three networks are always trying to gun one another down.

Good shows help a network build power blocs; *Herr* Silverman taught us that. Once you build a power bloc, you're able to sweep certain nights, and then you slowly but surely expand outward. When we started our second year, ABC took shows that were doing well and split us all up because it wanted to sweep *every* night. So for that reason, it shifted *Mork & Mindy* from Thursday to Sunday nights and scheduled us opposite *Archie Bunker's Place*. As a result of all that maneuvering, two or three ABC series got canceled, including a very good one called *Angie*. It was a simple case of greed, and it didn't work. Then, when the network realized things were going poorly for our show, it got panicky and started putting in all these sexually oriented stories: "Mork becomes a cheerleader for the Denver Broncos!" I think people who'd always watched the series just looked at that stuff and said, "Jesus, what's *this?*"

PLAYBOY: Was that your reaction as well?

WILLIAMS: It didn't piss me off as much as make me wonder *why*. Everyone was then doing T and A shows, so I guess the network guys said, "Let's put Mork in drag—that's *always* funny." But that was going far away from what we had originally had, a gentle soul who was suddenly becoming kind of *kinky*. The producers were torn between the network's saying, "We need stories we can promote" and their own feelings about supporting the characters. Well, because the network wanted a T and A show it could promote, there I was with 32 cheerleaders. [*Sings*] "We've got 32 girls, 64 nipples—and what can we talk about now?" Just count 'em, folks: 32 girls, 64 nipples—65? Ah, yes, the Venusian woman on the end; bless you, my dear. Right after that, we had a two-part show with Raquel Welch playing one of three dynamite-looking aliens who come down to Earth, take me prisoner and then try to get information out of me through sensuous tortures. Raquel was in a wild Bob Mackie outfit that had the guys on the set breathing *very* hard, and one of the other girls was a Playmate, Debra Jo Fondren, with long blonde hair braided all the way down her back. The planned tortures included putting me in a hot tub and having the Playmate whip me with her *hair*. I was not unhappy when they decided against going with that. [*In a child's voice*] "Daddy, Daddy, look—Mork's into *bondage!*" Then they came up with this little ball that was like a vibrator, and the girls were supposed to rub it up and down my body until I got crazy and gave in.

Shows like those changed us during the second year, and they weren't a help. By our third season, the network guys were *desperate* for stories they could promote. It was almost like, "Mork changes sexes! Watch out—he's got everything going now, and Mindy doesn't know *what* to do!" We continued to get our ass kicked, but they kept looking for promotable stories. "Are you ready for this, America? Mork becomes an iguana!" And then last year, in their search for promotable stories—that became the key to each week's show—we discovered that Mork and Mindy were going to have a child. How well could ABC *sell* that child? They almost forgot about the stories and the characters themselves. Right about then, I knew it was time to turn around and say, "They're near the east gate, *mein Herr*."

PLAYBOY: Were you opposed to having Mork give birth to Mirth, the Jonathan Winters character?

WILLIAMS: No, having him on the show was one of the main reasons I stayed with it. For me, it was like the chance to play alongside Babe Ruth. I'd always wanted just to *meet* Winters. When I was a kid, my parents would say, "All right, you can stay up a little longer to see this wonderful man fly around the room and do all his crazy stuff." I found out much later that Jonathan's shows never did well in the ratings, but an awful lot of people I've talked with remember those shows, and they vividly remember things that he did. And I mean exact lines and whole routines.

PLAYBOY: Such as?

WILLIAMS: My favorite was King Quasi of Quasiland. His country was five feet wide and 11 miles long, and its main exports were rope and pasta.

PLAYBOY: Were you instrumental in getting Winters on the series?

WILLIAMS: No, I wasn't, though the producers knew I wanted to work with him. Jonathan had done one episode in which he played another character's brother; the chemistry between us that night was terrific, and we got fantastic feedback on it. The first time I saw Jonathan on the set, he came up to me and said, "How are you, young man? My name is Willard Cespar and I'm here to check on violations of the building code." Somebody asked him what he'd been doing, and Jonathan started playing an old guard working the gate at Paramount, and then he did a thing about starting a telethon to keep Lucille Ball off the air. When the decision was made to have him play Mirth, I was happy about it and the network people were *ecstatic*. They had something else to promote: the new crazy man and the king.

PLAYBOY: As you mentioned a few minutes ago, Winters has never been very successful on TV, and some industry observers felt that making him a regular was like a kiss of death for *Mork & Mindy*. Do you think that's true?

WILLIAMS: No, I don't. I sometimes believe Jonathan thinks so, but it's not true; he didn't kill the show. In fact, he gave it a big boost, because the ratings shot up like crazy when Jonathan first came on. We did a couple of very good early stories about Mirth, like one in which he gets flak from the kids at school and then brings me to class as his show-and-tell project. But then we got back to doing bizarre stories that had no semblance of reality, and the show's ratings went *way* down. For a little while, I thought, God, maybe I'm not goosing up like I used to; maybe the old mad energy is gone. But I decided that wasn't true, because people still liked my performances. I think the show just had a confused base. The combination of that and going up against *Magnum P.I.* was finally too strong. In San Francisco, guys were walking around saying, "Who *is* that man on *Magnum P.I.?* Do you think he'll put on another Hawaiian shirt and undo one more button?"

PLAYBOY: How did you take the news that *Mork & Mindy* was being canceled?

WILLIAMS: Well, there was a period during which I thought, Oh, fuck, man, they're out to kill us *all!* After that, it was, All right, let us die gracefully. My feeling now is that we did some good stuff—some *strange* stuff, too—and I know that we made an impact on our time.

PLAYBOY: Are you referring to eight P.M. on Thursdays?

WILLIAMS: Where does it say the interviewer is supposed to make jokes? By the way, why is the red light on your tape recorder winking at me?

PLAYBOY: That's Japanese Morse code warning us that we're about to run out of tape on this cassette. We'll only be a second . . . there, we're back. What happens to Mork now? Will we ever see him again?

WILLIAMS: No, I don't think so. It was wonderful while it lasted, but I wouldn't want to bring the character back. When something like that ends, you just say thank you and put it away. In Mork's case, he ended with a kind of videonasia. I carefully lowered the volume on my TV set, let loose the vertical hold, put down the rabbit ears and let him go gently into that last good night. Mork was my day job for four years, and now it's over. The show was a crapshoot that worked out, and the freedom I had on it was incredible. If *Mork & Mindy* had been totally scripted, I don't think we would have lasted more than seven weeks, but the producers saw an energy happening between Pam and me, and they didn't want to mess with it. So they let me improvise, and in the script, there'd be notes for me to say something on the theme of such and such, and I'd just go off and expand on it.

PLAYBOY: Isn't that unusual in a TV series?

WILLIAMS: As far as I know, it is. But you have to remember that Mork supposedly was an open book, a sieve who'd picked up his knowledge of the planet from years of watching Earth television. He was a little like a comic-book character called Zippy the Pinhead, somebody who absorbs everything that comes in but who puts it back out a little out of context, like a word processor with dyslexia. It helped that Mork was an alien, because in some ways there were no real boundaries as to what he could say or do.

PLAYBOY: You never ran afoul of network censors?

WILLIAMS: Sometimes, but we always had wonderful censors. We had a Filipina lady who was great, and then we had a black censor who was really something else. I tried to sneak a few Yiddish phrases past him, but he knew all of them. It turned out that the guy spoke Yiddish and was also studying other languages. He got some interesting greetings: "What's happenin', bro'? What is a *putz*? Yeah, Jack, that's cool." In one show, a guy delivered flowers to Mork, and I told him, "Here's your tip: Don't eat Mexican food when standing next to an open flame." I couldn't *believe* they left that in! Mostly, the network's censorship worries had to do with product references. For instance, we had a major hamburger chain sponsoring the show, and one time, I did something about a hamburger chain selling kangaroo meat. I said, "Look, Min, my hamburger has another hamburger inside its little pocket, and there's *another* little hamburger inside *that* one." No chance. Another time, I was going to talk about sugar and then go into a hypoglycemic fit, but one of ABC's major sponsors was a candy manufacturer, so I couldn't do it.

PLAYBOY: Did ABC executives treat you as if you really *were* an alien?

WILLIAMS: They really didn't know what I was. When we started the series, the network guys would all come in and sit together, and at first they didn't laugh, but then they couldn't help laughing. Starting with the first taping in front of an audience, it seemed like everyone was having a good time, and the more freedom I was given, the more I enjoyed it. It was the kind of playfulness I'd experienced in nightclubs but hadn't thought I'd ever be able to get on TV. I mean, I'd guested on certain TV shows where they were specific: "Mr. Williams, your line is 'Lola, Jimmy's home now.'" There was no deviating from the script, but in *Mork & Mindy*, I was allowed to work the way I do onstage. In the middle of a monolog, I could suddenly go off into different accents and characters, and nobody would blink.

PLAYBOY: Did other cast members want to improvise their roles?

WILLIAMS: No, probably because we all knew that if you've got too many people going off and getting crazy, there's no reality base. The series needed some normal characters or else people would have thought, Jesus, *everybody* on this show is out of his fuckin' mind.

PLAYBOY: It's a little difficult to believe that you won't miss *Mork & Mindy*. Is that entirely true?

WILLIAMS: Oh, no; there's a painful aspect about the series's going off. But the thing that's always kept me sane is performing live, and even while shooting the series, I'd drop in and entertain at Los Angeles clubs like The Comedy Store and the Improvisation. It's therapy for me, and one night, I did an improvisation with some friends who were suddenly saying, "Mr. Williams, you must understand—it's time to let go of the series. Pam Dawber is going on to Broadway, but you'll still have films, records and nightclubs to play with." And then I said [*in a little girl's voice*], "No, I want *this* doll. I want my *Mork* doll! Oh, look—its head comes off." That helped me explore my feelings about the series's going off, and after that it was, Yeah, okay, I can deal with it. I can go on to other things, like films. Well, one night not long after *Popeye* had come out, when I was improvising, somebody yelled out, "What about *Popeye*?" I said, "You're a *cruel* person. For your information, it's playing in Hollywood on a double bill with *Heaven's Gate*." That helped me expunge the initial pain I felt about *Popeye* and, again, I could explore that by doing lines like, "If you watch it backward, it really *does* have an ending." But that wasn't really meant to attack the picture. It was just my way of dealing with the pain and disappointment I felt about the way *Popeye* was received. At the same time, I'm proud of the picture, and I'm proud of my association with Robert Altman, who directed it.

PLAYBOY: *Popeye* wasn't a total dud, but it certainly wasn't the blockbuster most people thought it would be. What went wrong with it?

WILLIAMS: *Popeye* was a nice fairy tale with a loving spirit to it, and I think most people—especially movie critics—were expecting a combination of *Superman* and a Busby Berkeley musical. In some ways, I expected that, too, but in the end, I think that what Altman got was a very gentle fable with music and a lot of heart. I recently found out that a lot of people are buying videotapes of *Popeye*, and their kids watch it four or five times a month. That makes me feel good, because although adults were expecting what they'd seen in cartoons for years and were disappointed when they didn't get it, no one tells children what to expect. You don't *have* conversations in which a woman says, "Jimmy, I think this should have been a *bigger* film," and little Jimmy answers, "Yes, Mother, but it works for *me*."

PLAYBOY: Altman says that he conceived of *Popeye* as a morality tale about a young man searching for his lost father.

WILLIAMS: That's probably why it missed, because people wanted to see the *Popeye* they remembered from when they were kids. I knew that when we were making the movie, and I could feel what was missing. For instance, we needed a couple of slam-bang musical numbers that really tore the tits off the place. Same with the action: When the cartoon Popeye started dancing, walls would come down, windows would break, people would go flying out the door and Popeye would be swinging Olive Oyl around with her body parallel to the floor. Instead of all that, we shot in a real small space where you couldn't kick out the jambs. A lot of the movie was filmed on a sunken steamer that was sitting on the end of the bay in Malta, and that kept things confined. So we wound up seeing the softer side of *Popeye*. [*In a fey voice*] "I enjoyed *Popeye* because the *clothes* were so interesting. And I *loved* those rubber forearms. I want to *meet* this man. If I give you money, will you put those arms on for me?"

PLAYBOY: How long *did* you spend getting made up each day?

WILLIAMS: About an hour and a half, and after that, they'd strap on the latex arms; they tied me off almost as if I were a junkie. In some of my fight scenes, I'd lose all the circulation in my arms and they'd lock up, so we'd have to stop shooting. I'd ask for a little blood, and they'd untie me and say, "Relax, Robbie, relax." Once the circulation got going, they'd tie up my arms again so I could fight for another half hour. It was very strange and very strenuous.

PLAYBOY: Did you have to put in a lot of preparation for the role?

WILLIAMS: Oh, yeah. Gymnastics, fighting, tap dancing and so forth.

PLAYBOY: *Tap* dancing?

WILLIAMS: Ah, this must not be a happy day for you, Mr. Interviewer. [*Sings*] "Let's get cynical, cynical. . . . You learned how to tap-dance, Mr. Williams? Where did you use it in the film?" You want to see a screening of *The World According to Garp* now; can we start on that one? "Did you really wrestle, Mr. Williams? I mean, did the other guy have to *let* you pin him?" Yes, I learned how to tap dance, and I worked hard on my one song in the film, and I often practiced Popeye's speaking voice, which sounded like a frog farting under water. That was all in a good cause: It was my first movie, it was being directed by Robert Altman and it was being filmed in a strange country.

PLAYBOY: How strange *is* Malta?

WILLIAMS: Imagine San Quentin on Valium. Malta is a small island populated by nice, warm but very tough people who've never been conquered. The Maltese have a language of their own, which sounds Arabic, and they always speak loudly. They also speak English the same way. A guy will come up within two inches of your face and say, *"How are you today? I like you very much!"* "Gee, could you whisper?" *"I am whispering!"* We all lived just off the set in a kind of compound—*Stalag* Altman—with guards at the front gate and barbed-wire fences around us because the studio was afraid people would come in and steal stuff. We were there for six months, working six days a week, and soon after we got to Malta, it started raining and hardly ever stopped. That stretched out our shooting schedule, and we'd just sit there for days, going bats and feeling trapped.

PLAYBOY: What did you do for kicks?

WILLIAMS: Well, there are no great entertainment centers on Malta, and on weekends, we used to drink. They had this very strange wine available on the island: cabernet muck. There aren't a lot of vineyards on Malta, and the few grape presses I saw were covered with spiderwebs, so obviously the wine was mainly chemicals. When the English had a naval base on Malta, they built a few pubs, which are still there. We'd visit them on Saturday nights and get a little loaded and then sleep all day Sunday and go back to the grind on Monday.

PLAYBOY: How did you happen to get the part in the first place?

WILLIAMS: I heard about *Popeye* when Robert Evans asked me to be in the picture. Dustin Hoffman originally was supposed to play Popeye, and he also was supposed to do *Garp*; if there's another film you don't want to do, Dustin, just tell me and I'll be there. *Mork & Mindy* was real hot when he backed out, so I guess Evans thought, Well, we'll get Williams and let's see what happens.

PLAYBOY: What did you think of your work in *Popeye*?

WILLIAMS: I thought that I had guts and my performance had depth, but while we were doing it I felt confined and I really wanted a chance to explode. I thought that would come when we had our big boffo ending, but suddenly Paramount pulled the plug on the film and said, "You people have to come home. You're tired and over budget, and if you stay any longer, you're going to be there on your own." So there *was* no boffo ending. On the last day of shooting, we were struggling desperately to come up with an ending, and we all knew it would take great special effects to pull it off. I'd pictured Popeye flying through the air, sort of like the cartoon thing in which he becomes a tornado with his legs spinning around at warp four. And I know that I was supposed to punch an octopus out of the water and have it go whirring into space, but that didn't happen, either.

PLAYBOY: Why not?

WILLIAMS: Because when we were ready to shoot the ending, the special-effects guys had already left Malta. We were backed against a wall, and we all knew it. Shelley Duvall, who was terrific as Olive Oyl, was supposed to be attacked by an octopus, but the one that was built for the movie couldn't *do* anything. The Disney studios had half investment in *Popeye,* and if anyone had let them know that the octopus couldn't even manipulate its arms, I think they would have sent over a couple of guys and we would've had an octopus that could blink, wink, blow bubbles and smoke underwater. Shelley had to do a scene with the octopus grabbing her, so she literally wrapped its tentacles around her like a wet rubber boa and had to sell the fucker as hand-to-hand combat; that's when I was supposed to show up and launch the octopus into outer space. We blew it up instead, but you couldn't tell what had actually happened. I've got distance from it now, but *Popeye* was real painful for me, especially when it came out and got knocked so heavily by some reviewers.

PLAYBOY: What had you expected? That Popeye would be the kind of role Superman turned out to be for your buddy Chris Reeve?

WILLIAMS: Absolutely. When I was training for *Popeye,* I thought, This is it, this is *my* Superman, and it's gonna go through the fuckin' roof! I also had that dream of getting up to thank the academy, but I got beyond the this-is-it stage as soon as we started shooting. After the first day on *Popeye,* I thought, Well, maybe this *isn't* it, and I finally wound up going, Oh, God, when is it gonna be *over*? The process really becomes good when you're having such a great time doing the movie or you're so deeply involved in it emotionally that you forget about your fears. *Oh, no! Gene Shalit's coming toward me—he's got a blow dryer! Help!* You start thinking about that again just before a movie's release.

PLAYBOY: *The World According to Garp* is scheduled to open around the country before this issue reaches the newsstands. Are there Shalits currently lurking somewhere in your mind?

WILLIAMS: The hopes and the fears are there, sure, but everything else about *Popeye* and *Garp* is different, starting with the directors. Altman and George Roy Hill represent two extremes. It was incredible to go from an Altman, who gives you all that freedom, to a Hill, who says "You've got to do it *this* way"; they're like the yin and yang of the directing school. Hill knows *exactly* what he wants. On the day we started shooting *Garp*, I improvised a line and Hill called a wrap for the set. I thought, Okay, you've made your point. I won't do *that* again.

The roles themselves were opposites. Garp was like an oil drilling. I had to dig down and find things deep inside myself and then bring them up. Heavy griefs and joys, births and deaths—*Garp* is an all-encompassing look at a man's life.

PLAYBOY: How do you think the movie and your performance will be received?

WILLIAMS: I don't know, but the advance word is good, because since I did *Garp*, I've been getting a lot of scripts. There was an initial wave of parts offered to me when people found out I wanted to do films, but after *Popeye*, the number of screenplays sent to me tapered off. It comes in waves; Hollywood's really like that. "Ah, he's *hot* again." Studio executives go to screenings of just about every film before it's released, and I guess some of them liked what they saw in *Garp*. Of course, if the picture doesn't do well, they may start recalling all the scripts I've been looking at.

PLAYBOY: Do you have another movie lined up?

WILLIAMS: No, and right now, I'm just interested in learning what I can about movies, because there are two possibilities: I can act in other people's films or I can eventually write and act in my own. I hope I can play a supporting character in the next film I do, so that I can sit back and watch people work rather than take the burden of being a major character, as in *Popeye* and *Garp*.

PLAYBOY: At this moment, we're sure, a lot of actors are giving you a *great* deal of sympathy.

WILLIAMS: Oh, yes, I can hear them now: "Fuck you, scumbag. Oh, how *tough* it must be, Robin, playing all those leading roles. I've been playing a spear carrier for several years now, you motherfucker, so I can really appreciate your problem." Yes, I just want to explore *minor* roles for a while, folks. "Mr. Williams, you might very *well* begin exploring minor roles. You might even begin to explore the Zen concept of not working at all, you lucky asshole." Ah, but I want to explore *all* possibilities. "One of the major possibilities, Mr. Williams, is that you might be on unemployment like the rest of us, Jack. So enjoy your major roles while you have them, and you can play supporting roles later on—like when your career tumbles to a quick end. Perhaps one day, you can appear underwater as fourth bubble in *The Lloyd Bridges Story*."

PLAYBOY: If you're through conversing with yourself, Robin, it sounds to us as if you intend to follow Woody Allen's example and jump into movies exclusively.

WILLIAMS: No, I'll always do live comedy, even if it should mean performing on the streets, with a little pig-nosed amp and a shitty microphone. And I'm not ruling out television, either. I'd like to come back and do something once in a while.

PLAYBOY: The Robin Williams special?

WILLIAMS: The Robin Williams mundane. A lot of my friends have been massacred trying comedy or variety TV specials. What happens is that you'll do a special and the network guys will put it on any time they need to fill an hour. They can really screw you up by televising the show before there's a chance to promote it. On top of that, most specials have a similar format—complete with guest stars—and they get *creamed* for having a similar format. It's going to be hard, but I'd like to find something to do that would be fun and totally freeform. So TV's only a possibility, but there's no question about my continuing to work in clubs.

PLAYBOY: You said before that nightclub work is therapeutic for you. In what way?

WILLIAMS: In a *lot* of ways. When I was doing *Mork & Mindy*, working the clubs was a way for me to keep my creative energies flowing without getting all flustered. It also provides the chance to explore other sides of myself. I have a piece about Dr. Jekyll and Mr. Williams, a comedian. Mr. Williams would end his act by saying, "Well, fuck *you*, Jack!" and then would walk offstage and go back to being himself. [*Imitates Boris Karloff*] "Thank you; is my coach ready yet? I have to go home now. What's that? I didn't really say *fuck*, did I? How strange. You must have me confused with someone else."

Club work also allows you to improvise. I've had two dreams come true: the chance to work with Jonathan Winters and the chance to improvise with Richard Pryor. We did two nights of improvising at The Comedy Store, and the energy we generated was *incredible*. Improvising with other people is real fragile stuff; sometimes you come up with a piece that's funny only for the moment, and then there are wonderful nights when you create a piece that can stand on its own anywhere, any time. It's like musicians jamming. Comedy jamming, I guess, would have to be called comming. "What are you doing?" I'm comming. "What, is it good for *you*?"

Incidentally, is this good for *me*? I can already see the newspaper stories: "In an interview for *Playboy*, Robin Williams talks about comming. . . ."

PLAYBOY: No, too rough for the family trade. Moving right along, Robin, we'd like to know why you want to stay active in virtually *every* phase of show business.

WILLIAMS: I just like keeping several things going at once. People see you on television in *Mork & Mindy* and get an idea of who you are, and then they see the same guy on Home Box Office using those strange words, and it shows them another dimension. I like changing profiles but not just for career reasons. I'm so hooked on improvising that I'd like to put together an ensemble group for TV or maybe do a record with some of my friends. Contact with live audiences is important to me, so I'm going to continue to fine-tune my act, and I'll probably go on tour later this year. As I've already told you, I want to continue acting in movies, and I hope to write some, too. But there's something else I'd like to do in movies, and it's a long way off: I directed one of the last episodes of *Mork & Mindy*, and eventually I'd like to direct my own movies.

PLAYBOY: Now that you're a successful actor, of *course* you want to direct.

WILLIAMS: "Now that you play basketball, you'd like to coach, *wouldn't* you? C'mon, Missa Bradley, don't go into politics. New Jersey don't need you, Missa Bradley—we got Springsteen." Yes, I've *always* wanted to direct. My first film will be a very simple one, and to make it, I'll need only $10 million. The film will be about a boy, his dog and his budget.

PLAYBOY: The studios will beat down your door. Let's get back to your work as a stand-up comic. Do you still get nervous when performing in clubs?

WILLIAMS: There's total fear every time you go on, and it doesn't matter whether you're playing in front of 20 people or 200 or 2000. You get the same feeling every time, and if you don't, you're fooling yourself. Before you go on, your body issues an order: "Jettison all excess baggage." Some people actually throw up before they perform, and others act like animals before a fight; they take a dump to get rid of anything that might possibly slow them down. At that point, the adrenaline shoots way up—there's a lot of initial banging up and down. After that, I get the yawns for a little bit, and then I'm up again and *ready*.

PLAYBOY: Would you think something pure was slipping away if you felt more relaxed about performing?

WILLIAMS: Oh, no; being relaxed is wonderful, and I'm not saying that manic is good, either. When you're manic onstage, that's when you're desperate; and the faster you talk, the more you're afraid. The ultimate relaxation is when you're working and you're totally in control. You feel as if nothing can go wrong and stuff just comes out of nowhere—that's the joy of it. My wife, Valerie, once told me she thought it was good for me to go onstage at comedy clubs as long as I wasn't doing it to get stroked. Because you *can* go out there and play that game of "Hi, I'm Mr. Incredible—aren't I cute?" If you're not exploring and coming up with new things, then it becomes a massive jerk-off.

PLAYBOY: What's the latest routine you've developed in clubs?

WILLIAMS: Last week I walked into a store and bought a used red beret for a dollar, and the next night, I put it on at The Comedy Store and started doing a piece that I want to work on. [*Imitates a Hispanic tough*] "Hello, I am a Guardian Comedian. Jokes are dangerous things. Don't use them at home unless you have a premise and a punch line. Remember: Two Jews do not walk into a bar without a reason. If you are heckled, prepare to deal with the heckler. If his heckle works and you have no response, you are dead."

PLAYBOY: If we asked you to analyze your comedy, how would you do it?

WILLIAMS: The New Federalism of Humor. I don't know; I've never *tried* to describe what I do.

PLAYBOY: Try.

WILLIAMS: I've heard other people describe me as a comic genius. *I'll* settle for that—will you?

PLAYBOY: Try again.

WILLIAMS: Thanks a lot. The only answer that occurs to me—I'm being straight now—is that my comedy is like emotional hang-gliding.

PLAYBOY: Fair enough. In terms of becoming a comedian, did it take you very long to learn how to hang-glide?

WILLIAMS: Long enough. The first couple of pieces I did were what you might expect from a young comic. I had this thing about Lawrence Welk going, "Tank you, tank you. Now let's all get down and get fonky. The boys in the band will now play for you a luffly melody, *Chumping Chack Flash.* Play that fonky Muzak, white boys. Folks, I want you to know that efery one of the boys in the band is a real mother-focker in his own right." The other piece I did when I started out was about a quarterback on acid who'd go up to the line of scrimmage and instead of calling signals would say, "Well, hike when the energy's right." In the beginning, you find yourself doing a lot of drug humor, and when you can't be funny, you can get some laughs by saying motherfucker a lot. One of the initial reviews I got tore me up, because it said I was a "scatological pubescent," and that was true. It hit me right on the nose. In the beginning, you're also imitating everybody you've ever seen—for me, it was touches of Winters and Pryor. But all of a sudden, you get to a point where you go, "Ah, I can be *me*. I can develop my own stuff." And you *do*.

PLAYBOY: Mort Sahl says that the current generation of young comedians specializes in very lightweight humor. Do you disagree?

WILLIAMS: Sure I do. Sahl raps all young comedians as being too namby-pamby, but he's wrong. He says they don't talk about anything but products and advertising, the reason being they don't have any guts or balls. Well, I think a lot of people are now doing political humor that's just as powerful as Sahl's and only half as bitter. Really, there's been a *massive* resurgence of political humor, which is something we haven't had for a long time.

PLAYBOY: Why do you think it's happening now?

WILLIAMS: Probably because it's easy to pinpoint Ronald Reagan on things like his being a former actor, his age, his tax cuts and even his hair. When Reagan was governor of California, Jonathan entertained at a dinner for him. He played Maude Frickert remembering Ronnie as a kid and said, "Even *then*, your hair was orange." Nancy's also in there for her share because of things like her dishes and the little gun she was packing. I still think Nancy does most of his talking; you'll notice that she *never* drinks water when Ronnie speaks. Reagan's also got some wonderful people in his administration, starting with those Pentagon types and their designer cruise missiles. Of course, the French are going the Americans one better with their Michelin bomb: It destroys only restaurants under four stars. And then there's James Watt, the only Secretary of the Interior who's ever wanted to sell the interior.

PLAYBOY: James Watt claims that much of what he's said has been misunderstood.

WILLIAMS: So does John McEnroe. "Mr. McEnroe, did you call the umpire an asshole?" "No, I said passing shot." Maybe we can get McEnroe's father working for the government. "No, no; James Watt didn't really *mean* that he wants to lease the Grand Canyon to the oil companies."

PLAYBOY: Several observers of the current comedy scene believe your humor is a lot gentler than that of your contemporaries. Any reason that might be true?

WILLIAMS: Maybe it comes from the fact that I come from an upper-middle-class family; maybe slightly upper but not *that* much.

PLAYBOY: You and your family did live in a 30-room house on 20 acres, didn't you? Most people would define that as upper class.

WILLIAMS: Yes, but the house was rented, and we didn't heat all the rooms.

PLAYBOY: Once again, Robin, you have our sympathy.

WILLIAMS: And once again, you've nailed me. From the burden of doing major roles, I now have to re-evaluate growing up in a cold house in the suburbs of Detroit. "Daddy, Daddy, come upstairs—Biffy and Muffy aren't happy. We have only seven servants. All the other families have 10."

PLAYBOY: Were you popular with the other kids in the neighborhood?

WILLIAMS: There *were* no other kids in the neighborhood. There was nobody around to play with except the maid's son. Mom and Dad had each been married before, and they each had a child, but my half brothers, Todd and Loren, were a lot older than I and I didn't see them until I was around 10. Todd always extorted all my money. He'd come into my room and say he needed some beer money, and I'd say, "Oh, gosh, yes, take it *all*." My mother would get furious, because Todd would get into my piggy bank and walk out with $40 worth of pennies.

PLAYBOY: Growing up alone in a 30-room house sounds as if it must have made for a very lonely childhood. Did it?

WILLIAMS: Yes, but I got started kind of early in floating and finding stuff to do. For instance, I made up my own little friends. [*In a child's voice*] "Can I come out and play?" "I don't know; I'll have to ask myself." We had a wonderful dog named Duke that would play hide-and-seek with me, and I could always find Duke, who thought that if he couldn't see me, I couldn't see *him*. Duke was dumb; I'd always spot—or hear—this big tail going *whop! whop! whop!* on the parquet floors. Pretty early on, I banished myself to the attic, where I had a huge army of toy soldiers. I must have had about 10,000 of them, and I had them separated by periods in boxes. I'd have time-machine battles, with Confederate soldiers fighting GIs with automatic weapons and knights fighting Nazis.

PLAYBOY: That doesn't seem quite fair to the knights.

WILLIAMS: We didn't care about *fair*; we needed a warm-water port. I'd throw all those soldiers into battle and build castles in the attic, and I always made Carl, my turtle, the king. Unfortunately, one day I flushed Carl down the toilet, because I wanted him to be free. I told Mother, "I let Carl go. He's *happy* now." Yeah, it was *real* lonely after Carl left.

PLAYBOY: Did your parents spend a lot of time with you?

WILLIAMS: Yes, and we've always been *very*, very close. Picture George Burns and Gracie Allen looking like Alistair Cooke and Audrey Hepburn and that's what my parents are like. Dad was a trouble shooter for Lincoln-Continental in the days when Lincolns were strong rivals to Cadillacs, and for a long time, we bounced back and forth from Detroit to Chicago. He has a very wry sense of humor, and Mom is always flying around, very bubbly and effervescent. Even when I was very young, she'd recite all these nasty poems to me. One of her best: "Spider crawling on the wall, / Ain't you got no sense at all? / Don't you know that wall's been plastered? / Get off that wall, you little spider." She thought that was great. Her favorite was a short one: "I love you in blue, / I love you in red, / But most of all, / I love you in blue." Mom also had an inexhaustible supply of jokes and stories. The one I remember most was a book supposedly written by a 19th century English princess who was famous for throwing parties. The title of the book—Mom swears it's real—is *Balls I Have Held.*

PLAYBOY: Would it be fair to say that your mother gave you your start in show business?

WILLIAMS: I got her energy and funkified sense of humor, and I got a grounding thing from Dad. I never met my grandmother on Mom's side, but Mom says she was a great character who just *loved* to watch men wrestle. There's probably a lot of happy madness that's been passed down in the family, with characters from *Arsenic and Old Lace* all over the place.

PLAYBOY: Do you recall the first time you consciously performed?

WILLIAMS: Yes. I started telling jokes in the seventh grade as a way to keep from getting the shit kicked out of me. Mom and Dad had put me in public school, and most of the kids there were bigger than me and wanted to *prove* they were bigger by throwing me into walls. There were a lot of burly farm kids and sons of auto-plant workers there, and I'd come to school looking for new entrances and thinking, If only I could come in through the *roof*. They'd nail me as soon as I got through the door.

PLAYBOY: Why? Because you were a rich kid?

WILLIAMS: How could they know I was rich? Just because I'd say, "Hi, guys, any of you play lacrosse?" They thought lacrosse was what you find at *la* church. Because of Dad's job, we had to move, and I finished the seventh grade at a private school for boys, where I went from dealing with *shtarkers* to intellectual bullies. All these hyperintellectuals would really lay into me with lines like "That was a very *asinine* thing to say, Williams." I remember one kid was into heavy calculus in the seventh grade, and everyone else would go, "Wow, cross sections of a *cone*. Gee, Chris, I wish *I* could do that." That was one side; the other side was physical abuse. The real problem was that everybody was going through puberty or about to, which produces a lot of tensions. That, combined with going to an all-boys' school, gave us all a certain extended view of women for a while.

PLAYBOY: Was it tough to meet girls?

WILLIAMS: We'd have only brief contacts with them. They'd bring in a busload from an all-girls' school and dangle them in front of us at a dance. Then, just when you were asking, "Was that your *tongue?*" they'd pack the girls back up on the bus. I'd be chasing it, shouting, "Wait, come back—what are *those* things? What do you *use* them for?"

PLAYBOY: Did you get into a lot of trouble at school?

WILLIAMS: Just once. The school's motto was *Monsanto incorpori glorius maxima copia*, which in Latin means, "When the going gets tough, the tough go shopping." The faculty was dedicated to making sure we acquired poise, and one way to do it was to have us make speeches during lunch. One day, when I was in the ninth grade, I did a comedy speech and people liked it, but I told a Polish joke. When I sat down, I immediately found out from my friends that our big, heavy assistant headmaster was Polish. Before lunch was over, Mr. Kroski came up to me and said, "Williams, may we talk for a moment?" Yes, sir, Mr. Kroski, I sure must have lost my head.

PLAYBOY: What else do you remember about that period?

WILLIAMS: All my friends were Jewish, which is why I know so much Yiddish. I went to 14 bar mitzvahs in less than a year, and it was great. My friends made me an honorary Jew and used to tell people I went to services at Temple Beth Dublin. Being an honorary Jew was a real challenge, but I knew I could master the art of guilt. That's about when I took up wrestling, too. After getting pushed around for a couple of years, in my first year of high school, I decided, Fuck it, I'll take control of this thing. So I did a lot of callisthenic work and got on the wrestling team.

PLAYBOY: Were you a good wrestler?

WILLIAMS: I was undefeated in my freshman year, but then I had to go to the state finals, where I was matched against some kid from upstate Michigan who looked like he was 23 and balding. I remember the guy asking me, "Are you a *grappler*?" Grappling is what you do when your opponent has twisted you up in such a way that you're about to bite your own balls. Really, parts of your body will be in places you never dreamed they could go, and you think about that when the inside of your knee somehow gets behind your *neck*. I dislocated my shoulder and had to quit during my sophomore year, but wrestling was fun for me. If you're a small guy, which I was—I competed at 103 pounds—wrestling finally gives you the chance to take out your aggressions on somebody your own size.

PLAYBOY: Did that put an end to your athletic career?

WILLIAMS: No, I was on the football team for a week. They put me at safety, and in my one and only scrimmage, the other squad ran every offensive play at me and over me. It was not easy for a 103-pound safety to stop a 200-pound running back. Toward the end of the practice, when the coach told me to get back in there, I asked him if he'd mind painting me white so that I could disguise myself as a yard marker.

After that, I played soccer, which was fun, because a little guy can dart in and out and not get creamed too bad. In those days, you didn't have soccer teams if you didn't have foreign-exchange students. We had an Abdul who didn't like too much contact, and if someone caught him with a flying tackle, he'd get up and say, "Thot's eet, I going now." He was an Egyptian playing on a team made up mainly of Jews, with a couple of goyim like me thrown in. Abdul and I were friends, but there were days when he suspected that *everyone* was out to get him. "You, too, Thobbie," he once told me. "You pipple all trying *tockle* me." I said, "That's not true, Abdul. We just don't *pass* to you very often."

By the end of my junior year, I had my act together. I was a good student—a member of the *magna cum laude* society, in fact—and I was going to be president of the senior class. I was looking forward to a very straight existence and was planning to attend either a small college in the Midwest or, if I was lucky, an Ivy League school. But just before my senior year, my dad retired and we all drove out to our new home in Tiburon, California, just north of San Francisco in Marin County.

PLAYBOY: Did you have any expectations about life in California?

WILLIAMS: I had no idea what it was about, but the surprises started when we got near San Francisco and I saw this gray stuff rolling over the hills real *fast*. It was the first time I'd ever seen fog pouring in, and I thought it was poison gas. It scared the piss out of me.

PLAYBOY: Did Marin County's often-satirized lifestyle send you into deep cultural shock?

WILLIAMS: In terms of cultural shock, it probably would have been easier for me to move to Mexico. I had *total* cultural shock. Marin has the image of people bobbing for Quaaludes, but it wasn't quite to that stage when I got there. Sausalito, for example, is now all shops and hot-and-cold running quiche, but in 1969, it was a lot less of a tourist town. I got a job at the Trident restaurant, which had the most beautiful waitresses in the world. They were also the *strangest* waitresses in the world. They wore spray-on two-piece macramé outfits that looked like a pair of socks. It was like, "Sonja, your *nipple*'s hanging out." And she'd say, "I know; I'm trying to get tips." Girls literally had to audition for their jobs. They'd come in and get their pictures taken, and most of them were these lovely *mondo organo* earth princesses. They'd go up to a table and tell people, "Hello, I'm your waitress. How's your energy today? Our lunch special is the Gestalt sushi—we give you a live fish, and you take the responsibility for killing it."

In the Midwest, we knew about organic chemistry, but we'd never heard of organic food. The waitresses told me, "You come from the Midwest and give us cars; we give you avocado, alfalfa sprouts and wheat berries." The first time I tried organic wheat bread, I thought I was chewing on roofing material. A lot of customers at the Trident were on holistic diets and drank things like *mu* tea; which I thought came from a cow's bowels. "Robin, you just don't understand; there's so much *energy* in *mu* tea and ginseng." I was sure ginseng was an ethnic thing: "Gin sing today?" "No, Juda sang, Gin's gon' sing tomorrow."

PLAYBOY: What was school like out there?

WILLIAMS: It was wonderful—and very, very *weird*. I went to Redwood High School, which had courses in 16mm filmmaking and a lot of psychology-type classes. It was the height of the encounter period, and in a lot of classes, teachers would get everybody together for an energy hug. I remember one teacher would sometimes just stop what he was doing and then a few kids would start pounding out a beat and everybody would get up and dance around the room. There was also a black-studies department, even though there was only one black kid in the school—and he didn't want any part of it. He said, "I know I'm black, so just leave me the fuck alone and let me go to school. I don't have to be in no black-*studies* program."

It was incredible to go from a private all-boys' high school to a place where there were Gestalt history classes and where kids were always flying around on acid. The first time I walked into one of the bathrooms, a bunch of guys were in there, all spaced out. One kid took me aside and whispered, "Don't *wake* them." I didn't.

PLAYBOY: You obviously regarded your new classmates as wackos. How did they feel about you?

WILLIAMS: Well, at first, I still carried my briefcase, and guys would either ask, "Who's the geek?" or stare at me and say, "Wow, a briefcase—how un*mellow*. You're really creating negative energy." In the Midwest, if your classmates thought you were creating negative energy, you'd hear, "Yo!" followed by a right cross to the jaw. It took me a few weeks before I showed up at Redwood High without a tie on, and within a couple of months, I finally took the big step and went to school in jeans.

PLAYBOY: Why was that a big step?

WILLIAMS: At Detroit Country Day School, we always had to wear decent slacks and our school blazer, which was blue for the sea that brought us here and gold for the harps we hoped to find. Right after I started wearing jeans, somebody gave me my first Hawaiian shirt, and after that, I was *gone*; I got into a whole wild phase and I learned to totally let go. Among other things, I learned to say "For sure," which Californians pronounce fur*shirr*.

PLAYBOY: Among other things, did you try drugs?

WILLIAMS: Fur*shirr*. Before coming to California, I hadn't even known what grass looked like. One of the first times I smoked it was on an astrological scavenger hunt—people who had the same astrological sign would pile into a bus and they'd drive all over the county searching for things like lost mandalas. The only problem I had with grass was that it got me real sleepy, so I didn't get into it and never have. At the time, though, there was a more important reason I didn't want to smoke it. I was on the cross-country running team, and I thought it would be bad for me.

PLAYBOY: How did you think marijuana would harm you?

WILLIAMS: I thought that if I smoked grass, it would screw up my endurance. My hero then was Frank Shorter, who later won the Olympic marathon, and I grew a mustache so that I could look like him. Shorter's running mate was a guy named Jack Bachelor, and I and a teammate named Phil Russell used to fantasize that we were Frank and Jack. Our cross-country team would run up and down those beautiful Northern California hills, and I remember going up a steep trail high on Mount Tamalpais and coming to the edge of it—and there, below us, was the fog sitting on Stinson Beach. That gave me a beautiful Zenlike feeling of *satori*, and I ran right down into the ocean. The other guys warned me not to go into the water, but it was too beautiful to resist. The moment I jumped in, both legs went out on me. It was like my body's saying, "You use me so hard for an hour and then you do *this* to me? How's about if I cramp up both your legs and make your testicles disappear right up through your scrotum? Think you'll remember not to jump in the water *next* time?"

PLAYBOY: Did that cause you to change *your* training habits?

WILLIAMS: I got stoned only once on a training run. I remember we came over a hill and there, in the middle of the trail, was this strange thing—a turkey vulture. Marin has a lot of them, and I thought, Well, it'll just move aside. But when I got close, it went *hssssssss* and spread its wings, and I turned to the rest of the guys and said, "Oh, Jesus, I *knew* this would happen if I got stoned. I can't *deal* with it!"

PLAYBOY: Did you ever have a full-fledged freak-out on drugs?

WILLIAMS: Just before graduation, a friend gave me peyote without telling me what it was. I said, "Why is this mushroom so *mangy?*" and he said, "Don't worry about it." A little while later, I could see that he was having some problems. I said, "Gosh, your face is turning into Silly Putty, and why is your *head* expanding? Your *eyes* are moving now—why do you have one eye on your chin? Uh-oh, your face is starting to *melt*."

The closest I came, I guess, was three years ago, at the Bread and Roses music festival in Berkeley. During a performance, somebody gave me some cookies that would supposedly give me a buzz. I hadn't had anything to eat that day, so I thought it would probably be okay to eat half a cookie. It wasn't. A few hours later, I was sitting at a pool, and all of a sudden it became difficult for me to breathe and I couldn't move. Some little kids came over and asked for an autograph, but I wasn't even able to sign my name—I couldn't do *anything*. Some people get very vivacious and outgoing on drugs; I just get debilitated.

PLAYBOY: So you're telling us that despite all the dope references and the rumors, you've never really gotten into drugs?

WILLIAMS: No, never. And I never will. I mean, somebody once gave me a Valium and it stayed in my blood for a couple of days. I was like [*shakes his head, out of it*]. Most times, anything I try, I have the opposite reaction to what I'm supposed to have.

PLAYBOY: Does that include cocaine? Instead of speeding you up, it makes you nod out?

WILLIAMS: Yeah, I get passive and just hold back. Most people get talkative; I don't say anything to anybody. It's always weird, because I don't have regular reactions to any of those things. I don't like doing any of the heavies, because normally my energy is just up when I'm performing.

PLAYBOY: At a *Mork & Mindy* taping we attended, a couple of teenagers in the audience asked you how many lines you do every morning. Presumably, they meant cocaine or, possibly, speed. Did that surprise you?

WILLIAMS: No, because if you've got energy, that's their assumption: "Good God, he's got all this energy; what's he really doing? You doing *speed*, man?" They assume you gotta be doing that shit and that it goes with the territory.

PLAYBOY: It doesn't? On a *Tonight Show* some time back, you told Johnny Carson—

WILLIAMS: That cocaine is God's way of saying you're making too much money. Just kidding. That was part of a bit I used to do about those great reasons to buy cocaine: severe impotence and paranoia. [*Imitates an L.A. swinger*] "Hi, honey, Mr. Wonderful's here." [*In a woman's voice*] "Come on, I'm waiting." "I'll be with you in a second. [*Angrily addresses his penis*] Come *on*, damn it!" No, the best drug in the world for me is performing.

PLAYBOY: What's the high like?

WILLIAMS: Imagine sex in a time warp. [*Sings in a high-pitched voice*] "Oooh, oooh, I'm coming. Over a period of hours." When it works, there's nothing better. When it doesn't, there's nothing more horrible and painful. You get the sweats, you get furious and sadness sets in.

PLAYBOY: How did you feel when you performed Saturday night?

On the day after John Belushi's death, Williams spent the afternoon being interviewed by Playboy. *That night, the* Playboy *interviewer met him at The Comedy Store in Hollywood where Williams put in a surprise 45-minute appearance.*

WILLIAMS: It was good, but there was a strange mood in the air. It was just kind of up and down.

PLAYBOY: It seemed strange to us that none of you comedians mentioned Belushi's death.

WILLIAMS: No one will; I don't want to for a long time. It's too personal. No one would, out of respect and kindness. I think it'll be a long time before anybody really puts it together. That's why I couldn't talk about it and probably won't for a long, long, long time. Maybe I never will. We were all feeling the same thing, but we didn't want to talk about it—so as not to open up a can of worms for somebody. You know, there were a lot of reporters there.

[*Subsequent to that exchange, rumors surfaced that Williams and actor Robert De Niro, a close friend, had met with Belushi several hours before he died of an overdose. In June, Catherine Evelyn Smith, the woman who had spent Belushi's last evening with him, said in the* National Enquirer *that she had given Belushi a fatal injection of heroin and cocaine. She also claimed that Williams and De Niro had shared cocaine with Belushi that night.* Playboy *set up a final interview session to discuss the rumors and Smith's allegations, but three days before Williams was to meet with* Playboy, *the Los Angeles district attorney's office announced that it was reopening its investigation of Belushi's death. At that point, Williams's lawyers counseled him not to comment further on the matter until the district attorney's investigation was completed. Williams took their advice.*]*

PLAYBOY: Let's talk of lighter things, Robin. Before we began discussing drugs, you were telling us how alien California seemed when you moved there. Was there anything about the state that *didn't* strike you as bizarre?

WILLIAMS: Yes, the women. As far as any war between the sexes, California girls were all for disarmament and wanted the boys to drop their weapons immediately. In Michigan, everybody was still observing the native courting rituals of the North American Caucasian: the parking of the car, the meeting of the mate's parents, the admiring of the father's shotgun collection and stuffed rabbit heads. I think my last vestige of my Midwestern upbringing was my choice of a career: When I graduated from high school, I went down to Claremont Men's College, because I knew that it specialized in political science and I was determined to become a foreign-service officer. One of the eight freshman courses I signed up for was an elective in theater, and after my first day in class, I was hooked. The school's theater seated about 80 people, and we formed an improv group called The Synergy Trust and filled the place every Friday night. I'd never had so much fun in my life, which was probably why I didn't show up for any of my other classes. When finals came around at the end of the year, one professor said, "Who is this man?" Another professor commented, "If I *knew* who he was, I could give him a failing grade." I don't claim to have total recall, but I can still quote the entire essay I handed in for my macroeconomics final: "I really don't know, sir." The following year, I was back up north, studying theater at Marin Junior College.

PLAYBOY: Did you have any regrets about your premature retirement from the foreign service?

WILLIAMS: No, and if I'd gone through with it, I probably would've ended up as a hostage somewhere, preferably inside the Belgian Embassy, with a crowd outside refusing to let me go until we shipped them more Brie.

Meanwhile, I'd made a conscious decision to become an actor, and Marin J.C. had a superb theater department. The school's auditorium housed a replica of the old Globe Theater stage, and we performed Shakespearean plays there.

PLAYBOY: What did your parents think of all that?

WILLIAMS: Dad said to have an alternative career waiting in the wings and recommended welding. Mom said, "Your grandmother would be very proud," and wished me good luck. I *had* good luck that year, mostly because I fell in love with the ultimate California girl. She was blonde, Bambiesque and *very*, very gentle.

PLAYBOY: What's the difference between a girl from California and a girl from Michigan?

WILLIAMS: A handgun. That girl was my first great infatuation. I remember running home and saying, "Momma, Momma, look; I'm writing *poetry*." Mom said, "Let me see some of it. Hmm, it doesn't rhyme." I said, "I know, Mother. It's freeform, like the ebb and flow of the sea." Mom told me that was a very shabby simile and offered me the use of her car. "I don't need it, Mother. My heart has wings—I can *fly* to her house." Mom just looked at me and said, "I know, son, I know." Anyway, I was at the junior college for two and a half years, and I was also studying with The Committee in San Francisco. I did a lot of acting during that period, but I knew that if I stayed in San Francisco, all I could look forward to was becoming a big fish in a little tide pool. It was time to kick forward and go on to the next level. I'd heard that Juilliard had just started its acting school, and that sounded good to me, because it was in New York. I had visions of Broadway in my mind, so I auditioned for a scholarship.

PLAYBOY: Was the audition held in New York?

WILLIAMS: No, in San Francisco. Juilliard holds auditions in every major city and in some minor ones, too. You know, of course, that they have theatrical recruiters out beating the bushes for talent. Alumni will tell them about an Othello down in Georgia, an Iago they saw in Iowa; and sometimes, they'll bend the rules and redshirt a couple of Prosperos and maybe a foreign-exchange student from Denmark, whom they'll bring in for only one play, *Hamlet.*

When I went to audition, they were seeing about 50 people a day, and when they got to me, I did a speech Malvolio makes in *Twelfth Night* and Leper Lepellier's flip-out scene from the novel *A Separate Peace*. Next thing I knew, I was in New York.

PLAYBOY: Was that a heavy adjustment for you to make?

WILLIAMS: I was the walking epitome of fur*shirr* meets yo' ass. On my first day in New York, I went to school dressed like a typical California kid: I wore tie-up yoga pants and a Hawaiian shirt, and I kept stepping in dog shit with my thongs. My first week there, I was in a bus going uptown to see an apartment when an old man two seats in front of me suddenly collapsed and died. He slumped over against a woman sitting next to him, and she said, "Get *off* me!" and moved away. Somebody told the driver what had happened, so he stopped the bus and ordered everybody off, but I wanted to stay and *help*. The driver told me, "He's *dead*, motherfucker, now get off! You can't do *shit* for him, so take your raggedy California ass and get outa my bus!" I knew that living in New York was certainly going to be *different*.

PLAYBOY: Was it difficult as well?

WILLIAMS: Not really. New York appealed to me because I'd been in danger of becoming terminally mellow, and it peeled away that layer very quickly. I'd be walking down the street and six Puerto Rican drag queens would go, "What you doin' here, baby? Want to go upstairs, *muchacho?*" New York forces you to toughen up, but I never got to the New York blinders stage, which is when you always look straight ahead, even if someone's getting mugged 10 feet away. I got there in September of '73; one of the first things I learned was the Brooklyn alphabet: fuckin' A, fuckin' B, fuckin' C. . . .

PLAYBOY: Were Juilliard's teaching techniques vastly different from those of the colleges you'd attended?

WILLIAMS: Yes, they really were. In the other places, you'd do scenes and then discuss them, but at Juilliard, we worked on all the skills needed by an actor. It's a little like the army; they break you down and then they build you back up. In my first few days at school, I learned that I didn't project out, that I talked too fast and that I swallowed my words. One of the first things I tried in class was a religious monolog Dudley Moore had done in *Beyond the Fringe*. I thought I did fine, but my teacher, a man named Michael Conn, hated it so much that he said, "You have two choices: Come back and do it again or give up any thoughts you have about an acting career." He really was furious with me, and it was because I'd only imitated what I'd heard and hadn't tried to find new things that would make the piece *mine*.

PLAYBOY: Did that shake you up?

WILLIAMS: It did, but that's what it was supposed to do—they wanted to reorient you and get you out of easy patterns. A *lot* of teachers were intense, including a New Yorker named Gene Loesser, who'd stop you in the middle of a reading and shout, "What the fuck do you think you're *doing?*" What we were doing was working our asses off; between all the acting, speech, movement and even fencing classes, we'd be at Juilliard from eight in the morning till nine or 10 o'clock at night. In the same way that the Juilliard School of Music didn't acknowledge jazz or pop, the acting school emphasized the classical approach. John Houseman, who was principal of the acting school, gave a speech one day in which he said [*imitates Houseman*], "The theater *needs* you. Don't be tempted by television or the movies. The theater needs new plasma, new blood." And then, a week later, we saw him in a Volvo commercial.

PLAYBOY: Did you have any run-ins with Houseman?

WILLIAMS: He talked to me once when I was blowing a literature course. In a very elegant way, Houseman told me to pull it together. That wasn't easy. Me and Chris Reeve had come in together as advanced students—Chris had gone to Cornell—and we had to catch up to the other students who'd been at Juilliard for a year. Chris lived about five blocks away, and we used to go up to the roof of his apartment building and drink cheap wine and talk about present and lost loves. Except for my friendship with brother Reeve, that first year was rough, especially at Christmastime. I couldn't afford to go back to California for the holiday, and it was the first cold, cold winter I'd experienced in many years—and New York seemed unbearably bleak and lonely. One day, I just started sobbing and couldn't stop, and when I ran out of tears my body kept going; it was like having emotional dry heaves. I went through two days like that and finally hit rock bottom and realized I had a choice: I could either tube out or level off and relax. At that point, I became like a submarine on the bottom that blows out some ballast and gets back up again. [*Imitating Georgie Jessel*] "Yes, I'm glad you asked. Once in a while, it's *good* to have a nervous breakdown. A little emotional house cleaning never hurt anybody."

Once all my anxieties were behind me, the rest of that year was easy, and the following year was even better, mostly because of a girl I'd met who'd recently come to New York from California. She was a free spirit who thought nothing about walking through tough neighborhoods wearing white lace gowns. I told her that if she kept it up, she'd get killed, and she said, "No, my aura will defend me." Her *aura*? I said, "Your aura's not gonna do shit against a straight razor." I was wrong. She'd blithely walk down the most dangerous streets in Manhattan and guys would stop her and say, "Hey, what's happenin', dear?" or "Yo, you lookin' good *today*, baby." Her best defense was not having one. We had a very wonderful time, and then I went back to California for the summer—and *really* fell in love. That was a transformation point in my life.

PLAYBOY: How so?

WILLIAMS: Well, it began with my not wanting to leave my girlfriend. When I came back to Juilliard in the fall, Chris had left to do a soap opera, and the amount of actual training I got dropped off: Juilliard used third-year students to perform shows on the road. We'd go to the Bronx and play at tough high schools and then we'd go to very elegant places upstate where the audiences were straight out of *Night of the Living Lacoste*. I really *missed* my lady friend, and I began running up $400-a-month telephone bills—and at the time, I was having trouble just making the rent. The tension of a long-distance romance was such a drain that before spring came, I dropped out of Juilliard and went back to San Francisco. As soon as I got back, I realized why I had left: I was at an impasse there, and it was time to take another step forward.

PLAYBOY: What did you have in mind?

WILLIAMS: I wasn't sure, but I knew I'd reached the end of the line at Juilliard. When I got back to San Francisco, the girl and I lived together for about a month and then it just fell apart. I went into a massive depression, and when I wasn't accepted by the couple of San Francisco theater companies that actually pay their actors, I joined a comedy workshop. It didn't take me long to put together my first stand-up routine, and the guy who ran the workshop, Frank Kidder, had us perform on weekends at a place called The Intersection on Union Street. It was a former religious coffeehouse, and before we went on, there'd be poetry readings. I liked the feminist poets best. I remember one poem that really plucked at my heartstrings:

Man. / With your big penis. / Big-prick violence, smashing windows. / Do you only want to come? / Can't we go somewhere?

PLAYBOY: Did you put your acting career on hold at that point?

WILLIAMS: Yeah, I did that immediately. Comedy had always been an outlet for me, but I'd always treated it as a guerrilla activity. It became primary for two reasons: It was a form of therapy that helped me get over the relationship, and it also allowed me to support myself for the first time. I'd do $25-a-night gigs and I'd actually make enough to pay my $100-a-month rent. I was self-sustaining, and I could say, "No, Pop, I don't need that check, but thanks." I played a lot of tiny clubs, like The Holy City Zoo in San Francisco—I met Valerie there—and the Salamander in Berkeley, which was a *very* strange place. One night, the guy who ran the Salamander shot a customer just because the man had asked for change.

It happened pretty quickly for me after that. Before long, I was getting good time slots at bigger clubs and I started making decent money. When Valerie and I had been together for about six months, it was time to take the next step and join the great migration south.

PLAYBOY: To Los Angeles?

WILLIAMS: Right. San Francisco comedians were finding work down there, and a couple of them had gotten on *The Merv Griffin Show*. I pulled up roots then and convinced Valerie to come with me even though it was going to be tough for her. Valerie is a modern-dance teacher, and there isn't too much of a call for that in Los Angeles. I mean, Twyla Tharp doesn't choreograph The June Taylor Dancers. Valerie went with me, though, and a few days after we got there, I auditioned at The Comedy Store and was hired for $200 a week. After that, I worked the Improv and other clubs, and after about six months in L.A., George Schlatter saw me at The Comedy Store and hired me for *Laugh-In*. I went into that show with *such* heavy illusions.

PLAYBOY: What were they?

WILLIAMS: I thought that I'd made it into the big time and that I'd have a big house and everything else that goes with being on a hit TV show. Unfortunately, doing a remake of a show that was one of the milestones of TV was a little like doing *Jaws VI*: How are you going to top the original? Are you gonna have the shark come up on land and *gum* people to death? *Laugh-In* sure sobered my ass up. The show lasted 14 weeks, and most of the time, I played a redneck or a Russian. My best line: Frank Sinatra was on *Laugh-In* one week, and I went up to him and said, "Mr. Sinatra, I'm so happy to meet you I could drop a log." I was afraid they'd want to fire me and that I'd have to explain that I'd never meant to upset Uncle Frank. Thank God, he laughed.

PLAYBOY: Before *Laugh-In* went off the air, you were hired as a regular on *The Richard Pryor Show*. Why didn't *that* series make it?

WILLIAMS: Richard got nailed by the network censors in the opening shot of the first show, and that was the beginning of his frustration with TV. It was sad, because he went into it with so much hope. I don't know if you remember this, but the first show was supposed to open with a close-up of him saying, "I'm on TV—*me*, Richard Pryor—and I didn't have to give up a thing." Then they were going to pan down on him and he'd be nude until the camera got below his waist, and after that, he'd have nothing down there—sort of like a Barbie doll. Well, that shot was shown on every newscast at all hours of the day, and they had big photos of it in *The New York Times*—but NBC cut it out of the show. After six or seven weeks, he was so disappointed that he'd just do his old nightclub act as his monolog; they'd run film on him for 45 minutes, and after the broadcast-standards people got through editing it, they could use maybe three minutes.

That was the first chance I ever had to uncork on TV, and it didn't happen again until I got the part of Mork on a *Happy Days* episode. When I auditioned for it, I made every bizarre noise and gesture I could think of, and the director, Jerry Paris, hired me and pretty much let me play it the way I wanted to. The show got some positive feedback, and for whatever reason, ABC decided to use the Mork character in a spin-off series.

PLAYBOY: Two weeks after *Mork & Mindy* went on the air, it became one of TV's top-rated series; and since then, you really *have* been in the big time. Do you ever worry that your career might suddenly collapse as abruptly as it took off?

WILLIAMS: I've thought about that, sure. Sometimes I think I might wind up like that old sleaze-bag character I do, sitting in a bar on Pico Boulevard and saying, "Remember me? I did a lot of good stuff in my time." The other extreme is that I wind up like Reagan, saying, "Valerie and I are happy to be in the White House. I'm glad I've succeeded Monty Hall as President, and I'll try to keep *Let's Make a Détente* an active part of our international policy. Next week, I'll be introducing my Gestalt tax plan: You can pay what you want but only if it feels good."

PLAYBOY: How do you think your future *will* turn out?

WILLIAMS: I have no idea, but I'll settle for Valerie and me living on our ranch in Napa and one day passing on the things I've learned to a child of ours, who'll sit there saying, "*Really*, Daddy, I saw *Popeye* yesterday—did you *have* to squint?" As far as being an actor or a comedian, I'll always perform, because show business is in my blood. Or maybe it's in my feet. Wherever it is, I don't think I'll ever stop.

January 1992

A candid conversation with the fastest mind in comedy about the secrets of acting, the exhilaration of stand-up and the pitfalls of life in Hollywood

In many ways, Robin Williams is just a big kid. Watch him play with eight-year-old son Zachary. Williams is positioned in front of the laptop computer, joystick in hand, as planes fly at him on the screen. He pops them off with childlike enthusiasm. "This is *great!*" he says, racking up kills. "Spielberg loves these, too, you know." Williams is just back from his day on the set of *Hook,* in which he plays, appropriately, Peter Pan, the boy who wouldn't grow up. And what about Zachary, Williams's son and playmate? He stands by quietly as dad downs more planes, patiently waiting his turn.

In other ways, Williams has grown up quite nicely. The stand-up comedian with the quicksilver mind who became an overnight sensation in *Mork & Mindy* has matured into something of a rarity—a true genius in the world of stand-up comedy, as well as one of the country's most respected dramatic actors. Many comics have had success in the movies, but few have enjoyed the esteem that Williams does (or the two Oscar nominations). Nor have many overcome the personal demons Williams faced early in stardom when drugs and alcohol threatened to destroy his career, if not his life.

Now 40, married for a second time and the father of three children, Williams is at his peak. He appears in movies of substance, not mindless comedies, and he has created a family life in Northern California far from the temptations of the Hollywood fast lane.

When *Playboy* first interviewed Williams in 1982, his career was at a crossroads. *Mork & Mindy* had nose-dived in the ratings and was canceled after a four-year run. His first movie, *Popeye,* had been a bomb, and his second, *The World According to Garp,* earned few rave reviews. But his stand-up comedy routines were legendary, racing from a sometimes simple premise—with mimicry, one-liners, characters and anything else he could think of—to cover an encyclopedia of subjects, leaving his audience breathless. *The New York Times* described them as having a "perfervid pace and wild, associative leaps," and worried that his "improvisational method seemed tinged with madness."

Much has happened to Williams in the 10 years since that first interview. After the death of acquaintance John Belushi, he stopped using drugs. His first marriage fell apart in a very public manner, and he's still angry about the way the press covered his divorce and marriage to the woman who had been his son's nanny; his father, a Detroit automobile industry executive, died. Despite the personal upheaval, his professional life started to jell. His stand-up routines became, in the words of *The New York Times*, "sharper and less frenetic." His successful concerts, albums, videotapes and cable specials put him in the top rank of comedians.

In 1986, he joined Whoopi Goldberg and Billy Crystal to found Comic Relief, a yearly benefit for the homeless that appears on HBO. So far, it has raised more than $18 million. He also makes appearances in support of literacy and is an advocate of women's rights.

But it was his development as an actor that surprised many. Not all of his film roles were memorable, especially at first, but as his list of credits began to build, so did his reputation. He followed *Popeye* and *Garp* with *The Survivors* (which also starred Walter Matthau), *Moscow on the Hudson*, *Club Paradise* and *Cadillac Man*. His performance in *Good Morning, Vietnam* earned his first chance at an Academy Award; his second came with *Dead Poets Society*. He followed that by co-starring in *Awakenings* with Robert De Niro, and with a tasty, morbid cameo as a "defrocked" psychiatrist in *Dead Again*. His performance in *The Fisher King* has received excellent reviews. And, of course, he's headlining one of the most anticipated Christmas films—*Hook*, in which he co-stars with Dustin Hoffman (who plays Hook), Julia Roberts (Tinkerbell), Maggie Smith (Wendy) and Bob Hoskins (the pirate Smee).

Director Terry Gilliam has worked with Williams twice, most recently in *The Fisher King* and earlier in *The Adventures of Baron Munchausen*, in which Williams appeared as a giant-headed man in the moon. "The thing with Robin is, he has the ability to go from manic to mad to tender and vulnerable," says Gilliam, who was a founding member of Monty Python. "He's the most unique mind on the planet. There's nobody like him out there."

To catch up with one of our national treasures, we sent contributing editor Lawrence Grobel (whose previous interviews include Marlon Brando and Robert De Niro) to spend three weekends with the Pan Man. Grobel's report:

"Since Robin was smack in the middle of making *Hook,* I was aware he was giving up precious family time to do the interview. Yet, once we started talking, I knew it couldn't be rushed. Williams is a stream-of-consciousness talker, and ideas bounce off him like atoms in a blender. Give him a topic—any topic—and he can do five minutes.

"When he was on a roll, he would often lean toward the tape recorder to make sure nothing was garbled or lost. But he can also be quiet and serious, concerned about social issues and politics. And sometimes, when his pregnant wife, Marsha, would enter the room, he would simply become very loving, almost apologizing for spending this time away from her.

"Throughout our time together, Williams was open and friendly, often more concerned about my welfare than he was about his own. When my car failed to start after one of our sessions, I called my wife to come get me and Robin volunteered himself, his publicist and his gardener to push the car out of the way until a tow truck arrived. The thought of these three men struggling with a car up a steep hill—and the ensuing chiropractic bills—worried me enough that I tried to start it one more time. This time it worked. 'It's okay. I yelled. I'm outa here.'

"'Wait!' Robin yelled. 'You better call your wife.'

"How can you not like a guy who's willing to risk his back pushing your car and then reminds you to call your wife?"

PLAYBOY: This is our second time with you. How did the first interview affect you?

WILLIAMS: To tell you the truth I can't remember it.

PLAYBOY: You can't remember it? That puts us in our place.

WILLIAMS: I can't remember doing all the *Mork & Mindys,* either. It isn't because of the drugs or anything. I didn't even read it when it came out.

Most interviews I didn't read, for fear of having said something strange or having stepped in a hole. So it was fear. Now I'm not afraid. I do read them now, so I won't repeat myself and so I can see what point I am in my life by what I've said. I will read this one.

PLAYBOY: You've described being interviewed as "two lepers doing a tango." Isn't it really one leper—the interviewer—and the subject, who doesn't want to be touched?

WILLIAMS: Eric Idle described it best; he said it's one-way psychotherapy. I'm telling you these things and you're going, "Great." I'm agonizing over some issue and you leave when it's over and say good-bye, and I'm going [*Bob Goldthwait voice*], "Aren't you going to help? Aren't you going to give me any advice?" It's like pouring out this stuff and then you write it down and people will read it, but I don't feel any better. It's like jerking off in a wind tunnel. Whoosh!—it blows back in your face!

PLAYBOY: It all depends on who's asking the questions and the chemistry between you. A lot of journalists aren't as trustworthy as you'd like them to be, and if you can't trust them, you don't open up.

WILLIAMS: [*Shouting into tape recorder*] That was *him*. And I'm *not* Bruce Willis. *He* said it. It was his line. But it's true nine times out of 10, they haven't read your book, they haven't seen your movie, they don't know dick about it. You're waiting for those three questions that you can't deal with. Or the standard ones [*William F. Buckley Jr. voice*]: "What are the influences that make you who you are?" There's always a Jonathan Winters question and one about your mother with the rubber band in her nose. After doing 10 years of interviews, you look for that.

PLAYBOY: We'll try to avoid some of those questions and ask a few new ones. For instance, did it take a lot of persuasion to play Peter Pan?

WILLIAMS: Yeah, I had to convince myself that I could play this.

PLAYBOY: What's the basic story line?

WILLIAMS: Peter's children have been kidnapped. He's grown up and become a man. But then Hook kidnaps his children to bring him back, because he's had no one to fight with for so many years and he's become bored. And the only way to save my children is to go back and fight him as Peter Pan.

PLAYBOY: Did you grow up with Mary Martin as your image of Peter Pan?

WILLIAMS: Oh, yeah. It's weird that Peter Pan has always been played by women, except in the cartoon, where he's a boy. If you read the book, he's a great character. He's forgetful, selfish, cruel—he has all these different aspects to him. Very heroic. But he's an 11-year-old, right on the cusp of sexuality. He's got all these things going on and he's adventurous. And he doesn't really give a shit about anything else. He has this great quote: "Oh, the wonderfulness of me." You hear that from an adult, you go, "Eat my shorts."

PLAYBOY: Did it take a lot of work to get into the character of Peter?

WILLIAMS: It took a lot of hard work to try and get this really anal tone, to find one that is kind of lost but still believable as a man-boy—as a guy who suffers from a Peter Pan complex because, in reality, he is Peter Pan! Once in a while he'll be talking and all of a sudden the Pan will come out and he'll think, Oh, I've got to kill that, that's like, in me. [*In deep* Exorcist *voice*] "Demonic possession. Happy thought." And finding that tone to make it boyish, lost, yet still a guy who makes a living basically screwing people as quickly as he possibly can. [*As the grown-up Pan*] "Damn it, Hook, you know what this place cries out for is development."

PLAYBOY: How much do you work with Dustin Hoffman as Hook?

WILLIAMS: We have about four scenes, with a huge scene at the end, the fight. It's just full out. It's a verbal confrontation. Physical, obviously, with the fighting. And no holds barred. It has to be that way. It has to be everything you've expected Hook and Pan to be. It's truly a learning experience. You sit down and you learn each day, because Dustin comes and he helps. And I write for him. I'll say, "Try a line like this." Because he's so deeply into character, sometimes he can't see to improvise it or to find a line.

In the book, Peter makes fun of Hook, he does his voice. And it gets quite brutal—he kills 14 men, plus Hook. They get offed by this little boy going, "Here's my happy thought, you fuck!" So it has all those levels in it.

Want to know the dark side of Peter Pan? Look at the Khmer Rouge. That's the most frightening army in the whole world, because it was an army of 12-year-olds and they committed most of the atrocities, they were the ones who could get rid of people with no compunction. It's the perfect age for an army—11- and 12-year-olds—because they have all that rage, all the power of pubescence, and they don't give a shit about anything.

PLAYBOY: Does Hoffman play a mean Hook?

WILLIAMS: There's a cruelty to it, but there's also a kind of wonderful comedy as well. It has to be a champagne villain. He has a great quote in the book: "No little children like me." That's a motivating factor.

That's why he hates them. He hates youth and innocence and joy, and he's out to destroy them. Plus he's quite frightening. He uses his hook as a weapon. It's not just some fashion accessory.

PLAYBOY: Speaking of accessories, will Peter have his shadow?

WILLIAMS: They do a wonderful thing with the shadow at the end. There's a great sequence with the young Pan and his shadow, wonderful animation. If they're still doing it, it will be amazing.

PLAYBOY: Has Spielberg lived up to your expectations?

WILLIAMS: Steven has been amazing. At first you think, here's a guy who basically deals in visuals. But no, he knows every movie that's ever been made. He's seen every movie twice. So he knows if someone did something before. And from that, he can give you an idea that goes beyond that. The weird thing that I never expected from him was this humanistic, behavioral directing. I thought he would be more into special effects. Just the opposite. The special effects he likes, they're fun—but he'll suggest pulling back, or adding a little bit more, trying things to make the story have a reality base. If it works, it'll play because the human element works, because of the interrelationships of the characters, not because of all the effects. The effects will be like this wonderful icing. But if the cake sucks, the icing won't mean shit.

PLAYBOY: Since Tinkerbell is played by Julia Roberts, who aborted her wedding to Kiefer Sutherland during the making of *Hook*, there's a lot more interest in her than just six inches of interplay.

WILLIAMS: God, the press on all that was just amazing. Helicopters buzzing her and Kiefer's house. Imagine what that's like at 23 years old. Imagine what it's like for 18-year-olds who get really famous. You're dealing with your sexuality and the world is coming at you like the Super Chief. How can they be balanced in fantasyland? It's like Disneyland staged by the Marquis de Sade. [*As Igor*] "It's the B&D ride. Shut up! You're good, but not that good." [*In high squeaky voice*] "Hi, everybody, it's Masochist Mouse!" [*Piercing scream*] I mean, who thinks it's real? It's like thinking that Disneyland exists. And going, "There really are big mice." [Jeff] Katzenberg [a Disney executive] will call, "Hi, Robin. Why do you keep attacking Disneyland?" I'm not, it's a motif.

PLAYBOY: Is it true that *Hook* is costing more than $70 million?

WILLIAMS: I don't even ask. I don't want to know. I'm not playing with you. I just don't want that pressure. You can't go around worrying about the cost of the movie. No one took any money up front. We said, "Okay, we'll take it in the back end. We don't want to add any more to this."

PLAYBOY: Bob Hoskins plays Hook's main pirate, Smee. What was he like to work with?

WILLIAMS: He's got the most natural grit of anybody I've ever seen. The other day we were supposed to do this scene in a pirate bar, and we're drinking and I was supposed to spit out this fluid. He had this idea. He said, "You know what would be great? You ever spit fire?"

I went, "Pardon me?"

"Spit fire."

"No, I haven't."

"Let me show you how," he said, and he took me outside. He used to do it in a circus. And he lit this thing, like a piece of cotton, and took some kerosene and said, "Don't you fucking do this with gasoline or you'll kill yourself," and then blew with his cheeks, and it was like a blowtorch! I tried it and it didn't do much. He said, "Relax," and showed me again, and after I did it again, out came this flame and I went [*Cockney accent*]: "R-i-i-ight! I spit fire!"

But when we went to do it in the scene, the fire marshal came and said, "You ain't got enough room in here to blow fire, so bag it!" So we didn't do it in the scene. But I did it with him. And that's what it's like working with these guys. It's terrifying thinking of the consequences, but then you get into it and it's like, "Wow! What a great way to stretch."

PLAYBOY: Did you ever stretch too far—to the point where you were overacting?

WILLIAMS: Oh, yeah. They tell me, "Why are you making the Greek tragedy face? To let people know that you're sad?" Bob Hoskins told a great story about doing *Richard III*. He said the first night he was doing it and acting his ass off, everything was *big*! And the audience was snoring: Do not listen to this play while operating heavy machinery. The next night, he asked this old guy who was in the repertory company, "What the fuck am I doing wrong?"

"Here's the trouble, boy: They know you're in deep shit. Now all you have to do is *tell* them."

And that night, he came out and said, "Now is the winter of our discontent," in a regular voice, not throwing it to the audience, and they listened.

With film, it's even more so. The moment you push it or go for a laugh, people know. That's one reason people are so fascinated with Brando—he can keep you transfixed just by looking. And he seems so dangerous in that way, even if you find out later he was thinking of nothing at all.

PLAYBOY: Can you imagine Brando as an aged Peter Pan? Or as Hook?

WILLIAMS: Brando as Pan would be great. They say he has dinner with Michael Jackson once a month. That would be something that would make *My Dinner with Andre* seem like a cartoon.

PLAYBOY: Wasn't Jackson considered for Peter Pan?

WILLIAMS: I think he and Steven had it planned for a while. They were waiting for a script for a long time. If anybody is Peter Pan, he has the credentials. He could play it up the wazoo.

PLAYBOY: We came up with some other names of potential Pans.

WILLIAMS: Want me to guess? Michael J. Fox. Or, wait, I'm blanking on his name. He's a friend sometimes. Did *Big*.

PLAYBOY: Tom Hanks.

WILLIAMS: Tom Hanks, thanks. He's a friend. [*Castigating himself*] "You idiot, you can remember people only by their credits!" Tom, I know your name, I just blanked, 'cause I'm thinking about you playing Peter Pan, you might be taking the part. Let's see, a real interesting choice if you wanted to get a punk Peter Pan would be Gary Oldman. That would be like: "Right! I'm flying. Fucking *fly-y-y-y-i-n-n-n-g-g*! You see it? Follow me, Tinky. Here's *my* happy thought." Who else? Tom Cruise, if you want a kind of Top Pan. What's your list?

PLAYBOY: John Candy?

WILLIAMS: [*Raucous burst of laughter*] He did it! Did you ever see the one where he played Divine playing Peter Pan? It was great. [*Laughs*] "Look at me, flying high." There's that great joke about Kate Smith playing Peter Pan, but the chains broke.

PLAYBOY: How about Linda Hunt?

WILLIAMS: Whoa. [*Strong laughter*] The European directors's versions. Now we're getting into interesting casting. Gérard Depardieu as Pan. [*French accent*] "Luk out, everybudy, luk up here, I'm flying. I have happy thoughts. And then I have sad thoughts. It's the sad thoughts that keep me on the ground for a brief moment. Then I fly again."

PLAYBOY: How about Steven Seagal?

WILLIAMS: [*Tough-guy whisper*] "Yeah, right, I'm, uh . . . are you Hook?" [*Grabs an imaginary arm, snaps it, becomes Hook screaming in pain. Then back to Seagal's voice*] "Look at you now, you've got two hooks, no waiting." He's amazing. Here's a man who practices *aikido*, the gentlest form of martial arts. Yet there's more carnage in his movies than I've ever seen before. The stuff Seagal does makes the Chuck Norris stuff seem so wuss. When Seagal puts people in those locks and he does that snap move—that one where this guy's arm just popped out—it was the most physical, brutal thing I've ever seen in movies.

PLAYBOY: How about Al Pacino as Peter Pan?

WILLIAMS: [*Pauses, thinks, defeated*] I can't do him.

PLAYBOY: How about De Niro?

WILLIAMS: [*Whistles. Becomes De Niro's character in* Taxi Driver] "What? You want me to fly? You want me to fly? Excuse me? I have happy thoughts. I have happy thoughts. You want me to fly? Right. Lost Boys. Right." Raging Pan. [*Changes to De Niro as Jake La Motta*] "'Scuse me. 'Scuse me. What? I'm supposed to fly? Pardon me. Yeah, kiss . . . my tights. 'Scuse me. I'm flyin'. Can't you see? I'm off the ground. I'm flyin'."

PLAYBOY: And in the end, do you and the Lost Boys and Wendy all fly away, like *E.T.* without the bicycles? Just sprinkled with dust?

WILLIAMS: That'll be at the end. I have to fly home with my family, I have to take my son and daughter back. It is interesting playing it after reading all the literature about the Peter Pan syndrome. It's a very Victorian tale that Barrie told. Basically about abandonment, orphans, dissociation from parents. And also the end, when he comes back to see Wendy, and she's old and he can't deal with it, so he takes her daughter. Here's this girl who gives him her heart and he goes, "Yeah, thank you, you're too old, kiss my ass, I'm outa here." [*Suddenly goes into Al Pacino's character in* And Justice for All] "I'm outa order, you're outa order, I'm flying, I've got my happy thought." Pacino Pan. "I'm outa dust, you're outa dust, you're old, you're wrinkled, go!" How about Bette Davis as Wendy? "Get over here. Shut up! Get over here, you little creep. But you are! You're a fairy!"

PLAYBOY: With Pan in the can, will you be glad to get out of Los Angeles and return to your home in Northern California?

WILLIAMS: Yeah. This place is strange for me. It's a fantasy life, just very surreal. It's a city where they have drive-by shootings, two-shot minimum. When you're in L.A. for more than a month, you bump into your career too much. You start reading the trades, looking for your name. You get paranoid about how you're doing. We're living in this rented house in this security area in Bel Air where you go, fuck—this is a fortress. There's a gate, a little beeper, a guy that comes if you press the beeper. What is that? Is that the way it's supposed to be? N-o-o-o-o. But it's the reality of this place and that's why I don't live here. People do pretty horrible business things to each other and still try and hang socially here. I don't come down and hang out here. The house we just bought in San Francisco is at the mouth of the bay and you can go from there through this beautiful park and up along the western beaches. It's incredible. It's nice to have distance between you and the world.

PLAYBOY: You talk about horrible business things. Have you ever been screwed over?

WILLIAMS: Yeah, I'm still getting fucked with. You're not immune from it at any level.

PLAYBOY: Are you talking about being passed over for the Joker in *Batman* and losing the lead role in the upcoming film *Jack the Bear* to Danny DeVito?

WILLIAMS: What they do a lot of times, they bait people. They'll say, "Robin might do this, are you in or out?" A lot of things are word of mouth and a lot of people are offered something and then, immediately, it's taken away and given to somebody else. There are many stories of Gene Hackman getting offered a film and then they're pulling him because Paul Newman comes back.

PLAYBOY: Were you used as bait to get Jack Nicholson to play the Joker?

WILLIAMS: Yeah. I was a little pissed by that. He'd been offered it six months before and then it was given to me. I replied, but they said I was too late. They said they'd gone to Jack over the weekend because I didn't reply soon enough. I said, "You gave me till Monday, I replied before the deadline." But it was just to get Jack off the pot.

PLAYBOY: And what happened more recently with *Jack the Bear?*

WILLIAMS: That was a case where something was written for me, developed for me and they gave it to somebody else. It was just a breakdown in the system. But I don't want to harbor hatred, anger. I just have to keep working. Otherwise, how do you separate yourself from not wanting to go and buy an automatic weapon, kick down the studio doors and say, "I'm coming"? That's why stand-up is great. It really helps to defuse that.

PLAYBOY: But haven't you also had problems in that area, as well? Didn't some magazines print complaints from comics accusing you of stealing their material?

WILLIAMS: I don't believe that shit. I bought that rap for a long time with a certain guilt, thinking, You're right, I'm no original. Yeah, I hung out in clubs eight hours a night, improvising with people, playing with them, doing routines. And I heard some lines once in a while and I used some lines on talk shows accidentally. That's what got me that reputation and that's why I'm fucking fed up with it. If I found out I used someone's line, I paid for it—way beyond the call. But thinking that I'm sitting around listening to people and saying, "Oh, that's great, I'll use that." No, that's horseshit. To say that I go out and look for people's material is bullshit and fucked. And I'm tired of taking the rap for it. People used a lot of my stuff, too. You're supposed to just go, "Well, that's flattery." And sometimes people give you lines. A drunken guy came up to me years ago on the street and said, "Robin, here's something for you: 'Cocaine is God's way of saying you're making too much fucking money.'" A lot of times people come up and tell you this stuff. And you have to be careful. Did they hear this somewhere else? That's why I avoid anything to do with clubs. People keep saying, "Why don't you do The Comedy Store?" I don't want to go back and get that rap again from anybody.

Another thing is, I don't want to take anybody else's time. I got tired of [other comics] giving me looks, like, what the fuck are you doing here? Maybe sometimes, don't you understand, if I show up, it might bring other people to see you? You idiot. People come to some of these clubs hoping to see people like me, once in a while, and that's great if they can see you beforehand.

PLAYBOY: If you don't go to clubs to work out the frustrations of the movie business, what do you do for release?

WILLIAMS: Sometimes I get it with groups of friends. Invite people over and go, "Two-drink minimum." I miss it, yeah. It's just hard to find the clubs right now because they are so jammed. You don't want to bump anybody. If I go on any place, it's usually in the middle of the week, late at night, unannounced. When no one else is fucking there, so no one can say, "You took my line."

PLAYBOY: Does stand-up help you with your acting?

WILLIAMS: The outrageousness and aggressiveness of it is perfect sometimes for acting. But the other side of acting is to peel all that away, just take off all the armor.

Someone asked Nicholson, "What is acting?" And he said, "Why should I tell you the fucking tricks?" Every person is driven by some deep, deep, deep secret and finding it drives you through.

PLAYBOY: Do you look for those secrets?

WILLIAMS: Yeah, you look for that, to help fuel the whole thing. I don't know the great secrets of acting, I'm just now learning that it's getting to the point where you don't act. Some sort of Zen concept where you finally realize that what you think is acting, you shouldn't do anymore.

PLAYBOY: If acting is ultimately letting people in, doesn't that contrast with stand-up, which often means being aggressive to keep people at a distance?

WILLIAMS: It can be as aggressive as you want to be, depending on how fearless you are. Sometimes you want to keep people at a distance—people who have had four cocktails, 12 beers, going, "Blow me!" Do you really want to let them in? Come, let me share with you my deepest secrets. But sometimes you do, you'll find the right group of people and you'll just talk about shit that will amaze you. But you should be careful, because you might start talking about something you're not ready to deal with.

PLAYBOY: Has that ever happened to you?

WILLIAMS: No, I kind of watch over that. Some issues are deeply personal. I get near them and think, I'm not ready to deal with that yet. When you're comfortable with it, you can be free about it. If not, it's open-heart surgery.

PLAYBOY: Do you have an interior voice that sometimes censors you?

WILLIAMS: It's a voice that tells you, *danger.* There was a night at the Holy City Zoo [in San Francisco] where four guys started to get nasty. It became very confrontational. Are you up for it? Depends. Are you up for the fact that the worst thing you say escalates to violence? Can you deal with that? It can get a little prime. I never drank or did drugs onstage, but there were times when I thought I was going to go crispy, mainly because I was hung over. And one time, someone gave me a line of coke before I went out. For me, cocaine made me paranoid, and being onstage is not exactly the place to go when you're paranoid. It was a short trip to hell. When I drank, the audience would send up a kamikaze switch—vodka and lime juice—chilled. They just want to see you drop. Kill the comic, flatten the boy. Watch the little furry guy go down. And one night, I almost did. I had four of them. I don't remember what I said, but people said it was pretty funny. I was dancing with chairs. But I didn't want that lack of control.

PLAYBOY: Vincent Canby once described your monolog as "so intense that one feels that at any minute the creative process could reverse into a complete personality meltdown." Have you ever felt that could happen?

WILLIAMS: Where it's beyond "Love me, please love me, or I might destroy myself"? It's like comedy terrorism. But all I'm doing is taking and expanding out from an idea. You say a sentence and some word will trigger another word and sometimes they'll all turn back onto each other and you'll come back to the original premise. Then, when you really feel great, you're just freeforming and there's no connection between the inspiration and the bit. Then you don't know what it is. It becomes one of those out-of-body experiences. At the Improv in San Francisco one night, just before the Gulf war started, I hadn't been onstage in a long time and all this stuff I'd been thinking about just exploded. Marsha said, "I've never seen you so together and yet so free." Even Garry Shandling, who was there, said, "You fucker." I did a whole piece about the Christian religion, where it started off as a mom-and-pop religion where Mom was a virgin and Pop was God, and then it got organized and you can't have a pop anymore, it has to be a Pope, kiss the ring. The bit just got so large it almost got frightening. It was getting near the edges of people's credulity, where you start to fuck with the premise of what they hold near and dear.

PLAYBOY: Do you ever worry that you'll run out of ideas?

WILLIAMS: No, there's a world out there. Open the window and it's there. The world is changing now, it's beyond arithmetic. It's like into some Malthusian nightmare. In two seconds, governments are gone. Oops, it's Lithuania—no, it's Yugoslavia—no, it's two countries. It's changing that quick. And there's so much to play off. We're living in this momentary society. If you want to be topical, that's the danger.

PLAYBOY: What happens when you're out there improvising and you suddenly draw a blank?

WILLIAMS: Oh, that happens a lot. To the point where you hit Premise Prairie. Nothing there. What do you do? Oh, God, the great abyss. Do you fall back on something old? Or do you die the death of deaths and try to go on? Can you find the courage to push yourself beyond the cliché and go to the next step? If you take the chance, sometimes you'll find something so magnificent that it was worth dying for, and sometimes you'll find nothing and have a horrible night. To go deeper with it, that's the most interesting challenge.

PLAYBOY: Have you ever been envious of another comic's routines?

WILLIAMS: I was just envious of other people's daring. Like Richard Pryor's ability to be so bold in talking about himself. Total candor. Now he's this fragile man. I've seen him go onstage and people start yelling shit and he doesn't know how to respond to them. Where in the old days he'd go, "Fuck me. Go away, motherfucker! Blow me! Suck my dick! I'll put it out here, bring your little dumb ass. . . ." One night, about five years ago, he went on, Eddie Murphy went on and I went on, and Richard was kicking again, it was great. When he kicks, there's no one in the world better. No one has ever done what he does. He is the king of that. He did the best performance movie. And his stand-up, he set the rules. Then destroyed the boundaries.

PLAYBOY: Has he gone places where you've drawn the line?

WILLIAMS: I don't want to talk that personally. Richard took it to the level of self-immolation. To the level of destruction. Some people have taken it to the point of disemboweling themselves onstage, to rage, to total anxiety. When Sam Kinison was starting out, it was incredible because it was so painful, and hilarious because he was talking about relationships. "I'm married . . . *a-g-h-h-h-h-h!*" And what struck you was the fact that this schlub had been through all this, and then he took another turn and got into a whole other area.

PLAYBOY: Who are the comedians who make you laugh?

WILLIAMS: Up until recently, if it's stand-up, you've got to say Pryor, George Carlin. Kinison. Bob Goldthwait. Charlie Fleischer for obscure comedy—he does wonderful, strange impressions. Among comics, if you asked who's their favorite, usually Jay Leno is in the top three, if not the top, because he is so quick and he's the most topical of anybody. He has that Elvis jaw, that face you could cut windows with, but he has a rock-hard view of the world that cuts through shit on either side. Like he was doing all those Sununu jokes, just beating the shit out of him. Then he had a great line about Russia starting a democratic party; he said, "Why don't they use ours, we're not using it?" He can fire both ways.

PLAYBOY: What do you think of David Letterman and Arsenio Hall?

WILLIAMS: Doing television sucks material out of you like a vacuum cleaner on speed. Letterman is doing the same stuff he was doing years and years ago, this acerbic thing where he'd just let people hang themselves. He's brilliant at that. Arsenio is an interesting combination of *schmoozing* and doing great characters.

PLAYBOY: How often do you rely on finding comedy through characters?

WILLIAMS: Characters are just a free way of talking as yourself. One night, I did that with Terry Gilliam. I created this ax murderer, a character he said was really frightening but hilarious. This very sweet guy who had killed people. Gilliam would ask me questions and I just started going with it.

PLAYBOY: You've worked with Gilliam on two films, *The Adventures of Baron Munchausen* and, more recently, *The Fisher King*. He seems to be an unusual director.

WILLIAMS: He's like John Huston, one of those people who has a vision, a way of seeing the world. Some people think it's askew, some think it's brilliant. Terry shoots stuff that has a half life. You walk out and it hits you. Whew! Shit! Fuckin' 60 foot samurais! Red knights! Icarus! Simple things! He creates images that are shot into your skull.

PLAYBOY: In *The Fisher King*, you're playing a role more like Leonard, the character De Niro played in *Awakenings*—the innocent who winds up in a hospital with semicomatose people. Have you considered the irony?

WILLIAMS: It is somewhat ironic that I end up in a catatonic state. It was strange. And almost similar, except my character is lying down and his was in a wheelchair. The thing that appealed to me was not, "Oh, it will be great, now I'll get to play the other part." It was that the story was so interesting and the characters were so balanced. It has this wonderful strange going-back-and-forth quality to it—where one moment it's very funny and the next it's horrifying. That's what I liked about it.

PLAYBOY: You shot *Awakenings* at a Brooklyn mental hospital. How tough was that mentally?

WILLIAMS: It was grueling, because there were real folks there on the bottom two floors. There was a ward that we never saw, of violent, criminally insane guys. You'd hear them screaming sometimes. It was depressing. It would make even Kafka go, "Too much." It's really the dark side.

PLAYBOY: That touching scene when Leonard awakens—were you off camera doing things to make him laugh?

WILLIAMS: Bob would say, "Surprise me." So I did Harvey Fierstein talking to him. "Leonard, sweetheart, lose the puppy on the pajamas. Come over here, darling, did Mom bring you that terrycloth robe? Do you want some slippers?" I could drop him doing that.

PLAYBOY: You've worked with De Niro and now Hoffman. What did you get from them?

WILLIAMS: Dustin's a guy who will try anything. He prepares up the ass, too. He's doing makeup tests, trying to make himself look totally different, trying to transform. I've been on three films that he was supposed to do: *Popeye, Garp* and *Dead Poets*. I should be just hanging out by his house. "What did you pass on? Yeah? Okay, that sounds good. What else?"

From Bob, you get the power of silence, of the deep-diving man. It's scary. To be in the same room with Bob and you're acting with him. [*Becomes interviewer*] "What are the fun things you want to do?" [*Answers in a high-pitched voice*] "I want to run a marathon with Frank Shorter, box with Mike Tyson and act with Bob De Niro." You see how little he does and you think, What the fuck is this? But he knows how powerful he is. It's total economy. Borders on rarefied. He knows exactly to the vowel what's too much.

PLAYBOY: Oliver Sacks, the doctor who wrote *Awakenings*, said he thought that the way your unconscious and preconscious mind worked was a form of genius.

WILLIAMS: Oh, God, coming from him! Really? I feel like the Rain Man: "That's okay, that's okay, gotta go now, gotta make in my underwear. Thanks, Oliver, gotta go, gotta go." Oliver thinks on levels that I've never dreamed of, because he has so much information. And he differentiates between the mind and the brain. The brain controls bodily functions and whatever. And then there's this thing called the mind, which has to do with soul, with elements of philosophy, with things that are so deep and profound and beyond anything that you can analyze, but in essence, it drives it all.

PLAYBOY: So what do you think of his assessing you a genius?

WILLIAMS: Can I call myself a genius? *N-o-o-o!* I can say I get flashes once in a while. These riffs that run through you and you know it's something you've never done before, and that's great. There are people who live in that zone. Have you read [physicist] Richard Feynman's book [*Surely You're Joking, Mr. Feynman*]? These people fascinate me. If there's any profession I envy, it's that. Imagine what it's like to be Stephen Hawking and to come up with the Theory of Everything. But he's got the job and he's doing it great. I wonder if there are guys who collect just scientists' autographs. "Excuse me, pardon me, Mr. Oppenheimer, seen all your bombs, could you please sign this? God bless ya. Could you put your name near your particle?"

PLAYBOY: Would you put any actors in the pantheon of geniuses?

WILLIAMS: The Brando man. Mr. Nicholson. Mr. De Niro. Mr. Hoffman, just because he keeps trying different things. Al Pacino. Duvall for his great characters. The younger ones? Probably one of the finest actors on film is Gary Oldman. And actresses? Meryl [Streep]. Susan Sarandon. [*Pauses*] God, this is hard, it sounds like I'm pimping for work.

Another genius who lives in that painful zone is Carrie Fisher. She's constantly pushing herself to find new stuff and says brilliant things on a pretty consistent level. She's very literate, lives on that painful edge, almost beyond that edge.

PLAYBOY: Geniuses in other arts?

WILLIAMS: God. Did you ever hear the music of Keith Jarrett? Some of the piano pieces just pour out of him.

Other geniuses? There are people who push the parameters. They take you someplace else. Musically, who keeps pushing the envelope? Just in terms of songs, you think of someone like Tracy Chapman, who tries things. Paul Simon. People may now think he's getting redundant because he's done another ethnic album, but no. Think of Bob Dylan. Think of who the people are you'd want to talk to. They must have some kind of genius if you're thinking, I want to know what makes that fucker tick.

What makes Dylan go [*improvises as Dylan*]: "Time is enriched/ Where does that poetry come from?/A man who changes religion more than he can change his shoes. I'm a wandering Jew from Malibu/Whaddya say we gotta do?/Look at me rip off Zimmerman!/I was a Christian, then Hasidim/For the things I truly need."

He writes some great poetry. And it kicks. Your may wonder what he is saying, but it's wonderful stuff. In comedy, you think of Pryor. But that's genius born of total pain. George Carlin. He just keeps pushing it. He doesn't care. He did a great piece in Comic Relief about golf courses and graveyards. He lives in that zone where stuff keeps coming through him.

In literature, [Kurt] Vonnegut. No one is consistent, no one bats a thousand.

PLAYBOY: Ever read James Joyce?

WILLIAMS: Tried. Read the first couple lines of *Ulysses*, then went, whew, thanks, I'll wait till the punctuation's in.

PLAYBOY: You seem to transform yourself from movie to movie, jumping from the sensitive teacher of *Dead Poets* to the sleazy car salesman of *Cadillac Man* to the vulnerable doctor in *Awakenings*, the wounded knight errant in *The Fisher King* and now the boy-man Peter Pan. Are there any films you've made for reasons other than artistic ones?

WILLIAMS: *Club Paradise.* They said it would be a box-office smash, a great combination of people, we'll kick ass, etc. And then [*explosion sound*] my ass got kicked. That's when you get screwed. Jump off with your passion, not as a whore. I believed in *The Fisher King* and in *Hook.* In the stories. With *Hook*, it's not blowing people away, stabbing and slicing and killing—it's about heart and family and love and orphans and interesting and deep issues for all of us in an age of greed. And *Fisher King* I did because it's about bottom-line compassion, about redemption, about not taking people on initial value but looking deeper. It's about dependency and strange relationships that come and go.

PLAYBOY: Is that why you did *Dead Poets Society?*

WILLIAMS: It talks about something of the heart and of pursuing that which is a dream—and in some cases, to a tragic end. Originally, my character was supposed to have leukemia, which would have been *Dead Poets Love Story*. Then Peter Weir said, "Let's lose that. Focus on the boys." Lose the melodrama and it becomes much simpler and much better.

PLAYBOY: Brando says that comics are people with a lot of anger and pain. Have you felt much pain and anger?

WILLIAMS: No. Number one, I didn't go through a very tough childhood. I used to joke about it. Say, "I was 16 before I had my first Mercedes." Or, "I had to work all summer long just to go to Europe." I had a wonderful childhood. All I suffered from was a lack of a lot of parental contact and being raised basically by the black maid. There may have been some uncomfortable moments, but no anger or bitterness. It's not, "Shit! Fuck! This world sucks!" I just made this incredible fantasy life because I had only myself to play with.

PLAYBOY: Did you have any kind of rite of passage into manhood?

WILLIAMS: You mean put your penis on a rock, bang your balls with this big stone and now you're a man? No. Was it Confirmation? No, because I'm Protestant, idiot! There's no Confirmation. There's just escrow. I really made the transition to manhood when I went away to college, moving away from home to where there was no one dictating what choices I had to make and I went berserk for one year. I just went, "Fuck this! There are girls to sleep with! And improvisational-theater classes, where you don't have to learn any lines and people laugh." I did all the shit that I ever wanted to do. Flunked out of all the political science classes, but found what I'm doing now. It was this weird catharsis. Total freedom. Like going from Sing Sing to a Gestalt nudist camp. Everything opened up. The whole world just changed in that one year.

Then came the second transitional period, when I was about 30, when I started to talk to my father [shortly before his death]. That was like the *Wizard of Oz*, where you look behind that curtain and you see the man for what he is. There was this little man behind the curtain, going, "Take care of your mother and I love you and I've been very worried about certain things. And I'm afraid, but I'm not afraid." It's an amazing combination of exhilaration and sadness at the same time, because the god transforms to a man.

PLAYBOY: How strict was he when you were a boy?

WILLIAMS: Not very strict at all. He was stern. He looked like a retired English viceroy, he had that kind of laid-back way about him. I never heard my pop yell, except once when I flipped my mother the bird. That's the one time I got smacked. They were yin and yang, my parents, who gave me a kind of perfect balance to do what I do now. My mother's this outrageous character who's so sweet and basically believes in the goodness of people. And Dad had seen the nasty sides of people. He had been in combat. She told me, "There are no boundaries." And he gave me this depth that helps with acting and even with comedy, saying, "Fuck it. Do you believe in this? Do you really want to talk about it? Do it. Don't be frightened off." Somewhere in his early life, he had to give up certain things, certain dreams. And when I found mine, he was deeply pleased. He was working his tits off to make this life and he had been screwed over by too many people in the automobile industry, which uses you and discards you just like the movie industry. He had seen that my life was in transition and that I was starting to take control.

PLAYBOY: Weren't there some problems with your parents' taking you out of boarding school to live with them?

WILLIAMS: No, I wanted to go back home because I wanted to be with my family. My mother's so naive about certain things. *The National Enquirer* called her and said, "We're doing a story and we'd like to have some photos." She gave them photos of my father and me and some school photos. They used these pictures to imply that my father was this tyrant and I came from this horrible existence and that's why I was funny.

PLAYBOY: And how did your mother react when she saw that story?

WILLIAMS: She felt used, and she was. But that is also balanced with her desire to sometimes be in the limelight. Normally, if I'm with her and I see cameras, I say, "Let's go, Mom." And she turns into Bette Davis. She's saying, "Stop! Let's talk to them." It gets interesting. But it can sometimes feel like psychic rape. Like the *People* interview. When you do these things, you get halfway through and you realize, My god, they're sticking it to me. It's like this feeling of violation. And what's weird is they're stabbing you with your own kitchen utensils. "That's my fork!"

PLAYBOY: Let's talk about that *People* cover, where they sensationalized your leaving your wife Valerie for your child's nanny, Marsha. There was a very strong anti-*People* reaction within the entertainment industry because of that, wasn't there?

WILLIAMS: I think so. They went from being a magazine people wanted to do to a magazine people were wary of. It was really a hatchet job, a setup, an ambush. A very low blow. And it cost them. Celebrities got very worried, like, Why should I do a story with you?

PLAYBOY: Would you ever do another story with them?

WILLIAMS: No. Not while the management is the same.

PLAYBOY: They described your life then as being at "the apex of a triangle of tension."

WILLIAMS: The tension was only that I was trying to tidy up the last ends of my first marriage and get on with my life with Marsha. And the fact that I didn't want to talk about that, because I was trying to be respectful of my first marriage and end it decently. And then it just exploded. But I was so angry and horrified that the interview turned this way, it was like being mugged. At the end, they said, "We have to ask you certain questions or you don't get the cover." Fuck it, I don't need a cover that badly. I sat down and talked to the reporter very personally and said, "This is what's up, this is the truth." And they didn't put any of it in. They made it seem exactly what they wanted to do from the very beginning: Marsha broke up the marriage. Which is total horseshit.

PLAYBOY: What is the truth?

WILLIAMS: I had been separated and away from my wife for a year by the time Marsha and I became involved. And the reason my marriage fell apart had nothing to do with Marsha, it was with a total other woman that I can't even get into now for legal reasons.

PLAYBOY: Is this the woman who sued you, claiming you gave her herpes?

WILLIAMS: I can't discuss it, it's what's called a gag order, you're not allowed to discuss it till it gets settled. I had this wanderlust and so did Valerie. And Marsha was working as my assistant at that time. She would just talk me down. I was not suicidal but fucked up. My wife was living with another man, I was just out of my fucking mind. I was very indignant and self-righteous and Marsha said, "Listen, asshole, there's no reason to be indignant, you were no prince, she was no saint." After about a year, I started into therapy. I was living in a house on the beach and started to get my life together and I fell in love with Marsha. And that's why my life was saved by her, not ruined by her. That was a troubled time, and enough said.

PLAYBOY: Marsha has called herself your safety net. How strong is she?

WILLIAMS: It's more than just a safety net, it's a reality check. She's real honest about everything. If I start to get too insecure, she'll say, "Stop it, you're great." And she's very creative, too. She was a weaver, but she gave it up to help me with my work. She was writing with me, she would write on *Good Morning, Vietnam*. She makes sure everything runs. Not that I have a huge entourage. I mean, I've got her, I've got . . . I mean, she's not an entourage. [*As interviewer*] "How many in your entourage?" [*Pompously*] "Well, the family. Zelda, who I can write off as a roadie." [*As the child Zelda*] "Daddy, can't carry bags, bags heavy."

PLAYBOY: You moved your family to New York when you did Samuel Beckett's *Waiting for Godot* with Steve Martin at Lincoln Center. How was that experience?

WILLIAMS: Painful. We put our ass out and got kicked for it. Some nights I would improvise a bit and the hard-core Beckett fans got pissed off. We played it as a comedy team; it wasn't existential. Like these two guys from vaudeville who would go into routines that would fall apart into angst. Basically, it's Laurel and Hardy, which is how Beckett had staged it in Germany.

PLAYBOY: Did you and Martin learn anything from each other?

WILLIAMS: I learned about physical comedy and the nuts and bolts about timing from him, because, obviously, when I do my act, I have as much timing as an Uzi! And his is the comedy of pause, of waiting, of holding back. I don't know what he learned from me. Perhaps about how not to be that anxious or obsessive. I also got to know about his appreciation of art. I've seen some of the art he has bought and I thought, Wow, while I was off putting half my profits up my nose, that's what you were doing. You were buying that. He trades paintings as if they were baseball cards.

PLAYBOY: During the early 1980s, when you were snorting your profits away, how out of control did you get?

WILLIAMS: I was totally out of control for a while. It was either fear or just a sheer wanting to run away from it all. I couldn't imagine living the way I used to live. I don't remember it as being anything except quick, with this series of people flashing through my life. Now people come up to me from the drug days and go, "Hi, remember me?" And I'm going, "No, did I have sex with you? Did I take a dump in your tool box?" It was kind of like my head was in a bell jar. I got crazier and crazier and then petered off.

PLAYBOY: When did it stop?

WILLIAMS: After John [Belushi] died. A month or two after that.

PLAYBOY: A lot was made of your visit to Belushi the night before he died, but you were reluctant to discuss openly exactly what happened. Have you ever talked about it?

WILLIAMS: I discussed it with the grand jury. I went to see John, he didn't want to see me and I left. And that was it. It was blown into this whole evening of debauchery. Like we'd been out together all evening.

PLAYBOY: Why didn't Belushi want to see you?

WILLIAMS: I have a strange feeling it was some sort of miscommunication or a setup in some way, because I went there and there were these strange people there—his friends—and he was loaded. I asked, "Are you okay?" He said, "Yeah, I've taken a couple 'Ludes." He didn't look like he wanted me there and I split. And next day he's dead. It was like seeing an elephant go down. Here's this guy who was a beast, who could do anything, and he's gone. That sobered the shit out of everybody.

PLAYBOY: Did you know Belushi well?

WILLIAMS: I knew him vaguely, I was with him a couple of times. Drinking once. There was one time that was magnificent, because we both sat and watched Jonathan Winters perform. That was the sanest I ever saw him.

PLAYBOY: That brings us to one of those questions you're often asked: What is it about Jonathan Winters that so inspired you?

WILLIAMS: It was like seeing a guy behind a mask, and you could see that his characters were a great way for him to talk about painful stuff. I found out later that they are people he knows—his mother, his aunt. He's an artist who also paints with words, he paints these people that he sees. I knew how his act worked when I went to his house and saw his special room. Then I wanted to have a special room like that.

PLAYBOY: What was in his special room?

WILLIAMS: Just things he's collected, pictures of presidents that he's performed for. Kachinas, little dolls, lead soldiers, antique toys, an entire wall of antique pistols. I went, "You're like me, we both collect information, we collect images and we play them back in this kind of room." You can see how it affects his art, it's his room, his mind room. And now I have a room like that.

PLAYBOY: What do you hold to be most valuable in your room?

WILLIAMS: Einstein's autograph. An English naval cutlass my father gave me. And my most precious object is another thing my father gave me, a little carved netsuke called a Peach Seed Man. It's a little boy popping out of a peach seed. When my dad gave it to me a couple weeks before he died, he said, "This is you."

PLAYBOY: Before children start seeing you as Peter Pan, do a lot of them still recognize you as Mork? Do you still get a lot of "*Nano nano*" when you walk down the street?

WILLIAMS: Some of that still goes on, but that's in their brains, in the memory bank of a country because it comes from TV. Watch the way people watch TV, it's hypnotic. Just sit back and you've got cable and 95 choices and you don't really care much about anything else. Eventually, you don't know about history, you can't remember if there really was a Civil War, and eventually people get slaves again. You can have a president who basically reads cue cards and it seems okay, because he's just like the guy on the series with the family with the little black child and it seems all right, because he's kind, and when he's angry, it's TV angry, where you get kind of angry but you don't go, "Fuck off!" You basically get where your eyes dim and the world seems all right and you kind of tighten up so much that your sphincter doesn't open. Then people at home can be TV pissed and they can go to a TV war and watch it. We basically fought a war, watched it on the TV set, and you can buy the tapes, sucking on the glass teat.

PLAYBOY: It's been almost a year since the Gulf war. Any opinions on that?

WILLIAMS: Getting involved in the Middle East is like tap-dancing in quicksand. There have been similar struggles for about 2000 years. What did we fight for? We fought for these Kuwaiti princes who, for most of the time, were in Zurich going, "Service! I am very upset about my people, hold on. . . . Put the plate over here and the champagne over there." And when they came back, the first thing they did was rebuild their pools. Everything went back to where it was before, except Saddam has fewer toys. Why was it a big surprise that as soon as the war was over, he'd go back to doing the same things, business as usual? I don't believe the war changed much. We'll probably have to do something like that again in the future. These are people who don't play by rules.

PLAYBOY: Before George Bush became president, you said he was the kind of guy a rattlesnake would refuse to bite out of professional courtesy.

WILLIAMS: And look how right I was. [*As John Wayne*] If you take John Wayne and tighten up his ass, [*now as Bush*] there you have George Bush. I do political voices once in a while just because you gotta keep making fun of the great Bushmeister. He's just incredible.

PLAYBOY: Do you think there's anybody among the Democrats who has a chance against Bush?

WILLIAMS: It's hard, because you're fighting an image. You've been fighting eight years of Mr. Warmth and now George has proved he has the *cojones*, so who are you going to fight with? You have to come back with someone of notable character and charisma—not things the Democratic Party is going out of its way to look for, if you look at the last two candidates. Bill Bradley could be quite wonderful, he could debate the piss out of Bush, but he doesn't have that charisma. Gore Vidal? Just watch him redecorate the White House! [Mario] Cuomo? He's certainly charismatic and powerful, but there's the sheer ethnic thing of people going [*backwoods voice*]: "Cuomo? He's a cuomosexual. What the hell's that? I ain't votin' for no Cuomo!" With no holds barred, I would say Barbara Jordan. This woman is as powerful as anyone you'll ever hear. She has this dignity. She's a black woman from Texas and she kicks ass there. She's amazing, sounds like Roosevelt when she speaks, has that kind of voice. If she was feeling better, I'd say bingo!

PLAYBOY: Do you think that poking fun at our problems can do anything to help solve them?

WILLIAMS: What's changed for me in the last four years is rather than just sit and criticize, you say okay, what can you actually do to start wading into it and make it work, instead of just saying, "You're wrong, that sucks, they're ripping us off." Now we have to fight from our local community up, and work on schools and for the homeless. All that's left now in a lot of our schools is reading, writing and arithmetic, everything else is considered catsup.

PLAYBOY: You do a lot of work for the homeless through Comic Relief. Do you also do things for education?

WILLIAMS: Yeah, plenty of stuff, charity things for schools and literacy programs. We're raising a nation of overweight, unintelligent people. The cities have broken down, the educational systems suffer cutbacks. The reality is, we're broke. Art exhibits, nudity in films and magazines, abortions, it's all up for grabs now.

PLAYBOY: Do you think abortions will eventually return to being illegal?

WILLIAMS: Poor people will either be forced to have the children or to go to these horrible doctors who function on the fringe. Making the decision to have an abortion is no easy choice for anybody, and if it isn't a hard choice, then the woman's not really going to make a great mother anyway.

PLAYBOY: Have you ever gone through it?

WILLIAMS: Long, long, long time ago, and it was because we were too young and it wasn't right. Here's what bothers me more than anything about those who believe in the right to life: They don't support the second part of the process, when they have all these children. Amend "right to life" to "right to a decent life." They don't support the education, they don't support the health care. If you are going to have a society where it's mandatory to have a child, let's make it mandatory to make this child's life wonderful. I don't want to deny life to anybody, but sometimes you have to choose—and it's a horrible choice, I'm not denying that. To deny people that choice forces them into the other dilemma, and then you raise children who are not loved and who go through a living hell of not being wanted, or are tossed off and live in homes or institutions, or who grow up numb.

PLAYBOY: Does the answer lie in better birth control?

WILLIAMS: Here's the best birth control in the whole world—if you have no pills, no diaphragms, no other forms of contraception, here it is for ladies: If he comes at you with that little thing in his hand, just laugh at it! *Ha, ha, ha.* We can't deal with that. It'll be gone, the little thing will be outa there. Assault with the macaroni, put it away!

I did a recent piece about sex in the 1990s: It's you and you. Put on the special song that only you like. And you don't have to fake orgasm, because it's just you. *Ménage à mono.* In an age where there is this incredibly deadly virus that could take us out as a species, it puts a whole other spin on it. We all look pretty ridiculous during sex. Even Warren Beatty looks pretty fucking stupid at the moment he fires the fool. Whatever strap-on attachment you use, you still look like a poodle and someone has to get a fire hose.

PLAYBOY: You've always been fond of dick jokes, calling it Mr. Weasel, the Throbbing Python of Love, Mr. Happy—

WILLIAMS: The One-Eyed Weasel with No Conscience. For a while, it was the essence of my act. The ultimate dick joke was this tribute the American Cinematheque gave me. It wasn't a tribute, it was a roast. It was a rough night.

PLAYBOY: Why was it rough?

WILLIAMS: Basically, it was an evening talking about me and my dick. It was Robin and Friend. Me and Señor Schmuck. After a while, I felt I should have gone, "Ladies and gentlemen, let him speak for himself." [*As his dick*] "I love the guy and when he's not choking me, he's a fabulous person."

PLAYBOY: Why didn't you do it?

WILLIAMS: How could you follow Billy Crystal, who came out with a giant penis on his head?

PLAYBOY: Wasn't that the tribute where Chevy Chase insulted Disney's Michael Eisner?

WILLIAMS: Yeah. He said, "Michael, do you mind if I pee in your mouth?"

PLAYBOY: How uncomfortable did that night get?

WILLIAMS: It was uncomfortable only in the sense of the outrageousness of it. It got pretty intense. It was like a Friars roast, and I don't think people expected that. I went to Martin Scorsese's Cinematheque tribute and no one went, "Yo! Marty! You bastard, over here." His was more of a real honor. I think people came to mine thinking it was going to be an honor and it was, "Blow me. Why don't you just put your dumb dick on the table?" And Chevy's thing, and then Billy came out as a dickhead. Everyone unloaded. It was a microwave, not a roast. It was actually written up in *Spy*. They used it as an example of the decadence of Hollywood. I guess all I'll be remembered for is my dick.

PLAYBOY: You're forgetting Popeye.

WILLIAMS: Oh, Popeye, with that face like rubber. I felt like a guy robbing a bank with a condom on his head.

PLAYBOY: Guess you're right. But at least you'll be remembered.

WILLIAMS: When in doubt, go for the dick joke.

PLAYBOY: There were a lot of dick jokes made at Pee-wee Herman's expense after he got busted for allegedly fondling himself in an adult theater. What did you think of all the fuss that was made about that?

WILLIAMS: It was insane. And really frightening. It goes back to the days of Fatty Arbuckle. People forget that. Disney and CBS immediately dropping his stuff. Wait a minute, he's not been proved guilty, what are you doing? Even if it was true—exposure for masturbation—it's like being busted for loitering in a Buddhist monastery.

PLAYBOY: Will this ruin his career?

WILLIAMS: I think his appearing at the MTV awards was a sign that the majority of people who matter are not going to buy that shit. He came out as Pee-wee and nobody seemed to mind. They weren't going, "Begone, demon seed."

PLAYBOY: The Senate didn't buy the charges of sexual harassment against Judge Clarence Thomas. Did you see the hearings as a new mine for future dick jokes?

WILLIAMS: It was incredible. Never did a Congressional hearing have so many references to penises. They kind of lifted the rock and showed you the underside of government. Clarence Thomas never gave any opinions to the Senate. They should have a show called *Bar Search*, with Ed McMahon, where they would go around the country. "Here we are in Pinpoint, Georgia. He's a judge, he's also a dancer."

PLAYBOY: Judge Thomas will probably be on the Court in the year 2020, when you'll be 70. What do you think the world will be like then?

WILLIAMS: [*In various announcer voices*] It will be one giant film corporation. It will be Sony-Disney-Carolmount. There will no longer be any governments. It will be one nation, under God, indivisible, with circuits and VCRs for all. There will be cold fusion. We'll actually be able to power our cars with our own feces. The emissions problem will be a little intense, but just light a match.

PLAYBOY: This being the start of a new year, did you make any resolutions?

WILLIAMS: I used to when I was a kid. I used to give up a lot of things for Lent, too, and then I still got hairy.

PLAYBOY: At least that won't stop you from working. *Toys*, to be directed by Barry Levinson, is next for you. What's that about?

WILLIAMS: A toy factory taken over by an ex-general who starts making functional war toys. And that's about all I can tell you. Someone just sent me a script to play Harvey Milk—do you think that will offend some people? That'll be an interesting choice for my career, won't it? He really brought a whole city to consciousness.

PLAYBOY: The city was San Francisco and the consciousness had to do with gay men. You're obviously aware that gays have taken you to task for portraying them effeminately in some of the routines you've done for Comic Relief.

WILLIAMS: I understand what they're talking about and I have tried to cut back a little. I can see their point, because they've always been portrayed as being that way. But don't tell me that if you walk down a street in San Francisco, you won't see a lot of people like that. I've been taking a lot of shit for firing at Jesse Helms, too. These born-again Christians were shooting down AIDS research money at a time when it could take out the species. How do you not offend anyone? Finally, you just say fuck it, I have to do what I do. If it pisses you off, I still do other things that piss other people off. I've got the born-again Christians after my ass because I defend gays, and gays are mad at me because I do effeminate characters. You can't keep modifying or you're like a chameleon in front of a mirror.

PLAYBOY: You also managed to piss off John Cardinal O'Connor, who objected to your comment about Marsha's pregnancy when you said you intended to make a movie of it, called *Fetal Attraction*. He said it was in gross bad taste. Does that concern you?

WILLIAMS: No, it doesn't. It was really strange, because I've said things much rougher than that. I think what offended him more than me saying it was the fact that it was quoted on the news and that people laughed. Well, sorry, John, don't mean to bum you out. I guess having babies is kind of rough when you're sitting there surrounded by choir boys. If I'm excommunicated, does that mean I don't get cable?

PLAYBOY: Jesse Helms, Cardinal O'Connor, some militant gays—and we thought everybody liked you.

WILLIAMS: I'll give you a list. The weird thing in Hollywood is they'll still smile at you, but the bottom line is they're thinking, You prick, you scumbag, I hope you choke on your own shit! Why don't you gag on your own genitals?

PLAYBOY: Does this come from jealousy?

WILLIAMS: Sometimes they don't like the way you look. "You're not funny, fuck you." In New York, a guy came up and said, "You the guy on TV?" "Yeah, I am." "You suck! You bite donkey dick, get off, you're so fucking bad!" Perhaps he had a bad day. But then you start to free up and have a good time with it and hope that a few people like what you do so you don't have to sell stuff like male hygiene spray. [TV commercial voice] "Foul Ball, for the man. Want to get rid of that special smell? Foul Ball."

PLAYBOY: You spend a lot of time in New York—making films, doing plays or shows. Do you like going back there?

WILLIAMS: It's great to go back for a while and get the shit peeled off you, get sandblasted: "You think you're so hot? I don't think so." My favorite part of New York is the park and the zoo, where you can see the animals wondering, What the fuck am I in a cage for? Look at that lady in bicycle shorts at 300 pounds. Why am I an object to stare at? Look at her.

PLAYBOY: What's more important to you: your life or your work?

WILLIAMS: A balance of the two. Time is really this delicate thing. Working your tits off during the week, then find time to come home at night and not be so self-involved. "So, enough about me. Now, what do you think about me?"

PLAYBOY: Any fears of your losing that balance?

WILLIAMS: Recently, Jerzy Kosinski killed himself; supposedly, the reason was that he just didn't want to become a vegetable, he didn't want to lose his sharpness. There's that fear—if I felt like I was becoming not just dull but a rock, that I still couldn't spark, still fire off or talk about things, if I'd start to worry or got too afraid to say something. As long as you still keep taking the chances and you're not afraid to play Peter Pan. . . . What if it fails? "I don't care, I'm having a great fucking time." If I stop trying, I'd get afraid.

CHRIS ROCK

A candid conversation with America's best stand-up comic about why black people are so cool, why Marion Barry is scary and why there's nothing sexier than a big ass

If President Clinton isn't Chris Rock's biggest fan, he ought to be. Consider how the 34-year-old comedian recently defended the chief executive during a tour stop this past winter in Atlantic City:

"They let Clinton off last week. Let him off! That's right, just let him go," said Rock, pacing back and forth onstage, eyes wide with mock surprise. Suddenly, he stops. "Wait . . . who's booing? What the fuck you booing about? How you gonna boo head? Have you really thought this over? What the fuck did Clinton do? He lied about a blow job so his wife wouldn't find out. Is that so fucking hard to figure out? You got to have a trial for that shit? Get the Supreme Court involved? You could have taken that to *The People's Court.*"

Most comics would have stopped there. Not Rock. "Some of this is Hillary's fault. That's right. I put blame where blame is due. Women, you know your man better than anybody else. You know if you got the crazy, needs-a-blow-job-every-day man. Sometimes you got to save your man from himself. Sometimes you got to sacrifice your lips for the good of the country. Hillary let us all down. She's the first lady. She's supposed to be the first one on her knees. Monica shouldn't have stood a chance. 'What you want, girl? Get out of here. I got this under control.'"

Rock certainly has things under control. For almost five years he's been the hottest comic in the country, the darling of the public and his peers, a book author, recording artist, movie actor and host of HBO's *The Chris Rock Show.* Credit his fearlessness at tackling issues such as race, politics, relationships, doctors, insurance, taxes, family dynamics, porn, pimps, crack, black leaders, false role models and the difference between the mall white people go to and the one they used to go to. Despite his success, Rock makes regular visits to the Museum of Television and Radio to study the likes of Woody Allen, Richard Pryor, Ernie Kovacs, Flip Wilson, Don Rickles, Groucho Marx, Steve Martin and Charlie Chaplin. And he still hones his material before last-call audiences at comedy clubs. Then it's all taken to the concert stage where, as in his Emmy award–winning HBO special, *Bring the Pain*, Rock works the audience with almost evangelical fervor.

Offstage, Rock is surprisingly calm and unassuming. He's a watcher, a thinker, curious. "I don't have to be the smartest person in the room," he says. "You don't learn that way." In other words, he's personable but not easy to get to know. But he can explain that too: "The only people easy to get to know are drug dealers and prostitutes. No matter where I go, people ask, 'How come you're so quiet?' Even in the library where you're supposed to be quiet. But I don't want to waste my powers. If Superman flew around all the time he might not be able to save Lois when it counts."

Rock was born on February 7, 1965 in South Carolina. His father, Julius, a union trucker, and mother, Rose, moved the family to Brooklyn. Eventually they settled on Decatur Avenue in Bedford-Stuyvesant, on one of the nicer blocks in a notoriously bad part of town. The family was close, and Rock, as the oldest of six, quickly absorbed his parents' work ethic. He took on odd jobs and, as he got older, often accompanied his dad on rounds delivering the *New York Daily News*. He was also bused to a nearly all-white school, where he was regularly beaten up and came to learn the many epithets whites have for blacks. He didn't make it through high school—by choice.

Once, in 1983, when he was 18, working at Red Lobster and a huge Eddie Murphy fan, Rock waited in line at Radio City Music Hall to get a ticket to Murphy's show. But when he heard about an open-mike night at Catch a Rising Star, he left Murphy behind and headed to the club, tried out, made the cut and joined the comedy circuit. One night in 1987 it was Murphy's turn to watch Rock, and he liked what he saw. With Murphy's backing, Rock appeared on an HBO *Uptown Comedy Express* special. In 1990 he followed in Murphy's footsteps on *Saturday Night Live*.

Three years and a couple of memorable characters (including Nat X) later, Rock asked *SNL* executive producer Lorne Michaels to let him go his own way. The pressure to be the new Eddie Murphy had taken its toll. He also admits that he didn't work as hard on the show as he did at partying and spending his newfound money. Even so, he appeared in a few films (including *New Jack City*), was briefly on *In Living Color*, made an album (*Born Suspect*) and, in 1993, starred in the rap parody *CB4*, which he co-wrote and co-produced. It opened at number one at the box office, but from there both the film and Rock's career went downhill. He ended up right back where he started: playing little clubs. And there was another problem. His act had gone limp. One night in Chicago, upstaged by comedian Martin Lawrence, Rock came back to his senses. As he told *Vanity Fair*, "Martin just annihilated me. Blew my ass away. That was a pivotal moment, because I wasn't really prepared. I'd been working with too many white guys."

The reality check paid off. Rock recommitted himself to his craft, often traveling the country with comedian Mario Joyner, "the funniest man I know." (Joyner is also one of Jerry Seinfeld's best friends.) Rock took more risks onstage and started talking about things that really interested him.

In 1996 *Politically Incorrect* host Bill Maher asked Rock to be that show's correspondent at the presidential conventions. Rock also taped *Bring the Pain*, featuring his new strutting stage manner as well as his popular Niggas vs. Black People routine. It was only a small part of the special, and Rock doesn't do it anymore, but it hit home.

Rock followed the special with an album (*Roll with the New*), a best-selling book (*Rock This!*) and an HBO variety–talk show (*The Chris Rock Show*), now in its third season. He also relaunched a movie career, with roles in *Lethal Weapon 4*, Kevin Smith's *Dogma* and *Nurse Betty* with Morgan Freeman. He's writing films as well, with Paramount greenlighting his remake of *Heaven Can Wait*, called *I Was Made to Love Her*. Finally, there's another HBO special, *Bigger and Blacker*, taped at the Apollo Theater in Harlem, and a new album by the same name. And let's not forget his role as pitchman for 1-800-COLLECT and his playing the voice of Li'l Penny for Nike.

Playboy asked Contributing Editor David Rensin, who co-authored Rock's book, to hook up with the comedian while he toured to get ready for his HBO special. Rensin's report:

"Most people who don't know him think Chris Rock in private is just like he was in *Bring the Pain*: loud, in your face, wearing a silky silver jacket and unable to sit still. Nothing is farther from the truth. Rock says he never wore that ensemble again. He's also more prone to lose himself in his Walkman than cut up after a show. Where many performers are superenergized and looking for trouble, Rock is easy-going and happy to watch a film on the tour bus with his players—Ali LeRoi, Lance Crouther and his wife, Robin Montague, and Wanda Sykes, all writer-performers on *The Chris Rock Show*. He may be the boss, but he acts like one of the gang.

"After a show at Princeton University, we traveled to the Trump Marina hotel and casino in Atlantic City. At two A.M. the troupe convened for breakfast in the coffee shop. Rock led a freewheeling dialog that covered favorite music from the 1970s and 1980s, favorite comedians, sports, the neighborhood, and relationships. Later, in the casino, Rock wanted to cut loose and gamble a bit, but then a phalanx of low-rollers approached for autographs. Said one obviously single woman, 'You're gorgeous. I want to marry you someday.' Smiling, then sighing, Rock begged off and said, 'My life has changed. I used to blend in around white people.'

"We were scheduled to begin our first session after lunch in his hotel room, but at the last minute Rock decided that we should go to the local mall for CDs and a radio, and do the interview as we shopped. We'd made mall runs together before, but this time there were no pals along—and no bodyguard. We entered on the upper level and hadn't been inside 30 seconds when we heard the first of what would become an afternoon full of variations on, 'Yo. It's Chris Rock. Is that Chris Rock? Hey man, how you doing?' and autograph requests. Rock motioned toward the tape recorder and politely declined—unless there were children involved—and just told me to keep walking and talking."

PLAYBOY: Everyone's staring.

ROCK: Keep walking. I'm from Brooklyn. If you come from a bad neighborhood you learn to notice everything around you. What I notice is there's no one in here who can whip my ass. Besides, I got you with me.

PLAYBOY: And you feel safe? All right, let's start with the accolades. *Vanity Fair*: "Funniest, smartest comic working today." *New York Post*: "Utterly fearless." *The Washington Post*: "His show is unfailingly funny." Lorne Michaels: "Chris is the shock of ideas." For a guy who only a few years ago called himself washed up, how much do you like what you hear?

ROCK: [*Laughs*] What do you want me to say? It's great. I'm glad they feel that way. They're all good sources and none of them had to say nice things about me before, including Lorne. I'm just glad I could do something they like.

PLAYBOY: How has all the attention changed you?

ROCK: I feel like Travolta in *Phenomenon*, when he got zapped by the light. Nothing's going wrong. Yet. I still live in the same house—I just haven't been there much because I'm extremely busy. But when I go around my old neighborhood and see my old friends, the differences between me and them still seem minuscule. I had a good dad and another guy didn't; I didn't get high and another guy did. That's scary. I sometimes feel like I'm one bad break from being back there and never making it out in the first place.

PLAYBOY: What do you miss most about your old life?

ROCK: Being able to take a walk by myself. Now if I'm alone everyone assumes I want company. Being famous is like having big tits. People always stare. In some ways that's good, because a girl with big tits can go anywhere and people always want to do whatever they can for her.

PLAYBOY: Sure. In hopes of getting laid.

ROCK: With me I guess it's the hope of getting money or hanging out—and then getting laid. My friends are always trying to drag me somewhere so they can get laid. Tell anyone you're my manager and watch what happens. [*Laughs*] I guess I've got some huge tits right now. But that's okay. I deal with all of it because they're my fans. It's like each one bought a thread on this coat I'm wearing. They bought the tips of my shoelaces. They helped pay for everything I've got. So the handshakes, the hugs, they're good. People are just trying to connect. It could be much worse.

PLAYBOY: As in no one's paying attention?

ROCK: No. As in they could be burning my football jersey and smashing my Heisman trophy.

PLAYBOY: How much does it bother you that O.J. is still able to go to the mall?

ROCK: I'm not happy about it. I'm not rejoicing. Yeah, we know he did it, but he's one guy I don't think is going to kill again.

PLAYBOY: When does celebrity get most weird for you?

ROCK: When I get to hear about which star someone in my family wants to fuck. When people want to know my mood before they speak to me. I used to see this around Eddie Murphy and Lorne Michaels. "How's he feeling? What's his mood?" It's hysterical. When I say something offhand and it comes back to me. If I'm mildly interested in something, my whispers are heard miles away. The next thing I know, someone is in my office wanting to make a deal. The other day I said, "You know, *The PJs* was funny last night." Two days later my manager gets a call: "They hear you like *The PJs*. They want you to be a voice on the show." For all I know I was overheard in an elevator. When people give me stuff I don't need. I get free food when there are homeless folks who can't get any. I get sneakers. I don't need sneakers; I can buy sneakers. It's all about big tits. And it's ironic that the guy who no one listened to, everybody listens to now. The guy everyone used to beat up, a lot of people are scared of now. The guy who couldn't get laid, everybody wants to fuck now.

PLAYBOY: That sounds like a positive development.

ROCK: I just wanted the opportunity to make people laugh in as many different forms as I could: books, albums, my TV show, as a producer, in the movies and, first and foremost, as a stand-up comic. All I wanted was options. And now I have them, because all being rich and famous really means is that you've got more options.

PLAYBOY: Didn't you once say that fame was bullshit?

ROCK: Here's what I meant: People say, "I want to be rich and famous like you." No, they just want to be rich. Believe me. Fame is only cool if you want to meet somebody.

PLAYBOY: And you have. We read about you in the gossip columns, at one big event or another, like Puffy Combs's birthday bash.

ROCK: I knew Puffy 10 years ago. I was a little sluggo-ing comedian and he used to drive some guy's car. I've known a lot of these people forever. Look at Lauryn Hill. To most people she just got famous. I did a gig with her and the Fugees seven years ago at some little college. I played Super Nintendo with Will Smith 10 years ago, in Philadelphia at his crib, when I was in town doing a gig at the Funny Bone for $800. Talented people tend to hang out together. They know who's got the stuff. If you respect someone's work it's worth a dinner or two. Plus, when you're all in the same business there's the safety factor. We don't need shit from each other. We're not put in the position to turn people down; that happens too many times when you hang out with people who don't do what you do. Does that make sense without making me sound like a snob?

PLAYBOY: Is that something you and your friends discuss?

ROCK: Who asked for what is one of the biggest topics of conversation. Everybody tries to top each other: "So-and-so wants me to help him buy a Ferrari." "So-and-so asked me for 50 large." "My uncle is trying to buy a fleet of school buses." Everybody's got some crazy tale. The best I ever heard was when a friend of mine, who will remain nameless, went on a date with a girl and had sex with her, and before she even left she asked him to help her buy a house.

PLAYBOY: Did he?

ROCK: No. But I told him, "Your time together must have been really bad for her to say 'You owe me now!'"

PLAYBOY: Will these observations ever end up as comic material?

ROCK: No. When I'm onstage I make $300 a week—though maybe I should give myself a raise to $500 for the millennium. No one wants to hear about my money. Nobody wants to hear about me hanging out with whoever's famous. Nobody wants to know about what a hassle it is sometimes to sign autographs. The fans just want me to be one of the guys. Be down. People want to hang out with their favorite comedian. They want to feel like he's the missing guy in their crew. "Fuck, I wish Chris was hanging." "Wouldn't it be great if Sandler was here tonight?" They want to feel comfortable with that guy. In their shoes, I did too.

PLAYBOY: How badly do you want Adam Sandler's kind of success?

ROCK: His success is nice. We both have the same philosophy: Work work work, work work, work work work. Album movie, movie, album movie, album. Get it out there. He's also one of the funniest guys. As big as he is, he's still underrated. He's a great stand-up comedian. Sandler's like Steven Wright with a dick—not that Steven Wright doesn't have one. I mean Sandler has an observational quality like Steven Wright, but his one-liners tend to be raunchier than Wright's.

PLAYBOY: And your approach to comedy is sort of like a fighter's.

ROCK: The crowd gives me a four-minute cushion: "Hey, he's famous. We saw him last month and he made us laugh." I try to hit them. Immediately. I don't try to fluff it that much, because a man's behavior is dictated by his physicality. I'm like a lightweight fighter, so I tell more jokes than a big guy. I've got to throw a lot of jokes. If Malcolm X were as small as Martin Luther King, he'd have believed in nonviolence, too. If Martin Luther King were as big as Malcolm X, he'd have been talking about "let me whup some ass." It's no coincidence that the little guy was nonviolent and the big guy was violent.

PLAYBOY: Why did you choose to become a comedian?

ROCK: It's the only good deed I can do. I've never been talented at anything else, like sports or school. The only other thing that sparked my interest as a kid was being a civil rights attorney, or a reverend—that is, if I could find a religion that didn't dog people out and wasn't on some level racist, sexist and homophobic. Yeah, I'd probably preach the gospel.

PLAYBOY: But your act is already more than jokes. As Lorne Michaels said, you're the shock of ideas.

ROCK: I'm just a comedian, man. Just a comedian. The media think I'm out there with an agenda. No. That's Jesse's job. That's Sharpton's job. Everybody's looking for the leader. Everybody's looking for the next guy, and they always try to pin it on entertainers and athletes. But I'm not a candidate, and I'm not a messenger.

PLAYBOY: So you say and no doubt mean, yet your fans take your observations to heart. And the critics see all sorts of wisdom in your observations.

ROCK: People also listen to Urkel. Oprah says what I say, in her own way. A million rappers: Ice Cube. Chuck D. Public Enemy. NWA. And they did it years ago. I just happen to be the quotemeister right now—people are repeating things I've said, in other contexts. I just talk about what interests me. That's the most important thing: Can I interest myself? I don't want to be bored up there, because you'll be bored if I'm bored. And I don't want to sound like other comedians. I don't want to have the airplane hunk about seat backs and tray tables.

PLAYBOY: So what's the gospel according to Chris Rock?

ROCK: [*Pauses*] If anything, I'm not a hater. I'm probably the only black comic who isn't homophobic, who doesn't have a big fag hunk in his act.

PLAYBOY: How do you feel about white people?

ROCK: I look at the individual. I probably could hate white people as a group, because when I went to school white kids would get together and beat the shit out of me. I'm still a little scared when I see whites in a group, but I've learned that all groups are stupid. What I hate is anyone who knows better yet chooses to be racist. On the other hand, if you don't know any black people and all you get is what you see in the news, I almost don't blame you for being a racist. But if you know a cool brother down the block, if you know me and you're still a racist, then you're a fucking idiot.

PLAYBOY: But you're not afraid to make fun of blacks or whites.

ROCK: [*Long pause, shakes his head*] I hate that hunk of mine, sometimes.

PLAYBOY: The "I love black people but I hate niggas" routine?

ROCK: Yeah, I'm so tired of that shit. Sometimes that's all people write about me, like I'm a one-joke comic or Ritchie Valens, only known for "La Bamba." They ignore everything else I've said and focus on that one thing.

PLAYBOY: It's certainly received the most attention.

ROCK: But if I didn't have the relationship stuff in my act, I wouldn't sell as many seats. No way in the world I'm playing these big houses just off so-called political shit. The relationship stuff sells the tickets, along with the stuff about insurance and doctors and malls. I talk about things that the average man cares about, stuff I care about. I've got insurance. I'm paying my mother's insurance bills. I'm thinking about the hypocrisy of the whole thing. Even when I was a kid, when I had my first car, it was like, Let me get this straight: The worse the neighborhood you live in, the more insurance you have to pay? Women in the inner city have to pay more for diapers and milk because they have to get them at the minimart because no grocery will build there? How fucking ignorant is that injustice?

PLAYBOY: True, but why does that make the "I hate niggas" material any less important?

ROCK: [*Sighs*] It's just that I hate white reporters talking to me about it without ever having watched *Bring the Pain*. They always ask, "How does a black audience deal with that stuff you're saying?" Take a look at the show! Were there any white people there that night? Not many. Were people laughing? Yes. What's the fucking question again? I'm in the middle of Maryland. Not even D.C., but the middle of the ghetto, in a theater that we spent money on to make look better—and it's full of black people. I purposely went into the hood to do it. But some writers act as if I did *Bring the Pain* in front of a joint session of Congress. I think what they're really saying is, "I like it, but how could black people possibly like it, since you're making fun of them?" Well, it looked to me like they were laughing. Whatever you see black people laughing at, that's what's funny to black people. It's like me going up to Garth Brooks after he plays the Grand Ole Opry and saying, "How do country people deal with your act?" Huh?

PLAYBOY: How are black audiences different from white audiences?

ROCK: For one thing, the black audience goes everywhere first. They dictate everything from music to comedy to fashion; they point to where the white audience is going to go. Who's going to be the hottest comedian in the year 2001? I don't know—but he's working in front of a bunch of brothers right now. Who'll be the hottest rapper? I don't know, but young black kids know right now. Black people are about the future. White people are all about the past and how to return to the fucking glory they had. Black makes everything cool. What are the Spice Girls without the black girl? Just three white bitches who can barely sing. What's the Rat Pack without Sammy Davis? A bunch of fucking alcoholics. My core audience is probably black, but I don't think white people want to see me water down my thing. The white people who are into me aren't afraid. They want me to be me.

PLAYBOY: Perhaps the question you don't like stems from white journalists having to be so cautious. They can't get away with saying nigger. They'd be crucified. So they don't understand when black people laugh at someone who does.

ROCK: White people can't go around saying nigger. That's a rule. Black people can; it's like calling your kid an idiot. Only you can call your kid that. Someone else calls your kid an idiot, there's a fight. You know, I said some ill shit in that special. I did jokes about porn and killing the president and hitting women. I had a guy beating a woman, and her complaining about it on *Oprah*. But no one mentioned that to me. Here's why: Race is big. It's the last frontier.

PLAYBOY: Who takes the truth about themselves better, blacks or whites?

ROCK: Probably blacks. We're used to being criticized and we deal with it easier. We're always expecting the hit.

PLAYBOY: How concerned are you about media backlash? You're on top now, but that also makes you a target.

ROCK: I don't worry about the mainstream media. They don't have much to do with making black artists succeed. There's no successful black artist without 90 percent of the black vote. Any black artist with longevity, black people already love, and he'd be successful—though maybe not stupendously—without the crossover. If white people had never gotten Richard Pryor he'd still have a big house and money. Bernie Mac, Jamie Foxx, Frankie Beverly, they all live really well. Steve Harvey lives really, really well.

PLAYBOY: Would black recognition be enough for you?

ROCK: Yeah.

PLAYBOY: So why the desire to cross over?

ROCK: Financial reasons. Black artists don't want white people to like them. That's real Uncle Tom. It's the money. Everybody wants to make the most dough they can because we're in an industry where you can be over at any moment. The idea is to cross over to white dollars, not to white people.

PLAYBOY: What's the best career advice you ever got?

ROCK: Before I taped *Bring the Pain* I bumped into Andrew Dice Clay. Anybody who knows Dice knows he can't help but give you advice every time he sees you—good or bad. But when you really think about it, who knows more about doing an HBO special than Dice? Who's gotten more out of being on HBO than Dice? Who filled up Madison fucking Square Garden? He said, "Watch *Rocky* and you'll remember why you got started. Everything will come back to you." They say I'm big, but I can't ignore a guy who filled the Garden. And he was right. I watched *Rocky* and it all came into focus. It's the best inspirational movie in the world. All schoolkids should be forced to watch *Rocky*. The lesson is try your best, no matter what, and you'll feel good at the end. Be better than your best. That's my career philosophy. Buster Douglas was a bum. But one night he fought Tyson better than his best, and he won.

PLAYBOY: Do you have any advice for Tyson?

ROCK: Watch *Rocky* [*laughs*]. Stop drinking. Mike is insecure. The last time I bumped into Mike was at some show at Roseland. We ended up going to Jersey to a party. It was two or three in the morning, and we were both sitting there trying to figure out if we could have gotten our wives if we weren't rich. This big motherfucker and this little guy, both from Brooklyn, connected on the same thing. We couldn't figure it out. Neither one of us was confident enough. Both of us were like, "Nah, nobody likes us for us." It says nothing bad about our wives and everything about us.

PLAYBOY: You recently went to Richard Pryor's birthday party. What's he like these days?

ROCK: It's really sad. He can't talk. Richard fucking Pryor, the greatest orator, the greatest comedian of all time, and he can't talk. What the fuck is that? It's like Fred Astaire being paralyzed.

PLAYBOY: What made Pryor great?

ROCK: He was honest.

PLAYBOY: The same has been said of you. According to HBO President of Programming Chris Albrecht, you can "get away with being honest in a way few people can."

ROCK: I don't get away with anything. I just do it. It has to be instinctual. The minute that I start to analyze my act, I'm dead.

PLAYBOY: Come on. Maybe you want to play it down, but you must think this stuff through.

ROCK: Sometimes when I come off the stage I feel like the Incredible Hulk, when he turns back into David Banner. Did I kill anybody? Did I hurt anybody? I feel like that a lot, especially when it's a good night. I get in a weird zone because my act gets my complete attention. In sex, my mind can drift, but onstage it's do or die. When I walk into a comedy club I want motherfuckers to be scared I'm going on. "Oh shit. I don't want to follow him." I don't want the he's-famous-let's-cut-him-some-slack funny. When Rodney Dangerfield walks into the Improv, they know he's getting ready to bring the noise. It's like, get the fuck back! This guy is 70-something and he's going to blow everybody off the stage. That's what I want.

PLAYBOY: How do you feel about once having been called the new Eddie Murphy?

ROCK: Every hot black guy is the new Eddie Murphy. But I think I've established myself as my own guy. The first time I heard it I felt a bit of pressure; more than, say, Damon Wayans or Sinbad did, because folklore has it I was discovered by Eddie Murphy. People were looking for that from me.

PLAYBOY: Is the folklore bullshit?

ROCK: The average person thinks I was driving a bus and Eddie said, "Hey, this guy is funny." I had been in the comedy business for a few years. Eddie said I was funny on camera and in print—which is a bigger thing than any manager or agent could do—and he got me on this show called *The Uptown Comedy Express*, an HBO special he developed and produced. When the funniest guy in the world says you're funny, well, you—

PLAYBOY: Feel like, Holy shit, what do I do?

ROCK: I just did what I was doing and people said, "He's funny, but he's no Eddie Murphy."

PLAYBOY: But only a few years earlier you were 18 and standing in line at Radio City on your night off from a job at Red Lobster, waiting to get a ticket to Murphy's show, when you suddenly split to do open-microphone night at Catch a Rising Star. Murphy was and is your hero, yet you blew off the show. What possessed you?

ROCK: Something called to me. Every comedian will tell you the same thing. There's no big revelation. It seemed like a better option than waiting in line.

PLAYBOY: Was it your first time onstage?

ROCK: Yeah. There was a guy on my block who co-managed R&B singer Freddie Jackson. He represented show business to me. I also knew *Saturday Night Live* was looking for people. So I told him, out of the blue, "Get me on *Saturday Night Live*." Obviously, I was an idiot at that point, thinking you could just get on *Saturday Night Live*. The guy said, "You have to go to the Comic Strip, you have to audition. You need to go to the clubs." I guess it put a little germ in my head—so one night I did it. Or maybe it was because I was at the end of a long-assed line and probably wasn't going to get in to see Eddie anyway.

PLAYBOY: How big a career jump was getting on *Saturday Night Live*?

ROCK: Huge. To this day, the biggest. It was the last break that actually changed my life. When I got on *Saturday Night Live* I moved from a studio apartment into a huge duplex, I bought a car, I helped my mother get a house. Nothing like that has happened to me since. Even today the quality of my life is pretty much the same. When I used to get $50 or $300 a gig, every gig would change my life. It meant I was going to eat differently. I might buy sneakers so I'd have a new wardrobe. Today the only changes are more artistic options, and a lot of white people speak to me.

PLAYBOY: What went wrong at *Saturday Night Live*?

ROCK: Lorne hired me because I was funny and because *In Living Color* had just come on. I don't think it was coincidence. The first year I was alone, which was perfect. If you're black you might as well be the only black person there. You're competing enough as it is to get a little screen time. Then it was me, Tim Meadows and Ellen Cleghorne. We all wanted to star in our own pieces, but we weren't all going to get on each show—even if all our stuff was great. The show is no different than society. But I'll never dog *Saturday Night Live*, because it's the best thing that's ever happened to me. Another problem is that I followed Eddie Murphy. Whatever I did was compared with him, and that's unfair. I had tough shoes to fill. I had the Larry Holmes gig.

PLAYBOY: What's your relationship with Eddie like these days?

ROCK: We're cool. I always looked at Eddie like my older cool cousin, the one, when you're a kid, that you can't wait to see because he's got the tapes and cool clothes. He's getting laid and he's got stories. I'm never going to be Eddie's equal, and friends have to be equals to be friends. But that said, we're better friends than we were before.

PLAYBOY: Didn't you also party a lot during your three years on *Saturday Night Live*, sometimes to distraction?

ROCK: We all partied. I also got a big-ass apartment, a convertible 'Vette. What's cornier than a red 'Vette driving through Brooklyn? How obnoxious is that? I was ridiculous. Lorne Michaels told me, and he was right: "Everybody loses their first money. No matter who you are, you're going to lose your first money." That first hunk I got, though it couldn't set me up for life, could have helped. But I lost it. I spent it on shit I couldn't afford: a car, not paying taxes. My whole life was just trying to fuck girls I had no business fucking—and I succeeded on several occasions [*laughs*]. Ah, those were the days.

PLAYBOY: Sounds like you miss them.

ROCK: I miss the innocence. Otherwise I was tired, I looked like shit. In pictures of me back then I look like I was on the pipe.

PLAYBOY: You were hot, left *Saturday Night Live*, made a couple movies and then you were gone. You couldn't even get an agent. What happened? How did you work your way back?

ROCK: After *Saturday Night Live*, I co-wrote, produced and starred in *CB4*. Probably made $18 million. We did it with Brian Grazer and Ron Howard's company, Imagine. Ron Howard was in the movie, but he cut himself out. He saw how shitty the movie was and said, "Hey, I can't be in this." In his scene he says, "When I first heard the song *Sweat of My Balls*. . . ." Ron Howard saying "sweat of my balls" is pretty funny. Cut to three years later and I get a call to do *Sgt. Bilko* with Steve Martin. I thought, great, but it was essentially an extra part. Two lines. I felt like shit, but you've got to do what you've got to do. A lot of guys wouldn't go to the audition. I do what I've got to do. The worst gig in show business is better than the best job out of it. I would have been the stand-in for the extra if I had to. And if I didn't take that extra part I wouldn't be where I am right now. That same year I did a guest shot on *Fresh Prince of Bel Air*. It was a horrible episode. I had to be Will Smith's ugly date, so I was in drag. Barely funny. I had to do it, though. From *Saturday Night Live* to *New Jack City* to *CB4* to being dressed up like an ugly bitch for Will Smith.

PLAYBOY: Did you have to kiss him?

ROCK: No, but I'm glad they offered me the part. I needed it at the time. And guess what? People on the street were going, "Hey, I saw you on *Fresh Prince*," "Hey, I saw you in *Sgt. Bilko*." It kind of kept me alive. It's not shoveling shit, but I definitely went backward to get forward. I did *Sgt. Bilko* because it was Grazer, Steve Martin, Dan Aykroyd, Phil Hartman. I got to be around all those guys, even if it was only for two days. There was some value in doing it. Association brings assimilation, as my mother says.

PLAYBOY: How often do you get back to the old neighborhood?

ROCK: I still talk to people there. But one of the last times I went around I almost got carjacked. This guy was following me; I ran a light and he ran the light. When you grow up in Bed-Stuy you have an extra sense for trouble. The next thing I know, I'm on a high-speed chase with three cars behind me. I was probably going about 60 or 70 miles an hour through the streets of Brooklyn, running lights.

PLAYBOY: What would have happened if they'd caught you?

ROCK: They would have taken me to my crib, made me open up, taken everything, duct taped me and maybe killed me. They wanted my shit. And kidnapping's big. This is what's going on now. The only guys my age with dough who aren't entertainers sell drugs. Drug dealers keep their money in their house. I don't keep money in mine, but these young guys probably think I have a million dollars under my bed.

PLAYBOY: Sounds like you can't really go home again.

ROCK: I'm not going back there like "look at me." I like to sit on the stoop and talk. Usually it's okay. When I first get there it's an immediate, "Chris is here!" But that always happened no matter what job I had. As far as my neighborhood is concerned, I made it 10 years ago when I was in the movie *I'm Gonna Git You Sucka*. Do you know how far that is from Bed-Stuy and hanging out watching my friends sell lactose as coke? Or making crack: cocaine, lactose, vitamin B-12, a little baking soda. The common Friday night thing was to get with a bunch of friends at six o'clock. But then people started getting high and no one would go anywhere. It would start with the first beer, to the first joint, to the first snort, to freebasing. Every fucking Friday. I never got or get high, thank God.

PLAYBOY: Did that self-destructive experience make it any easier for you to understand Chris Farley's death?

ROCK: No. I took it really hard. He was a great friend. A good, jolly—I know that's a fat word—guy to be around. He needed hugs but he was quick to give them, too. When I was off the show, with no career, he and Sandler were the only guys who'd call to see how I was doing. Farley was way funnier than we've ever seen him be. He was more like W.C. Fields than the character he usually played. He had a "get away from me kid, you bother me" funny mean streak, but then he'd give the kid a big hug. But in movies he always played this fat guy who didn't know any better, who straightened up at the last minute. The last time I saw him I pretty much had to get rid of him. I was in Chicago, on tour, and Chris came to see me. He was so fucked up. He was screaming. He wanted more booze. We had made plans, but I had to say, "You know what? I'm going to bed." It was only midnight. Right then he kind of straightened out for a minute: "Come on, Rocker. Come see my apartment. Come on, Rocker." I couldn't, and that's the last time I saw him. He died a month after that. I miss Farley a lot. Phil Hartman, too. It made for a really shitty year, losing both of them. The worst thing that they did was try to make other people happy offstage. They went out of their way for other people for the sake of their own happiness, and it killed both of them.

PLAYBOY: What was your relationship with Hartman like?

ROCK: Phil was a mentor. He was the most prepared guy at *Saturday Night Live*. He could also show you about the good life. Sometimes he'd call me into his office and say, "Hey, look at this picture of my new boat." "Hey, here's the house I'm buying. You work hard, you can get this, too." But Phil had a weird marriage. He was always going through some shit with it, and I never liked to spend time with them as a couple. Every now and then he'd talk about it. I remember him saying, "Okay. If I lose half my shit I'll have to be on the show another three years." In part because of what happened, I'm really into my own happiness and my own comfort now in a way I wasn't before. I'm probably a rougher person to be around than before they died. I would never rock the boat. I'd go along with the program even if I was miserable. The old me would take shit for a while and then explode. After Farley and Hartman died, and died not happy, the idea of toeing the company line made me think, Fuck this. I'm more assertive now. I've found the courage to say no. They say life is short. No, it's not. Life is long. Life is excruciatingly long if you make bad decisions and do things you don't want to do.

PLAYBOY: Let's talk about what you want to do—and what you have done for three seasons: *The Chris Rock Show*. Why did you want to try talk on cable, particularly when you could have had your own sitcom?

ROCK: I had nothing else happening at the time. I was bubbling under, doing *Politically Incorrect*, doing Li'l Penny. I had done *Big Ass Jokes*, which won the Cable Ace award. I was on a little upswing. It was HBO's idea. It was like, whoa, get my own show? This is great. We made the deal before *Bring the Pain*, and the success of the special just made things go quicker.

PLAYBOY: You're a TV interviewer now. Who's your role model?

ROCK: Bob Costas. Best in the world. I saw Bob Costas interview Little Richard once. At the time Little Richard was a fucking joke to me. Just a clown. When Costas got through with him, I was Little Richard's biggest fan. I saw Bob do that with a lot of people. He had all the best questions.

PLAYBOY: What have you learned?

ROCK: I look at an interview like I look at a woman I'm trying to get with. You have to avoid the obvious, especially if you're not a good-looking guy. I'm not, so it's all going to be verbal. If she's tall, don't mention it. If her name is Eve, don't say a joke with Adam in it. The second rule is to never ask a question if you know the answer. If somebody's got a hit movie, "Boy, your movie's really big. How does it feel?" What are they going to say? They're going to say it feels great. Why ask that? Rule three is you can get away with a lot if you say "with all due respect."

PLAYBOY: When you interviewed Magic Johnson why did you concentrate on his HIV? What wasn't obvious about that?

ROCK: Who has asked Magic Johnson, "How has it affected your business?" I even gave Magic one of those hard-to-ask questions: "Do women still hit on you?" His ego wants to say yes, but he has to say no. He kind of went in the middle of it: "Women like successful men." That's what you're looking for. He was great. He was the best guy I've probably had on this year. [*Smiles*] You know, I think he's got a new strain of AIDS, the kind that makes you gain weight and make money.

PLAYBOY: Why wasn't he any good when he did the interviewing?

ROCK: Magic Johnson is supposed to suck at being a talk show host just like I'm supposed to suck at being point guard for the Los Angeles Lakers. It's no dis to him. He gave it a good shot.

PLAYBOY: Will former D.C. mayor Marion Barry ever come on your show—especially after you made fun of him in *Bring the Pain*?

ROCK: I bumped into Marion Barry. He shook my hand. He said I shouldn't do the jokes. And as I looked in his eyes I realized, if he wasn't the mayor or a public figure, he'd beat the shit out of me. He's not the mayor right now. If I bumped into Marion Barry again he'd probably kick my fucking ass. No doubt in my mind. If nobody was around, Marion Barry would beat the shit out of me.

PLAYBOY: So that's why you have a bodyguard.

ROCK: Yes. Just for Marion Barry [*laughs*].

PLAYBOY: What's your take on the tragedy at Columbine High in Colorado?

ROCK: It's a big gun problem. And you know, one kid was on Prozac, but the toxicology report found no Prozac in him. I don't want to sound insensitive, but whatever happened to just being crazy? Everyone's looking for reasons, but no one's mentioned that maybe those guys were just fucking nuts. When I was a kid, those kids would have been put on a yellow bus and sent to a little classroom away from everybody, and nobody would have been shot. When I went to school, there were probably a couple kids who didn't belong, but no one got shot.

PLAYBOY: Maybe it's just frustrated middle-class white kids with access to guns who don't know how else to deal with not being popular.

ROCK: Right. Black people can't go, "I'm going to buy machine guns." They'd never leave the store. The cops would be called immediately. You can't buy any bomb-making stuff either if you're black. You can't even say "bomb" if you're black. As soon as you say "bo" you're arrested. B-o. You don't even get to the m. It's true! There are no black serial killers, right? You know why that is? Because a brother does one murder and they get him. It's like we're fucking suspects for everything. The white man gets the benefit of the doubt. I'm sure there are black people who would love to be serial killers, but they've never been given the chance. It's really sad. The law comes down on us too fucking hard.

PLAYBOY: Can the media and the Internet and goth music be blamed for what happened?

ROCK: Blame the media? What was Hitler listening to? How come no one ever questions what Hitler was listening to? What movie did Hitler see that fucking set him off? He was just a crazy, evil guy. This whole "listened to" thing is bullshit to me. If you're dumb enough to kill somebody because you listen to Marilyn Manson, then we ought to get you early. We ought to eliminate you right away. What's Milosevic listening to? He's killing everybody, and I'm sure he's not listening to Marilyn Manson. What were they listening to during feudalism? The only people happy about those kids being shot are JonBenet's parents. They're like, "Hey, boy, now they're going to leave us alone." [*Pauses*] That's a joke.

PLAYBOY: Let's move on. Your movie career is in high gear. Besides the stuff we've seen you in, what are you being offered?

ROCK: Mostly con men. A numbers runner in Beverly Hills. Or I steal cars in Beverly Hills. That's the big thing: a fish out of water. You know what? I've got money and I'm famous and when I'm in Beverly Hills I am a fucking fish out of water. I walk into Barneys and I can afford whatever I want, but I'm still a freak. Jerry Seinfeld walking through Bensonhurst is a fish out of water. You don't need to be a fucking drug kingpin to be a fish out of water. Eddie called me a couple months ago and said, "I see what you're doing, the supporting actor thing here and there. Don't do that no more. You have to star in your next movie. Now's the time. Strike while the iron is hot. Don't fucking blow this."

PLAYBOY: Did you take his advice?

ROCK: Yes. I can't just wait around to be cast. The really successful guys are the ones who develop their own shit. So I co-wrote a script with my guys, and Paramount greenlighted it and we're going to start shooting in January.

PLAYBOY: What's it about?

ROCK: It's a remake of *Heaven Can Wait* or *Here Comes Mr. Jordan*. It's called *There Goes Mr. Rock* [smiles]. No, it's called *I Was Made to Love Her*.

PLAYBOY: You're in Kevin Smith's newest film, *Dogma*, as Rufus, the 13th apostle. The movie's subject matter—a critique of Catholicism—has caused a fair amount of controversy. Is that what attracted you to the project?

ROCK: Kevin's other movies, *Clerks* and *Chasing Amy*, just spoke to me.

PLAYBOY: What was it like working with Smith?

ROCK: Kevin holds the most intense rehearsals. When you get to the set, your lines and blocking have to be second nature. You're prepared. You're in shape. It takes hours—morning until night. I wanted to do it, especially since I'm not an actor like the other people in the movie: Matt Damon and Ben Affleck, Linda Fiorentino, Alan Rickman, Salma Hayek. I need the extra work and it was like free acting school. It's definitely the best work I've done. It broke me out of all my moves.

PLAYBOY: How did that compare to your *Lethal Weapon* experience?

ROCK: In the beginning I was really scared because it was the fourth one, like *Alien 4* and *Batman 4*. Part of what convinced me is that the script turned out good. Also, Joel Silver admitted to me that number three wasn't all that great. I figured, okay, if you're going in with that attitude, four is going to be okay.

PLAYBOY: How much did you have to bulk up?

ROCK: I just had to fight my ass off and get my lines up. I don't mean that in a bad way, but I was pretty much an extra. *Lethal Weapon* was a weird movie. I'd been filming for a month, or at least I'd been on the set for a month, and I hadn't done anything. Then, one day, the whole cast did *The Rosie O'Donnell Show*, and I did well. I killed 'em. But I'm a comedian. I'm supposed to do better than Danny Glover and Mel Gibson on a comedy show. When Joel Silver and Dick Donner saw it they said, "We've got to get him in the movie more!" It's like I'd inadvertently auditioned for a movie I was already in. From then on it was like, "Hey, we've got this scene for you." "Hey, what about this scene?"

PLAYBOY: In *Nurse Betty* you work with Morgan Freeman. Do older black men want to mentor you?

ROCK: Morgan's more of a mentor than Danny. I guess I look for it. I ask questions. Maybe I'll linger longer than I should. My dad's dead and I love guys my dad's age: "Tell me something I don't know, please." Any black guy in his 50s or 60s, I'm like, "Please talk to me. Pleeease." Danny is kind of eccentric; also smart and well educated. He knows African history, is very politically active. He told me about his college days, about the Panthers. It's a perspective I'm just not going to get from a white guy. In *Nurse Betty* Morgan Freeman has to kiss someone. Turns out it's the first time he has had to kiss a woman on-screen—and he's 60-whatever years old! That's got to be hard. Morgan is one of our best actors and, due to petty racism, no one's ever paired him with a woman, ever. Morgan fucking Freeman. You know how many ugly white guys get women in movies? When he told me I couldn't believe it.

PLAYBOY: Which of his movies is your favorite?

ROCK: Believe it or not, the most significant Morgan moment for me, and this sounds crazy, is *Deep Impact*. He plays the president of the United States, he's a black guy, and no one said shit. His color is never mentioned in the movie or in reviews. He is such a commanding presence that it's obvious he's the president. I don't think there's another black actor who could play the president without it being a big deal.

PLAYBOY: According to you we already have a black president: Bill Clinton.

ROCK: Yes, but I said it two years before all this impeachment bullshit, because of how much he was persecuted. I hate hearing people saying it now.

PLAYBOY: Why?

ROCK: Because after the Monica Lewinsky thing it was used to make it sound like this: Since Clinton—our black president—has low morals, so do my people. That's not what I meant. In an interview with *The New York Times*, the reporter asked me about Clinton and really tried hard to get me to say that. "Why do blacks support Clinton?" "We feel persecuted," I said. "We feel overwatched." He wanted me to say, "Because we all cheat," or whatever.

PLAYBOY: Most blacks supported Clinton.

ROCK: Blacks supported Clinton because Clinton supported blacks. It's that simple. Clinton appointed black people without making a fucking big deal out of it. He just did it. Any time the Republicans want to show off they say, "Hey, we've got J.C. Watts here! We've got a black guy." They have to point it out, which is racist in itself. Let's just be people. Clinton hires black people and doesn't say shit. If one fucks up, he'll hire another one. He'll hire the best person for the job, whatever their skin color.

PLAYBOY: Do you think Clinton committed perjury?

ROCK: Clinton was on trial for lying about something that wasn't even a crime. There was no crime committed before he had to answer the questions. That's what they tried to take him down for. That's ridiculous. Perjury because he didn't want to say he fooled around? Do you get an extra sentence if you tell the judge, "I wasn't speeding"? That's some shit they made up for John Gotti and Al Capone. Clinton is not Al Capone.

PLAYBOY: You mentioned Oklahoma Representative J.C. Watts. Do the words black Republican bother you?

ROCK: Not theoretically. It just confuses me that they want to hang out with guys who clearly don't like black people. Don't they realize that white Republicans are just letting them hang out so nobody can say they don't have any black guys around? It's a bold move on his part. It's nothing special to be a black Democrat, so that's one way to make a splash.

PLAYBOY: How did he do on your show?

ROCK: Even though he played to an uptown crowd that was probably 99.9 percent Democrat, he had the fucking audience. And he worked it. He explained his position in a coherent way that people could understand. I got some jabs in, but he had the audience—until he fucked up because he didn't know who George Clinton is [laughs]. I asked, "What do you do when George Clinton comes to town?" He said, "Who's George Clinton?" and the air went out of the studio.

PLAYBOY: How much does it bother you when you don't have the crowd?

ROCK: I've got the crowd. It's my show. It doesn't matter. That's why a lot of talk show guys fuck up. They think they have to get every joke. I figure if they like the guest, they like me. If everybody's funny, I'm funny. Do you want to be Magic Johnson and pass the ball and get everyone involved or do you want to be someone who scores 80 points a game but doesn't win shit? When Michael Jordan started passing the ball he started winning. Johnny Carson is the greatest assist man in the history of the game. The biggest mistake guys make is thinking they have to be the only funny one on their show. When I had on Darryl Hughley, he killed. He was so funny. That meant I looked great.

PLAYBOY: Speaking of assists, why did you decide to fund the Howard University *Lampoon?*

ROCK: We need new black writers. It's the only way for us to get decent TV shows and movies. We can't sit around waiting for white guys to write good black shit. I'm reading submissions now. Then I'm going to assemble and edit the first issue.

PLAYBOY: Do you like any of the stuff that you've seen?

ROCK: Most of it's okay-to-bad, but that's how it is with all art. I figure if the writer is 18 and I get hold of him now and work on the bad habits, he might be a real writer in a year or two.

PLAYBOY: You're far more sophisticated than these kids. Can you let them be who they are?

ROCK: Yeah. I know they're kids. I'm not looking for stuff for my show. This is a college comedy paper. That's right: I grade papers. I'm Professor Rock.

PLAYBOY: What is the worst job you had as a kid?

ROCK: [*Laughs*] I used to clean up dog shit. No one walks their dogs in the freezing New York winter; they just let them shit in the backyard. When the spring thaw came there were a bunch of people on the block with shit all over, and I was the shit boy. The phone would ring: "Hey, can you come over and clean up my backyard?" They wouldn't say "clean up the shit," but I knew what time it was.

PLAYBOY: How old were you?

ROCK: Probably 12, 13. I took any job I could get. I liked having my own job. That's why sometimes it's weird to hear, "You're rich, you have all this now." I've always had more money than my friends because I've always worked.

PLAYBOY: How do you explain the early work ethic?

ROCK: My dad worked all the time, so I figured I should. It wasn't even the money. If you're a little boy, you want to be a man. And to me, a man worked. I shoveled snow when it was cold and shit when it thawed. And you know what? It wasn't fun, but if I had to shovel shit again I wouldn't waste a day. Back then I never said, "How dare this happen to me!" I was a kid; I was supposed to be shoveling shit.

PLAYBOY: Do you own a dog today?

ROCK: My wife got one about a year ago. But I'm not cleaning shit no more.

PLAYBOY: How about having kids?

ROCK: I'm not ready.

PLAYBOY: Does the pressure your dad faced—and died of—to support a family scare you?

ROCK: I can afford a kid, but I don't want another job right now, let's put it that way. On the other hand, I'd be a real good dad, and I'd probably stop doing comedy on some level and become the guy doing it all for his kids. I used to look at my dad and think, What does he really want to do? Does he really want to come home all tired? He was beat. Beat the fuck down. We'd be out there playing stickball or whatever and he'd try to throw the ball at you. He'd throw it twice and his arm would fall off. He had to go in the house and rest. He was just tired a lot. I don't want to be that fucking tired.

PLAYBOY: Aren't you anyway?

ROCK: Not like him. I'm sure my father wanted a family to take care of and to get the love you can only get from a family. But, at the same time, he worked every fucking day. I haven't really done anything for all this shit I have. My dad worked. He supported people. He had kids. The kids wanted to go to school, the kids wanted bikes. The wife wanted something else. I work, but I'm not under the stress my dad was under. All my stress is based on worrying how I'll be perceived if I do bad work. It's not the same. I'll still eat. I really miss my dad. His death changed me, made me go into a shell I'm still not out of. Made me take more risks because it could be over in a second. It makes me sad that he didn't live to see what I've done. He would've eaten it up. We'd be going to the fights; we'd have season tickets to the Mets. My dad would be at the Dodgers spring training right now in Vero Beach. If he were still around, I would have made it all happen.

PLAYBOY: How much does your mom enjoy your success?

ROCK: She's having a ball. She has a house in South Carolina, runs a daycare center. She never shies away from doing stuff. I have to tell her not to: "What do you mean you're doing *Ricki Lake?*" [*Pauses*] My whole family is doing fine. They're all working. Brian works on the show; he's a production assistant and he's worked his way up. I'm not one who likes to pay people to do nothing, to just hang out with me. My brother Andre just bought a truck to haul garbage from New York to Pennsylvania. He has the steadiest gig as far as I'm concerned. I have the shakiest job in the family. But I can still appreciate what's happened to me and to my comfort level. The difference between me and my wife is that she complains about the maid and I can't believe I have a maid. I'm dumbfounded. I like that I can buy two slices of pizza. I've never been hungry in my whole life, but if you want more, you should be able to get more.

PLAYBOY: On the subject of getting some, we've noticed on your show that you seem to have a fondness for Latin women. Would you care to explain?

ROCK: Gorgeous women. Look at them. Have you ever been to the Puerto Rican Day parade? It's the most beautiful thing in the world. They are beautiful people. I love my people but, boy—

PLAYBOY: Latina for you is exotic?

ROCK: It's exotic. American jails are filled with men over drug offenses and shit. Latin jails are filled up with men going crazy over their women. They are passionate about their women. If you fuck with them they'll lose their mind and kill you. Why? Their women have the best pussy in the world. Puerto Rican girls, man. Gorgeous. In bed it's "Mommy," "Poppy." What's better than some woman calling you Poppy?

PLAYBOY: And you would know from experience?

ROCK: I've been called Poppy a couple times, but long, long ago.

PLAYBOY: What do you love physically about black women?

ROCK: Probably the black ass. I hate women who hide the big ass. Don't hide the big ass. It's for all of us. Share this gift. Share your big ass with all of us. We don't have to touch it or anything, but don't hide the big ass. Let us see it. Let us worship it. Let us pay it compliments. Let us tip our hats to the big ass. Love the big ass. And I'm not alone. Brothers love ass. There was an episode of *Real Sex* on HBO. They went from a black strip club to a white strip club. It was so funny. The white strip club was all about tits. The black strip club, ass. It was all about ass.

PLAYBOY: When you look in the mirror now, what do you see?

ROCK: A skinny guy who needs to get his teeth fixed. I could also use an extra 15 pounds.

PLAYBOY: Let's wrap this up. Bill Cosby blazed the trail for Richard Pryor, who opened it up for Eddie Murphy, who set the stage for you. Will the success you've had make it tougher or easier for the next guy?

ROCK: I hope it will be easier, but maybe tougher artistically, like Richard Pryor made it tough. He did stuff 20 years ago that no one has matched, partly because he's brilliant and partly because he got to do it first.

PLAYBOY: What did you do first?

ROCK: I can't say without sounding like an idiot. [*Pauses*] I talked about race in a different way; I'll go that far.

PLAYBOY: Are you worried about the next new guy?

ROCK: I never look at anything as a competition. Someone else's success never comes out of my paycheck. I don't need my friends to fail for me to succeed. To me it's just, "Let's do good work." The function of the comedian is to get as many laughs as he can by doing whatever works for him. Everybody wants to buy his mother a house. Whatever you do to get that house is the right thing. We all do our own things, from Dice to Eddie Murphy putting on a leather suit. One of the happiest times in my life was when I was eight years old and my friends and I had cool bikes—and they were all the same bikes. I was happy because everyone was equal.

 October 1993

JERRY SEINFELD

*A candid conversation
with TV's top-rated comic
about the important things:
sneakers, masturbation, dating
teenagers and making a hit
show about nothing*

This is the introduction to the *Playboy Interview*, the part you read
before you get to the questions and answers. It's an important part.
Just read what this month's subject, comedian Jerry Seinfeld, says
about it.

"I think the introduction is one of the best parts of the interview.
I also like where they go '[*laughs*]' and '[*smiles*].' But to tell you the
truth, in the introduction you always pick up some juicy little personal
tidbit, like the subject just came back from tai chi. You also get the
thing about when the interviewer drove up to the house and what the
guy was wearing, what he drank. You find he does some little thing
you didn't know about, like eating potato chips through the whole
interview. I remember someone once ate french fries. I thought, Wow.
He eats french fries. That's what I'm interested in.

"Plus, when something is in italics it calls a great deal of attention
to itself. A word in italics almost seems to vibrate on the page. And
this is a whole page of italics."

Five years ago, Jerry Seinfeld was a thin, single, mild-mannered,
obsessively neat comedian working the stand-up circuit, making a
name for himself as a bright and funny guy. Today, he's a thin, single,
mild-mannered, obsessively neat comedian and TV star whose hit
sitcom, *Seinfeld*, has garnered amazing media coverage and critical
acclaim—especially for a show that is admittedly about nothing.

"Nothing" fits Seinfeld's particular brand of comedy—some call it
observational or deconstructionist—like a glove. Seinfeld plays Jerry
Seinfeld, who, of course, is a 39-year-old, thin, single and obsessively

neat comedian living in an Upper West Side New York apartment. He has three friends: Elaine (Julia Louis-Dreyfus), the ex-girlfriend, now platonic gal pal; George (Jason Alexander), the balding and unemployed paragon of low self-esteem; and Kramer (Michael Richards), the eccentric neighbor who proves you can get by in life no matter how unusual your hairstyle. When they're not gathered in Seinfeld's apartment or sharing a booth at a local coffee shop, they're living life at its most mundane and uneventful, asking questions such as "Why do I get bananas? They're good for one day," confronting what *Entertainment Weekly* called "the little adjustments of daily urban life that no network in its right mind would turn into a sitcom."

In the wrong hands this would not be particularly funny. It would possibly even be boring. After all, how funny can an entire show about waiting for a table in a Chinese restaurant be?

Pretty funny, according to *Washington Post* TV critic Tom Shales, who wrote that *Seinfeld* can be "painfully amusing and amusingly painful." In one show, the four characters lose their car in a mall parking garage. In another they ride the subway. Recently, Jerry's car had a horrible odor he couldn't get rid of.

Seinfeld specializes in unusual topics: masturbation and who can go the longest without it, breast implants, pooper scoopers and the perils of trying to make friends as an adult. Other shows wouldn't touch these subjects with a 13-episode commitment, unless there were a few hugs and a life-affirming moral attached. *Seinfeld* eschews hugs. And morals. And anything that smacks of neatly summing up life in 22 minutes.

When it debuted, *Seinfeld* was a critical hit and a cult favorite. Cult favorites, of course, don't impress network executives unless the cult starts to grow—and the *Seinfeld* cult did. *TV Guide* said: "The yen for *Seinfeld*'s idiosyncratic hipness is on the upswing," and went on to describe the sitcom as "resolutely minor crises played out with excruciatingly wry precision that has distinguished the show as 'thirty-something,' comic style." Eventually, *Seinfeld* was holding its own on Wednesday nights on NBC—until ABC's *Home Improvement* moved in next door. The more mainstream *Home Improvement* clobbered *Seinfeld* in the ratings, so NBC moved *Seinfeld* to Thursday, following *Cheers*. The viewership expanded instantly, and NBC turned to Jerry in much the same way it turned to Bill Cosby 10 years ago—to anchor its all-important Thursday-night lineup.

Despite his youthful appearance, Seinfeld is no overnight sensation. The middle-class kid from Massapequa, Long Island had an uneventful childhood. He wasn't popular, he wasn't unpopular. He wasn't part of the in-crowd, he wasn't a ladies' man. He had ambition, but it was largely unattainable: to be Superman. Instead, he decided to become a comedian. His first funny venture was taping interviews with his parakeet.

Seinfeld's late father, Kalman, was a salesman and a funny guy, but the son never considered trying to out-funny his father. And when Seinfeld graduated from Queens College, started doing stand-up and then decided on a career making people pay to laugh, his folks supported his decision.

There were a few odd jobs along the way: selling light bulbs over the phone, peddling jewelry on the sidewalks of Manhattan. Seinfeld got two nights and 70 bucks a week emceeing at the Comic Strip, and he knew he was on his way. He simply didn't realize what a slow trip it would be.

Other comics seemed to make it overnight. Garry Shandling, who first appeared on *The Tonight Show* about the same time as Seinfeld, became a big name, a Carson substitute and the star of a cable series, while Seinfeld continued playing small clubs and flying in coach. Shortly after being cast as the governor's joke writer on *Benson* for a few episodes, he showed up for work to discover he'd lost his job. No one had bothered to tell him. So Seinfeld went back to the comedy circuit, traveling 300 days a year, hitting the talk shows and doing a fairly lackluster cable special.

Slowly but steadily his success grew. Clubs turned into arenas, sold-out signs began appearing on box offices and TV producers saw him as the next Bob Newhart.

And then one day, after he and comedian pal Larry David finished performing at Catch a Rising Star, they came up with the idea for *Seinfeld*. Originally, it was just about two guys talking, dissecting the world—something comedians tend to do offstage with other comedians. NBC ordered a pilot.

Working on *Seinfeld*, says Seinfeld, is like being in a submarine. The hours are long and constant, and the responsibilities are shared among a small group, with little network interference. Seinfeld, Larry David and a tight inner circle come up with the ideas and write the scripts. Seinfeld also has to come up with a couple of minutes of material every week for the onstage monolog that winds through the show.

Although there's time for little else but work during the TV season, all the work has paid off. *Seinfeld* is solidly in the Nielsen top 10 and was nominated for 11 Emmys. Seinfeld himself is a media rage. There's a line of greeting cards, and the cast can be seen on boxes of Kellogg's low-fat granola. He even has a book out of observations on life called *Sein Language*. This is what he told the press at a New York comedy club when he announced the publishing deal: "I'm not really an author. I've been writing for 17 years. I'm just presenting it differently. I'm numbering the pages."

Here's the point in the introduction that Seinfeld likes so much—where we tell you that we asked Contributing Editor David Rensin to meet with Seinfeld and have him expand on all the stuff we just told you. Rensin had this to say about his experience:

"I met Jerry on the set. He looked just like he does on TV. Who says the camera adds 15 pounds? He gave me a Polaroid camera and asked if I would take a picture of him and his baby to put on the makeup-trailer wall next to everyone else's 'with baby' pictures. Seinfeld's baby turned out to be a 1958 baby-blue Porsche Speedster.

"During our first session, at Jerry's newly remodeled, largely unfurnished, 6500-square-foot Hollywood Hills home, he offered me a glass of water. There were no tables so I set it on the carpet next to the couch. I had my legs up, trying to keep my shoes off the couch (with middling success). When we were done, Jerry hopped up and snatched my glass off the carpet before I could bus it myself. He wasn't taking any chances of a spill.

"Frankly, interviewing a guy who is supposed to be just like his TV character makes one wonder what to talk about. What was I going to ask him? Why do you like cereal so much? Does the TV Jerry own as many pairs of sneakers as you do? Why are you so neat? Actually, I did have a few questions designed to get at the man behind the man whom everyone thinks they know so well. But before I could ask even one, Jerry posed a question of his own."

SEINFELD: When are we going to get to the sex part?
PLAYBOY: The sex part?

SEINFELD: Yeah. I think people want to know what I'm doing sexually and what my experiences have been, what kind of sexual prowess or power I may have because of my position. What instructions were you given as far as "Find out about his sex life"?

PLAYBOY: Okay. Do you have sex?

SEINFELD: Yes, I do.

PLAYBOY: Good. And now—

SEINFELD: Is that it? Is it over?

PLAYBOY: What's your hurry?

SEINFELD: You're such a tease.

PLAYBOY: Stick around.

SEINFELD: There's something else besides sex I want to talk about. I would like to blow the lid off the three quotes under the three pictures. I wasn't saying any of these things when the three pictures were taken. They are the three best pictures and the three best quotes, but they're completely unrelated to one another. In fact, if any of this is under the pictures, I'm telling you right now that there's no camera here.

PLAYBOY: What if we let you choose the quotes?

SEINFELD: Great. So put "This is not what I was saying when these pictures were taken. In fact, if any of this is under the pictures, I'm telling you right now that there's no camera here" under the first. And "When are we going to get to the sex part?" under the second. I'll think of a third as we go along.

PLAYBOY: Fine. There's one last thing to clear up. Are we talking to the real Jerry or the TV Jerry?

SEINFELD: What do you mean?

PLAYBOY: One of your TV show's conceits is that the real Jerry and the TV Jerry are supposed to be the same guy.

SEINFELD: They're not that different. But I'm the real Jerry.

PLAYBOY: Can you prove it?

SEINFELD: I have no script [*holds up his hands*].

PLAYBOY: That must take away all your image worries.

SEINFELD: I found an acceptable image that was really pretty much me, and that's how I've done everything. That's why I was able to do the show and why I've succeeded as a comedian. I don't have the energy to maintain an image.

PLAYBOY: So, people who stop you on the street must really think they know you.

SEINFELD: They know me better than they know Dan Rather. You couldn't predict what Dan Rather would do in most situations, but I think you could with me. I wouldn't mind an "Excuse me" before a total stranger starts talking to me. That's the most amusing and most bizarre thing about celebrity. I'm walking down the street, someone walks up alongside of me and says, "So, how come Elaine and you got together only that one time?" They don't say, "Excuse me, could I talk to you for one second?" Nothing. We're just talking as if we've been talking for blocks. This happens all the time.

PLAYBOY: By the way, how *was* sex with Elaine?

SEINFELD: Well, you can see that she's very expressive. The way she moves, she has a physical fluidity. You can see that just by watching her talk. It's not a big leap for someone with imagination.

PLAYBOY: Which our readers—

SEINFELD: Probably don't have.

PLAYBOY: Why do you say that?

SEINFELD: If you have a good imagination, you usually don't need visual aids. I don't mean to offend, but who's going to get this deep into the interview anyway? They're probably at the centerfold by now.

PLAYBOY: They might have turned to it first.

SEINFELD: That's right. [*Laughs*] And now they're falling asleep.

PLAYBOY: Whom would you stop on the street just to meet?

SEINFELD: Abraham Lincoln. I'd say, "I'm sorry, I'm sure you get this all the time, but I just think you're fantastic."

PLAYBOY: Seriously, are strangers so taken with *Seinfeld* that they insist their lives are perfect material for the show?

SEINFELD: That's a compliment. I'm doing something that seems so taken from their own lives they can't help but assume that everything in their lives must be funny.

PLAYBOY: Are they right or wrong?

SEINFELD: They're wrong. They may be funny enough to get them through that moment at the water cooler, but they're not funny enough to be on television in front of millions of people and have them buy a Geo Prizm as a result. I take it as a comment on my skill as a comedian. It seems like nothing. It should seem like nothing. It should seem like something anyone could do.

PLAYBOY: What are the levels of comedy?

SEINFELD: Making your friends laugh, making strangers laugh, making strangers laugh for money and making people act like you.

PLAYBOY: Do civilians always try to make you laugh?

SEINFELD: Could you explain that to me, please? What the hell is that phenomenon? If I meet singers, I don't go, "Hey, what do you think of this?" and sing. Why would you invite that humiliation by trying to be funny around a comedian? To make a comedian laugh, you have to be funnier than you are when you make your friends laugh. Funnier than you've ever been in your life. What are the odds that you're going to succeed? Why do you try?

PLAYBOY: Are you kind to amateurs?

SEINFELD: I'm very kind. Everyone has a few fake laughs they use to get through life. The snort, the snort-chuckle, the nod-smile, the "That's good!" But they're all just nice ways of saying "Stop. Please stop."

PLAYBOY: So the constant attention of strangers—

SEINFELD: I'm annoyed. But if you're not cranky and annoyed, you can't be a comedian. Any good comedian is, by definition, highly irritable. Even I, though I may not seem to be, am constantly irritated.

PLAYBOY: What irritates you?

SEINFELD: Everything. I just hate everything and everybody. And that's why I'm so funny. If I didn't have all these sensitivities, I'd have nothing to talk about.

PLAYBOY: Do you owe your public?

SEINFELD: That's where the money's coming from, isn't it?

PLAYBOY: That's an elegant way of looking at it.

SEINFELD: That's my job: to understand what's going on in life, to figure it out. The news, books, magazines and films cover a certain portion of what's going on. But there's a lot of stuff that's not touched on, and that's my job. To tell you the truth, 75 percent of the world is not touched on except by comedians.

PLAYBOY: Which you do in your TV show—

SEINFELD: Wait. What about the sex part?

PLAYBOY: First the TV show.

SEINFELD: Oh, *Seinfeld*. Yes, I've seen it. It's quite a charming little piece of work, isn't it?

PLAYBOY: Especially for a show that's supposed to be about nothing. What exactly does that mean?

SEINFELD: It's actually about details. We joke that it's about nothing because there's no concept behind the show, there's nothing intrinsically funny in the situation. It's just about four people. There's no thread. No high concept.

PLAYBOY: But isn't Hollywood built on concept?

SEINFELD: That is the concept: no concept.

PLAYBOY: Which, as we've already mentioned, fuels the perception that your real life is just as it's portrayed on the show.

SEINFELD: I play myself as I was before I got the show. I understand that people would like to think that they're looking into my actual life. It would be fun if that were true. People want to get to know people they see on TV. That's why they read interviews. That's why they watch talk shows. Other cultures accept performers as they view them. Americans see performers whom they like and they want to know, "Hey, what's behind that? How did they get to be that way? How do they come up with their ideas?"

PLAYBOY: What do you think is behind this obsession?

SEINFELD: I guess Americans are just nosy. They want a little bit more. It's the same concept behind extra-strength pain relievers. What the hell is extra strength? We don't know how much strength they were giving us, and we don't know how much more "extra" is. But we're giving you extra, and Americans like that idea. We'll throw in the floor mats when you buy a new car. It's that little something. Then, when they've found out enough about a person, they start to hate him. Then they move on to the next person.

PLAYBOY: Thanks. You've just explained the entire—

SEINFELD: Cycle of celebrity.

PLAYBOY: Can you deconstruct anything?

SEINFELD: Deconstruction. That's a very good word for what I do. I have a friend who's not a comedian, he's a computer analyst. He's always going, "See, there's something funny about this saltshaker, but I can't see it. You could see it." And it frustrates him. He's looking at the saltshaker and I'm looking at the saltshaker, and he knows there's a joke there. He can't find it.

PLAYBOY: Have you found anything you can't deconstruct?

SEINFELD: Yeah, sure. I can't crack most things. You don't realize that the joke is the diamond. The joke is the fleck of gold after going through a ton of rock. And you're saying to me, "What's rock?" The whole world is rock. I've found this little lump of gold—my comedy material—and I've made it into an act.

PLAYBOY: Do you enjoy your job?

SEINFELD: I am my job. Everything else in life pales by comparison to the interpretive experience: seeing something, interpreting it, shaping it, communicating it and being affirmed for it. Every time something funny is discovered, it's an absolute miracle. And the most amazing thing is when I have only three minutes to think of something funny. We shot a show recently where George borrows his father's car and it gets destroyed by a gang—it's actually more complicated than that. We're in this scene where I'm standing next to George and his father's car. The door is ripped off, the engine's destroyed, the windows are all smashed. We're shooting, it's late, it's cold, we need a line. What can I say? I love that.

PLAYBOY: What did you come up with?

SEINFELD: I said to him: "You know, a lot of these scratches will buff right out."

PLAYBOY: Why do you come to a scene like that without a line?

SEINFELD: Because—I knew you were going to ask that, by the way—we were going to try to make the joke with a camera shot. But once we were all standing by the car, it needed what they call a button.

PLAYBOY: So this is the thrill of comedy.

SEINFELD: I've learned that when I really need to think of something funny, I'm often able to do it. I never knew I could do that. I always thought it took hours. But I found out that sometimes the mind can work faster when it's under pressure, even comically.

PLAYBOY: Were you this quick when you were younger? Or were you quick but not funny?

SEINFELD: We have ourselves a nice little setup here, haven't we? It's worked very well. I probably was quick when I was younger, but I didn't know it, so it's the same as not being quick. Here's what it comes down to: You need talent, you need brains and you need confidence. Those are the three things you need to do virtually anything. Confidence is a fascinating commodity. There's no upper limit on the usefulness of it, as long as it doesn't bleed into arrogance. You need as much of it as you can get.

PLAYBOY: Considering your current popularity, you must be overflowing with the stuff.

SEINFELD: That's what I've gained from this show. And that's what I wanted from day one. I didn't want a successful TV series, I didn't want money, fame—any of the things any normal person would want. I wanted the confidence I would have if I could do it.

PLAYBOY: How do you know when it becomes arrogance?

SEINFELD: When you're losing. When you start making bets that you're not winning. I've always had a lot of confidence. But I wanted more.

As a comedian you're never as good as you want to be. To me that means being strong enough to take your time with an audience. Young comedians—most comedians—work onstage at a breathless pace, and that's out of fear. I do it, too. It keeps it going. But when you can slow down and hold people, that's being good enough. I love seeing Bill Cosby tell a story slowly. Comedy strength is slowness. Jack Benny is a perfect example. He would come out onstage, wouldn't say anything. He would just stand there and the people would start to laugh. I mean, that is comic strength. But to wait for the laugh, that's balls. And I say balls only because it's *Playboy*.

PLAYBOY: Can you apply this to other things?

SEINFELD: It applies to everything. Of course it applies to life. The good things in life, the most interesting things in life, are the things that distill life—like comedy, like baseball and art. Whatever takes the experience and kind of crushes it down into something you can grab. That's why you go to a movie. That's why you read a book. That's why everybody likes epigrams and aphorisms. You feel, like, if you go to a movie, maybe you'll experience more of life in that two hours than you would in just your own life. That's what a lot of entertainment is: a condensed life experience.

PLAYBOY: Let's get back to *Seinfeld*. Is it true that all the cast members hate one another?

SEINFELD: Yes. We're at one another's throats constantly. [*Laughs*]

PLAYBOY: How are you dealing with Kramer's transformation into a pop-culture superstar?

SEINFELD: I think he's bigger than I am. Michael Richards has a unique talent, which needed to find a place. Before this show, nobody was using him properly. He's like this engine, just running and running. It's not in gear, it's not driving anything. And if you don't hook it up with something, it's going to turn on you. Having a talent is a kill-or-be-killed thing. Especially comedic talent. It has to be focused on other people, or it turns on you in the most vicious way.

PLAYBOY: And then what happens?

SEINFELD: You become self-destructive. Or you have to leave the country. I know a guy who had to leave the country.

PLAYBOY: Isn't he just killing himself in some other country?

SEINFELD: No, he's forgotten about it. He's away from it. He doesn't have to see all his friends on TV and know that he's funnier than they are but he's not doing anything.

PLAYBOY: How are you taking your own transformation into an icon?

SEINFELD: Great. Unfortunately, right now I'm out of control.

PLAYBOY: If you're talking about the line of *Seinfeld* greeting cards, that does seem over the top.

SEINFELD: Yeah, I wasn't too happy with the greeting cards. It seemed like a good idea then. We were approached by a reputable merchandiser, and at the time we weren't doing well against *Home Improvement*. We needed every bit of promo we could get. By the time the stuff came out, the landscape had changed. It's not really right for us anymore.

PLAYBOY: Is that what you mean by being out of control?

SEINFELD: No. For 98 percent of my career I was completely at the wheel. All my performances, my level, my workload—it was all under control. Now I'm just hanging on to this thing. My career has now developed a life and a power of its own, and I am just a passenger. I don't like peaks. I always wanted to have a plateau kind of career. I shudder when I see these people skyrocket and then flame out in a second. I wouldn't want Madonna's kind of career, where you constantly have to make battleships disappear. I'm more into watchmaking. I'm most interested in having a body of work, to say that I created all this material and I did these shows.

PLAYBOY: So you're in this for the long haul?

SEINFELD: I will have longevity. I'd like to play the London Palladium when I'm 100, just like George Burns. No, make that 110. But I still can't believe it can go on the way it has for much longer. I mean, I'm almost out of things to say. No, I'm just kidding.

PLAYBOY: Enough about you. Why is *Seinfeld* a hit?

SEINFELD: It has an urban flavor. It's about single life. Everyone is single at some point. But mostly it's about being offbeat. Almost everything we do is offbeat. Even ordinary things somehow come out offbeat. We don't want to do stuff we've seen. We try to step into real life. When *Roseanne* does a show about teenage abortion, that's real, too. But our field of expertise seems to be more minute.

PLAYBOY: Who's the audience?

SEINFELD: The bored, the disaffected, the disenfranchised. The tired, the huddled masses. I did a bit about that on the show. "Must we specifically request the worst people in the world? Why don't we just say our doors are open and we'll take whatever you've got? Do we have to say, 'Give us your tired, your poor'? Do they have to be tired? People who don't return calls—anybody who can't do something—send them over." You have to expose yourself to the show for a while, develop a taste for the characters, the situations, the jokes, the stories. It's not everyone's cup of tea.

PLAYBOY: It wasn't when it was on Wednesday nights.

SEINFELD: *Home Improvement* was killing us. It has a broader appeal.

PLAYBOY: Why are you doing better on Thursdays?

SEINFELD: I don't know.

PLAYBOY: Your co-creator, Larry David, said that if people didn't watch on Wednesdays he didn't want them to watch on Thursdays.

SEINFELD: I never agreed with that. I wanted people to watch it. The show is funny. There's not much good comedy on TV, period. Funny is hard. It's like Michelangelo's *David*. I was just in Florence. I saw the *David*. I also saw some of the other statues littered around the city—the legs were too thick, the proportions off—and it was clear Mike knew what he was doing. Sitcoms are hard because there are so many people involved, and good comedy is always specific. Our show is basically run by Larry David and me without any interference. That's one reason the material is good. We're not trying to please anybody but ourselves. It's not homogenized, it's not run through the system.

PLAYBOY: And how would that change things?

SEINFELD: We did this line in the show a couple weeks ago where an ex-boyfriend of Elaine's was being operated on. Kramer wanted to watch and wanted somebody to go with him. He says, "C'mon, c'mon. Go with me." We're sitting in the coffee shop and I go, "All right, all right, I'll go with you. Let me just finish this coffee and we'll go watch them slice this fat bastard up." That is not the type of thing that lead characters in successful sitcoms say. It's not what you would call likable, at least not in the traditional network sense. But that's what's great about the show. We're at the point where people understand the characters as human beings and they'll accept that. What makes it fun for me is being that honest—because that's what I would say in real life—without hurting my likability.

PLAYBOY: You've said that after five seasons you're gone. *Time* magazine recently posited that your show might be around for 10.

SEINFELD: I can guarantee you we won't do 10. I don't want to be in people's faces. This show is going to be off way sooner than anyone would believe.

PLAYBOY: So do you worry about being overexposed?

SEINFELD: Yes, I do. There are certain movies where the promotion is so well-coordinated and so pervasive that, before the movie comes out, I hate it, just because they're so good at telling me about it. They've done such a complete job of selling that it breeds resentment.

PLAYBOY: And yet you've been everywhere lately.

SEINFELD: I was working yesterday with a magazine photographer, and the wardrobe woman and I were talking about this. They wanted to do a cover line on me—America Loves Jerry Seinfeld or something like that. I said, "That's not good. That's going to make people hate me. If you say that about someone, it defines a relationship with the public and then propels it to end badly. A love affair is a relationship, and that has to end badly." And she said, "It's going to end badly anyway, no matter what." That's true: It ends badly anyway. So you might as well experience the peak of passion with whatever relationship we're talking about, whether it's with a person or, in this case, a professional relationship with the public. It's going to end badly. Everything ends.

PLAYBOY: How does a *Seinfeld* evolve?

SEINFELD: Somebody comes up with an idea for a show—it could be just one line. And just hearing that one line makes you laugh. "Jerry picks up his car from the valet and there's a smell that won't come out." "Jerry and Kramer go to watch an operation, and a Junior Mint falls into the body." Virtually every show that we've done can be boiled down that way. It's not like "Jerry's nephew comes to visit for a week." That doesn't make you laugh.

PLAYBOY: What's the one-liner for "The Contest"?

SEINFELD: Jerry, George, Kramer and Elaine decide to see who can go the longest without masturbation and who can remain master of their domain.

PLAYBOY: How would you do a one-liner for a show about this interview?

SEINFELD: We already did that. It's "The Outing." A reporter overhears Jerry and George joking around and then writes that they're gay. Not that there's anything wrong with that. [*Pauses*] You know, I was thinking about that show this morning. My friend Mario was in the kitchen, because he's staying here. I was thinking, Gee, I wonder if this guy from *Playboy* thinks there's something going on.

PLAYBOY: Frankly, that did immediately come to mind.

SEINFELD: Oh, really? That's so funny!

PLAYBOY: Also, "Hey, he's a damn good-looking guy."

SEINFELD: [*Laughs*] Oh, that's funny. Too bad we've already done the show. No, Mario's just a comedian friend of mine.

PLAYBOY: But you've heard the rumors?

SEINFELD: Many. Somebody told me the other day that he heard I had special phone numbers for different levels of women. I don't know what the hell that meant. And obviously I've heard that I'm gay. I've been told that everybody at NBC in New York thinks I'm gay.

PLAYBOY: Now's your opportunity to state unequivocally that—

SEINFELD: I'm not gay.

PLAYBOY: When you're in the heat of passion—

SEINFELD: Do I think of men? No.

PLAYBOY: Do you fold your clothes before you have sex?

SEINFELD: No. I generally don't wear clothes during sex. Wait a second, wait a second! Are we up to the sex part?

PLAYBOY: We're getting closer.

SEINFELD: All right!

PLAYBOY: Has a guy ever approached you?

SEINFELD: Once, in Rome. I decided to take a trip to Europe on my own, to see if I could meet people. This was a complete miscalculation of my personality. I don't talk to anyone. I spent 10 days there without having one conversation, except with this guy. I was so thrilled to have someone to talk to, and I didn't realize that he was hitting on me. But then it became obvious.

PLAYBOY: Is this misperception part of the reason that you did "The Outing" episode?

SEINFELD: No. That was actually Larry Charles's idea. He's our supervising producer. And when I heard it, not only did I think it was a great idea on its own but I also thought, perfect! It's not something I'm uncomfortable with. I used to be. When you're younger, if someone thinks you're gay you get really upset about it. But now I just laugh. It means people are thinking too much about you.

PLAYBOY: Why do you take on topics like masturbation, nipples on Christmas cards and bad smells when other shows don't?

SEINFELD: If I may be so immodest, it takes some pretty skillful writing to do these things and make them comfortable for people to watch on a mass level. Anybody can write a funny show about masturbation. But can you do it in an artful way that offends no one and, in fact, is even funnier than if you had come right out and talked about it? It takes skill. And when we re-ran that show last May we got our highest rating ever.

PLAYBOY: It's a classic show. Right up there with the birth of Little Ricky.

SEINFELD: And, of course, the first time Little Ricky jerked off.

PLAYBOY: Why did you think you could pull it off?

SEINFELD: I'll ignore your choice of phrase there. If it's something no one else has done before, it's challenging.

PLAYBOY: Were you just trying to see if you could get the material past the censors?

SEINFELD: We're not trying to get away with anything. That's a completely different sensibility. I want to see if I can do what I want to do without pushing people's moral envelope, or whatever. And if we can't, then we don't do it. We wanted to do a show in which Elaine would be stuck in a subway and miss her stop, and be on her way to Harlem. Kind of explore her fear of having to get off the subway in Harlem. We couldn't find a way to do it without people getting the wrong impression. It was coming off racist. It was too small a needle to thread, so we abandoned it.

PLAYBOY: How did you hook up with the show's co-creator, Larry David?

SEINFELD: We've known each other since about 1976, 1977. We were both doing stand-up. But stand-up isn't his form. It's too crass for what he does. Larry has a brilliant flair for staging and direction. There is no show without him. He has, more than me, created this enterprise. My skill has been to help him interpret his ideas. He filters things through me. I contribute lines and jokes.

PLAYBOY: Do you wish you could have done it all by yourself?

SEINFELD: No. I have stand-up for that. I'm not out for the credit. I'm just glad to be doing something that's not bad TV.

PLAYBOY: What do you watch on TV?

SEINFELD: I could never watch sitcoms before I started doing one. But now they're really interesting because I see what they're trying to do, where they're succeeding, where they're failing. It used to be only *The Honeymooners*, sports, news, animal shows.

PLAYBOY: The Discovery Channel?

SEINFELD: Yeah. *Shark Week*. I always love how one animal is the star each week. And you want him to kill whatever he's trying to kill because you're on his side. If it's the lion, you want him to get that boar. The next week it's about boars. Now you're hoping that the boar gets away from the lion. Your loyalty is so fickle with these animal shows.

PLAYBOY: What did you watch as a kid?

SEINFELD: *Rocky and Bullwinkle, Jonny Quest, Spider-Man, Batman. Flipper* was a big favorite. Comedywise, Ed Sullivan, Red Skelton, Jonathan Winters, the Smothers Brothers.

PLAYBOY: Was yours a happy childhood?

SEINFELD: I had a lot of fun. I rode my bike a lot, went swimming. I was a Cub Scout. I had a Schwinn Sting Ray, blue metallic with, of course, the banana seat. The first one in Harbor Green to have one. The other kids went nuts. I was very proud of that.

PLAYBOY: What did you want as a kid that you couldn't get?

SEINFELD: The Schwinn Sting Ray. And once I got it, I was very happy. It's pretty much the same with the Porsche. At about 13, I realized I wanted a Porsche, and I was unhappy until I got it. Now I have it and I'm happy.

PLAYBOY: What's next?

SEINFELD: Nothing. I'm set.

PLAYBOY: How were you with girls?

SEINFELD: Uneventful. I kind of withdrew from a lot of social activity. I didn't like group mentality and group behavior. I wanted to focus in on one person. I wanted to tell that person what I think about nuances and details and substructures. And you don't do that in groups.

PLAYBOY: Not when you're just eight years old.

SEINFELD: And even now you don't. You go to parties and it's all breezy bullshitting, chitchatting. I like that up to a point, but then I'm bored by it. I want to sit with somebody and get down to the nuts and bolts.

PLAYBOY: When you're at a party, where do you stand?

SEINFELD: I'll tell you what happens when I go to a party. I'll open the door and I'll walk in. And I'll keep walking—and it usually won't be far—until I hit a spot where someone stops me or I see someone I know and I start talking. That is the spot I will stay in for the entire party. I sometimes wonder: Why can't I get deeper into the room?

PLAYBOY: Any clue?

SEINFELD: I guess it's because I immediately try to make the best of the situation I'm in. I think that's a key component of my personality. I'm not as interested in changing my situation as I am in improving the one I have, which I think is good. I mean, I always do the best I can with what I have.

PLAYBOY: Is that your philosophy of life?

SEINFELD: No, it just occurred to me. But I'd like to change that. I would like to walk through more of the room and be at four or five different places by the end of the party. [*Looks down at his new sneakers*] The tongue on this shoe is really short. And you know what? That makes or breaks a shoe in my book. Look at how short that is. That is no goddamn good. This will never be one of my favorites.

PLAYBOY: You've said that small talk is excruciating for you. Do you give the impression that you don't want to talk to people?

SEINFELD: I generally don't want to. Most people are not equipped to discuss the things I want to discuss, which is sneaker tongues and things like that. They haven't thought about it, they have no ideas about it. That's why Larry David and I just go on forever. He's equipped to discuss anything.

PLAYBOY: Would you talk about sneaker tongues if somebody else brought it up?

SEINFELD: Yeah, I love it. I light up when somebody else brings it up. I go, "Okay, now I have a player here. Let's talk."

PLAYBOY: You're always buying and wearing new pairs of sneakers. Do you have a sneaker fetish?

SEINFELD: I've always liked sneakers—that was something I responded to even at six years old. I drove my mother crazy about getting me sneakers. She wouldn't let me wear them in the winter. She would set a day when I was allowed to start wearing sneakers again.

PLAYBOY: What kind did you wear?

SEINFELD: Keds. My favorite ones were the dark-blue kind that you could get only in the city. On Long Island they had only black. I've got a picture of me wearing them in my first grade class. Every other kid in the picture has regular shoes on. I'm in high tops.

PLAYBOY: Apparently this runs deeper than anyone suspected.

SEINFELD: All comedians have an obsession about their feet. If I see a comedian during the day with a pair of shoes on, I stop him, grab him and go, "What is going on?" You just never see it. Comedians hate shoes.

PLAYBOY: Why?

SEINFELD: Comedians like to be comfortable. But more than that, it's clinging to your youthful mood. I always wanted to be ready to play ball if anyone suggested it. I didn't want to have to go home and change. Your shoes are important because they define your relationship to the earth. I like to have something playful on my feet.

PLAYBOY: We hear that you don't keep them if they get as much as a tiny scuff.

SEINFELD: Another media-driven scandal. Not true. But I do give old pairs away to the less fortunate—who at this point are pretty much everybody.

PLAYBOY: How many pairs do you have?

SEINFELD: Right now I'm a little low. Probably 15 or 20. I really need to get some more.

PLAYBOY: Let's investigate a couple of your other notable quirks. What about your love of flossing?

SEINFELD: More bullshit. I flossed after lunch one day at the show, and a magazine writer decided that meant I'm obsessed with flossing. I floss twice a day. That's what my dentist told me to do, so I do it.

PLAYBOY: What about your involvement with Scientology?

SEINFELD: I took a couple courses a number of years ago that I thought were fabulous. I learned a lot and I had a good experience with it.

PLAYBOY: You're not an unwitting dupe of the church?

SEINFELD: No, I've always had the skill of extracting the essence of any subject I study, be it meditation, yoga, Scientology, Judaism, Zen. Whatever it is, I go in to get what I need. To me, these are supermarkets. I go in to get my supplies, then I leave.

PLAYBOY: Most of your friends are comics. Why is that?

SEINFELD: I love funny people.

PLAYBOY: We hear time and time again that most comics are venal, self-centered and not nice.

SEINFELD: There are guys driving bread trucks who fit the same description. I feel comfortable with comics. We understand one another. Here's a good question for you the next time you interview a comic: If you had to be stuck in a room for the rest of your life with one person, and either you would be funny or that person would be funny, which would you prefer? That's a good one, isn't it?

PLAYBOY: What's the answer?

SEINFELD: I would prefer that the other person be funny. To not laugh is worse than to not be funny.

PLAYBOY: Many comics might choose the other option.

SEINFELD: Not the good ones. If you're up there for yourself, you're not as good as if you're up there for them. That's how I break them down. That's how I cut the comedy community in half. For whose benefit are you onstage?

PLAYBOY: Is that why you've said there should be no stars in comedy?

SEINFELD: Yes. Stars can succeed by concealing who they are. Comedians can't.

PLAYBOY: But you've become a star.

SEINFELD: Well, not in my mind—and that's the one we're talking about. Do I look like a star to you?

PLAYBOY: Nope, just a regular guy. How have the experiences of your friends who have become famous prepared you for the change in your own life?

SEINFELD: They haven't. Jay Leno is really the only one I knew well, and I watched him take off. But you have no idea how you're going to respond to it. Jay and I are very different. Jay's the ultimate public-service guy. I mean, when he gets 30 calls about a joke that was offensive, he calls every one of those people and finds out why or apologizes. I don't respond to the public that way. This is my thing, take it or leave it.

PLAYBOY: Is it true that you and Jay sit around and critique comics just for fun?

SEINFELD: All comedians do it. Comedians gossip endlessly. They love to bullshit their lives away; that's why they became comedians.

PLAYBOY: Weren't you once considered as the guest host for David Letterman?

SEINFELD: He said that one time in an interview. I don't think that was ever at a serious stage. He mentioned me as a fill-in if he were on vacation or something.

PLAYBOY: Are you interested in being a talk-show host?

SEINFELD: No. I could never maintain the illusion that I really give a damn about when this person's movie is coming out, or show any interest in the person. The brilliance of Letterman, the genius of Letterman, is that he can conduct an interview with someone he does not respect without compromising himself and, at the same time, he lets us know how he feels. I'm amazed by that. I could never play that edge the way he does.

PLAYBOY: Explain the differences between Jay and Dave.

SEINFELD: Jay reads the books. Every day they screen the movie of the guest who's coming on the next day. Leno does incredible research. He is like John Riggins of the Washington Redskins. He was the kind of guy to whom you would give the ball and he would plow into that line over and over again.

PLAYBOY: What about Dave?

SEINFELD: Letterman's a little more offbeat. Letterman is like Crazy Legs Hirsch.

PLAYBOY: Since both Letterman and Leno are your pals, how did you feel watching them jockey for position before Dave decided to go with CBS?

SEINFELD: It was as uncomfortable for me as it was for them. But they were cool about it. They understand the inherent brutality of show business, and that was just one of those episodes. Two wildebeests are walking down the street and the lion's in the bushes. Somebody's going to get eaten. But it seems to have worked out well for both.

PLAYBOY: Did you talk to Dave and Jay during the battle?

SEINFELD: Yeah. They both felt it was terrible that it had to be like that. But friends compete in sports all the time. Look at Jordan and Barkley. There is no acrimony. Luckily, they're two professional guys who are fairly secure.

PLAYBOY: Is it difficult to choose which show you're going to appear on?

SEINFELD: No. Being on Carson was like being on your dad's show. Being on Letterman or with Leno is like being on your friend's show. I kind of miss the fear. I don't feel out of place anymore. I miss putting together the suit and tie, very conservative so as not to offend.

PLAYBOY: Now you don't depend on talk-show appearances for a living.

SEINFELD: Now who gives a shit?

PLAYBOY: There are some who are afraid to go on Dave's show.

SEINFELD: But that's just a matter of being funny. With the Carson show there were all these other points of protocol that you worried about: the okay finger versus the not-okay finger at the end of your set, the suit and the idea of "What if I went on without a tie? Oh my God!" It was like throwing a Molotov cocktail. I don't think about things like that now.

PLAYBOY: How many times were you on with Carson?

SEINFELD: Thirty.

PLAYBOY: Did he wave you over to the couch the first time?

SEINFELD: No, it was like the fourth or fifth.

PLAYBOY: Was it devastating?

SEINFELD: No, I knew this was the process. I wasn't one of these phenoms where the guy gets called over his first time, hits a home run in his first at-bat. I always did well, but they have to warm up to you. They tell you, "Mr. Carson thought you were very funny." That type of thing.

PLAYBOY: And no one inspires that kind of fear now?

SEINFELD: I can't put myself in the position of just starting out anymore. Now, if I did *The Tonight Show* and they said, "Mr. Leno didn't feel that your material was strong enough," I'd say, "I didn't think he was so funny, either."

PLAYBOY: What about you and Howard Stern?

SEINFELD: We have a lot of fun.

PLAYBOY: You have a lot of fun with a guy who recently said he wishes your house would fall off the mountain, that you would get cancer and die?

SEINFELD: Yeah, he's funny. People don't understand the Howard Stern character. We were laughing our asses off.

PLAYBOY: Wait. Supposedly, his feelings were really hurt because of something you said about him in an interview.

SEINFELD: He was offended. He's a sensitive guy, if you can believe that. I called him an amusing jerk. So I went on his show and told him that I stand by my comment. We had this really hostile exchange. Then, as soon as he'd go to a commercial, we'd both be laughing. That show is all playacting.

PLAYBOY: Was that all set up from the beginning?

SEINFELD: It's just kind of understood. He makes fun of me, I make fun of him. It's friends ragging on each other for the fun of it. Hey, if I really thought he didn't like me, why would I give a damn about him and go on his show?

PLAYBOY: What does Howard want to know that you won't tell him?

SEINFELD: He's always asking me about dates and women.

PLAYBOY: How did you feel when he grilled your ex-girlfriend, comic Carol Leifer, about your sex life?

SEINFELD: I was a little embarrassed about that, especially since we broke up 17 years ago.

PLAYBOY: She said you were good.

SEINFELD: Yeah, she was just being sweet. Nobody remembers.

PLAYBOY: And he grilled her not only about your sex life but also about your penis size.

SEINFELD: Hey, that's kind of personal. Come to think of it, I like Don Imus better. And I mention that because I know it will really irritate Howard, which is always gratifying to me.

PLAYBOY: This might be the perfect time to interject a guest question from a young woman—and fan—who watched "The Contest" and wanted to know if in fact you are the master of your domain.

SEINFELD: No. My empire has crumbled.

PLAYBOY: She wanted specifics on frequency. And when—in the morning? In the evening?

SEINFELD: I'll need her home number.

PLAYBOY: Creams? Oils?

SEINFELD: Well, we're definitely into it now. Tell her that the show, while being lifelike and entertaining, is basically an exercise in fiction. I'll tell you something interesting about me. It's probably my biggest secret, the biggest skeleton in my closet. I didn't discover masturbation until after

I lost my virginity. I don't understand how everybody else knew about it and I didn't. Nobody told me about it. I don't know how they found out about it. I didn't know this technique was available to me. I don't know how it happened, but somehow I was absent that day. And when I discovered it, I thought, Well, that's the end of that. I'm never going to get upset about a woman ever again!

PLAYBOY: How soon after your first sexual encounter did you learn—

SEINFELD: Right after. Nah, just kidding.

PLAYBOY: So who told you?

SEINFELD: It was my college roommate. We were talking one day, and he told me.

PLAYBOY: Were you embarrassed?

SEINFELD: Are you kidding? I would love to tell people about this. What a tremendous gift to give another human being, to tell them, "You know, here's what you can do. . . ."

PLAYBOY: Is that basically how it happened?

SEINFELD: That's a funny version of it.

PLAYBOY: Which parent told you about sex, and what did he or she tell you?

SEINFELD: I don't really remember how I learned. They said they showed me a book or played me a record or something. They swore they told me all about it, but I don't recall it. I think I learned from that book, the David Reuben book, *Everything You Always Wanted to Know About Sex (But Were Afraid to Ask)*. I found a copy when I was in high school, and that was helpful.

PLAYBOY: Don't get excited. This isn't the sex part, but since you brought it up, when did you lose your virginity?

SEINFELD: I'm not sure whether I was 19 or 20.

PLAYBOY: Not sure?

SEINFELD: I'm not positive, to tell you the truth. I remember the place. I remember whom. I was in a relationship, so it wasn't a seduction.

PLAYBOY: A lot of men lose their virginity at a much younger age.

SEINFELD: I'm not pushy. I remember being upset about it having taken so long. Might have been 20. I should probably call it a "technical" at 19, but the red light—sorry about the metaphor—came on when I was 20. So I'm willing now to admit that as a teenager I never had sex. And I was the master of my domain. And I'll tell you this: At the age of 39, I've almost caught up with everybody else. I think I'm even.

PLAYBOY: Why so late?

SEINFELD: I hated the idea of upsetting a woman in any way, so the slightest amount of resistance would deter me. I had no persistence at all. Still don't, really. If she is at all reticent, I'm out of there. It kills the mood for me. I don't want to sell anybody anything. It's one area of my life where I'm extremely—

PLAYBOY: Shy?

SEINFELD: Yeah. Still very shy about it. I'm not pushy.

PLAYBOY: Of course, now you don't have to be.

SEINFELD: No, I still have to be.

PLAYBOY: How much has fame changed the equation?

SEINFELD: It's changed it, but it hasn't really improved it. In some ways, women are put off by it. They think I'm dating millions of women, they think they won't be special. They think I'll take them for granted.

PLAYBOY: True?

SEINFELD: No.

PLAYBOY: Are you willing to make the first move now?

SEINFELD: Yes, I am. I feel confident enough to do that now. [*Gets up and goes into the kitchen*] Do you mind if I do these dishes?

PLAYBOY: You like doing dishes?

SEINFELD: I like the water and I like the soap [*soaps some glasses and plates*].

PLAYBOY: Do you like to iron?

SEINFELD: No. I like vacuuming, though. I like the way the carpet looks after I'm done. I like those lines the wheels make.

PLAYBOY: While we're in the kitchen, maybe we should mention your fascination with cereal. The *Seinfeld* kitchen is jammed with cereal boxes. You have stashes in your Los Angeles and New York homes. Why?

SEINFELD: It's the first thing I could make when I was a kid. I was proud of it. I love milk.

PLAYBOY: So cereal is just a means to an end?

SEINFELD: I think so. I really like anything with milk.

PLAYBOY: Your face will soon be on a box of cereal, right?

SEINFELD: Yeah. Kellogg's low-fat granola. [*Takes a small package from the cereal box*] I love things like this: They put the raisins in a special packet. I guess it keeps them moist and juicy.

PLAYBOY: What's your favorite cereal?

SEINFELD: I constantly change my allegiances. Right now I'm in this Cheerios mode. I'm sure the Kellogg's people won't be happy to hear that. [*Scrambling*] Cornflakes, though—you really can't beat cornflakes. If you had to have one cereal the rest of your life, it would have to be cornflakes.

PLAYBOY: Let's turn to your cereal days as a comic. When did you know you had made it?

SEINFELD: When I turned in my waiter's apron in September of 1976. I was working at Brew and Burger on Third and 53rd. Ten to two—lunch. I got a gig emceeing at the Comic Strip. I already had one night, then I got another night, and it was like 35 bucks a night. I thought I could make it on 70 bucks a week. So I turned in the apron. I went out to visit my parents. I remember standing on the platform of the Long Island Railroad in Massapequa. That was the highest moment of my career. I was a comedian. I had made it.

PLAYBOY: Has anything compared to that since then?

SEINFELD: No. That was the transition from man to superman.

PLAYBOY: You've always said your dad was a funny guy. Did he think you had a shot at a career in comedy?

SEINFELD: Oh, yeah. He was extremely encouraging about it. He was a salesman, and that's a similar type of life. You're really not doing any legitimate kind of work, you're just making a living talking people into things. That isn't too much different from what a comedian does.

PLAYBOY: What did he sell?

SEINFELD: Signs.

PLAYBOY: Signs? Seinfeld?

SEINFELD: A coincidence. Anyway, I had been doing comedy for a few months by then. My parents were fine with it. They weren't quite sure what I was doing. They really didn't know how serious I was about it. But they always took everything in stride. Their life didn't revolve around me. If I was happy, they were happy.

PLAYBOY: Whom did their lives revolve around?

SEINFELD: Everybody did what they wanted to do. We were all just kind of roommates. My parents never really had families. My mom grew up in an orphanage and my father left home when he was young. They got married late in life—they were both in their mid-to-late 30s. They were independent people.

PLAYBOY: Would you call yours an intimate family?

SEINFELD: No. We went on vacations together and we always had dinner together, but it wasn't that kind of cloying, got-to-talk-every-day thing. My mother doesn't call me every day. There was plenty of breathing room in the family. It was a healthy atmosphere.

PLAYBOY: What is your definition of intimacy?

SEINFELD: There are certain families in which people are all over one another. They look like newborn puppies. It's too much.

PLAYBOY: Would you describe yourself as an intimate person?

SEINFELD: It's hard to be intimate all by yourself. But I'm comfortable with intimacy, if that's what you're asking. I just haven't been involved with anyone seriously in quite a while. I have had a number of legitimate relationships, but the past few years I haven't. I've been too busy and it's been too difficult. And sometimes I wonder if I've lost the knack of it. Of course, I'm minimizing the whole experience by using the word knack. But I don't think so. No human being is immune to love and how it can change you.

PLAYBOY: Ever been in love?

SEINFELD: Yeah, a few times.

PLAYBOY: What's the shortest amount of time it's taken you to say "I love you"?

SEINFELD: A month.

PLAYBOY: Were you holding out?

SEINFELD: No, it seemed about right. I'm into timing.

PLAYBOY: Speaking of timing, you're 39, straight, never been married. What's going on?

SEINFELD: I've been busy.

PLAYBOY: Well, maybe this will make things easier. We have some phone numbers we've been asked to pass along.

SEINFELD: [*Looks at slips of paper*] What is this? Where'd you get these?

PLAYBOY: This one is from a woman who said, "Tell Jerry I'm a nice Jewish girl." And this is from a woman who—

SEINFELD: What do these women think? Why would I call someone like this? I don't know who they are. [*Flustered*] I mean, this is really quite mind-boggling. I find this astounding. I don't know them, they know me. Do they understand that TV works only one way? They get to see me, but I don't get to see them. This basic fact of electronics seems to get past a lot of people. It's beyond me. I don't know, maybe some people are that indiscriminate. I'm extremely careful about who I spend my time with.

PLAYBOY: The tabloids had a field day with one of your recent dates— with a 17-year-old.

SEINFELD: I was in a tabloid rocket to the moon. I'm telling you, that was too fun. That was so much fun. That was just absolutely hilarious to me.

PLAYBOY: Excuse us. We need to get a pan to catch the dripping sarcasm.

SEINFELD: [*Laughs*] I guess I haven't quite adjusted to celebrityhood because it's still hard for me to believe that anyone gives a damn who the hell I go out with or what I do.

So anyway, I met this girl, Shoshanna [Lonstein]. She's a very sweet girl and she's very pretty. I didn't know how old she was. I knew she wasn't 40. I took her to a basketball game and that was the whole thing.

PLAYBOY: Did you meet her in the park like they say?

SEINFELD: Yeah, but the rest of it is all—

PLAYBOY: Is she 18?

SEINFELD: She's 18 now.

PLAYBOY: When did she tell you her age?

SEINFELD: When the article came out.

PLAYBOY: You took her to the basketball game and now the tabloids are calling you a cradle snatcher.

SEINFELD: Cradle snatcher! It was a wonderful article. I couldn't believe how nice they were about it.

PLAYBOY: Nice?

SEINFELD: Everybody was saying, "I don't see anything wrong with it. If they like each other. . . ." My manager couldn't believe it. He said I'm bulletproof even in the tabloids. They had every chance really to stick the knife in and they didn't do it. They could have said anything: I'm taking advantage of her, she doesn't know what's going on, her parents are upset, my mother wanted to disown me. They could have made up anything.

PLAYBOY: How did Shoshanna feel about all the attention?

SEINFELD: Didn't bother her a bit.

PLAYBOY: Kids today.

SEINFELD: The great thing is you can go out on a date and pick up a little babysitting money on the side. That pays for the pizza. She's a very nice girl.

PLAYBOY: What have your friends said about this?

SEINFELD: It's really strange. The reactions ran the absolute gamut from horrified to just busting buttons with pride that they know me. Guys I hadn't heard from in years called to say, "Congratulations! Good for you." Women I know wouldn't even call me back. My assistant punched me. She saw me and literally punched me, she was so mad. It was reviled by women in their 30s and by Jay Leno.

PLAYBOY: Leno?

SEINFELD: Leno was just terrified. To him any potential public-relations imbroglio, any appearance of impropriety, is the most terrifying thing in the world. He was scared for me, just out of concern as a friend.

PLAYBOY: Did he do anything in the monolog?

SEINFELD: No, he would never do anything like that. But my mother was thrilled because Shoshanna is Jewish and Syrian. My mother's Syrian. And all my aunts and uncles on the Syrian side, this is what they expect. They figure 15, 16 is the right age [for a woman] for me, because that's the way they do it in Syria. So they're going, "Eighteen? She's a little over the hill, but if you like her. . . ."

My women friends, some of them were really hostile about it. They didn't like it. First of all, they think I look for this. Like this was an ambition of mine. But the fact is, I don't meet that many women I like, period. So when I like someone, I don't care about her race, creed or national origin. If I like her, I don't care. I don't discriminate. If she's 18, if she's intelligent, that's fine.

PLAYBOY: So, is it love?

SEINFELD: No, no, it was just a couple cups of coffee.

PLAYBOY: And a basketball game.

SEINFELD: I'm also dating a woman who's 39. I'm trying to pander to whatever personal prejudice people have. See, the thing is, my own age isn't really real to me. I look in the mirror and I just don't feel 39. I don't feel any different than I was when I was 23. And I don't look that much different. So it's weird. Look, I don't have impossible qualifications. All that I want in a woman is sweet, smart and sexy.

PLAYBOY: Frankly, we're surprised you weren't more careful about going out in public with Shoshanna. The walls have cameras.

SEINFELD: Can you believe it? Can you believe how naive I can be?

PLAYBOY: What's your idea of a fun date?

SEINFELD: To me the ultimate date is dinner and a movie. My fantasies are all of normalcy, because I don't get to do a lot of these things. As you know, I'm a great fan of the mundane anyway. So, to me, dinner and a movie—I can't imagine a more fabulous evening than to have enough time to do that and to have scheduled that so it works. And then you have coffee later. That's just orgasmic for me.

PLAYBOY: Having gone from a successful stand-up career to this saturation in the media, how has your popularity, on a percentage basis, increased the number of female opportunities available to you?

SEINFELD: [*Laughs*] We're getting there! I feel it coming now. The sex part! Yeah! The sex part! You can't keep it from me any longer. You can't hide. This is the sex part. [*Laughs*] No, the percentage is the same: It's all women, 100 percent. A percentage increase in the number of female opportunities? Hard to believe we're not in a Citibank board meeting here. I know you want an answer to this question, but here's the problem: Along with the saturation there's a price. And that price is the enemy of all living things: time. I can go out on a date maybe two or three times a month, 10 months out of the year. That's a maximum. It's a funny situation. You get yourself to this point in life where you have a nice job, a nice car, a nice place to live, you know where the good restaurants are—and you can't go.

PLAYBOY: Is that a problem for you?

SEINFELD: No, it's a problem for my dates. That's why I'm not involved—the kind of woman who would put up with that is not the kind of woman I want.

You know, I never imagined being at this particular point in show business. Currently, I can do almost anything I want. I can meet almost anybody I want. I'm what they call "hot" right now, this second. Come back tomorrow, it could all be different. I have to manage that. It's a good word, heat, because it has a destructive quality to it. I'm careful about it. The fire heats the home and can also burn it down, as my father used to love to say. But as long as I'm at this apex, I want to experience it to the maximum and make the most of it.

PLAYBOY: Does this mean you'll be a lonely guy for a while longer?

SEINFELD: No. I'm never lonely. Even when I'm alone I'm not lonely. That's another reason I'm a good comic: A lot of time alone never bothered me.

By the way, I would like to meet all the women I'm in this issue with. It seems like I should. I think when people read an issue they assume that all the people in the magazine know one another. Like they were all there that day. One guy's getting interviewed, the Playmate's getting photographed, someone else is doing a wine ad and there're a bunch of football players in some other room getting their picture taken. And they're all at the Mansion. I think that's the Playboy image.

PLAYBOY: Maybe we should have a party in your honor and invite everyone in the issue. Will you come?

SEINFELD: Absolutely. Besides, I've never been to the Mansion. And I really think you owe me that.

PLAYBOY: And something else, as well.

SEINFELD: Yeah, the sex question. Have we done it? I think everyone is looking forward to the sex question.

PLAYBOY: We're sorry, but we have run out of time.

TINA FEY

A candid conversation with TV's comic "goddess of the geeks" about 30 Rock *versus* SNL, *having a filthy mouth, and those disappearing sexy glasses*

Tina Fey can't seem to shake her image as queen of the comedy nerds.

In the beginning it probably had something to do with the glasses. When she was co-anchor of Weekend Update on *Saturday Night Live*, her trademark black-rimmed glasses made her look like a cross between a naughty librarian and Velma from *Scooby-Doo*. But her geeky charm wasn't in appearance alone. Fey's caustic wit and wry delivery made it clear she wasn't another airhead comedienne willing to play dumb for laughs. If the world needed reminding that smart girls can be funny and sexy, Tina Fey proved it.

While she has often been called the thinking man's sex symbol, she would probably prefer something a little less pretentious. After all, this is a woman who frequently refers to herself as a supernerd. *Time* magazine came closest to summing up Fey's appeal when it crowned her "goddess of the geeks."

Fey rarely wears glasses since leaving *SNL*, but the nerd spirit remains. On the NBC sitcom *30 Rock*, now in its second season, she plays Liz Lemon, the head writer for a late-night comedy sketch show bearing more than a passing resemblance to *Saturday Night Live*. Liz is the antithesis of a perky, self-confident leading woman. She's insecure, clumsy, rotten at love and, above all, dorky as hell.

It would be easy to dismiss Fey's geeky persona as a carefully calculated veneer designed to win over fans. But Fey the Emmy-winning comic isn't all that different from Fey the shy and gawky teenager who grew up in Upper Darby, Pennsylvania. Born Elizabeth Stamatina Fey in 1970, she had a mostly sheltered upbringing with parents Donald and Jeanne and older brother (by eight years) Peter. By the time she got to high school she was already establishing herself as an outsider. Fey was a straight-A student and active in extracurricular activities such as choir, drama club and co-editing her high school newspaper.

She was also fiercely opposed to her school's culture of drugs and sexual promiscuity—which, by her own admission, made her unpopular with the cool kids. So she and her social circle—the "AP-class brainiac nerds," as she calls them—would sit in the cafeteria and make jokes about the more popular students from a safe distance. Although Fey admits she could be scathing and even cruel to her classmates, she was just as hard on herself. In a caption accompanying her high school yearbook photo, she predicted she would someday become "very, very fat."

After graduating from the University of Virginia with a degree in drama in 1992, she moved to Chicago to join the legendary Second City, where she performed sketch comedy six nights a week and met her future husband, musician Jeff Richmond. In 1997 she was hired as a staff writer for *Saturday Night Live* and a few years later became the first female head writer in *SNL*'s then 25-year history.

In 2000 executive producer Lorne Michaels plucked her out of obscurity to become co-anchor of Weekend Update, first with Jimmy Fallon and then, in 2004, with Amy Poehler.

Like every breakout star from *Saturday Night Live* before her, Fey made the leap to feature films, with 2004's *Mean Girls*, a biting satire of teenage girls and the emotional violence they inflict on one another. Next up is *Baby Mama*, Fey's movie collaboration with her former Update co-anchor Poehler, about a single career woman (played by Fey) who hires an eccentric surrogate (Poehler) to have her baby. And if that's not enough to keep Fey busy, there's *30 Rock*, once marked for death but now one of NBC's most highly rated and award-winning shows.

We sent writer Eric Spitznagel to interview Fey at the Beverly Hills Hotel in Los Angeles, where they sipped coffee by the pool and talked for most of the day. He reports: "Tina is two very different women trapped in the same body, the yin and yang of comedy. Half her personality is what you would expect: She's intelligent and poised, like a feminist superhero. But the other half is an introverted underdog who makes up for her lack of confidence with a biting sense of humor. If life really does imitate high school, then she's the hot cheerleader everybody wants to sleep with and the band geek who makes fun of you for being so shallow."

PLAYBOY: Did you want to be the star of *30 Rock*, or would you have preferred to remain behind the scenes?

FEY: My original deal was to create a show for NBC as a writer only, but when we came up with this idea, I figured, Why not? Let's take a shot. Well, not at first. Before I said yes, I talked to Amy Poehler and asked her, "Am I getting too old for this? Do people want to see me anymore?" She helped me think like a male comedian. When Ray Romano and Jerry Seinfeld got their shows, I don't think they had a moment like, Am I good enough to do this? I need to stop worrying so much about what other people think.

PLAYBOY: How much of *30 Rock* is based on your experiences at *Saturday Night Live*?

FEY: It depends. Some of it's personal to me, and some of it's personal to the other writers. I tried to remember what it felt like when I started at *SNL*, before I was comfortable managing people. It's weird to sit down with somebody my own age and tell them, "You need to try harder."

PLAYBOY: Can you remember a particular moment at *SNL* when you had to be the boss and didn't like it?

FEY: God, yes. Tim Herlihy, who was my co-head writer, threw me to the wolves in the most hilarious way. We had had a string of bad shows, and he said to me, "Okay, we have to tell the writers they're not cutting it." So we called this big meeting, and I was already a little nervous because I had been co-head writer for only a couple of weeks. We walked in, and Tim turned to me and said, "All right, go ahead." He made me scold the writers, who were essentially my peers. I was like, "Me? Wait, what?"

PLAYBOY: Did you have a lot of conflicts with the other *SNL* writers?

FEY: Not really, but we did an episode on *30 Rock* last year about Liz finding out a co-worker had called her the C word.

PLAYBOY: You mean cunt?

FEY: Yeah. That happened to me. Somebody at *SNL* called me that word, and my response was "No! My parents love me. I'm not some child of an alcoholic who will take that kind of verbal abuse!" It was such a strong out-of-left-field reaction, so it was easy to turn that into comedy.

PLAYBOY: Is it safe to assume Jack Donaghy, your fictional boss on *30 Rock*, played by Alec Baldwin, is supposed to be Lorne Michaels?

FEY: I would say he's Lorne Michaels–esque. There's a whole other corporate end of Donaghy that's nothing at all like Lorne. But he was definitely the inspiration. I may be the only *SNL* alumnus who has created a character based on Lorne who's not lying about it.

PLAYBOY: Who's been lying?

FEY: Well, maybe not lying but at least not advertising it. I've always wanted to do a special for Turner Classic Movies, screening all the films with characters based on Lorne. There's *Scrooged*, *Brain Candy* and the *Austin Powers* series. I think there are a few more. When you work for *SNL*, Lorne is such a huge part of your life. It's like the movie *The Paper Chase*. The guy idolizes his professor and thinks the professor is messing with him. At the end of the movie the student finally has the courage to talk to him, but the professor doesn't even know who he is. That's what it's like with Lorne. Everybody wants this personal relationship with him.

PLAYBOY: Did you have that?

FEY: To an extent. We aren't best pals or anything, but I consider him a friend. Lorne always encourages you to enjoy the finer things in life. He's big on saying things like "You should buy a huge apartment because then you will come home and be like, 'Wow, who lives here? Oh yeah, that's right. I do.'" It's kind of sweet the way he wants everyone to get rich.

PLAYBOY: Was Michaels intimidating to work with?

FEY: Sometimes. We would do dress rehearsals for a live audience on Saturdays at eight P.M., and each writer would go under the bleachers and watch his or her sketch on the monitor with Lorne. He would stand next to you, and it was terrifying. You're accountable for everything. The worst was if the sketch was dirty or had a lot of fart jokes. He would say things like "You must be really proud" or "Mmmm, call the Peabody board."

PLAYBOY: Is he aware he's a character on *30 Rock*?

FEY: Oh yeah. He doesn't always comment on it, but sometimes he will call me and say, "Boy, I was all over this week's episode."

PLAYBOY: What about Liz Lemon? Is she basically another version of you?

FEY: There are two big differences between Liz and me. One is that apparently my character's jugs are a lot bigger.

PLAYBOY: Really? We hadn't noticed that.

FEY: Yeah, whatever. I think our costume designer is trying to draw the viewers' eyes up until I lose the rest of this baby weight. I was doing a movie with Dax Shepard, and we were talking about *30 Rock*, and he said, "By the way, those things are blazing hot on your show."

PLAYBOY: And the other difference between you and Liz is . . . ?

FEY: She's not married. I was saved by having met my boyfriend before I worked on *Saturday Night Live*. I was already dating Jeff, who is now my husband. Many times when I was at *SNL* I would survey the writers' room and think, Oh, thank God I'm not coming to this job single.

PLAYBOY: The pickings were slim at *SNL*?

FEY: I could've gone on four weird dates with Colin Quinn. Or I could be married to Norm MacDonald and living in Arizona.

PLAYBOY: Liz briefly considered quitting her plush TV job in New York and moving to Cleveland. Have you ever been tempted to do the same thing?

FEY: Oh sure. Sometimes the struggle to live in New York makes you think you're really living your life, but you're actually only struggling to get from place to place. You say things like "I did two errands, and I got home!" But is this my dream life? I think everybody occasionally has the fantasy of moving somewhere else. Sometimes New York gets to you. Some days I win, some days New York wins.

PLAYBOY: What's with all the *Star Wars* references on the show? Are you a closet sci-fi geek?

FEY: Not at all. I just think it's funny. For a while we tried to have at least one *Star Wars* reference in every episode, but somewhere along the way we dropped the ball. I think my character knows a little more about *Star Wars* than I do. I have basic girl-nerd knowledge, but I wouldn't be able to pull a name like Admiral Ackbar out of my butt the way Liz Lemon does.

PLAYBOY: Liz once described her sex life as "fast and only on Saturdays." Does that seem healthy to you?

FEY: I think it's an attitude everybody has sometimes. And it's not one I've seen reflected in the post–*Sex and the City* world. Especially for married people with kids, there is a lot of fake-it-till-you-make-it. "We're all exhausted. Let's just go ahead and do it." And then you think, Oh, that was a great idea.

PLAYBOY: You've done only a handful of kissing scenes on *30 Rock*, and you've always looked uncomfortable. Why is that?

FEY: I don't know. It wasn't a big deal with Jason Sudeikis, who plays Liz's boyfriend, because he's a buddy. We actually auditioned a lot of actors for that role. How can I say this so Jason won't be offended? The L.A. actors were what Amy and I call "L.A. tight." They're all skinny and ripped and don't look like real dudes. Jason will read this and ask, "What are you saying? I need to work out more?" But there's something too perfect about them. I like to keep it East Coast loose.

PLAYBOY: Were you a big fan of sitcoms as a kid?

FEY: Of course. The late 1970s were a sweet spot for half-hour comedy. There was one night of the week—I think it was Saturday, but I'm not sure—that had the best shows. There was *The Bob Newhart Show* leading into *The Mary Tyler Moore Show*, or the other way around, and then *The Carol Burnett Show*. That was a big night. I remember getting into trouble once as a kid, and the only threat my parents used was that I wouldn't be allowed to watch that lineup. It was all they had to say: "We're withholding quality television from you." I was really sweating it.

PLAYBOY: Did you watch those sitcoms again when you were creating *30 Rock*?

FEY: Oh yeah. I tried to make *Mary Tyler Moore* the template for our show. I also watched a lot of *That Girl*, but mostly because there was a *That Girl* marathon on TV and my husband TiVoed all of it.

PLAYBOY: Was he helping you with the research?

FEY: I think he just has a crush on Marlo Thomas.

PLAYBOY: Well, who doesn't?

FEY: I know, right? Actually, every woman he's had a crush on has been a straight path to me. Marlo Thomas, Kristy McNichol and Julie Kavner when she played Rhoda's sister. It's a trajectory that leads right to me. The only one missing is Dustin Hoffman as Tootsie.

PLAYBOY: Did your daughter, Alice, get your comedy genes?

FEY: I think so. In our house the baby is the funniest, followed by husband Jeff, and I'm a distant third. I'm too tired. I'm funny, but I'm not room funny.

PLAYBOY: How has Alice demonstrated her sense of humor?

FEY: She has started doing spit takes. She will take a huge drink of water and let it dribble out. I guess it's not really a spit take, more of a *blerch* take. Even before we noticed and laughed at it, she was doing it just to crack herself up.

PLAYBOY: Does it matter to her if she has an audience?

FEY: Oh yeah. She's not stupid. She won't do it until she has your attention.

PLAYBOY: Were you a funny baby?

FEY: Not like Alice. She likes to engage people and make them laugh. I was more of the weird kid who came home after school, put on my colonial-lady costume from Halloween and did little skits for myself.

PLAYBOY: How long did it take before you realized you could make other people laugh?

FEY: I think it was in middle school. I remember thinking, Oh yeah, I may not be superpretty. This comedy thing may be my best move.

PLAYBOY: Was comedy a way of hiding from your insecurities?

FEY: I wasn't really insecure. I was quiet and nerdy, and comedy was a way to ingratiate myself with people. I had a buddy named Jimmy McDonough who was the class clown; he was louder and more outspoken than I was. I could never do that, put myself out there and be disruptive in class. I would sit on the sidelines, coming up with vicious burns about the popular kids.

PLAYBOY: You did an independent-study project on comedy in eighth grade. Do you remember anything about it?

FEY: I remember the only book I could find as research was *Joe Franklin's Encyclopedia of Comedians*. It was about old vaudeville guys like Joe E. Brown and Rudy Vallee. But I was way into comedy. I would watch *An Evening at the Improv* every time it was on. I miss the golden age of stand-up. I miss the brick wall.

PLAYBOY: Did you dream of becoming a cast member of *Saturday Night Live*?

FEY: Well, sure. But that's not a unique dream. Everybody wants to be famous when they're young.

PLAYBOY: When did you decide being a writer would be enough?

FEY: When I figured out it was an option. By the eighth or ninth grade a few English teachers were encouraging and helped me realize writing was something I could do. When I was in Chicago, doing improv at Second City and places like that, it seemed clear the closest I would get to *SNL* was writing for it.

PLAYBOY: You became *Saturday Night Live*'s first female head writer. Before you, *SNL* had a reputation for being a boys club. Do you think you changed that?

FEY: Well, there are still more men on the writing staff than women. But it has never been a woman-haters club, at least not when I was there. The more women around, the more integrated the comedy will be. People like what they like. If mostly guys are writing the show, then the material will skew toward jokes that guys like. It's not malicious or intentional. It's what makes them laugh, so that's what they write.

PLAYBOY: *Saturday Night Live* is notorious for being a competitive, cut-throat environment. Did you ever have a feud with anyone on the show?

FEY: Will Ferrell tried to stab me once. We had been up all night writing skits for the guy from *Dawson's Creek*—James Van Der Beek. And you know, it was *SNL*, so we were all hopped up on goofballs, out of our minds on quaaludes and horse antibiotics. I foolishly made a disparaging joke about Will's skit. I was like, "Really, dude? A hat salesman who's afraid of hats? That's the best you can come up with?" And he lunged at me with a letter opener. I remember thinking, This guy's a genius. It would be an honor to be killed by him.

PLAYBOY: Other than the occasional stabbing, how did the writers and cast members let off steam?

FEY: The usual ways. We tried to make one another laugh. There was a lot of same-sex fake rape.

PLAYBOY: What's your happiest memory from *SNL*?

FEY: Besides the same-sex raping?

PLAYBOY: Yes, besides the rape.

FEY: Well, a few days before a show, every sketch is read out loud in front of all the writers and actors, and you live or die in that room. Making everybody else in the cast laugh was always more satisfying than having something on the show. It happened for me only once or twice.

PLAYBOY: What's your worst memory?

FEY: The worst was probably in late 2001. I was sitting in my dressing room on a Friday night, working on my jokes for Weekend Update, and Lester Holt came on the news and said anthrax had been discovered in 30 Rockefeller Plaza, and I was in 30 Rockefeller Plaza. I stood up, got my stuff and walked out, right past Drew Barrymore, who was hosting. I didn't even tell her there was anthrax in the building. I went to the elevator, walked up Sixth Avenue to Central Park West and went straight to my house, sobbing the whole way. Those were bad days.

PLAYBOY: Were you reacting out of fear, or were you angry you had been put in that situation?

FEY: It was fear. There was a palpable feeling that we were probably all going to die. That was before we knew, Oh, this is the kind of anthrax cats get.

PLAYBOY: Did you ever have a bad experience with a host that made you wish you were in another line of work?

FEY: Well, in late 2005 Paula Abdul did a guest bit on the show, and she was awful. I was pregnant at the time and probably a little moody, but

I remember thinking, She's a disaster! I gotta prop this lady up and get her on TV.

PLAYBOY: How was she a disaster?

FEY: In the ways she generally appears to be. It was an *American Idol* sketch, and she wanted to change parts. So Amy Poehler had to play her. A year later I saw her on a flight. We both looked at each other like, Do I know that girl? And then we both had the same moment of recognition, and she was like, *Uuuggh.* I saw it register on her face that she had had a terrible time with us.

PLAYBOY: Since leaving *SNL* permanently, in 2006, you rarely wear glasses. What happened?

FEY: I still wear them and occasionally need them to see. They're not props, but I don't wear them all the time. Sometimes I use contacts. When I was auditioning for Weekend Update, I tried doing it with and without the glasses. One of the writers on *SNL*, T. Sean Shannon, watched my audition and said [*in a smarmy, vaguely Southern voice*], "You want the job, you oughta leave them glasses on." [*laughs*] So I followed his advice, and it kind of worked out for me. Getting rid of the glasses was rough. Even now I will go on a talk show and worry nobody will recognize me without the specs.

PLAYBOY: Which used to work to your advantage. It was like your Clark Kent disguise but in reverse.

FEY: Exactly. It helped for a while, but I don't think it's fooling anybody anymore.

PLAYBOY: So losing the glasses wasn't a conscious decision to change your image?

FEY: Oh no, not at all.

PLAYBOY: But you do know that by retiring the glasses, you're breaking a lot of nerd hearts?

FEY: [*Laughs*] Yeah, I know it's a nerd fetish that should probably be respected. Just like Mr. T should never show up in public without his Mohawk.

PLAYBOY: What do you think of your male fan following? There are websites devoted to you that verge on the obsessive. Is that flattering or creepy?

FEY: It's all good, I guess. As long as they don't try to kill me. Everyone around me gets upset by it occasionally. But I prefer not to think about it or question it.

PLAYBOY: Why do you think your fans are so drawn to you?

FEY: Maybe because I seem very attainable.

PLAYBOY: Attainable? But you're married.

FEY: Not in that way. Attainable as opposed to a supermodel.

PLAYBOY: Some older male comics like Jerry Lewis have argued that women aren't funny. Does it piss you off, or is it easy to ignore?

FEY: The only people I've heard say that are Jerry Lewis and Richard Roeper. That's not a strong showing. Yeah, Richard Roeper is *hi-larious*. Remember his radio show? Me neither. It's irrelevant to me that Jerry Lewis doesn't think I'm funny. I'm not writing a movie for Jerry Lewis; he's not running a studio. It's not a thing for me. That's not a burden I need to carry. But what's unfair is when one woman tries to do comedy and isn't funny and it somehow reflects on all women. Nobody watches a terrible male standup comic and says, "God, men just cannot do this." There are just as many awful comedians who are men.

PLAYBOY: The late Michael O'Donoghue, the first head writer for *Saturday Night Live*, once said, "It does help when writing humor to have a big hunk of meat between the legs."

FEY: I do have one, but it's been flayed open to a vagina.

PLAYBOY: So you don't agree with that sentiment?

FEY: Well, the thing is, he said it, and then he died. So I don't know. Maybe he was wrong.

PLAYBOY: Was he just the product of a different era and a different way of thinking about women and comedy?

FEY: Probably, yeah. But if I had been at *SNL* during the 1970s, I think I would've gotten along fine with him.

PLAYBOY: Really? You wouldn't have come to blows?

FEY: He liked to be shocking, and I have a filthy mouth.

PLAYBOY: You do? Why are we learning this now?

FEY: Probably because I try to filter all the filth before saying anything out loud. But backstage I have an incredibly foul mouth. I've noticed this pattern, especially in comedy. There's a big difference between the men and women in the business. The guys probably attended college but didn't finish, and they have a problem with authority. Almost all the women attended a very nice college, they graduated and were always obedient, good students, but comedy was their one outlet for expressing themselves and not being so prim and proper.

PLAYBOY: Was that true for you?

FEY: I think so. Growing up, I was a very good kid. I went to college. I didn't drink, didn't smoke, didn't do drugs. Comedy was the one place I was able to misbehave.

PLAYBOY: What's the secret to delivering a mean-spirited joke and making an audience love you for it?

FEY: I know there's a secret, but I don't remember it anymore. It has something to do with smiling a lot. I think you can't clamp down on a gag. There's something you gotta do: You can't look like you love it too much.

PLAYBOY: What about your comments about Paris Hilton on Howard Stern's radio show?

FEY: Oh right, that. [*laughs*]

PLAYBOY: One could say you were tough on Ms. Hilton. You called her a piece of shit and made fun of her hair.

FEY: Okay, here's the thing. I went on *Stern*, and they were very nice to me and, well, I think part of it was. . . .

PLAYBOY: You were drunk, weren't you?

FEY: It was eight in the morning, so as always I was *loooaded*. No, I think what was going through my head was, How can I protect myself? I don't want to talk to Howard too much about myself. I want to throw out some gossip steaks. That kicked in instinctively. I'm sorry I used such terrible language about her. Even my mom said, "Oh, that was awful." Not long after it happened, I went to my gynecologist, and she said, "Are you all right? I read what you said about Paris Hilton in the paper, and that's very hostile."

PLAYBOY: Now that enough time has passed, do you feel any different about her?

FEY: I regret sinking down to that level of discourse. But Paris is a terrible role model and a terrible young woman. She needs to be ignored. I work with people who have 12-, 13-, 14-year-old girls who are fascinated by her. They look up to her, and that's not great. You can buy videotapes in which you can see her bejanis.

PLAYBOY: Her what?

FEY: Her bejanis. You know, her lady bits. Her beholio.

PLAYBOY: Those are the most adorable pet names for the vagina we have ever heard.

FEY: Somebody told me that when she did *Larry King* she said she had never done drugs. Is that true?

PLAYBOY: It is. She also said she isn't a big drinker.

FEY: I don't know if she drinks, but she has done some drugs, y'all! There's a generation of girls in Hollywood who think they can say stuff in the press and make it true. It's not only Paris; a whole bunch of them do.

PLAYBOY: You don't seem to have much sympathy for the blonde Hollywood girls with bulimia.

FEY: When I was in high school, bulimia didn't even exist yet. Remember the movie of the week *Kate's Secret*? It came out in 1985 or 1986. I think somebody famous was in it.

PLAYBOY: Meredith Baxter?

FEY: Yeah, that's the one. When it came out everybody was like, "Wait, you can do *what* now?" It was such a foreign thing to us. Nobody had anorexia or bulimia when I was in school. That movie and when Karen Carpenter died were the first times anybody had heard of those disorders. But now everybody knows, and they all give them a shot.

PLAYBOY: It's like marijuana. Everybody tries it at least once.

FEY: Which, I would like to say for the record, I never did either. I never tried any drugs. I may as well get it in print, so years from now when my daughter is reading back issues of *Playboy*, which I'm sure she will do, she will know her mother was drug- and bulimia-free. And here's the other thing. How can I articulate this properly? When I was growing up, to have a good body you actually had to have a good body. You know what I mean? You had your shape, and whatever your God-given shape was, that was your shape. But now—and this is what these young Hollywood ladies seem to do—even if you don't have a great body, you can lose a lot of weight and get superskinny, get a fake tan and fake tits, and you're in the game. Just get super-duper skinny. Some women are the real deal, like Jessica Alba. She has an amazing, gorgeous body. But for some of these other chicks, the closest they can get to a body like that is to remove everything that's there and add a little something on top. It's like the ladies you see in *Playboy*.

PLAYBOY: Wow. You really want to talk about this here?

FEY: I don't want to seem like a bad guest, but I have a few gentle theories. If you look back at old *Playboys* from the 1960s and 1970s, the Playmates represented the girl next door, and some of them had maybe different-size boobies, perhaps with brown nipples or large areolas. There were even ladies with their actual hair or with hair that wasn't blonde.

PLAYBOY: Do you say this because you're a brunette? Are you lashing out against blondes for the dark-haired sisterhood?

FEY: I just take personal offense. Really, you would be so disgusted to fuck a brunette? It would make you sick? [*laughs*] It's the Joyce DeWitt part of it. I remember as a little kid watching *Three's Company* and thinking, Oh man, that's who is representing us? C'mon, can't Jaclyn Smith be the brunette? Joyce DeWitt was cute, but they gave her a bowl cut and made her wear a football jersey and panty hose. That look was rough. So yeah, I guess you could write all this off as jealousy.

PLAYBOY: Would it help if you dyed your hair?

FEY: No, it goes deeper than that. It's this weird fetish with ladies who look like erasers. Holes is holes, as I like to say, but I don't understand the cultural obsession with these weird mental children with orange skin and bleached-out Barbie hair and boyish hips and big fake choppers. They're so close to being trannies. I sometimes feel like, Who *are* these creatures? And they certainly don't exist only in this magazine. They're everywhere, and that's a reflection of our culture. It's like the difference in our food since the 1970s. It has become overprocessed with all the trans fats. Maybe we need to get organic with these ladies.

PLAYBOY: You are a feminist role model for a lot of young girls. Do you feel qualified to be that person?

FEY: Sure, why not? I could probably be a better-educated feminist. For my generation, we're all figuring it out as we go along. You have to follow your gut. The line in the sand between what's okay and what's not keeps changing. You can have a strong, empowered character—like a Carrie Bradshaw on *Sex and the City*, a show mostly for ladies—and sometimes she's in her underpants. It's easy to forget you can be both.

PLAYBOY: You were in your underpants, or at least your bra, in the opening credits of *Mean Girls*. Was that a statement about your empowered sexuality, or did you just feel the film needed some gratuitous nudity?

FEY: I don't think anybody was super-aroused by it, so I'm probably off the hook. But I will admit we didn't execute the joke the right way. It was better on paper. We should have cut it.

PLAYBOY: Your *Mean Girls* co-star Lindsay Lohan has been struggling lately with drugs and alcohol. Have you reached out to her and offered advice?

FEY: I haven't because I feel I know enough about addiction, from a distance, to say that only somebody who is truly and intimately close with a person should ever attempt to intervene. I made a movie with Lindsay four years ago. I don't know her. I genuinely like her, but you can't fix people from the outside.

PLAYBOY: You saw addiction firsthand with Chris Farley. He died a few months after you were hired for *Saturday Night Live*.

FEY: That's right. He hosted the show in October 1997, and he passed away in December. That was the only time I have ever been around someone and thought, This guy is gonna die. He looked really unwell. I guess that's a lesson learned. Sometimes if you see people who look like they might die, they might die. And again, it's not something you can do anything about. Because you have to be really close to them even to attempt to help, and ultimately only they can help themselves.

PLAYBOY: What about your *30 Rock* co-star Alec Baldwin?

FEY: What about him?

PLAYBOY: There was the scandal this past April when his irate voice-mail message to his daughter was—

FEY: That's separate from me.

PLAYBOY: You never talked with him about it?

FEY: Oh good lord, no. It's none of my business.

PLAYBOY: Even as one parent to another?

FEY: Oh my goodness. No, sir.

PLAYBOY: So you and Alec have a relationship that's 100 percent professional?

FEY: Absolutely. And I wouldn't want people in the office coming up to me and inserting themselves into my business.

PLAYBOY: I guess there's a perception that everybody in show business is family.

FEY: I know. Isn't it insane? They think everyone knows everyone.

PLAYBOY: It's hard not to laugh at the red-carpet interviews when somebody like David Duchovny is asked if he has any advice for Britney Spears.

FEY: It really is.

PLAYBOY: Has that ever happened to you?

FEY: Many times. I went to the opening of Martin Short's play in New York, and I was talking to a reporter on the red carpet. He said, "What brings you to the show?" And I said, "Oh, I think Martin Short's really funny." "That's great. So anyway, do you think John Mark Karr killed JonBenet?" And I was like, What? I guess there must have been a development in the JonBenet Ramsey case or something. But what does it have to do with me? I am not going to answer that! Because if you do—well, not as much if you're me, but if you're Ben Affleck and you say something—they're going to clip it on the news. "Ben Affleck thinks that guy killed JonBenet Ramsey!" And you're like, What the hell just happened? I've been sucked into answering those questions, but thankfully nobody cares what I have to say.

PLAYBOY: Being asked about JonBenet Ramsey is one thing. But Baldwin is someone you actually see and spend time with, so it's not unreasonable to think you may have an opinion about him.

FEY: But Alec and I have never really hung out. We've talked about trying to have dinner together for the better part of a year now, but we've never gotten around to it. And it's not only Alec. I don't have a social life with anyone on the show. There's no time. It's an unbelievably intense work environment. Sometimes I write for 10, 12 hours a day. Then at night I have huge amounts of homework: reading what everyone else is working on, going over outlines and polishing my own scripts. It's like a marathon.

PLAYBOY: A marathon, eh? So you need to drink a lot of water, and sometimes when you're getting close to the finish line you fall apart physically?

FEY: Oh yes. And there's also vomiting and pooping in your pants. And the Ethiopians always win.

PLAYBOY: In your new movie, *Baby Mama*, you play the straight person to Amy Poehler's wacky surrogate mom. Is it weird to let somebody else get all the funniest lines?

FEY: Not at all. I love it. I'm not one of those actors with a big trunk filled with characters. I've got maybe two or three at most. I enjoy being the one who reacts to all the funny things happening around her. It's different when you're only an actor and you feel like, Oh, I have all the setups and everyone else has the punch lines. For me it's just as satisfying to write something for somebody else and watch them take it to another level and get the laugh.

PLAYBOY: *Baby Mama* is a comedy about, well, babies. Isn't there an old show-business rule about not acting with children or animals?

FEY: That's right. They will upstage you because they're adorable. The same can be said of Amy Poehler. I shouldn't have acted with Poehler. She climbs everything and curls up in your lap, and she's cuter than babies.

PLAYBOY: That's a pretty bold statement.

FEY: Amy Poehler is cuter than a baby and a monkey combined.

PLAYBOY: Now you're going too far.

FEY: I never should have done it. I never should have agreed to do this movie with her.

PLAYBOY: Could you ever give it all up? Just abandon the movies, TV and your comedy career and never look back?

FEY: I could definitely live a quieter, less work-filled life. It happens to everyone at some point. It doesn't matter if you're ready to give it up; it gives you up. No one stays this busy all the time. There's such a small window of time when I will be allowed to do this. Right now they fly me out to L.A., and I get to stay in nice hotels and get taken out to dinner. But in 10 years, and probably much sooner, I will be flying on my own dime, and it will be coach and I will be staying at a hotel near the airport. At that point I hope I realize it's over. I don't want to be on some horrible reality show just because I'm desperate to be on TV.

PLAYBOY: Will a small part of you be relieved when it's over?

FEY: It will be a sad day. Because the minute the camera stops and it's not pointed at me anymore, I will probably gain a hundred pounds.

PLAYBOY: Isn't this exactly what you predicted in high school? That you would become "very, very fat"?

FEY: [*Laughs*] That's right. I still say it all the time, so when it happens, I'm covered.

INDEX